AF239711

Connectivity Matters!

Connectivity Matters!

Social, Environmental and Cultural Connectivity in Past Societies

---

Edited by Johannes Müller

© 2022 Individual authors

ROOTS Studies, Vol. 2

Series editors: Lutz Käppel, Johannes Müller and Wolfgang Rabbel
Associate editor: Andrea Ricci

Published by Sidestone Press, Leiden
www.sidestone.com

Imprint: Sidestone Press Academics

Layout design: ROOTS/Tine Pape and Sidestone Press
Copy editing and translations: Eileen Küçükkaraca, Kiel
Cover design and image editing: Tine Pape, Kiel
Cover image: Tine Pape, Kiel

ISBN 978-94-6427-027-3 (softcover)
ISBN 978-94-6427-028-0 (hardcover)
ISBN 978-94-6427-029-7 (PDF e-book)

Published with funding of the Deutsche Forschungsgemeinschaft (DFG, German
Research Foundation) under Germany's Excellence Strategy – EXC 2150 ROOTS –
390870439.

Preface of the series editors

As the outcome of overarching, interdisciplinary scientific research efforts within the Excellence Cluster 'ROOTS – Social, Environmental and Cultural Connectivity in Past Societies' at Kiel University, we are pleased to introduce the second volume of the publication series **ROOTS Studies**. This book series of the Cluster of Excellence ROOTS addresses social, environmental, and cultural phenomena as well as processes of past human development in light of the key concept of "connectivity" and presents scientific research proceeding from the implementation of individual and cross-disciplinary projects. The results of specific research topics and themes across various formats, including monographs, edited volumes/proceedings and data collections, are the backbone of this book series. The published volumes serve as a mirror of the coordinated concern of ROOTS researchers and their partners, who explore the human-environmental relationship over a plurality of spatial and temporal scales within divergent scientific disciplines. The associated research challenges revolve around the premise that humans and environments have interwoven roots, which reciprocally influence each other, stemming from and yielding connectivities that can be identified and juxtaposed against current social issues and crises. The highly dynamic research agenda of the ROOTS cluster, its diverse subclusters and state of the art research set the stage for particularly fascinating results.

The new book in the series is a presentation of the basic concept of social, environmental and cultural connectivity in past societies, as embodied in a diversity of disciplines in the Cluster of Excellence ROOTS. Thus, rather pragmatically driven ideas of socio-environmental connectivities can be found at the beginning, which formed the basis of the Cluster of Excellence in its research application. A discussion of the fluidness of the term connectivity and the applicability of the concept follow in another contribution. With various case and concept studies, we then advance into the perspectives that develop from the new interdisciplinary interaction. These include both rarely considered dependencies between nomadic and urban lifestyles, and aspects of water supply and water features, which represent an area of connectivity between the environment and agglomerated human settlement structures. In addition, diachronic aspects are presented in various studies on the role of connectivities in the development of social inequality, the use of fortification, waste behaviour, or the creation of linguistic features in written media. The contribution on linguistics and archaeology basically comments on the question of interdisciplinary connectivity of the two disciplines and the resulting perspectives. In sum, facets of connectivity research are revealed that are also being investigated in numerous other disciplines with further results in the Kiel Excellence Cluster ROOTS.

The editors of the ROOTS Studies series would like to take the opportunity to thank those colleagues involved in the successful realisation of the second volume. We are very grateful for the detailed and well-directed work of the ROOTS publication team. Specifically, we thank Andrea Ricci for his steady support and coordination efforts during the publication process, Tine Pape for the preparation of the numerous figures and the cover design and Eileen Küçükkaraca for scientific editing. Moreover, we are indebted to the peer reviewers and our partners at Sidestone Press, Karsten Wentink, Corné van Woerdekom and Eric van den Bandt, for their support and their commitment to this publication.

Kiel, March 2022
Lutz Käppel, Johannes Müller, Wolfgang Rabbel

Contents

Preface of the series editors   5

Preface of the volume editor   9

Introduction   11

Social, environmental, and cultural connectivity: A concept for   13
an understanding of society and the environment
    Johannes Müller, Lutz Käppel, Andrea Ricci, Mara Weinelt

On the concept of connectivity   25
    V.P.J. Arponen

Nodes of connectivity: The role of religion in the constitution of   35
urban sites in nomadic Inner Asia
    Jonathan Ethier, Christian Ressel, Birte Ahrens, Enkhtuul Chadraabal,
    Sampildondov Chuluun, Martin Oczipka, Henny Piezonka

Water supply, settlement organisation and social connectivity   71
    Annette Haug and Ulrich Müller

An archaeological perspective on social structure, connectivity   93
and the measurements of social inequality
    Tim Kerig, Johannes Bröcker (†), René Ohlrau, Tanja Schreiber,
    Henry Skorna, Fynn Wilkes

Connectivity and fortifications   115
Oliver Nakoinz, Anna K. Loy, Christoph Rinne, Jutta Kneisel,
Tanja Schreiber, Maria Wunderlich, Nicole Taylor

Connecting linguistics and archaeology in the study of identity: 139
A first exploration
John Peterson, Nicole Taylor, Ilja A. Seržant, Henny Piezonka,
Ariba Hidayet Khan, Norbert Nübler

The dimensions of refuse: Discard studies as a matter of   165
connectivity
Jens Schneeweiß

Ideology and identity in grammar: A diachronic-quantitative   187
approach to language standardisation processes in Ancient Greek
Dariya Rafiyenko and Ilja A. Seržant

Preface of the volume editor

In the fast-paced development of scientific methodology and theory, there are hardly any constants left, particularly in the humanities, which have existed and been recognised as viable concepts over many decades. Moreover, there is a diversity of the various scientific schools, distributed regionally and continentally, which develop ideas and concepts partly independent of each other. This fundamental situation has not changed much in light of the dominance of the English-speaking language in the "Western world".

It seems all the more surprising to me that the concept of connectivity not only necessarily tears down disciplinary boundaries. But that here, in particular, by linking many facetted aspects from ecological and climate spheres, and from cultural and social aspects of societies, they can be combined to form a basic element through which the interaction in and between human societies and resilient behaviour towards the environment can be experienced and explained – in the best case with sustainable consequences.

Connectivity is something that is comprised of the basic elements of human action, which includes, among other things, sharing and competition. It is something that establishes the ecological parameters of societies as determining factors for social developments, but also vice versa. At the same time, traditional terminologies dissolve, e.g., the concepts 'rural' and 'urban' are inseparable, just as the natural and cultural environments or even matter and spirit.

In this respect, 'connectivities' constitutes an exciting topic, the academic localisation of which is attempted in this book. We would like to thank the authors for their contributions as well as Eileen Küçükkaraca for scientific editing, Tine Pape for technical editing and Andrea Ricci for coordination efforts in the background. As is often the case, working with Sidestone Press went as smoothly as ever. Thanks are also extended to the DFG for funding in the framework of the Excellence Cluster 'ROOTS – Social, Environmental, and Cultural Connectivity in Past Societies' (EXC 2150 ROOTS – 390870439).

Kiel, March 2022
Johannes Müller

Introduction

Connectivity matters!

In order to develop resilient and sustainable structures, e.g., in the face of climate changes, connectivity within and between societies is decisive. This is at least a basic hypothesis of the Cluster of Excellence ROOTS. Accordingly, in our investigations we understand connectivity in general in the context of three different areas:

▶ social, environmental and cultural connectivity, i.e., the relationships that exist between the environment and society,

▶ methodologically, the connectivity between disciplines of different traditional categories, i.e., between life sciences, natural sciences and the humanities,

▶ the connectivity between the past, the present and the future.

Consequently, in the contributions presented here, the concepts of ROOTS concerning questions of social, environmental and cultural connectivity in past societies are examined, on the one hand, and relevant questions are discussed here in various case studies on the other.

The basic concepts on social, environmental and cultural connectivity developed in Kiel are first placed in the context of questions of social and ecological developments in relation to globalisation, but also to sustainability and resilience (cf. contribution by J. Müller *et al.* in this volume). In a detailed study, particularly on the question of the openness of concepts on connectivity and the role of capability with regard to a definition of connectivity approaches of human individuals, V.P.J. Arponen describes the fluidness of the term.

In the case studies, Annette Haug and Ulrich Müller first lay the foundation for a reception history of a connecting element between nature and culture in human settlements with a study that is specifically related to water in cities. The role of social inequality for questions of connections and commitments in human societies is presented by Tim Kerig *et al.*, whereby questions concerning "measurement" are elaborated. In a continuous study on the issue of connectivity in disputes and conciliation, Oliver Nakoinz *et al.* investigate the consequences of the corresponding conditions. In concrete terms, this can also be demonstrated in the framework of identity studies from the fields of archaeology and linguistics, presented by John Peterson *et al.*

In purely archaeological or linguistic terms, corresponding connectivities are reflected in material or non-material remains. This is traced by Jens Schneeweiß with regard to the question of behaviour associated with garbage just as much as in a study by Ilja A. Seržant and Dariya Rafiyenko concerning linguistic standardisations in language events.

Overall, we clarify how crucial the question of connectivity is for the most diverse areas of human society, relationships to the environment and for explanations of events, processes and structures.

Social, environmental, and cultural connectivity: A concept for an understanding of society and the environment

Johannes Müller, Lutz Käppel, Andrea Ricci, Mara Weinelt

Johannes Müller
Institute of Prehistoric and
Protohistoric Archaeology
Kiel University
Johanna-Mestorf-Str. 2-6
24118 Kiel, Germany
johannes.mueller@ufg.uni-
kiel.de

Lutz Käppel
Institute of Classics
Kiel University
Leibnizstr. 8
24118 Kiel, Germany
luka@email.uni-kiel.de

Andrea Ricci
Cluster of Excellence ROOTS
Kiel University
Leibnizstraße 3
24118 Kiel, Germany
aricci@roots.uni-kiel.de

Mara Weinelt
Cluster of Excellence ROOTS
Kiel University
Leibnizstraße 3
24118 Kiel, Germany
mweinelt@roots.uni-kiel.de

Abstract

In our daily experiences, we can observe how the existence and the degree of connectivities between society and the environment, as well as between and within societies, determine political, social, cultural, economic and even ecological life. 'Connected' societies appear to enable a more peaceful coexistence, whereas disentangled societies can be the basis for severe conflicts. Thus, connectivity often creates the possibility for resilient reactions, for example, to climate change or pandemics. Decisive in this respect can be the connection between the natural and the cultural environment (Guedes and Crabtree 2016; Müller 2018). Against the background of a more general perspective, various aspects will be discussed here, which represent connectivity as the most important concept for an analysis of the environment and society and their dynamic relationship. The use of knowledge about the past, for instance, the tracking of trends or reflections in distant times, enables a special view of the present.

Introduction

The connections of people with each other and with the cultural or natural environment represent a basic component of human society. Since humans as social beings fundamentally need corresponding connections with other humans on both a biological and cultural level, connectivities are a fundamental component of existence. The manifestation and organisation of this connectivity is important for both well-being and the capabilities that result for individuals and society.

Access to resources and the creation of new resources together with rules of access are of utmost and crucial importance.[1] This influences the possibility of being resilient to changes, particularly environmental change, and of developing forms of sustainability (cf. Becker *et al.* 2021; Giannakis and Papadas 2021). Thus, connectivity is a phenomenon, which is anchored in human and environmental history, and its recent manifestations can only be understood and, if need be, changed against the background of the general historical dimension (cf. Hodos 2017a). Recent and past developments are ruled by complex connectivities between social groups and their environments, occurring in both the short and the long-term. A diachronic and long-term perspective is indispensable for the understanding of our own current fragility (Kintigh *et al.* 2014). Both socio-environmental settings and connectivity are subject to continuous alterations at various spatio-temporal scales (Jennings 2017; Knappett 2017; Netz 2020). Events, processes, and structures are rooted in recurrent patterns, and possess both early precursors and long-term efficiencies. Key dimensions shaping these include environmental changes, dietary constraints, knowledge production, population agglomeration, social disparities, and conflict potentials. These constitute deeply rooted drivers within human-environmental relationships and in this way constantly shape the 'human condition' (Fuchs *et al.* 2019). By identifying, reconstructing, and interpreting socio-environmental dynamics in the past, we aim at amplifying fundamental knowledge in order to better address questions related to social, environmental, and cultural connectivity (Layton *et al.* 2006; Müller and Ricci 2020).

Definition of connectivity

Surely, various definitions of connectivity are possible from different perspectives (cf. ASEM 2017; Becker *et al.* 2021). In addition to numerous epistemological discussions on questions of perception and the creation of different reception concepts, we define connectivity in a pragmatic sense.

> *'Connectivity concerns the mutual links between individuals, groups, and societies, and their physical and biological environments. The extent and velocity of connections are intimately linked to environmental conditions, access to food and other resources, conflicts and social tension, as well as to the production, access, and distribution of knowledge and innovation. The complex mutual interactions between societies and environments as catalysed by connectivities create dynamics within and among both spheres, even creating scenarios of instability, crisis and collapse. Communities may respond to environmental changes through connectivity, for instance, by developing resource management strategies, by transferring knowledge through technological and social innovation, via different forms of mobility, or by adapting existing social structures and creating novel ones. Arguably, connectivity may*

---

1   We define resources as those scarce material and immaterial goods that help individuals, groups or societies to assure success in carrying out their intentions and advancing their ends (Rawls 1971, 92). This broad perspective on resources enables a sound theoretical framework to advance the understanding of, *e.g.,* socio-environmental connectivities.

enhance power and wealth, forms of cohesion, and personal support. Conversely, a lack or low degree of connectivity may correlate to disempowerment, poverty, marginalization, and inequality. Even though modern societies appear to be mainly integrated by abstract media (i.e. law, state administrations, money, and the internet), different and fragile modes of connectivity operate beyond this realm. These societal 'glues' originated in (pre-)historic communities and remain crucial in modern times' (ROOTS 2018).

Concept of connectivity

A specific operationalisation results from this definition that is derived from empirical observation. Within this framework, the concept of connectivity serves as a theoretical lens through which we understand and reconstruct the extent, rate, and nature of past social, environmental, and cultural processes and structures. The central idea is that dynamics can be described as the interdependency between society, *i.e.*, the network of social behaviour and interaction, environment in the sense of 'nature' in the form of natural living conditions, such as climate and vegetation, and culture as the domain of practices, discourses, and material expressions of human behaviour. We adopt and extend the term 'connectivity' to describe and analyse how the social-environmental-cultural milieu facilitates, impedes, or generates movement, interaction, and cohesion. Thus, the potential of certain social and natural drivers become linked in a manner that produces social, environmental, and cultural change occurring at various spatial, temporal, and social scales. It is necessary to explore the effects of connectivity on socio-environmental change in past societies through an integrated analysis of environmental conditions and human behaviours (Arponen *et al.* 2019; Widlok *et al.* 2012).

Social, environmental, and cultural connectivities in past societies are visible on different temporal and spatial scales. Thus, past environmental and archaeological archives of high quality might be explored in different landscapes, and in different social constellations. A combination of archaeological and palaeo-environmental methods is necessary to detect the socio-environmental dimension from local to global interactions.

Connectivities and globalisation

Connectivity might be seen in different scenarios and to different degrees. The connectivity between environments and societies is represented on different scales, from the construction of local interconnectivities between, *e.g.*, technologies of subsistence economies and the local environs, to global climatic hazards and societal transformations (cf. Kneisel *et al.* 2015). From a historical viewpoint, prehistoric and historical societies developed new forms of interconnecting, gradually becoming more complex and more numerous. At the same time, globalisation and de-globalisation processes occurred – processes we can observe today in the material record (Scholte 2017). Globalisation, viewed as a kind of combination of complex connectivities, involves

'a dense network of intense interactions and interdependences between disparate people brought together through a long-distance flow of goods, ideas and individuals' (Jennings 2017).

During processes of increasing connectivity and through the development of shared practices, the establishment of new links as well as an increasing 'awareness' of cultural differences can be observed (Hodos 2017b). In principle, an increase in connectivities involves a sharing of cultural customs and environments, and within localised learning processes (habitus) translocal influences and networks become active (cf. Furholt 2018; Shennan 2009). Moreover, this leads to the repeated character of certain phenomena in history, which in turn, leaves traces in environmental records and societal archives (Feeser and Dörfler 2015; Gronenborn *et al.* 2014; Zimmermann 2012).

However, we should recognise that recent globalisation led to a number of socio-economic tensions and a destruction of socio-cultural milieus, especially on a local scale (cf. Angelbeck and Grier 2012; Scholte 2017). In principle, the dialectic relationship between global phenomena and local reactions has to be noted.

Recent discourses

There can be no doubt that the renewed interest in human-environmental interactions and connectivities is triggered by current debates on globalisation and global change and their political and social implications (Martens *et al.* 2015; Schwab 2018). These discussions feature prominently in current research on ecology and climate change, as well as in the social sciences, and are increasingly encroaching on historical and archaeological research, fomented among other things, by political and socio-cultural debates.[2] In the debate on global change, climate and environmental change are often discussed as causes which might potentially lead to an increase in violent conflict and the creation of further social division. Moreover, it is assumed that environmental change causes, in certain cases, severe resource shortages which can consequently trigger migration waves ('climate refugees', 'economic refugees'), although this hypothesis remains to be empirically verified. Nevertheless, it seems clear that the capacity for societies to cope with rapidly changing living conditions remains central in this debate. Thus, the necessity of a 'grand transformation' to mitigate global warming and environmental destruction is postulated and its implications discussed in an interdisciplinary plenum. These debates, which are mostly directed towards future developments, have massive and controversial implications for our current national and international policies and economic developments (United Nations 2015). Although current human-induced climate change is unprecedented in its magnitude and velocity, these debates have, however, also directed attention towards comparable processes and phenomena in the past[3] (among others: Burke *et al.* 2021; Rockman and Hritz 2020). We need a much longer historical perspective to understand these phenomena.

In an otherwise very inspiring and ground-breaking diachronic historical study, well integrating humanities and natural science approaches and dealing

---

2   The significance of the topic was already documented by a number of recent conferences (*e.g.* "Transformations 2015 – People and the Planet in the Anthropocene", Stockholm, 2015; PAGES workshops on hazards and risks in natural and urban environments, Riederalp, 2017; Adaptation and Resilience to Drought: Historical perspectives in Europe and Beyond, Strasbourg, 2017).

3   Already the German Advisory Council on Global Change (WBGU 2011), a multi-disciplinary and independent advisory body tasked by the German Government, not only analysed and provided recommendations on how to address the current environmental predicament, but has also increasingly addressed and taken into account the historical transformations of human-environment interactions.

with the dimension of social complexity in a global view, the authors widely ignore the environmental component (Turchin *et al.* 2018). With respect to 'complex connectivities and globalization', in a recent handbook on archaeology and globalisation the editor remarks on the existence of complex past connectivities and networks, well resembling recent globalisation processes, and that scholars have as of yet rarely explicitly addressed them under the perspective of globalisation (Hodos 2017b, 3). Environment centred studies, in contrast, rather aim at comprehensive accounts of environmental development and transformations, and human impact patterns in their historical dimensions (*e.g.* Walsh 2013, who deals with the palaeo-environmental record in the Mediterranean from the Neolithic to the Roman Age).

New goals

In principle, we defined four general goals for research on social, environmental and cultural connectivity: (1) the development of a specific archaeological and historical anatomy of connectivities through a broad, multi-faceted and interdisciplinary handling of the dynamical socio-environmental interrelations in a diachronic perspective, (2) the analysis of individual cases of socio-environmental 'biographies' as historical incidences with their particular developments, diagnostics, triggers, and consequences, (3) the identification of environmental and social scales of connectivities as occurring on different spatio-temporal scales by the systematic comparison of individual case studies in a *longue durée* perspective ('timelines'), (4) and a narrative of the environmental, cultural and social history of change by inferring general characteristics of connectivities, primarily from the Palaeolithic to pre-industrial periods.

The confrontation with today's multifaceted socio-environmental challenges might enable us to identify major interrelated spheres of social, environmental, and cultural connectivity.

Aligned methodologies

In result, we might reveal the shaping of socio-economic and cultural systems, as well as their general structure, shape, and the reciprocal impact of them and socio-environmental globalisation processes. The link of site and landscape biographies, and studies on general 'socio-environmental connectivities', will enable both a downscaling and an upscaling perspective on the roots of connectivity.

In practical research, we see the necessity to establish connectivity between very different research archives. In fact, we are dealing with data

▶ which reflects natural and anthropogenic environmental development via environmental archives,

▶ which enables a reconstruction of dietary changes, in particular via the remains of animal and human bones,

▶ which allows a reconstruction of the social and economic sphere via the remains of activity zones and settlements with their architecture,

▶ which facilitates the reconstruction of ritual and social practices with moveable and decorated legacies of material culture,

▶ which determines the reconstruction of a selective reconstruction with written sources.

Accordingly, on the one hand, "biographies of landscapes, places, people" can be traced (cf. Kolen and Renes 2015). On the other hand, timelines of phenomena, such as climate-related environmental changes, can be drawn up. The connection of the more qualitatively influenced "biographies" and the more quantitatively shaped "timelines" requires, as interdisciplinary research, a methodical connectivity that can develop scientific narratives and models with corresponding discourses. Thus, we assume that in addition to aspects of spatially-scaled, very different connectivity patterns, the drivers of coping strategies and the shaping of socio-cultural processes can also be disentangled/deduced.

Examples of connectivity concepts

Three examples will serve to illustrate connectivity issues. Selected here are connectivities, which result from the setting of values, those which refer to the landscape and those which represent real networks.

The development of values

In order to create connectivities between people and groups, agreements concerning values and thus also valuation are indispensable (cf. Graeber 2002). In modern economies, the corresponding valuation is established, for example, according to market mechanisms in which economic or social aspects of the exchange of goods proceed as an exchange of goods with use and exchange values or exchange values that become use values (Baumgärtner *et al.* 2017). The multitude of economic writings since the end of the 18th century at the latest provides information about economic theory expertise, attempting to analyse the processes of value creation. Due to climate change and aspects of the sustainability of production and consumption, however, socio-ecological deficits, which are assumed according to a purely economic valuation, play an increasingly important role (Baumgärtner *et al.* 2017).

Irrespective of environmental aspects of value setting and the asymmetries within the framework of, for example, the worldwide globalised exchange of goods, the problems arising in our modern world demonstrate the necessity to also deal with other forms of value setting.

As has been known for a long time, a valorisation that enables connectivity takes place through a special form of "gift and return gift" practices. Following Marcel Mauss (1993 [1923/1924]), the character of a gift is mentioned as an explanation for numerous historical and prehistoric circumstances: an object, which is offered as a gift, contains not only the material part of the object but at the same time also a part of the giver. This is combined with the personal obligation of the recipient to do the same in form of a return gift. Accordingly, reciprocal relations are initially programmed that create a form of equality in relationships and in the exchange of goods and, moreover, in a type of moral community (Fontijn 2019). For non-market economies, in particular, the principle of gift and return gift is alternatively formulated, although modern economies also implement corresponding backdrops within the framework of alternative concepts.

Principles of valorisation can obviously be institutionalised and created in different contexts. In the context of *rite de passage, i.e.,* in rites of passage to death, we know of the valorisation of things and actions, and also of the depositions of objects, which are often carried out at special places in nature. The observed rule in many Neolithic, Bronze Age and Iron Age non-state and non-literate societies that only certain objects are placed in graves or depots with simultaneous taboos about what can serve as grave goods or as part of a depot, points to the development of a canon of values. In the burial ritual or in votive offerings for the dead, the actors are shown what is of value and how this stands together. The "destruction" of objects that are often deposited in specific and defined areas of nature indicates the valorisation of the objects of real exchange to the actors (Fontijn 2019). Since such practices have supra-regional connotations, they enable the development of networks according to the valorisation.

The development of landscapes

Of particular importance for the concept of socio-environmental connectivity is the concept of 'Landscapes' (cf. Taylor et al. 1993). Landscapes are results of social practices that are in themselves products of socio-environmental connectivities, in which both the authorships of societies and the changing pre-conditions of environmental developments are visible (Müller 2018). Topographies, which develop in association with the backdrop of ecological and climatic parameters, are distinctive, socially generated connected social spaces. In a historical perspective, recent landscapes become containers, in which 'landscapes' of the present and the past are coded and really connected. Modern landscapes are always past landscapes, past landscapes are always already future ones.
If so,

'the creation of cultural environments amplifies the meaning of landscape connectivities: Apart from natural conditions (individual: health and genetics; ecological: soil, climate, vegetation; technological: wind and waterpower, or natural resources), social constants (social hierarchies, ideologies) play a decisive role in the formation of landscape connectivities. Social environments, within this concept of landscapes, are not only reflected by material remains but also by the spatial imprints of mobility and sustainability. The development of social space under specific ecological conditions is linked to the ideological systems, which maintain societies, for economic reasons or ritual purposes, together.' (Müller 2018, 39).

In this respect, the 'landscapes' are a synonym for social, environmental and cultural connectivities, which include not only environmental, demographic, and social space but also the ideological changes regarding 'landscapes': the conception that individuals and societies have concerning 'nature' (Käppel and Pothou 2015).
The developments of human societies were shaped by the landscapes in which they took place and in turn shaped those landscapes. Both societies and landscapes evolved over time, partly interactively, partly under the influence of external factors like climate.
The intentional development and alteration of the landscape by human societies is a product of social structures and symbolic systems, including the ritual sphere (Ingold 1993; Käppel and Pothou 2015). Settlement structures, of which characteristics are determined by social groups and interactions and by natural conditions alike, are a significant component of any landscape. The layout of settlement systems and settlement hierarchies within specific environments, the division of local and regional environments in areas for domestic and sacral

uses, and the interrelation of identity groups by communication spheres provide options for analysing connectivites within human adaptation to and cultural reshaping of environmental premises. Ceremonial spaces and structures provide evidence of the conceptual space of connectivities and environmental frameworks of connectivities. Objects, which are in themselves a product of connectivities, may indicate, in their fabrication and in the materials used, trade networks as well as patterns of connectivities within their production.

From a historical perspective, consequences arise from the above-mentioned for the reception of what we find around us. Starting from environmental conditions, primary topographies, which develop in association with the backdrop of ecological and climatic parameters, are distinctive, socially generated social spaces (Burmeister and Müller-Scheeßel 2006; Fontijn and Cuijpers 2002). Exemplarily, the spatial distribution of social architecture has a determining effect on the landscape – whether one considers manor houses, megalithic tombs, railway lines or urban agglomerations. The construction of lines (*e.g.* railroad lines), landmarks (*e.g.* by megalithic tombs), dense demographic crystallisation points (*e.g.* by cities) or power representation (*e.g.* manor houses) changes the landscape as space that is perceived (Furholt and Müller 2011; David and Thomas 2010). 'Socio-cultural landscapes' are those, in which the constantly changing ecological topographies are integrated and used for the invariably socially founded anthropogenic overprint and exploitation of the 'natural' environment. Consequently, the *socio-economic* sphere is joined with the *socio-cultural* sphere. Accordingly, we perceive the 'landscape' as the *container* in which both socially shaped space and the natural environment converge: socio-ecological, socio-economic and socio-cultural. In the framework of such a simplifying, but clear definition of landscape, we can observe the landscape as space, where environmental conditions and social conditions merge for spatial design without necessarily yielding a dichotomy: cultural phenomena are always something new and independent.

Thus, 'landscape' is the product of primarily dynamic social processes, but also a relic of past social processes. In this context, the ecological aspects of landscape provide, on the one hand, the framework and, on the other hand, represent a socially relevant product themselves in light of high human influence. The impact of natural changes, for example, including short, medium or long-term climate changes, influences societies, but can also be intensified by societies. Correspondingly, the following is important for the different scales of social development: On a local scale, the local ecological environment already exhibits extreme human influence in Neolithic societies, for instance, through the over-exploitation of resources, which surely led to the abandonment of settlements. On regional and global scales, the sum of events leads to corresponding processes, which can be significant for structural formation.

Therefore, 'landscape' is also the space in which the reciprocal relationship between humans and the environment – between complex societies and individual questions – takes place and becomes visible connectivities. Accordingly, and by the newly developing initial situations, individual elements of 'landscape' acquire meanings, which can be comprehended as the reception of their own social conditions and the environment. These co-exist with the environment, which is usually perceived as 'natural', with its ecological and climatic parameters (Müller 2018, 43-44).

The development of social boundaries and networks

In principle, communication technologies are the infrastructural basis of connectivities. Today, just as we know, *e.g.*, the technologies for data streams in their constant development and connection between different real and unreal worlds, in the past there were trails, paths, streets, railway lines, waterways, telephones, etc. Connected with corresponding possibilities of communication, movements and mobilities of objects, animals and people ensure the exchange of information within the framework of connectivities (Becker *et al.* 2021). Important in such a context are here the indirect consequences of other aspects: not only the limitations of the communicative infrastructure due to environmental conditions and events, but also the limiting or stimulating aspects of other technologies.

Thus, we can observe the development of technologies that either depend on a significant level of communication and connectedness of people and groups, which cannot exist otherwise (*e.g.* the cooperation of villages and areas that is required for certain agricultural technologies or water management technologies and strategies) or technologies that are dependent on a restriction of knowledge and thus a rather low level of connectivity (*e.g.* nuclear technology). Accordingly, under the respective ecological and social conditions, we observe the emergence of communications or connectivity institutions, including integrative architecture, meeting and market places, libraries, churches, parliaments and the like.

Networks of very different quality represent both the implementation and the infrastructure of connectivities, such as institutionalised knowledge networks with libraries and archives, religious networks with temples, churches and, for example, pilgrimage routes or processional streets, field systems and spatial planning as a connection between environment and society as well as exchange and trade networks.

Networks consequently develop on very different levels and velocities and with very different consequences. Open, general interaction, secured by principles of sharing, leads to a far-reaching development of the exchange of goods or knowledge. In contrast, systematic restrictions become apparent, *e.g.*, with the introduction of tin bronze technologies, electromobility, or new animal husbandry practices.

Consequences

Social, environmental and cultural connectivity represents a concept that helps to describe the state of a society and the environment and their dynamic processes. In addition to institutionalised and interpreted connectivities, such as values, networks and landscapes, there are basic tendencies that cannot necessarily be described as positive or negative. Although an increase in social inequality and thus a decrease in connectivity lead to problematic developments, an increase in population agglomerations and thus an increase in connectivity do not necessarily lead to a greater freedom from conflict. Moreover, the expansion of economic networks in the framework of globalisation processes leads to stronger dependencies and thus a reduction of conflict risks, but at the same time, this also means the possibility of the global spread of diseases, inhuman ideas and economic crises.

Based on an initially value-oriented hypothesis, the concept of connectivity proves to be more of a description of interaction patterns and dependencies, and by no means a simplifying insight into "better" or "worse". In this respect, the original relevance of the term is put into perspective. Instead, we recognise a powerful tool, which enables a comparison of empirical studies with natural science, humanities and life science contents.

References

Angelbeck, B. and Grier, C., 2012. Anarchism and the Archaeology of Anarchic Societies. Resistance to Centralization in the Coast Salish Region of the Pacific Northwest Coast. *Current Anthropology,* 53, 547-87.

Arponen, V.P.J., Dörfler, W., Feeser, I., Grimm, S.B., Groß, D., Hinz, M., Knitter, D., Müller-Scheeßel, N., Ott, K., Ribeiro, A., 2019. Environmental Determinism and Archaeology. Understanding and Evaluating Determinism in Research Design. *Archaeological Dialogues,* 26, 1-9.

ASEM, 2017. Chair's Statement of the 13th ASEM Foreign Ministers Meeting in Na Pyi Taw, Myanmar, 20-21 November 2017, Annex I. *ASEM Connectivity,* 1-2 [online]. Available at: https://eeas.europa.eu/sites/eeas/files/asem_definition_connectivity.pdf.

Baumgärtner, S., Drupp, M.A., Meya, J.N., Munz, J.M., Quaas, M.F., 2017. Income Inequality and Willingness to Pay for Public Environmental Goods. *Journal of Environmental Economics and Management* 8, 35-61.

Becker, W., Domínguez-Torreiro, M., Neves, A.R., Tacão Moura, C., Saisana, M., 2021. Exploring the link between Asia and Europe connectivity and sustainable development. *Research in Globalization* 3, 10045. Available at: https://doi.org/10.1016/j.resglo.2021.100045.

Burke, M., Driscoll, A., Heft-Neal, S., Xue, J., Burney, J., Wara, M., 2021. The Changing Risk and Burden of Wildfire in the United States. *PNAS,* 118 (2). Available at: https://doi.org/10.1073/pnas.2011048118.

Burmeister, S. and Müller-Scheeßel, N., eds., 2006. *Soziale Gruppen – Kulturelle Grenzen. Die Interpretation sozialer Identitäten in der prähistorischen Archäologie.* Tübinger Archäologische Taschenbücher 5. Münster, New York, München, Berlin: Waxmann.

David, B. and Thomas, J., eds., 2010. *Handbook of Landscape Archaeology.* London: Routledge.

Feeser, I. and Dörfler, W., 2015. The Early Neolithic in Pollen Diagrams from Eastern Schleswig-Holstein and Western Mecklenburg – Evidence for a 1000 Years Cultural Adaptive Cycle? *In:* J. Kabacinski, S. Hartz, D.C.M. Raemaekers, Th. Terberger, eds. *The Dabki Site in Pomerania and the Neolithisation of the North European Lowlands (ca. 5000-3000 cal B.C.).* Rahden/Westf.: Verlag Marie Leidorf, 291-306.

Fontijn, D.R., 2019. *Economies of Destruction: How the Systematic Destruction of Valuables Created Value in Bronze Age Europe, c. 2300-500 BC.* London, New York: Routledge.

Fontijn, D.R. and Cuijpers, A.G.F.M., 2002. Revisiting Barrows: A Middle Bronze Age Burial Group at the Kops Plateau, Nijmegen. *Berichten van de Rijksdienst voor het Oudheidkundig Bodemonderzoek,* 45, 155-87.

Fuchs, K., Kirleis, W., Müller, J., guest eds., 2019. *Special issue: Scales of Transformation – Human-Environmental Interaction in Prehistoric and Archaic Societies.* The Holocene, 29 (10).

Furholt, M., 2018. Translocal Communities – Exploring Mobility and Migration of Sedentary Societies in the European Neolithic and Early Bronze Age. *Prähistorische Zeitschrift,* 92, 304-21.

Furholt, M. and Müller, J., 2011. The Earliest Monuments in Europe – Architecture and Social Structures (5000-3000 calBC). *In*: M. Furholt, F. Lüth, J. Müller, eds. *Megaliths and Identities. Early Monuments and Neolithic Societies from the Atlantic to the Baltic.* Frühe Monumentalität und Soziale Differenzierung 1. Bonn: Habelt, 15-32.

Giannakis, E. and Papadas, C.T., 2021. Spatial Connectivity and Regional Economic Resilience in Turbulent Times. *Sustainability,* 13 (20), 11289. Available at: https://doi.org/10.3390/su132011289.

Graeber, D., 2002. *Toward an Anthropological Theory of Value.* London: Palgrave Macmillan.

Gronenborn, D., Strien, H.-C., Dietrich, S., Sirocko, F., 2014. 'Adaptive Cycles' and Climate Fluctuations: A Case Study from Linear Pottery Culture in western Central Europe. *Journal of Archaeological Science,* 51, 73-83.

Guedes, J.A. and Crabtree, S.A., 2016. 21st-Century Approaches to Ancient Problems: Climate and Society. *PNAS,* 113, 14483-91.

Hodos, T., ed., 2017a. *The Routledge Handbook of Archaeology and Globalization.* London, New York: Routledge.

Hodos, T., 2017b. Globalization: Some Basics. An Introduction to the Routledge Handbook of Archaeology and Globalization. *In*: T. Hodos, ed. *The Routledge Handbook of Archaeology and Globalization.* London, New York: Routledge, 3-11.

Ingold, T., 1993. The Temporality of the Landscape. *World Archaeology,* 25 (2), 152-174.

Jennings, J., 2017. Distinguishing Past Globalizations. *In*: T. Hodos, ed. *The Routledge Handbook of Archaeology and Globalization.* London, New York: Routledge, 12-28.

Käppel, L. and Pothou, V., eds., 2015. *Human Development in Sacred Landscapes.* Göttingen: V&R unipress.

Kintigh, K.W., Altschul, J.H., Beaudry, M.C., Drennan, R.D., Kinzig, A.P., Kohle, T.A., Limp, W.F., Maschner, H.D.G., Michener, W.K., Pauketat, T.R., Peregrine, J.A., Sabloff, T.J., Wilkinson, H.T.W., Zeder, M.A., 2014. Grand Challenges for Archaeology. *PNAS,* 111 (3), 879-880.

Knappett, C., 2017. Globalization, Connectivitiees and Networks: An Archaeological Perspective. In: T. Hodos, ed. *The Routledge Handbook of Archaeology and Globalization.* London, New York: Routledge, 29-41.

Kneisel, J., Dal Corso, M., Kirleis, W., eds., 2015. *The Third Food Revolution?Setting the Bronze Age Table: Common Trends in Economic and Subsistence Strategies in Bronze Age Europe. Proceedings of the International Workshop "Socio-Environmental Dynamics over the Last 12,000 Years: The Creation of Landscapes III (15th – 18th April 2013) in Kiel".* Universitätsforschungen zur prähistorischen Archäologie 283. Bonn: Habelt.

Kolen, J. and Renes, J., 2015. Landscape Biographies: Key Issus. *In*: J. Kolen, H. Renes, R. Hermans, eds. *Geographical, Historical and Archaeological Perspectives on the Production and Transmission of Landscapes.* Amsterdam: Amsterdam University Press, 21-48.

Layton, R., Stone, P.G., Shennan, S. 2006. *A Future for Archaeology: The Past in the Present.* London: UCL Press.

Martens, P., Caselli, M., De Lombaerde, P., Figge, L., Scholte, J.A., 2015. New directions in globalization indices. *Globalizations,* 12 (2), 217-228. Available at: 10.1080/14747731.2014.944336.

Mauss, M., 1993 [1923/1924]. *The Gift. The Form and Reason for Exchange in Archaic Societies.* London: Routledge.

Müller, J., 2018. The Disentanglement of Landscapes: Remarks on Concepts of Socio-Environmental Research and Landscape Archaeology. *In*: A. Haug, L. Käppel, J. Müller, eds. *Past Landscapes. The Dynamics of Interaction between Society, Landscape and Culture.* Leiden: Sidestone Press, 39-52.

Müller, J. and Ricci, A., eds., 2020. *Past Societies. Human Devlopment in Landscapes.* Leiden: Sidestone Press.

Netz, R., 2020. *Scale, Space, and Canon in Ancient Literary Culture.* Cambridge: Cambridge Univesity Press.

Rawls, J., 1971. *A Theory of Justice.* Cambridge: The Belknap Press of Harvard University Press.

Rockman, M. and Hritz, C., 2020. Expanding Use of Archaeology in Climate Change Response by Changing Its Social Environment. *PNAS,* 117. Available at: https://doi.org/10.1073/pnas.1914213117.

ROOTS 2018. *Roots – Social, Environmental, Cultural Connectivity in Past Societies.* Proposal for the German Excellence Initiative. Availble at: https://www.cluster-roots.uni-kiel.de/en.

Scholte, J.A., 2017. *Globalization: A Critical Introduction.* London: Red Globe Press/Springer Nature.

Schwab, K., 2018. *Globalization 4.0 – what does it mean?* World Economic Forum Annual Meeting, 2018. Available at: https://www.weforum.org/agenda/2018/11/globalization-4-what-does-it-mean-how-it-will-benefit-everyone/ [Accessed: 13 March 2022].

Shennan, S., 2009. *Pattern and Process in Cultural Evolution.* Origins of Human Behavior and Culture 2. Berkeley, Los Angeles: University of California Press.

Taylor, P.D., Fahrig, L., Henein, K., Merriam, G., 1993. Connectivity Is a Vital Element of Landscape Structure. *Oikos,* 68, 571-73.

Turchin, P., Currie, T.E., Whitehouse, H., François, P., Feeney, K., Mullins, D., Hoyer, D., Collins, C., Grohmann, S., Savage, P., Mendel-Gleason, G., Turner, E., Dupeyron, A., Cioni, E., Reddish, J., Levine, J., Jordan, G., Brandl, E., Williams, A., Cesaretti, R., Krueger, M., Ceccarelli, A., Figliulo-Rosswurm, J., Tuan, P.-J., Peregrine, P., Marciniak, A., Preiser-Kapeller, J., Kradin, N., Korotayev, A., Palmisano, A., Baker, D., Bidmead, J., Bol, P., Christian, D., Cook, C., Covey, A., Feinman, G., Júlíusson, Á.D., Kristinsson, A., Miksic, J., Mostern, R., Petrie, C., Rudiak-Gould, R., ter Haar, B., Wallace, V., Mair, V., Xie, L., Baines, J., Bridges, E., Manning, J., Lockhart, B., Bogaard, A., Spencer, C., 2018. Quantitative Historical Analysis Uncovers a Single Dimension of Complexity that Structures Global Variation in Human Social Organization. *Proceedings of the National Academy of Sciences,* 115 (2), E144-51. Available at: https://doi.org/10.1073/pnas.1708800115.

United Nations, 2015. *Transforming Our World: The 2030 Agenda for Sustainable Development.* Resolution Adopted by the General Assembly on 25 September 2015. A/RES/70/1, 15-16301, 1-35. Available at: doi: 10.1007/s13398-014-0173-7.2.

Walsh, K., 2013. *The Archaeology of Mediterranean Landscapes: Human-Environment Interaction from the Neolithic to the Roman Period.* Cambridge: Cambridge University Press.

Widlok, T., Aufgebauer, A., Bradtmöller, M., Dikau, R., Hoffmann, T., Kretschmer, I., Panagiotopoulos, K., Pastoors, A., Peters, R., Schäbitz, F., Schlummer, M., Solich, M., Wagner, B., Wenniger, G.-C., Zimmermann, A., 2012. Towards a Theoretical Framework for Analyzing Integrated Socio-Environmental Systems. *Quaternary International,* 274, 259-72.

Zimmermann, A., 2012. Cultural Cycles in Central Europe During the Holocene. *Quaternary International,* 274, 251-58.

On the concept of connectivity

V.P.J. Arponen

Abstract

Despite some examples of systematised usage in the literature, the concept of connectivity is not a technical term with a commonly accepted definition or a steady meaning. Thus, we are to a good extent free to construe the meaning of the term, which this contribution seeks to do by relating it, on the one hand, to a Binfordian systemic perspective and, on the other hand, to a Wittgensteinian contextualism – the outlines of which are sketched in this paper. The paper argues, first, that while a multi-faceted Binfordian systemic meta-theory is in an excellent position to describe a comprehensive analytic framework with essential connectivities between systems and subsystems, there has also always been a reductivist tendency to ultimately reduce connective multiplicity to adaptation to the environmental system – a view that may ultimately be counter-connective. Second, the paper explicates the concept of a logical investigation as it emerges from the philosophies of Kant and Wittgenstein, rarely if ever discussed in archaeological and anthropological contexts. A logical investigation is characterised as a reverse-engineering approach to connectivity, reflectively testing archaeological interpretations by inquiring into the conditions that would be needed to be fulfilled by prehistoric human-environmental interactions for these interpretations to be plausible.

V.P.J. Arponen
Cluster of Excellence ROOTS
Kiel University
Leibnizstr. 3
24118 Kiel, Germany
vcrponen@roots.uni-kiel.de

Introduction

This article attempts to gain clarity about the concept of connectivity by situating it within a philosophy of archaeological knowledge.

The first difficulty we encounter is that, despite some examples of systematised usage in the literature (Kempf 2020), the concept of connectivity is not a technical term with a commonly accepted definition. The concept does not have a steady or regular meaning or use in archaeological or other scientific practice. As such, the concept of connectivity invites us to construe a place for it in the existing field of scientific debate and practice.

We adopt our starting point in the statement that, on the most abstract level, the concept of connectivity alludes to a scientific perspective that emphasises, so to speak, the elemental and compositional or, if you like, systemic nature of reality as studied in human and natural sciences alike. Imagery evoked here by the Enlightenment philosopher David Hume (2000, originally published in 1748) was one of billiard balls moving on the table and striking each other in a process manifesting interactions, or connectivities, between the different elements of the compositional whole of the system. Such imagery pretty well summarises the modern scientific worldview and its central ideas of the nature of reality involving compositional, elemental connectivities.

What Hume said next, however, opened up a second lane of approach to connectivity. For Hume went on to argue that, strictly speaking, the causal connection between one ball impacting another cannot strictly be observed. Like magnetism, we do not see 'causality' in a manner in which we see, *e.g.*, colours. Rather, Hume argued, causality is imputed onto the process by the observer based on their past experience of certain causes being followed up by certain effects, and the resulting expectation of colliding billiard balls and their changing trajectories. That is to say, the fundamental phenomenon of causality was not observable but had to be induced from observations of constant conjunctions of collisions and particularly changing trajectories.

In this context, Hume formulated his problem of induction by which name it is commonly known in philosophical literature to this day: no number of past observations of a conjunction of particular causes and effects can logically confirm the existence of a causal connection, which is inferred from past cases, and there is thus no observable causal necessity. Hume's basic imagery formed the basis of philosophical thought about the nature of the scientific method, for example, in the work of Carl Hempel (1981), an immensely influential philosopher in archaeology.

In any case, with this argument, Hume drew a wedge between causal reality and the human concept of it. In the self-confession of a second foundational modern philosopher, Immanuel Kant (1999, originally published in 1781) was awoken from his "dogmatic slumber" about the nature of causality by Hume's work. Kant went on to formulate a concept of philosophical idealism in which reality appears, so to speak, as a product of connectivities between human categories of understanding and reality itself. Philosophical Kantianism is the groundwork of 20th and 21st century relativism and the thesis of the social construction of reality (Jarvie 2007).

At the risk of opening up an old can of worms in the form of Charles P. Snow's two cultures debate (Snow 1998; Arponen *et al.* 2019), we can look back at the divergence of the Humean and Kantian traditions as evoking a contrast between natural and human scientific approaches. Ultimately, the examination of the presuppositions of these traditions will allow us to arrive at a reflective and differentiated concept of connectivity.

Connectivity and reductivism

In the Humean tradition, for example, in the Binfordian systemic meta-theory (Binford 1962), reality may be understood as a system consisting of interconnected subsystems, all in functional or other interaction with one another (Lerner 1994). This meta-theory was not Lewis Binford's invention, but reflected, alongside contemporary cultural evolutionary influences, as much in the mid-20th century as it does today, a very basic natural scientific, ultimately Humean "mechanical world view" that regards reality in terms of elements and their interactions (Merchant 1980).

New archaeology has often been associated with an empiricist theory of knowledge, or something that in archaeology has tended to be referred to as positivism. Empiricism, as it derives from the classic modern philosophies of Hume and John Locke (1690), posits a theory of knowledge focused on the idea of an interplay between the cognitive systems of knowing subjects, say, humans, and information we gather about objects, reality, or the world around us. Human knowledge, then, involves a careful collection and systemisation of empirical knowledge, essentially by way of iterative hypothesis formation and testing. This is an on-going and iterative process upon which, for example, generalisations or law-like statements can rest. The Hempelian model of scientific method articulates the same basic view.

Now, despite past critiques, there is no question that archaeology is fundamentally a data-driven science and, as such, quantitative methods of a broadly speaking Humean scientific archaeology continue to occupy a central place at the core of the archaeological practice, even experiencing a powerful resurgence (Kristiansen 2014). Equipped with a Binfordian meta-theory of interlocking subsystems, including subsystems down to level of cultural perceptions and maybe even individual cognition (Malafouris 2013; Tylén *et al.* 2020), such an approach can in principle offer a powerful account of human, cultural, social, political, and environmental connectivities.

That said, while the Binfordian meta-theory can in principle account for a wide variety of connective elements, in practice the scientific archaeological approach has often been earmarked by certain *reductivism to selected essentials*. That is to say, already for Binford, the environment was conceived as the most essential system (Gremillion *et al.* 2014; Larson *et al.* 2014). The other subsystems, such as any given cultural, social, and political repertoire of technical and conceptual know-how, were viewed as conducive to human flourishing within the environmental frame (or indeed detrimental to it, Diamond 2005; but see also Middleton 2017).

The concept of *affordance* in landscape archaeology could be seen as an attempt to rearticulate the Binfordian meta-theory. Affordances are objective physical properties of a given physical space as seen in relation to human opportunities that they afford. In other words, affordances offer human subjects, who act in that space, potentialities or opportunities of engagement with and within the environment (Gibson 1986). Such a concept of affordance went hand in hand with the development of computerised Geographic Information Systems (GIS). These systems could map the objective geographical space of affordances, which were then studied virtually. For example, Marcus Llobera (1996) saw here a promise of rigorous empirical methods being introduced into landscape archaeology – while spatial cognition had hitherto been studied, so to speak, analogically, *e.g.*, in Tilley's work through walks in landscapes. Interestingly, Llobera

(1996, 612) also pointed out that there was a danger of "environmental determinism" in landscape archaeology if affordances were seen to determine human action in the environment.

The precursors of reductionism can already be seen in the philosophical responses to the problem of induction. To recap, the problem was that human knowledge was understood as fundamentally based on generalisations from a limited number of observational instances, yet multiple mutually incommensurable generalisations could be logically derived from the same data. In other words, in induction, the data under-determines its interpretation. Philosophers of science noted that further criteria were thus needed to be able to sort formally equal and empirically adequate generalisations in those that were law-like and those that merely looked like it.

The list of criteria suggested in the course of the 20ᵗʰ century was quite long and diverse (Bird 2006), but there was a certain reductionist thrust towards separating the essential properties of phenomena for which an explanation was sought from their non-essential properties. For example, towards the end of his career, Hempel (1988, 23) began to speak of "provisos" which he characterised as statements that formulate *"essential, but generally unstated, presuppositions of theoretical inferences"* that define the object or process of study as of a certain kind. The under-determination problem was thereby combatted by positing that, when provisos first define reality in certain ways, it becomes easier to distinguish truly law-like generalisations from those that merely look like that. That is, provisos, so to speak, pre-define the object or process of study as of a certain kind and thereby provide a blueprint for the kind of generalisation we are looking for in the object of study. In other words, provisos can serve to reduce a given object or process to its essential properties that can be tracked by fitting generalisations.

One example of such reductionism could be, as argued above, the narrowing down of the essential aspects of the prehistoric human condition to human coping with environmental affordances. When that reduction is made, those interpretations that track the shape of human coping with the environment (say, hunting technologies and practices) are singled out as pertaining to the essentials.

A parallel reduction to the putative essentials by the deployment of certain provisos is arguably happening in the contemporary debate about aDNA in archaeology, which are used to make plausible the equation of shared aDNA with shared cultural traits and thus the equation of the movement or transfer of aDNA with migrational movements. The provisos in question pertain to ideas about the geographical co-occurrence of human biological reproduction and the transfer of the ways of a group by the parents, family, and kin to the offspring in communities. When the same DNA is then found in different times and spaces, the provisos seem to enable the inference to cultural similarity across time and space in these cases. Accordingly, the challenges of the conclusions of such aDNA studies have focused on challenging the provisos, namely, the

> *'premise that prehistoric communities were closed, internally homogeneous social entities with a shared uniform culture and a shared genetic ancestry'*
> *(Furholt 2020, 23).*

The particular details of the examples above notwithstanding, the moral of the story is that reductivism is antithetical to the concept of connectivity. If both are contained in the Binfordian meta-theory of systems and subsystems, then the meta-theory threatens to contain internal inconsistencies.

Connectivity, Kant, and Wittgenstein

Going back to the beginning of our story of the Humean problem of induction, we noted that the Kantian strand developed the story to a quite different direction from the one that, eventually, led to Hempel and New Archaeology.

We can distinguish two directions in the Kantian heritage. On the one hand, we have the idea of categories as potentially culturally specific and particular, which gave an overall relativist overtone to the philosophies emerging from this branch. Arguably, this has been the dominant branch to grow from the Kantian heritage in 20th and 21st century human scientific theory, including anthropology and archaeology (Jarvie 2007).

On the other hand, Kant's philosophy was originally conceived as an objectivist, scientific approach to the fundamental structures of human understanding. In this second sense, Kantianism gave rise to the idea of investigating what came to be referred to as the *logic* of understanding. In this concept of logic, it can be argued that we find a particular concept of connectivity. In what follows, we shall explore some aspects of this second, in my view, somewhat overlooked branch.

The nature of the Kantian 'logical investigation' can perhaps be best approached by considering Kant's famous contribution to moral philosophy: the categorical imperative (Kant 1785). The categorical imperative proposed that one should only act according to maxims that one can wish to become a universal law. Behind this approach is the idea that moral commandments form a necessary, universal scaffolding. That is to say, Kant reasoned that by its logic or nature as a certain kind of a system, morality makes demands on us from this categorical, universal, and necessary stance. As an Enlightenment thinker, Kant believed that critical reason could reveal the universal scaffolding of the logic of morals, just as it could, and in Kant's work did reveal the logic of human understanding in its categories of thought. This Kantian concept of a universal logic had its influence on a number of thinkers, one of them the anthropologist Claude Lévi-Strauss (Lévi-Strauss 1966). Lévi-Strauss' work posited universal, structural relationships that had their origin in parallel structures of the mind, but could also be found reflected, *e.g.*, in structures of kinship.

In the philosophy of language, the Kantian concept of logic found a use in the philosophy of Ludwig Wittgenstein (1889-1951), and it is here that we will now try to find a concept of connectivity (see contrast with Bintliff 2000).

Wittgenstein's almost exclusively posthumously published major works (most notably 1958 and 1975) used the concepts of language game (*Sprachspiel*) and form of life (*Lebensform*) to describe the context of language use. In Wittgenstein's famous dictum, meaning is use – that is, to describe the meaning of a concept is to describe its use, that is to say, its role and place in a form of life (Wittgenstein 1958, paragraph 43). To use Wittgenstein's favourite example, the meaning of a concept is analogous to the role of a piece in chess and described by an account of the role of the piece in the game of chess.

Wittgenstein's approach is Kantian, for it views concepts as belonging to a system of logic consisting of a context use. That is, concepts always imply a context of use, a world, or a form of life, of some kind. The Wittgensteinian philosopher Vincent Descombes (2000, 228) exemplified this thinking by way of a thought-experiment:

Imagine a Cro-Magnon man suddenly struck by lightning, and imagine that the electrical discharge makes his neuronal state identical to that of someone remembering that he has to go to the bank. According to the postulates of the materialist theory of mind, this Cro-Magnon man must have the thought that he must now go to the bank.

Descombes intended the thought-experiment to show that a particular thought always made sense only in context of a form of life. Hence, to think that one must go to the bank presupposes a context, a form of life, in which there are banks and the rest of the 'logic' or 'scaffolding' implied by the existence of banks (why and for what reason would one go to a bank and so on). Therefore, our Cro-Magnon man could not be said to be having the thought that he must go to the bank – the context for it is completely missing in the Cro-Magnon form of life. (By contrast, if the meaning of concepts was equated with a person thinking that concept, then it should be conceivable that we could accidentally, such as through a lightning strike, come to entertain thoughts for which there is no context in our lives.)

In philosophy, the Wittgensteinian (Kantian) approach has inspired, among others, work on discourse theory in which discourses are seen as processes with an in principle distinguishable logic from which entitlements, validity claims and the like can be derived (Habermas 1984; 1987). Again, in philosophy of language, inferentialism is the Wittgenstein-inspired view that meaning can be made explicit by analysing inferential connections emanating from statements to other statements (Brandom 1994).

Now, for archaeology, one implication of Wittgenstein's method of a 'logical investigation' is that it can introduce a certain, so to speak, reverse engineering frame of mind to archaeological reasoning. Reverse engineering is the process of inferring aspects of the internal construction of a device, its compatibility or incompatibility with other devices and other such aspects of possible functionality, from what the device looks like or how it is known to function.

In archaeology, a logical investigation of this kind could be used to interrogate the plausibility of archaeological interpretations by reflectively thinking back from the interpretation to the kind of form of life it presupposes as its context. This concept of a logical investigation can give rise to a concept of connectivity.

For example, recently, a controversy arose over the use of archaeogenomic studies to make inferences about family and kinship structures. The concept of "core family" now frequently appears in such studies (Furholt 2021; Mittnik *et al.* 2019), a concept that, however, harks back to the contemporary concept of "nuclear family". This is a concept belonging to quite a definite historical juncture characterised by the formation of core, nuclear father-mother-children families due to migration from rural to urban areas as the rest of the extended family resides in other geographical locations. There is no obvious logic in the Bronze Age or elsewhere that corresponds to the logic within which the concept of core family has its historical place (parallel to how there was no bank that a Cro-Magnon individual could wish to go to). Secondly, the concept of a core family in the contemporary context has a historical-material and socio-cultural definition, while the same concept used in archaeogenomic studies seems to above all simply refer back to genomic data in absence of further context. In other words, there is no plausible connectivity between the concept of a core family and the prehistoric context, which calls for an exploration of further anthropological models in terms of which to interpret the genomic data.

As a second example of the significance of this way of thinking about connectivity that I would like to present concerns the notions of social complexity, stratification, power and domination. Overall, the method is the same as above:

we inspect and evaluate models of stratification "thinking in reverse" from these models into the kind of social reality that these systems presuppose and could plausibly be said to exist in. In other words, leadership and systems of stratification can be seen to operate under particular historical conditions that enable as well as limit the operations of these systems.

For example, Martin Furholt *et al.* (2020, 28) discussed a number of prehistoric stratification contexts where the commoners could always in principle vote with their "feet and paddles" and abandon the system of stratification. In such conditions, it may not be plausible to think of stratification as a top-down, hierarchical, elite-focused phenomenon in which these elites pursue their self-interested aggrandising (compare Hayden 2014, 14), but rather, even if self-interested, these elites could arguably be forced to devote considerable energies in pre-empting "voting with feet and paddles" – or, alternatively, it could perhaps even be argued that there was a selective pressure favouring elites with a communalist rather than a self-interested ethos (compare "social actor vs. economic entrepreneur" in Roscoe 2012). The latter perspective could plausibly be grounded in an action-based, in contrast to resource-based, theory of value articulated by David Graeber (2001) for anthropology.

In sum, a logical investigation, therefore, can be characterised as a reverse-engineering approach to connectivity. It reflectively tests archaeological interpretations by inquiring into the conditions that would need to be fulfilled by prehistoric human-environmental interactions for these interpretations to be plausible. Such an investigation might be found to be valuable in that it serves to expose the sometimes contestable presuppositions behind particular archaeological interpretations by revealing their incompatibility with features of the prehistoric context they claim to fit into. Conversely, an investigation into the logical connections between phenomena and their context espouses a holistic awareness of past, present, and future fields of connectivities.

References

Arponen, V.P.J., Grimm, S., Käppel, L., Ott, K., Thalheim, B., Kropp, Y., Kittig, K., Brinkmann, J., Ribeiro, A., 2019. Between Natural and Human Sciences: On the Role and Character of Theory in Socio-Environmental Archaeology. *The Holocene*, 29 (10), 1517-1530.

Binford, L., 1962. Archaeology as Anthropology. *American Antiquity*, 28 (2), 217-225.

Bintliff, J., 2000. Archaeology and the Philosophy of Wittgenstein. *In:* C. Holtorf and H. Karlsson, eds. *Philosophy and Archaeological Practice: Perspectives for the 21st Century*. Gothenburg: Bricoleur Press, 153-172.

Bird, A., 2006. Philosophy of Science. *In:* J. Shand, ed. *Fundamentals of Philosophy*. London: Taylor & Francis.

Brandom, R.B., 1994. *Making It Explicit: Reasoning, Representing and Discursive Commitment*. Cambridge, MA: Harvard University Press.

Descombes, V., 2000. The philosophy of collective representations. *History of the Human Sciences*, 13 (1), 37-49.

Diamond, J., 2005. *Collapse: How Societies Choose to Fail or Survive*. London: Penguin.

Furholt, M., 2020. Biodeterminism and Pseudo-objectivity as Obstacles for the Emerging Field of Archaeogenetics. *Archaeological Dialogues*, 27 (1), 23-25.

Furholt, M., 2021. Mobility and Social Change: Understanding the European Neolithic Period after the Archaeogenetic Revolution. *Journal of Archaeological Research* [online]. Available at: https://doi.org/10.1007/s10814-020-09153-x.

Furholt, M., Grier, C., Spriggs, M., Earle, T.K., 2020. Political Economy in Archaeology of Emergent Complexity: a Synthesis of Bottom-up and Top-down Approaches. *Journal of Archaeological Method and Theory*, 27, 157-191.

Gibson, J.J., 1986. *The Ecological Approach to Visual Perception*. Hillsdale, N.J.: Lawrence Erlbaum Associates.

Graeber, D., 2001. *Toward An Anthropological Theory of Value: The False Coin of Our Own Dreams*. New York: Palgrave.

Gremillion, K.J., Barton, L., Piperno, D.R., 2014. Particularism and the retreat from theory in the archaeology of agricultural origins. *Proceedings of the National Academy of Sciences* [online], 111 (17), 6171-6177. Available at: https://www.pnas.org/content/111/17/6171.

Habermas, J., 1984. *The Theory of Communicative Action 1: Reason and the Rationalization of Society*. Cambridge: Polity.

Habermas, J., 1987. *The Theory of Communicative Action 2: Lifeworld and System, a Critique of Functionalist Reason*. Boston: Beacon.

Hayden, B., 2014. *The Power of Feasts: From Prehistory to the Present*. New York: Cambridge University Press.

Hempel, C., 1981. Turns in the Evolution of the Problem of Induction. *Synthese*, 46 (3), 193-404.

Hempel, C., 1988. Provisoes: A problem concerning the inferential function of scientific theories. *Erkenntnis*, 28 (2), 147-164.

Hume, D., 2000. *An Enquiry Concerning Human Understanding*. Oxford, U.K.: Clarendon Press.

Jarvie, I., 2007. Relativism and Historicism. *In:* S.P. Turner and M.W. Risjord, eds. *Handbook of the Philosophy of Science: Philosophy of Anthropology and Sociology*. Burlington: Elsevier, 553-589.

Kant, I., 1785. *Groundwork of the Metaphysics of Morals*. Translated by Mary J. Gregor, with an introduction by Christine Korsgaard. Cambridge: Cambridge University Press, 1998.

Kant, I., 1999. *The Critique of Pure Reason*. New York: Cambridge University Press.

Kempf, M., 2020. From landscape affordances to landscape connectivity: contextualizing an archaeology of human ecology. *Archaeological and Anthropological Sciences* [online], 12 (8), 174. Available at: https://doi.org/10.1007/s12520-020-01157-4.

Kristiansen, K., 2014. Towards a New Paradigm: The Third Science Revolution and its Possible Consequences in Archaeology. *Current Swedish Archaeology*, 22, 11-71.

Larson, G., Piperno, D.R., Allaby, R.G., Purugganan, M.D., Andersson, L., Arroyo-Kalin, M., Barton, L., Climer Vigueira, C., Denham, T., Dobney, K., Doust, A.N., Gepts, P., Gilbert, M.T.P., Gremillion, K.J., Lucas, L., Lukens, L., Marshall, F.B., Olsen, K.M., Pires, J.C., Richerson, P.J., Rubio de Casas, R., Sanjur, O.I., Thomas, M.G., Fuller, D.Q., 2014. Current perspectives and the future of domestication studies. *Proceedings of the National Academy of Sciences* [online], 111 (17), 6139-6146. Available at: https://www.pnas.org/content/111/17/6139.

Lerner, H., 1994. Lewis Binford and the New Archaeology. *Totem: The University of Western Ontario Journal of Anthropology*, 1 (1), 57-62.

Lévi-Strauss, C., 1966. *The Savage Mind*. London: Weidenfeld and Nicholson.

Llobera, M., 1996. Exploring the Topography of Mind: GIS, Social Space, and Archaeology. *Antiquity*, 70, 612-622.

Locke, J., 1690. *An Essay Concerning Human Understanding*. London: Thomas Basset.

Malafouris, L., 2013. *How Things Shape the Mind: A Theory of Material Engagement.* Cambridge: MIT Press.

Merchant, C., 1980. *The Death of Nature: Women, Ecology and the Scientific Revolution.* London: Harper & Row.

Middleton, G.D., 2017. *Understanding Collapse: Ancient History and Modern Myths.* Cambridge: Cambridge University Press.

Mittnik, A., Massy, K., Knipper, C., Wittenborn, F., Friedrich, R., Pfrengle, S., Burri, M., Carlichi-Witjes, N., Deeg, H., Furtwängler, A., Harbeck, M., von Heyking, K., Kociumaka, C., Kucukkalipci, I., Lindauer, S., Metz, S., Staskiewicz, A., Thiel, A., Wahl, J., Haak, W., Pernicka, E., Schiffels, S., Stockhammer, P.W., Krause, J., 2019. Kinship-based social inequality in Bronze Age Europe. *Science* [online], 366 (6466), 731734. Available at: https://science.sciencemag.org/content/366/6466/731.

Roscoe, P.B., 2012. Before Elites: The Political Capacities of Big Men. *In:* T.L. Kienlin and A. Zimmerman, eds. *Beyond Elites: Alternatives to Hierarchical Systems in Modelling Social Formations.* Universitätsforschungen zur prähistorischen Archäologie 215. Bonn: Habelt, 41-54.

Snow, C.P., 1998. *The Two Cultures.* New York: Cambridge University Press. Originally published in 1959.

Tylén, K., Fusaroli, R., Rojo, S., Heimann, K., Fay, N., Johannsen, N.N., Riede, F., Lombard, M., 2020. The evolution of early symbolic behavior in Homo sapiens. *Proceedings of the National Academy of Sciences* [online], 117 (9), 4578-4584. Available at: https://www.pnas.org/content/117/9/4578.

Wittgenstein, L., 1958. *Philosophical Investigations.* 2nd edition. Oxford: Basil Blackwell. Translated by G.E.M. Anscombe.

Wittgenstein, L., 1975. *On Certainty.* Translated by Denis Paul and G.E.M. Anscombe. Oxford: Blackwell.

Nodes of connectivity: The role of religion in the constitution of urban sites in nomadic Inner Asia

Jonathan Ethier, Christian Ressel, Birte Ahrens, Enkhtuul Chadraabal, Sampildondov Chuluun, Martin Oczipka, Henny Piezonka

Jonathan Ethier
Institute of Prehistoric and
Protohistoric Archaeology
Kiel University
Johanna-Mestorf-Straße 2-6
24118 Kiel, Germany
jonathan-ethier@hotmail.com

Christian Ressel
Institute of Prehistoric and
Protohistoric Archaeology
Kiel University
Johanna-Mestorf-Straße 2-6
24118 Kiel, Germany
ch.ressel@web.de

Birte Ahrens (Independent
Researcher)
Adolfstraße 53
Bonn 5311, Germany
ahrensbirte@gmail.com

Enkhtuul Chadraabal
Institute of Prehistoric and
Protohistoric Archaeology
Kiel University
Johanna-Mestorf-Straße 2-6
24118 Kiel, Germany
chenkhtuul@yahoo.de

Sampildondov Chuluun
Mongolian Academy of Sciences
Institute of History and Ethnology
Jukov st. 77
Ulaanbaatar 13343, Mongolia
sarnchuluun@gmail.com

Martin Oczipka
University of Applied Sciences
Fakultät Geoinformation
Friedrich-List-Platz 1
01069 Dresden, Germany
martin.oczipka@htw-dresden.de

Henny Piezonka
Institute of Prehistoric and
Protohistoric Archaeology
Kiel University
Johanna-Mestorf-Straße 2-6
24118 Kiel, Germany
hpiezonka@ufg.uni-kiel.de

Abstract

The study of past urban centres as a link to social dynamics and transformations evokes much interest among archaeologists. In investigating the multi-conceptual meanings of connectivity, these urban centres provide the stage for intricacies and constant shifts that are central to human history. Yet, the main narrative regarding urbanity is driven by settled societies, forging a discourse on preconceived notions of what defines an urban environment. As such, nomadic pastoral communities have been relegated to a footnote in the debate of the urbanisation process. In line with the concept of connectivity as a motor for urbanity, this study proposes to re-evaluate this discourse by investigating the role and impact of urbanisation in nomadic pastoral contexts through the lens of religion and the creation of sacred spaces. Although often seen as a passive voice, as part of the theatre's background, religion belongs here to the active agents that connect different actors (*e.g.* local populations, foreign relations, or the spiritual world) and participates in all spheres of urban dynamism, whether political, economic, or cultural. Thus, the writing of Anthony Leeds provides the first step towards a more inclusive approach through three interrelated specialisations, namely (1) localities preferred for ecological or sociocultural reasons, (2) components of technology, and (3) institutions. From this interaction, a model of urban nodes is proposed here as a principal connecting framework, where religion is seen as a generable force that produces and influences the core and its connections. To apply this model, this paper turns towards a diachronic approach with a focus on the Orkhon Valley in Central Mongolia. Four case studies were selected, which include the Uyghur city of Karabalgasun (8th-9th century CE), Karakorum, the capital of the Mongol Empire (13th-15th century CE), the monastic complexes of Erdene Zuu during the Ming dynasty (16th century CE), and Baruun Khüree under the Qing rule (17th-20th century CE).

Introduction

Historically, religion acts as a bonding agent, invested in the sociocultural dynamics of community formations. In its practice and institutionalisation, it can foster connectivity between people and their social groups, providing a common ground for potential and actual interactions. Although religion was never denied a particular centrality in societal development, its transformative and dynamic nature has often evaded archaeological and historical works, to be ranked as something set, as part of the background in an eternal status quo (*e.g.* Orsi 1999; Knott 2005; Cho and Squier 2013; Rüpke 2020). In opposition to this ahistorical and static assessment, religion continuously changes and becomes multiple in practice and definition. By permeating the sociocultural landscape of human interactions, religion plays an essential role in creating sacred permanencies or nodes (*e.g.* shrines, pilgrimage sites, and monuments), which can be at the heart of the establishment of settled communities and lifeways. From small villages during the Neolithic to the formation of large complex urban centres in the Bronze Age and then to the modern metropolises, such nodes provided guidance, anchored group affiliations, and took part in generating social and politico-economic vibrancy in place.

Nomadic pastoral groups, however, are more often than not excluded from this narrative as their sociocultural, economic, and political contribution to what has been considered the "civilised world" is perceived as fringed in a discourse tainted by an ethnocentric point of view of settled peoples (*e.g.* Bernbeck 2008; Honeychurch and Makarewicz 2016; Hammer and Arbuckle 2017). From the Nubian pastoral influence on the development of pre-dynastic and dynastic Egypt (Gatto 2011) to the Mongolian nomadic culture that at the height of its power dominated much of Eurasia (Perdue 2015), nomadic pastoral ways have had and continue to have an important role in forging human societies. Once this role is acknowledged, religions become an essential part of connecting these pastoralists to other pastoralists, settled communities, and their landscapes.

And yet, to understand this dynamism, one must dispense with a dichotomic conception of nomadism and sedentism and embrace a web of intricacies in which the actors are in constant relation and interaction with each other. In terms of religious implications, we will see that through acts of sacralisation and symbolisation, nomads can appropriate their surroundings by attributing unique qualities to landscape elements such as rivers, mountains, or rock formations (Eliade 1957; Chidester and Linenthal 1995). The appropriation of these now sacred, natural fixed elements will often lead to added values by creating places of worship, monuments, more permanent nodes of settlement, and ultimately urban sites. Through urban centres, religions expand their functions and interact with other spheres of society. Aside from providing ritual services and other religious duties, religions are central to political and administrative functions, on the one hand, and socio-economic and communal developments (*e.g.* schools or care centres) on the other. They also play a role in establishing and maintaining local contacts and contribute to networking between nomads, farmers, and urban populations through trade, temple festivities, or cultural and sporting events.

Within the scope of the present volume that aims at deciphering and understanding connectivities in past societies, this paper explores the role of religion as a component in urbanisation processes within pastoral nomadic societies and polities, investigating the World Heritage region of the Orkhon Valley in Central Mongolia as a case study. We implement an archaeological and ethno-historical approach to demonstrate through a diachronic perspective how sacred nodes integrate the sociocultural constitution and spatial development of sedentary and urban sites from the Uyghur Khanate period (744-840 CE) to the end of the Qing dynasty in the region (1911 CE). We will explore the different ways in which religions and ritual practices play a role in the constitution, the structural shaping, and the subsequent further development of sedentary centres and urban agglomerations within the nomadic setting, spanning the field from state religion as an aspect of power politics connected to imperial cities, cosmopolitan religious freedom and its footprint in cityscapes, to the role of sacred places in the emergence of modern urban nodes in the steppe.

Urbanity in nomadic settings: Definitions and concepts

Urban nodes seem to represent, in a certain way, an opposition to nomadic lifestyles, with their realisation of complex, controlled, and settled ways that are seen as the essence of 'civilisation' in persisting stereotypes of socio-economic evolution (cf. Childe 1950; Khazanov 2005). Even though it may depict reality in part, this perspective can also hinder our reflection on the subject and impede its malleability (Cowgill 2004; Smith 2016). The main problem lies in the definition of urbanity and the urbanisation process as well as its application which is often constituted by the ethnocentric perceptions of settled peoples (Honeychurch and Makarewicz 2016). Not unknown to these barriers, archaeology continues to carry the weight of some academic and popular assumptions that bound concepts of permanency and sociocultural complexification to the rise of 'civilisations' and settled actors.

Archaeologists have for a long time worked on defining, elaborating, and enumerating the different elements that constitute urban phenomena and the development of cities. An influential starting point was provided by V. Gordon Childe (1936; 1942; 1950) and his concept of an 'urban revolution', in which he established ten criteria that allow a distinction between the first cities and villages – from population density to monumentality and from the presence of full-time specialists to a ruling class.

Since then, the list has expanded and was reorganised to fit different questions and contexts, but most archaeologists recognise the flexibility in attributing traits and the difficult, if not impossible task to create a universal definition without being too generalist (*e.g.* Cowgill 2004; Marcus and Sabloff 2008; Weeks 2010; Smith 2016). Thus, definitions include economic responses (*e.g.* Christaller 1966; Trigger 1972; Tilley 1994), political and religious administrative centres (*e.g.* Fox 1977; Marcus 1983), or demographic density and heterogeneity (*e.g.* Wirth

1938). In the same way, modern inquiries on the question, which often influence archaeological responses, rely mainly on separating agricultural land and urban space, meaning that the urban realm is composed of non-agricultural activities (Weeks 2008; 2010). However, this criterion of non-agricultural can hardly be applied historically, as well as in our modern society where a resurgence of small green spaces for personal or communal food production on rooftops or allocated areas is observed.

These categories are interconnected and contribute to shedding light on the deep history of urbanisation processes. Yet, they are also a source of limitations and create new divides, as they trap the conceptualisation into rigid categories (*e.g.* Cowgill 2004; Smith 2016). In all these attempts to provide an inclusive answer, categorisation is bound to observations of similarities between similar entities, as judged by the predefined world of the scholar investigating the question. It follows what Anthony Leeds (1979; 1980; 2017) acknowledged as fundamental biases in the definition and application of urbanism.

> *'Most current discussion of "urbanism" and "urbanization" can be shown to be ethno- and temporocentric and based on a historically particular class of urban phenomena and urban forms of integration' (Leeds 1979, 227).*

From another angle, Leeds (2017) and John R. Weeks (2010) argue that the misconception stems from a dichotomy of 'rural' vs. 'urban'. For Leeds, this separation breaks the link between both entities, as both are connected in many ways.

> *'At a most general level, all human nucleation, from the smallest "tribal" villages to the largest megalopolises, have the same functions with respect to an inclusive society: facilitation of all forms exchange, transfer, and communications, while linking the nucleation or locality both with other localities and with the society at large' (Leeds 2017, 53).*

In other words, urban dynamism and influence extend beyond the limits of a city, whereas regional productions are often bound to urban centres, where the redistribution of goods is operated and local and international trade agreements are made, creating dependency towards the urban core. The dichotomic divide of a regional and an urban sphere, based on the type of production activity, is illusory. The main problem derives from the definition of urbanisation as a passage from rural to urban (Weeks 2010). Although we agree that transformations are part of the equation, centrality also plays a crucial role, understood as a concentration of interaction (Nakoinz 2019). Whether by the organisation and establishment of diverse specialised positions or by the accumulation of goods, centrality creates a network that incorporates the regional in its functions.

Although the topic was revisited many times since then, Leeds' criticisms are still relevant, especially when discussing urban formations among nomadic pastoral societies, like those dominating the Inner Asian steppes. The struggle to include these groups in the narrative has led Jan Bemmann and Susanne Reichert (2020, 1) – in a paper on Karakorum during the Mongol Empire (1206-1368 CE) – to define the remains as an 'imperial city in a non-urban society', developing in an environment they call 'anti-urban'. The authors efficiently demonstrate the difficulty of applying universal characterisations of cities and urbanity to the region, which they illustrate by applying Michael E. Smith's urban traits (Smith 2016), as they cover a wide range of vital facets and show flexibility that can not only be transferred from European and Mesoamerican patterns to Asia but also from period to period. Smith's approach initiates a polythetic study of urban attributes that encompasses traits with varying combinations, namely settlement size, social impact, built environment, and social and economic features (Smith 2016). After providing an extensive analysis of each trait in relation to the city of Karakorum, Bemmann and Reichert conclude that the inability of steppe cities to survive once the political power that created them disappears infers an absence of urbanisation, or more precisely of the transfer from a steppe society to an urban one (Bemmann and Reichert 2020). For the authors, urban society is connected to longevity and must surpass its creators to show inner transformations that last, at least, on a social level.

Such a conclusion brings us to an inherent problem in using checklists or packages to define complex notions in order not to fall for the same ethno- and temporocentric biases that Leeds warned us about. Instead of talking about a '*city in a non-urban society*', one should seek to reclaim the concept in relation to the functions and needs of the context. Bemmann and Reichert (2020, 138-139) recognise this point, but do not venture further to define it according to the data. Recent works that understand urbanity as a process of adaptation to changing conditions or contexts in a complex settlement system provide new approaches to this field (*e.g.* Nakoinz *et al.* 2020).

In the steppe, the bond between cities and nomadic herders is constituted across complex interdependencies. One economically provides foodstuffs and preserves the local traditions, whereas the other administratively, politically, and religiously organises, distributes, and provides other services otherwise difficult to obtain. Anatoly Khazanov (2005, 163-164) distinguishes three models of interrelations between nomads and cities: (1) Interrelations involving, *e.g.*, trade as well as cultural and religious contacts between nomads and cities in sedentary societies, (2) nomads conquering and controlling sedentary territories and states, utilising their urban potential, and (3) the creation of an own urban sector undertaken by some nomadic polities and states. Our paper explores examples of the third model, focusing on urbanisation from within the nomadic polities themselves. To come closer to an idea of nomadic urbanity, especially in the Mongolian steppe region, the holistic approach of Anthony Leeds provides a fruitful perspective, as it takes a low population density but a high degree of social and economic mobility into consideration. By refusing to oppose urban and rural, or even urban and rural societies, Leeds (2017, 71) argues that all kinds of human nucleation from the smallest to the largest are part of society as a whole and thus rather have to be understood as 'nodal points'.

Instead of classifying urban as a matter of population density or size, Leeds understands urban as the interaction, respectively the confluence of interrelated specialisations, which appears in society and tends to increase local specialisation. He distinguishes specialisations according to (1) localities preferred for ecological or sociocultural reasons, (2) components of technology such as materials, housings, tasks, activities, knowledge, and (3) institutions, which are translated by separating the function of ordered and characterised ways of doing things (Leeds 2017, 53). Thus, what can be understood as 'nodal points' or 'urban nodes' is, in the words of Leeds (2017, 54), '*always a matter of degree*' of interaction that '*is variously linked with other localities*'. Such an application should, however, also include the possibility of city de-urbanisation, disintegration, or abandonment. Accordingly, the range of archaeological urban attributes, as suggested by Smith, might become a helpful tool to analyse the specialisations and integrating functions of a node, rather than being used as a tool to evaluate and identify a settlement according to such attributes as *the expression of urbanism in the archaeological record*' (Smith 2016, 159). As nodes of connectivity, we imply a connection between Leeds' three specialties that include the concept of urban as part of a greater network, encompassing the city itself and its spheres of interactions and influences (*i.e.* rural, hinterland, or foreign connections).

When reflecting on 'urban nodes' in a nomadic context, one must also consider the given ecological conditions. Applying Leeds' concept of urban nodes to the Inner Asian steppe regions, we need to consider a high degree of mobility as part of the settlement patterns. Caroline Humphrey and David A. Sneath (1999, 182) point out that categories, such as 'nomadic', 'sedentary', and 'semi-nomadic', are broadly understood with regard to land use, but do not reflect the intricacies behind stationary and mobile dwelling types. Their appeal for rethinking the terminological and methodological principles for a more accurate understanding of systems of settlements in the region is also valid for a better understanding of urban ways of life in the Mongolian steppe from a diachronic perspective. The analysis of settlement patterns necessarily needs to consider the complexity of social and economic mobility according to their respective historical contexts. Historically, urbanisation processes and types of settlement in the Mongolian steppes cannot be reduced to economic factors, but also included military-strategic, religious, and other sociocultural considerations.

As Bemmann and Reichert (2020) demonstrated in their application of Smith's approach, the urbanisation processes as seen in the Near East or Mesoamerica with large complex systems should be viewed with caution when applied to the steppe regions. In Mongolia, we have something we can call unsettled settlements. These urban or city-like nodes transform in specific ways as part of their physical periphery. Yurt camps gather, interact with the sedentary core, and grow and shrink according to the seasons. In this unsettled way, the general definitions of urban and city must be reconsidered. Urban is here gravitational and generable. It creates a gravitational effect that attracts and supports full-time specialists in crafts and trade, religious authorities, and political and administrative institutions that initiate politico-economic and sociocultural activities, but that also, on an international scale, becomes a representative of its community. One aspect often overlooked in defining urban is this external relation. External ties are often mentioned as an economic motor, but external recognition and external political and sociocultural value should not be underestimated. Although urban is generally defined in its local and regional dynamism, it also attracts on a broader scale, reaching other nodal points or nations, designating a place of power in constant transformation, involved in many different translations (cf. Latour 2005; Sassen 2010; Hahn 2017).

Finally, the city generates not only food, tools, and other necessities but also structure and specialties, such as administrative duties, rules and regulations, scholarly works, and artistic emancipation. More importantly, it generates connections between people; it becomes a node of multi-faceted connectivities across Leeds' three specialisation categories. The city may or may not persist through time, and it only leaves permanent traces through accumulation.

Nevertheless, it becomes urban through its gravitational and generatable traits. Accordingly, we can question the degree of permanency of the urban. From an archaeological lens, fixed settlements leave remains that are easily recognisable and quantifiable. Thus, it becomes natural to equate urbanism with permanencies. As we will see with the Mongolian steppe region, many cities and modern urban centres developed out of mobile urban nodes. Yet, mobile urbanism had its limits, and eventually, even the most enduring tradition, in search of expansion, needs to settle.

As one may have noticed, religion is largely avoided in the discussion on cities and urban processes, and if integrated, it takes the form of a more or less ahistorical trait belonging to the status quo. From our point of view, however, religion is at the heart of these processes. It often integrates the plan or design before the first stone or wooden beam is placed. It is a cornerstone in constant development, connecting people, first through ritualisation, but soon after by becoming institutionalised and fundamental to urban design. As religion takes many forms, our attention will be turned towards the creation and use of sacred spaces. Henry Lefebvre (1992, 182) once eloquently postulated that urban phenomena are 'punctual' in the sense that they seek to 'localise' and 'focus'. As part of the sacred, many cities are founded on significant spaces and connect their founders among themselves and among farming and herding communities. Religions and the construction of sacred spaces also occur in accordance with Leeds' three categories of specialisation in the appropriation of space through means of sociocultural activities, the implication of specific knowledge and architectural constructions, and finally, the creation of a certain order through the regulation of its institutions. As the diachronic analyses of urban nodes in the Central Mongolian Orkhon Valley will show in the next section, the characteristics and specialisations of nodes have changed according to sociocultural, political, and economic processes, and, thus, have more or less always involved religious agencies and the production of sacred space.

The sacred, the profane, and space

In creating fixed nodes, religious people, or as Eliade coined them *homo religiosus*, transform their surroundings, the landscape, or specific monuments and items with unique properties, performing an act of separation between a sacred and a profane state. In the sacred, communal bonds are created, whereby intergroup communications and connections are established. As exemplified by Christian churches that became the *axis mundi* of a community, a pillar that mentally and physically centres the village, or through the erection of *ovoos*, sacred stone heaps in the Mongolian landscapes that add significance to a place, the sacred in all its abstraction becomes materialised. Although this process may appear to *homo religiosus* as both fundamental and natural, there is still no consensus on what defines the sacred. In interrogating the role of religion in connecting nomadic groups to urban centres, the conception of the sacred and the formation of sacred places appear to be fundamental.

Among scholars who investigated the nature of the sacred, Rudolf Otto (1917 [2014]) and Mircea Eliade (1957) provided the first extensive reflections on the subject. For Otto, the idea of sacred, or more precisely the idea of holy, is part of a 'non-rational' and 'non-sensory', extrasomatic experience and feelings that he designates as *numinous* (Otto 1917 [2014], 5-7). In that sense, the holy is *sui generis* and not taught, and can only be mentally evoked. *Numinous* experiences are thus, according to Otto, mysterious and entail both terror and fascination, which he named *mysterium tremendum*. Architectural and space sacralisation is in part with this process as it nurtures the religious experience. For Douglas R. Hoffman (2010, 6), the *mysterium tremendum* contains the keys to appreciate the connection between architecture and a religious or spiritual experience,

> *'as a physically inert form, architecture cannot teach per se, but it can provide the markers to awaken consciousness'.*

Although Otto's contributions to the idea of the holy cannot be overlooked, it was Eliade's work that established the theoretical and methodological foundations that continue to be relevant and central in debates surrounding the notion of sacred and sacred spaces.

From Otto's work, Eliade (1957) integrated the idea of *'ganz Andere'*, where the *numinous* manifests as something completely different, beyond human understanding, apart from a natural reality. What interests Eliade is the manifestation of the sacred and its materialisation, or its transfer from an abstract, non-sensory notion to reality, which he coined as a hierophany. Following this premise, in nature, space is homogenous and chaotic, and it is only through the process of sacralisation that *homo religiosus* establishes order, a cosmic order that is laden with meaning. If profane space can be quantitatively different, it stays the same qualitatively, whereas the hierophanic appropriation of space transforms *homo religiosus'* surroundings into a meaningful and heterogeneous place. By creating sacred spaces, a rupture emerges, and space is consecrated through cosmogonic repetitions. According to Eliade, *homo religiosus* searches to reproduce, to a certain degree, the world's foundations in line with the actors' belief system. When the sacred is attached to an object or place, it preserves its basic traits and, in the eye of the beholder, transmutes to something else at the same time. A sacrificial dagger is still a dagger, and it is only to the initiate that the hierophany, or the sacred manifestation, is gained, and the dagger reveals itself as sacred. *Homo religiosus* experiences a similar transmutation when looking at nature, where the cosmic sacrality can be reproduced. Eliade (2004 [1968], 17) expresses the connectivity between the nomad and the sedentary through this cosmic sacrality, as

> *'both live in a sacralized cosmos, both share in a cosmic sacrality manifested equally in the animal world and in the vegetal world'.*

Although nomads eventually find hierophanies in their mobile inventory, they nevertheless designate fixed nodes that are central to their world. Otto and Eliade's approaches to the sacred continue to influence research. However, opposition came in reorienting the perspective away from a sacred that manifests itself towards a sacred that is internally active in humans' actions (*e.g.* Smith 1978; Chidester and Linenthal 1995). David Chidester and Edward T. Linenthal (1995) identify two different views on the sacred: substantial and situational. If Eliade and Otto represent the former, in the situational view to which Chidester and Linenthal subscribe, the sacred is

> *'inevitably entangled with the entrepreneurial, the social, the political, and other profane forces' (Chidester and Linenthal 1995, 17).*

Following this definition, the sacred is meaningless or like an empty shell filled with proactive, cultural actions of ritualisation or consecration. Thus, it leads to different 'levels of reality' that proceed to a hierarchisation of power relations and othering processes. In that sense, the sacred is rooted out from an idiosyncratic and external position, to be embedded into the intricacy of humans' social and personal realities. As we will see with Central Mongolia, the interrelation of religion and sacred space goes beyond the religious act. It infers political and economic ramifications that are intrinsically bound to each other. Chidester and Linenthal strongly oppose the notion of manifestation and refer to the sacred as a human performance laden with violence due to the constant negotiation of the claims on the significance. For the authors, it is part of strategies of *appropriation*, *exclusion*, *inversion*, and *hybridisation*. Through these strategies, sacred spaces became interwoven with the creation of urban nodes, beyond the decision behind the localisation of the core, by weaving its thread in all aspects, such as Lead's categories of specialisation.

Jonathan Z. Smith (1978; 1987) also argues for a situational view, since for him, God's work is not at play here, but rather a human construct. Like Chidester and Linenthal, Smith refers to the creation of sacred spaces as part of a hierarchical system. However, he moves away from a traditional view that rituals answer the sacred in the form of an expression of the essence. Instead, he regards rituals as the vehicle to the connection human/divine, where the sacred and the profane are only the results in creating association and disassociation. In other words, the sacred indicates differences, creates distinctions, thus a hierarchical order with the sacred at the top of the ladder. In this case, rituals become a human creative process in which meanings are given.

Although situational and substantial approaches may seem opposite, they both have merits and flaws, but they can also be explored in conjunction. It is a question of angle. On an emic level, the substantial point of view reflects on the experience lived by the actors or *homo religiosus*, whereas the situational point of view emerges from a more reflective or anthropological analysis, it takes on an etic level. More recently, inquiries on the sacred took new paths by including new perspectives such as gender studies (*e.g.* Massey 1993; Tobler 2000; Massey 2013) or in seeking the sacred in profane or common places (Knott 2005; 2015).

This study looks at the sacred mainly from an etic or situational perspective, with few incursions on an emic level. As we have seen, the sacred plays an important role not only in connecting individuals and groups but also in connecting different aspects of human activities. The sacred has historically influenced decision-making in economic, political, and sociocultural development and urban design and its transformative nature in the negotiation between a nomadic pastoral society and sedentary urban centres. This paper traces these relations and the underlying connectivities for one of the cores of historic nomadic polities, the Orkhon Valley in Central Mongolia.

In the heartland of nomadic polities: Case studies from the Orkhon Valley, Central Mongolia

The Inner Asian steppes with the Mongolian high plateau form the world's current largest contiguous area of shared grazing land. This region has favoured mobile lifeways over millennia, while the development of permanent settlements and urban centres has been sparser and historically specific. As part of the UNESCO World Heritage since 2004, the Orkhon Valley in Central Mongolia has been an economically and geostrategic advantageous location for millennia, as well as a place of religious importance. From the focus point of the Old Turkic memorial sites in the 7th century CE to the centre of dominance of the Uyghur Khanate,

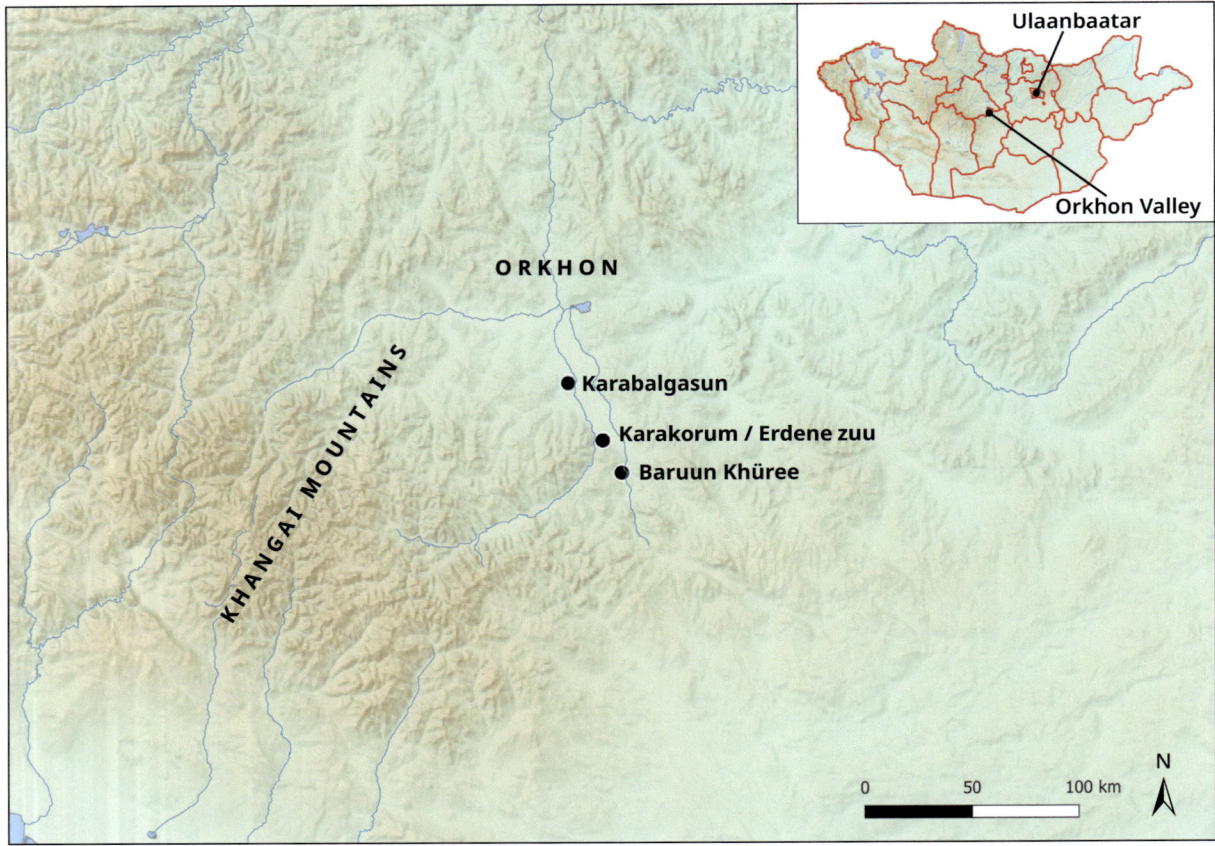

Figure 1. The Orkhon Valley in Central Mongolia and archaeological sites (map: B. Ahrens and J. Ethier).

and from Chinggis Khan's capital of the Mongol world empire to the Manchu aegis from the 17th century until the beginning of the 20th century CE, the Orkhon Valley was a central region in the formation of mighty capitals, military sites and religious centres (cf. Hüttel 2005; 2007; Bemmann *et al.* 2011a). Dominated by one of Mongolia's longest rivers, the Orkhon, the region is characterised by a diverse landscape composed of the Khangai mountain range with deep valleys that became the stage of cities and urban dynamism in a pastoral nomadic landscape (Fig. 1). The Orkhon Valley thus provides an excellent laboratory for the present study on the formation of urban nodes in a nomadic world and on the role of religion therein on a diachronic level.

The intricacies accompanying the religious history of Mongolia, and here the Orkhon Valley, is indissociable from its urban history. Through historical events, ritualisation, and special features in the landscapes, the Orkhon Valley contains numerous sacred spaces that include cities, monasteries, burial sites, ritual stone heaps, so-called *ovoos*, and other designated sacred areas (*e.g.* rivers and mountains). The sacralisation processes and expressions stem from different sources, with shamanism and Buddhism being the main belief systems, but other religions, such as, Manichaeism, Islam, and Nestorian Christianity, also influencing this region at the crossroads between various parts of Eurasia, intersecting with each other and conjunctively participating in the act. These sacred spaces often became the sites for the emergence of more permanent settlements. This is even more the case when we look at later periods, especially under Altan Khan and the Manchu influence between the 16th and the 20th centuries, where mobile Buddhist communities started to settle down and establish many urban centres. Thus, the Orkhon Valley was central not

Figure 2. Aerial view of the so-called 'imperial complex', interpreted as temples and a palace city at Karabalgasun (photo: M. Riemer, fig. 2, copyright: KAAK DAI, fig. 2).

only to the rise, *e.g.*, of Manichaeism and later of Buddhism in the country but also to repeated developments towards implementing permanent urban nodes in a primarily nomadic environment. In our study, we will review these developments for several prominent urban nodes in the region from the Uyghur period in the 8th and 9th centuries CE until the end of the Manchu Empire in the 20th century CE.

Karabalgasun, capital of the Eastern Uyghurs, 8th-9th century CE

One of the most prominent ruined urban sites of the Inner Asian steppe marking today's landscape is Karabalgasun (Fig. 2). The city was founded in 744 CE in the Orkhon Valley under Bayanchur Khan after the Uyghurs had assumed the leadership of a confederation of nomadic groups to replace the old authority of the Second Turkish Empire. Originally named Odru Balik, 'camp of the ruler', and later also known as Karabagasun, 'black ruin', the city served as the capital of the Eastern Uyghur Empire for almost a century, before it was destroyed in 840 CE by Kyrgyz invasions from the north (Hüttel and Erdenebat 2010). Located ca. 40 km north of the modern town of Kharkhorin, Karabalgasun is a monumental, architectural complex with an impressive citadel and an extensive, partly dispersed urban area covering approximately 44 square km (Franken *et al.* 2020) (Fig. 3). The constitution of this first major city in the Mongolian heartland, its layout and architectural hierarchy, is closely linked to the political and economic relations of the nomadic Uyghurs with sedentary societies such as Tang China and the Iranian Sogdians, where religion plays a significant role in forging and maintaining these power relations. The establishment of the capital city and other urban centres across the Uyghur steppe empire, stretching from current South Siberia across Mongolia in the Xinjiang province of China, are most likely related to influences and possible urban models of sedentary polities. Their emergence was based on the immense wealth the Uyghurs accumulated through their contacts and trade relations involving, *e.g.*, silk (Rogers *et al.* 2005; Franken *et al.* 2020).

Manichaeism as the Uyghur state religion

Around the middle of the 8th century CE (761-763 CE) (Moriyasu 2015), the Uyghurs, a Turkic-speaking group under Mouyu Khan, officially adopted Manichaeism as their state religion, thus becoming the first and only state to follow this path. Manichaeism is a Gnostic religion that, since its foundation by Mani (216-276 CE) in Persia, has spread, despite persecutions and bans, from Rome in the west to China in the east. Manichaeism developed into a universalistic religion based on Gnostic elements in which pre-existing written revelations and systems were integrated and reinterpreted (*e.g.* Buddhism, Christianity, and Zoroastrianism). The Manichean religion is characterised first and foremost by radical dualism, anti-cosmic optimism, and strict asceticism. The world is seen as a mixture of light and darkness (Eliade 1995, 171-172), in which light has to be detached from darkness and freed through cleansing actions. The complex cosmogonic-eschatological myth behind it, elaborated by Mani, shows above all elements of gnosis, but with the significant difference that this is a universal religion that should be accessible to everyone and not just to a few initiates (Eliade 2002, 328-335). Despite the universal claim of Manichaeism, the practical implementation of the numerous and strict rules of life could not have been for everyone. In the teaching of Mani, for example, strict vegetarianism was prescribed, as it was forbidden to kill or go to war. These regulations were in radical contrast to the nomadic way of life, based on livestock breeding and hunting with the repeated occurrence of warlike raids. The strictly hierarchical social order of the Manichaean believers also opposed the idea of a nomadic, more egalitarian social system (Kolbas 2005, 306).

The founding and rise of the Uyghur state during the 8th and 9th centuries CE in the Central Asian steppe was connected to several radical changes and upheavals that in a way opposed the nomadic way of life: The founding of large city complexes with a multicultural and multi-ethnic population in a nomadic environment, on the one hand, and the adoption of a new religion with strict regulations and a complex belief system on the other. Two reasons have been suggested for the conversion to Manichaeism of the Uyghur leadership. First, the rulers might have needed a representative world religion that differed from the other, rival empires (*e.g.* Buddhism in Tibet or Taoism in China) (Kasai 2020, 65). With the conversion to Manichaeism, the Uyghur state made itself theologically and politically independent and neutral towards its rival neighbours (Kovalev 2016, 5; Kasai 2020, 65). Second, the connection to Sogdian merchants and traders, who were mainly followers of the Manichaean religion, played an essential role in choosing Manichaeism as the state religion. At the time of the Uyghurs' conversion, the practice of Manichaeism was forbidden in most parts of Central and Inner Asia and was being persecuted. The Uyghur state was able to secure the favour of the Sogdian by adopting their religion, most likely aiming at economic advantages (Kovalev 2016, 59).

The broad influence of the Sogdians in the Uyghur state regarding trade, diplomacy, politics, material culture, writing, religion, and, last but not least, urban structures is significant and cannot be overlooked. The Sogdians, in turn, profited from trade with the Uyghurs, in which China was also involved primarily through silk trade (Kovalev 2016; de la Vaissière 2018, 224). These strategic motivations for adopting Manichaeism as the state religion suggest that it may have only been practiced by a smaller ruling elite and Sogdian merchants who had settled in Karabalgasun. For a nomadic population, it would have been difficult to implement and follow the strict regulations that have already been mentioned

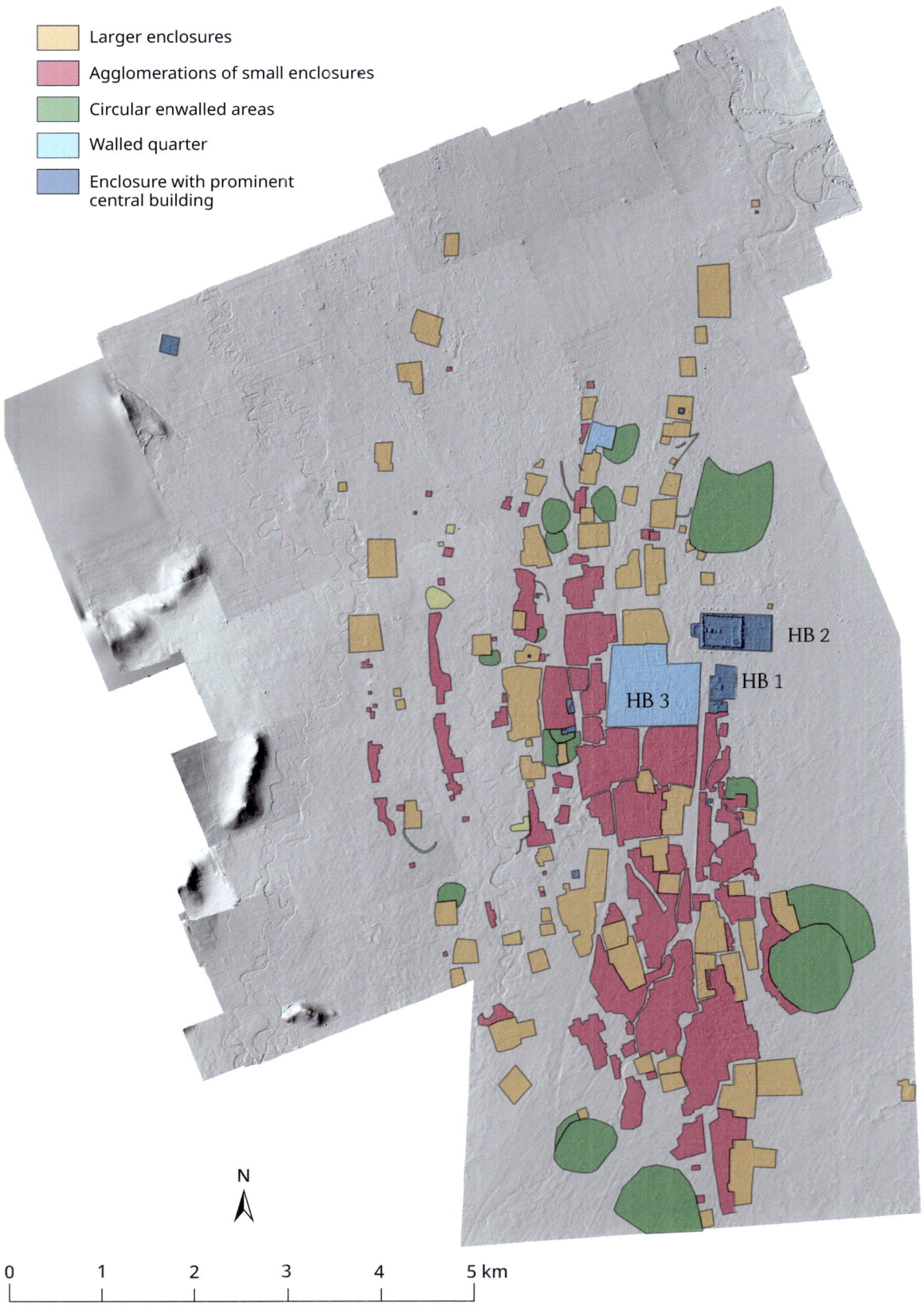

Larger enclosures

Agglomerations of small enclosures

Circular enwalled areas

Walled quarter

Enclosure with prominent central building

HB 2

HB 1

HB 3

N

0   1   2   3   4   5 km

Figure 3. The structure of the urban area of Karabalgasun (after: C. Franken *et al.* 2020, fig. 7).

(Kovalev 2016, 5). Whether the conversion to the Manichean faith and the turning away from the nomadic way of life of the Uyghur leadership also contributed to the empire's collapse cannot be proven. However, it can be assumed, as Roman K. Kovalev (2016, 5) notes, that the turn to urban luxury and consumption as well as socio-economic differences led to a turning away from the inherent strengths and advantages of the nomadic culture. Mobility, a simple way of life, and a classless organised military are seen as the factors that had once turned the Uyghurs into a unified nomadic and powerful state (Kovalev 2016, 5).

Between function and sacred space: The city layout

As part of a cooperation project since 2007 between the Mongolian Academy of Science, the National University of Mongolia, and the Commission for the Archaeology of Non-European Cultures (KAAK) of the German Archaeological Institute (DAI) and supplemented since 2008 by research conducted by Bonn University and the Mongolian Academy of Sciences, various plans and 3D surface models of Karabalgasun have been made using airborne laser scans and UAV flights, which impressively show the layout of the city with numerous details (Bemmann *et al.* 2014; Franken *et al.* 2020). In addition, several excavation campaigns over the last years have concentrated on investigating the areas HB1, HB2, and HB3 (Franken 2014; Franken *et al.* 2014; see Fig. 3).

The city's construction was partly carried out by Chinese and Sogdian craftsmen, who certainly influenced the architecture and the layout of Karabalgasun (Hüttel and Erdenebat 2010). Located in the centre of the east side of an almost semi-circular settlement structure is the so-called 'imperial complex', a temple or palace complex, which, thanks to its monumental construction, is visible in the flat steppe from far beyond the city limits (Fig. 3: HB2; see also Fig. 2). This complex consists of a rectangular enclosed space with formerly 12 m high walls made of rammed earth. The so-called 'citadel', a 60 x 70 m podium that was originally about 7 m high, is situated in the southern corner. The imperial complex with its reminiscence to Chinese palace architecture and the monumental citadel with elaborate sculptures, including apotropaic demon masks, is interpreted as an architectural representation of the claim to power of the Uyghurs (Franken *et al.* 2014). To the south of this temple or palace area, a double-walled area (HB1) is located, in which there are fragments of a famous trilingual inscription praising the ruler Baoyi Khan in Old Turkic, Chinese, and Sogdian languages. Due to the pedestal-like central building, it is assumed that this is a building with a special meaning, interpreted as a Manichaean sanctuary (Dähne 2015, 70). While the adoption of Manichaeism by the Eastern Uyghurs in the 8th century CE is well-documented by the aforementioned trilingual inscription stone from Karabalgasun and by other written sources (Moriyasu 2015; Yoshida 2020), clear archaeological evidence of this social and political upheaval has been lacking so far. The interpretation of the area around the inscription stone (HB1) as the '*Manichaean sacral complex*' (Dähne 2015, 70) is mainly based on the location of the mentioned inscription stone and the location of the complex south of the citadel, although further evidence, such as a detailed comparison of the architecture, is still pending. Thus, the actual function of the building remains unresolved. A large walled area (HB3), measuring around 900 x 1000 m and located south of the citadel, is currently identified as a craftsmen's quarters.

Around these three prominent areas, various smaller and larger ramparts and oval enclosures are grouped in a semicircle to the west, north, and south, becoming less dense towards the periphery (Bemmann et al. 2014; Franken et al. 2020) (Fig. 3). This spatial layout of the city with the palace and temple district on high ground at the centre is described in the literature as a mixture of a military camp and Buddhist ideas (Golden 2013). Considering the area covered and the dispersed structure, Karabalgasun has, in part, the character of low-density, agrarian-based cities (Fletcher 2019), possibly representing a specific example related to its hybrid constitution between external influences from sedentary societies and its local nomadic setting.

Karabalgasun as a node of connectivity with the hinterland and the wider region

Recently, pilot studies have tackled the questions of the structures at the periphery and the other quarters of the city. Since 2008, studies by the University of Bonn have shown that the area around Ordu Baliq was used intensively. There are signal towers or watchtowers that connected the various residences and cities in the Orkhon Valley in a dense network (Bemmann et al. 2020, 119) with elite burial grounds in the surrounding valleys (Erdenebat et al. 2011). A quarry about 50 km south of Karabalgasun seems to have supplied granite for column bases and possibly also other building materials and architectural elements (Bemmann et al. 2011b). Additionally, enclosed structures and related settlement remains at the fringes of the city area are assumed to be connected to food production and agricultural activities to supply the city's population. Bemmann et al. (2014, 359) suggested that these structures should be interpreted as gardens that were primarily used for growing fruits and vegetables, suggesting a possible link to the vegetarianism of the Manichaean religion. This interpretation requires further research as the cultivation of field crops does not necessarily have to be related to the strict dietary regulation of the Manichaeans, mainly because the conversion to the Manichaean religion can only be assumed for a small Uyghur leadership elite (Kovalev 2016, 5). Traces of intensive agriculture can still be seen in aerial and satellite images of the entire central Orkhon Valley and on the terrain itself (threshing rollers, millstones, strip of fields). However, dating these traces is extremely difficult, as the region continued to be intensively used for agriculture in later times and the findings have not yet been dated. Whether the following, much-quoted passage of Tamīn Ibn Bahr refers to Karabalgasun is discussed in research:

> '[...] this is a great town, rich in agriculture and surrounded by rustāqs full of cultivation and villages lying close together' (Minorsky 1948, 283; see also Waugh 2010, 103).

In scientific investigations of sediments, however, cereal-type pollen has only been detected about 40 km south of Karabalgasun (Lehmkuhl et al. 2011; Bemmann et al. 2014).

The city's hinterland was used for the supply, construction, and maintenance of the city and its residents and for communications with the broader region, as exemplified by the watchtowers. The extent to which this impact on land use led to conflicts with nomads, who continued to live a mobile lifestyle, and how this generally affected the local nomadic society has not yet been investigated; the effects of these interventions on the environment, landscape, and nomadic society have so far only been partially understood. An open question also concerns the general problem of who the inhabitants of Karabalgasun were. Did settled nomads live there, who had previously roamed the Orkhon Valley as cattle breeders? Was it a multicultural and multi-ethnic population, similar to the Mongol capital of Karakorum a few centuries later (*e.g.* Rohland 2019; see below)? Did traders, craftsmen, and scholars settle in Karabalgasun, or were the ruling elite and merchants the primary settlers? How exactly was this city supplied, by whom, and with what?

The current state of research enables the conclusion that the adoption of the Manichaean religion as a state religion by the Uyghur rulers went hand in hand with the physical manifestation of power in the monumental architecture and the hierarchical layout of the capital city of Karabalgasun as the centre of the nomadic empire. It is inherently linked to the political strategies of the rulers concerning their economic and political connectivity with influential sedentary polities of that time, including the Sogdian in Central Asia and the Tang dynasty in China. Although further research into the city layout and the creation and use of sacred space is much needed, the Uyghur case demonstrates the dynamic and connecting nature of religion in the city's development and, more importantly, as an urban node, as expressed by Leeds (2017). Through urbanity, Karabalgasun connected, on a larger scale, its actors to other urban entities, but, through Manichaeism, it bound a community.

Karakorum, capital of the Mongolian Empire, 13th-15th century CE

Arguably, the most famous urban formation in pre-modern nomadic Mongolia was the capital of the Mongol world empire, Karakorum. During the rule of the unifier of the Mongol tribes and the founder of the empire, Chinggis Khan (?-1227), the focal area of the expanding empire was concentrated in the ruler's home region, the Khentii mountain range, and the area of the Onon River in what is today Eastern Mongolia (Di Cosmo 2014/15, 68-69). The court was mobile and moved between seasonal stations, probably represented by the semi-permanent palace excavated at Avraga in the Kherlen River Basin (Shiraishi and Tsogtbaatar 2007; Shiraishi 2013). In the early 1230s, under the rule of Chinggis Khan's successor Ögedei, a decision was made to move the centre of the empire to the Orkhon Valley and install a royal residence and urban centre there. In 1235, significant constructions started at the selected site (Di Cosmo 2014/15; Reichert 2019, 68-73). Historical sources, including a later inscription from 1346, suggest that Chinggis Khan himself had selected the site for the new capital when he moved through the Orkhon Valley in 1219 during a military campaign, yet this interpretation is contested by some scholars (*e.g.* Sagaster 2005; Bemmann and Reichert 2020).

The site chosen for the imperial capital is located at the southern end of the wide plain of the middle Orkhon Valley. The region had been, already at that time, a special focus of nomadic formations from the Old Turkic period, which saw the erection of the major memorial sites of the khans at Khöshöö Tsaidam (*e.g.* Jisl 1960; Stark 2008, 76-78) and the installation of the capital of the Uyghur Empire, Karabalgasun (Fig. 1; see above). According to Thomas Allsen's influential interpretation, the Orkhon Valley was chosen as the new site for the imperial capital due to its importance and charismatic essence, based on its history as the centre of political power and its expression by previous polities (Allsen 1996), although

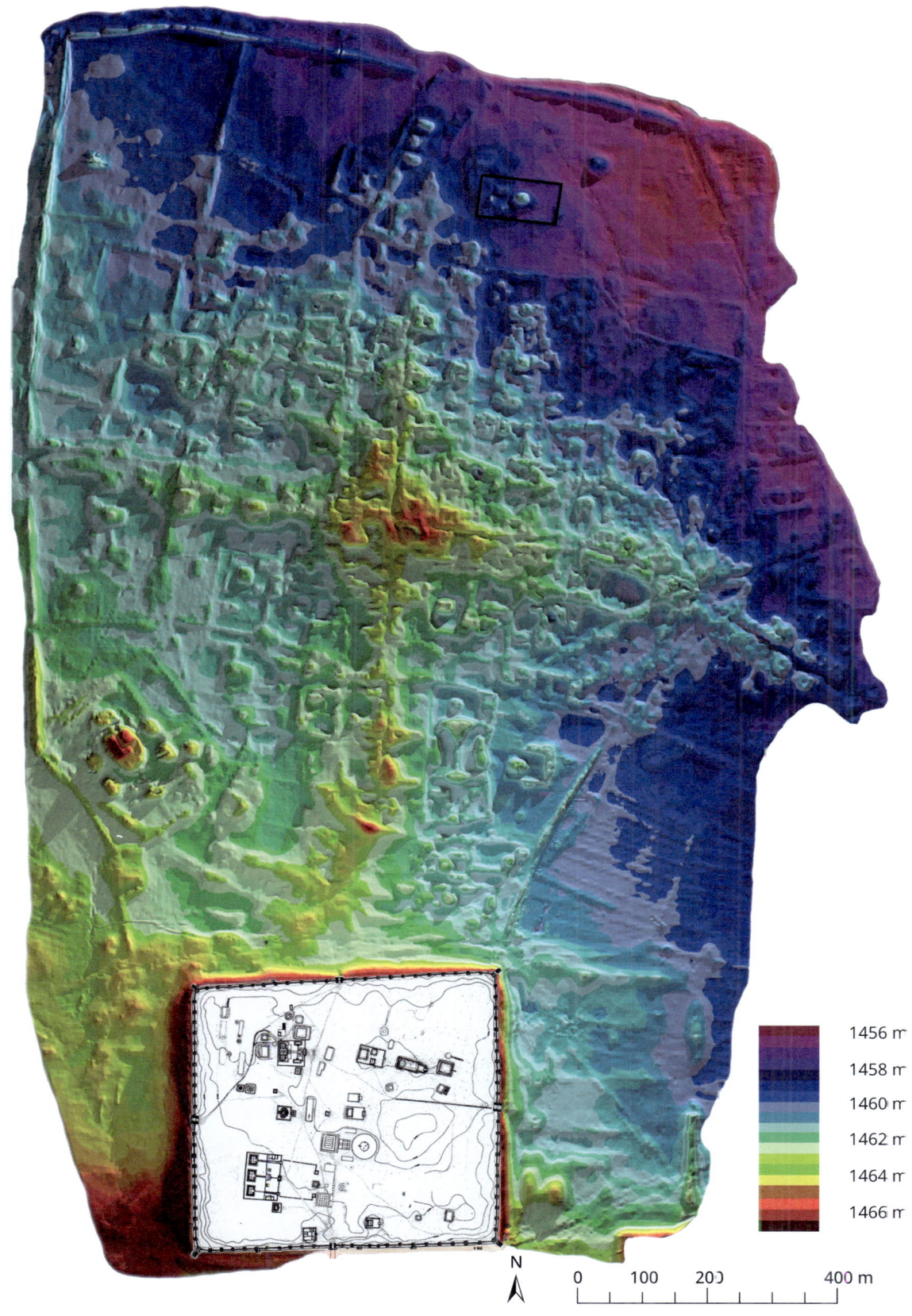

1456 m
1458 m
1460 m
1462 m
1464 m
1466 m

N

0   100   200   400 m

Figure 4. Surface elevation model of Karakorum and plan of Erdene Zuu (after: H.-G. Hüttel and U. Erdenebat 2010, fig. 5).

other researchers also take into account the favourable environmental conditions in the Orkhon Valley at that time, promising a stable economic basis for a longer-term fixed settlement as a capital city (Di Cosmo 2014/15).

The area is preserved as a field of low ruins and remains of walled enclosures in the vicinity of the modern town of Kharkhorin. Most of the area lies open with the southern part occupied today by the Erdene Zuu monastery (Fig. 4; see below). After several excavations at this site during the 20th century, more intense archaeological research set in since 1999 with the Mongolian-German Karakorum expedition (MDKE), including targeted excavations at key locations within the city area and vicinity (Becker 2007; Bemmann 2014). In addition to archaeological results, valuable information on the city, its structure, inhabitants, and history are provided by written sources, most prominently, the vivid account of the Franciscan monk William of Rubruck, who visited Karakorum in 1254 (Ruysbroeck *et al.* 1990).

Quarters and neighbourhoods: The layout and structure of a cosmopolitan city

In the detailed accounts of his stay at Karakorum, William of Rubruck (Ruysbroeck *et al.* 1990) described the city as an utterly cosmopolitan place, including a neighbourhood of Chinese artisans, a quarter of Islamic merchants and Nestorian Christians, French captives of war among its population, alongside Mongolian officials and other locals. He mentions numerous houses of worship, including mosques, Daoist and Buddhist temples, and a Nestorian Christian church, testifying to a city that reflected the religious freedom and tolerance that characterised the policy of the Mongolian Empire at that time (Erdenebat and Pohl 2009). According to Rubruck's description, twelve temples, two mosques, and one church were present during his passage (Ruysbroeck *et al.* 1990, 221). He also provided details on the Khan's palace that was located in the city.

The archaeological findings, although patchy, are in broad accordance with such a picture. The area surrounded by the city walls, excluding the location of the later Erdene Zuu monastery, amounts to ca. 135 ha, but settlement remains also extend outside this area (Bemmann and Reichert 2020) (Fig. 4). The preserved surface relief shows a systematic layout determined by two main streets running approximately east-west and north-south with a crossroads in the centre. The sub-rectangular city wall provided access to the city through four gates. Built architecture was mainly concentrated in the crossroads area, where excavations revealed a stratigraphy of successive building phases. The building remains and associated material culture in this area are interpreted as having belonged to a Chinese craftsmen's quarters (Pohl 2010; Reichert 2019). While the Muslim community has not been recognised from specific architectural remains, a burial group outside the city walls has been identified as an Islamic cemetery (Bayar and Voitov 2010). The excavation of a large and prominent structure at the western periphery of the city area was initially suspected to represent the remains of the Khan's palace mentioned in the sources. Excavations revealed, however, that this monumental building, which contained a significant number of Buddhist votive offerings, rather indicates a Buddhist temple, possibly the '*Pavilion of the rising Yuan*' mentioned in an inscription found in the vicinity (Cleaves 1952, 23; Franken 2015, 161-162) (Fig. 4). Another building structure that stands out in the elevation plan of the city is located in the northeast sector (Fig. 4). Excavations of this building complex suggest a religious function, belonging, according to structural evidence, to the Nestorian church (Hüttel 2012; Rohland 2019). Bemmann and Reichert (2020, 133) warn us of such a conclusion, as it mainly relies on two arguments that cannot be fully verified, namely, Rubruck's description of the city, indicating only one Nestorian temple, and building traditions. In his dissertation, Hendrik Rohland (2019, 159-194) examined the textual, architectural, and material evidence at our disposition regarding the Nestorian church in great detail. His conclusions express the ambiguity of the structure, but reveal the current interpretation to be the most plausible explanation, as, until new archaeological evidence proves the contrary, the presence of a Christian cross, the building tradition, and the written sources substantiate this interpretation. Otherwise, the elevation plan of the city shows areas seemingly without substantial architecture, especially along the periphery. It has been suggested that these might have temporarily been areas for the yurts (*gers*) of mobile occupants, temporarily residing within the city's walls, although this interpretation remains to be confirmed (Bemmann and Reichert 2020).

Ongoing discussions concern the evaluation of the city layout itself. While some scholars interpret the clear axial layout with the two intersecting streets as a model based on the Chinese's ideal city (*e.g.* Pohl 2010), it has also been suggested that it is an inherently pastoralist cosmological program that formed the basis of the city's structure, with the Khan's palace to the south and the city stretching northwards. Such a pattern would reflect the traditional spatial orientation of a Mongolian yurt, indicating the participation of Mongols in the planning of the layout (Wasilewski 1976; Bemmann and Reichert 2020).

Karakorum with its hinterland and the wider region: Economic, political, and religious connectivity

As reflected in its layout and structure and in its multi-ethnic population, the cosmopolitan constitution of Karakorum mirrors the political foundations of the Mongolian World Empire with its far-reaching connections to and communication with diverse polities and societies across Eurasia, including Chinese, Muslim, Christian, and even European actors. Like the historical accounts of Rubruck, the find materials attest to long-distance relations over thousands of kilometres, as exemplified by Chinese pottery from kilns located over 2000 km away (Sklebitz 2018). Besides its role as an administrative and political centre, it was also a place for specialists in science, religion, arts, crafts, and trade (de Rachewiltz *et al.* 1993; Reichert 2019; Bemmann and Reichert 2020). Food supplies for the city's population depended primarily on large-scale imports, *e.g.*, Chinese grain, although local cultivation attempts are also attested (Bemmann and Reichert 2020). Likewise, intensive trading connections also secured the supply of non-local raw materials for handicrafts and industries (Reichert 2019). The khans actively supported these merchant connectivities, which also benefited from the elaborated communications systems established throughout the empire to ensure the prosperity and prominence of the capital (Bemmann and Reichert 2020). At the same time, the Khan's court remained mobile with seasonal residences throughout the Mongolian heartland – the palace at Karakorum being just one of them (*e.g.* Shiraishi 2004).

At Karakorum, an urban node was in action, interacting and connecting the local actors with the social structure in place, the hinterland within a network of cities and mobile groups, and foreign institutions with economic and political power, but also religiously through the creation and use of sacred spaces stemming from heterogeneous backgrounds. Religious freedom was an integral part of the cosmopolitan and multi-ethnic character of the city and acted as a tool for political and personal gains. For example, Chinggis Khan wanted the development of an elixir of immortality from the Daoists and at the same time, their control, which he sought through the guidance of the Daoist sage, Changchun (Rossabi 2012, 47). Judging from both the written sources and the archaeological evidence, the different forms of worship places inscribed in the cityscape and their role in urban dynamism fulfilled Leeds' conceptualisation of urbanity, including localities, components of technology, and institutions, which partake in the core of economic and political life.

The Erdene Zuu monastery and the rise of Buddhism, 16th century CE

Through political decisions that led Khubilai Khan, a grandson of Chinggis Khan, to move the capital from Karakorum to what is now Beijing in China in the 13th century CE, the Orkhon Valley lost prestige and centrality in geopolitical and religious spheres. When the Mongol groups returned to the northern steppe regions after the end of the Yuan dynasty, their political situation was characterised by divides and disputes over political leadership. These processes ran parallel to the disintegration of the Mongol World Empire by creating several dominions of independent princes. With previous close ties between the Mongolian aristocracy and the Tibetan Buddhist elite then weakened, scholars have for a long time suggested that they became politically rather marginalised and re-strengthened their ties to shamanist practices (cf. Bawden 1968, 27; Moses 1977, 82). Larry Moses (1977, 84) explains the decline of Buddhist influence with the absence of urban centres 'necessary to support a monastic community'. By pointing out the connectivity between political power, religion, and urban nodes in the Mongolian steppe region, he writes:

> 'Buddhism had not become widespread in Mongolia proper during Yuan except in the imperial city of Karakorum and its immediate environs. As in past historical periods, the Mongol Buddhist monuments were associated with fixed urban sites. Those sites were then abandoned after 1368 A.D. in the face of repeated military invasions by Ming armies. Buddhist doctrine, written texts, statuary, and monastic communities were abandoned in the gradual reversion to tribalism that accompanied the Mongol retreat from the Inner Asian frontier with China' (Moses 1977, 82).

However, the idea of a return to shamanism was based on the absence of visible evidence, such as temple structures from this period, which, according to Isabelle Charleux (2006, 34-35), was caused by a higher degree of nomadic mobility, a lack of unity as well as limited access to resources. Only a few contemporary sources indicate that monks were actively involved in Mongolian political affairs during the Ming dynasty from the late 14th century onwards (Jagchid 1979). Archaeologically, the evidence supports this thesis by the discovery of what appears to be permanent monastic communities, e.g., at the Arjai Grotto in the Ordos region, Inner Mongolia (Wang et al. 1994; Batu and Yang 2005). Although difficult to assert its degree of influence based on the sparse evidence, Buddhism did not completely disappear from the steppes after the end of the Yuan dynasty.

It took until the second half of the 16th century CE for Buddhism to regain influence in the steppe regions. Early in this process, the Orkhon Valley became central again by the revival of the former urban node of the imperial capital as the site of the foundation of the Erdene Zuu monastery. The powerful Khalkh Mongol prince, Abadai Khan (1554-1588), whose dominion included the former imperial city of Karakorum, became a driving force in the spread of Buddhism among his people. He met with the Dalai Lama at the court of the southern Mongolian Altan Khan (1507-1582), whose support of Buddhism since the 1570s led to 'the great turning-point in the religious history of Mongolia' (Bawden 1968, 29-30). Among his deeds, Altan Khan revived the 'Dual Principle' of the Yuan dynasty, the political-religious alliance between the secular power of the state and Tibetan Buddhism, which had drastic ramifications for the Mongolian socio-political landscape. During his meeting with the Dalai Lama, Abadai Khan received the instruction to build a place for cult in his homeland (cf. Moses 1977, 103-104). As narrated in a biography of Zanabazar (1635-1723), the great-grandson of Abadai and a leading figure in the religious history of Mongolia, the Dalai Lama bestowed a relic of Shakyamuni Buddha and other religious objects to Abadai Khan and told him to erect a temple at an auspicious site in his territory, in an area named 'Old and New Orqon' (Bawden 1961, 37).

Erdene Zuu as a religious and political centre

Abadai initiated the construction of Erdene Zuu in 1586, in the vicinity of the old imperial capital of Karakorum and laid the foundation for an influential supra-local monastic centre, engaged in the spread of Lamaism in the Orkhon Valley and beyond (Gutschow and Brandt 2005). Laden with a rich history, Karakorum proved to be the ideal location in connecting the past with a renewed dedication to Buddhism, inscribing the foundation of the site into a sacred, meaningful space. However, archaeological and historical data indicate even stronger and long-lasting connectivity, as the site of Erdene Zuu was located at the same place as a previously existing Buddhist temple from the Uyghur period (Maidar 1972, 35; Bareja-Starzynska 2018, 135) and most likely also at the site of the Khan's palace of the imperial capital of Karakorum (cf. Rohland 2019, 25).

Religious and political spaces were interwoven in several ways into the monasteries' built structure. Some remarkable buildings were set up in the second half of the 17th century by Zanabazar, the first Jebtsundamba khutagt or 'Living Buddha' of Khalkh Mongolia (e.g. Tsultem 1982; Uranchimeg 2020). It was also during this period that two stupas were added to the ensemble in front of the three 'Zuu' temples (Gutschow and Brandt 2005, 353). These are good examples of how the sacred space of the monastic node was permeated by and interacted with the political sphere, as they were both dedicated to great supporters of Buddhism in Khalkh Mongolia and powerful nobles in the lineage of Chinggis Khan. Thus, the consolidation and extension of Erdene Zuu continued and developed further into a combined religious and political centre.

Over centuries, new temple buildings and memorials were added to the architectural arrangements within the monastic centre of Erdene Zuu, and, while artisans and carpenters usually came from China, archaeological evidence suggested that available building materials, such as bricks from the ancient Mongol capital of Karakorum, were at least partly used (Bareja-Starzynska 2018, 136). As described in the late 19th century by the Polish traveller Kotwicz, most temples in Erdene Zuu were constructed in a Chinese style, while only a few buildings showed Tibetan architecture with a flat rooftop or mixed styles (Bareja-Starzynska 2018). According to the report of Alexsej M. Pozdneyev (1971 [1892], 302) from the late 19th century, the monastic complex was comprised of 62 temples and additional housings for lamas, while outside the monastery enclosure, approximately 500 buildings were arranged along simple roads.

The origin of the monastery enclosures (*kherem*) with its stupas and large gates on each side cannot be precisely dated. The wall made from clay brick could only be reliably dated back to the early 18th century, whereby it possibly replaced a previous square earth embankment (Gutschow and Brandt 2005, 353). Concerning the characteristic stupas that create the unique appearance of the monastery, D. Maidar (1972, 35) mentions 108 of them that were successively added to the wall and its four corners, while the four large gates, each on one side, were constructed in 1803. However, his depiction relates to a cosmological, auspicious number while *de facto*, not more than 100 stupas were added, which were donated by wealthy Khalkh families (Gutschow and Brandt 2005). Generally, a monastery's wall needs to be understood as a feature separating the inside and outside spheres, with a physical and spiritual protecting function. As described for Erdene Zuu, the monastery is the residence of the clergy and *'the place to study, practice, and serve the community'* (Baasansüren 2011, 50). While lay people could enter the complex during the daytime for devotions, mediations, the receiving of teaching, and more, the gates would be closed at sunset before the evening meditations and prayers of the monks.

The construction of the Erdene Zuu monastery took place over almost two centuries, beginning during a political period of independent Mongol princes and the second wave of the spread of Buddhism in Khalkh, and continued during the Manchu reign over Mongolia. At least twice, it was the focus of Oirat war campaigns against Khalkh in the 1680s and 1730s. It was temporarily abandoned, then revived and renovated. Lamas and lay patrons continued the monastery's restoration and expansion, as Erdene Zuu became famous throughout Central Asia as a spiritual, educational, and artistic centre (Baasansüren 2011, 9). Hence, its role as a node of connectivity seems to have changed during this period. Erdene Zuu continued to be one of the most important Buddhist centres in Khalkh. It might have been due to the monastery's supra-local religious and political authority that the Orkhon Valley became the scene of the so-called 'battle of Erdene Zuu' between Oirat and Manchu troops in 1732. However, the presence of the Manchu military and particularly Chinese traders, who followed them, again changed the face of the region by situating the monastic node of Erdene Zuu within a region equally attracting clergy and believers as well as traders, peasants, and craftsmen partaking in the greater, regional network.

Baruun Khüree: The Orkhon Valley under the Manchu aegis, 17th-20th century CE

A few years before Zanabazar's birth, Northern China was conquered by the Manchus, who were Tungus-speaking nomadic peoples from the east, initially allied with the southern Mongol tribes until quarrels undermined their relationship. Internal conflicts and the failure to unite led to the subordination of the southern Mongol tribes under Manchu protection, which was officially proclaimed at the enthronement of the first Manchu emperor of Northern

China and the beginning of the Qing dynasty (1644-1911). While the Khalkh in the north kept their independence for a few decades, their situation was already overshadowed by a growing Manchu influence. According to Charles R. Bawden (1968, 54), it was a political consideration of the Tüsheet Khan Gombodorj, one of the leaders of the Khalkh, to (re-)introduce Buddhism as a unifying principle. In 1639, the Khalkh aristocracy accepted his son Zanabazar as a high Buddhist incarnation, who received the honouring title 'Bogd Gegeen' (Holy Enlightened) and 'Öndör Gegeen' (High Enlightened). Thus, Zanabazar was perceived as a 'Living Buddha' and as the reincarnation of a well-known Tibetan lama, the scholar Taranatha. He took up the third-highest rank within the Gelugpa, yellow hat order, and became a leading political figure, broadening his influence as a religious leader beyond that of a local noble (Bawden 1968; Kaplonski 2004). At a young age, Zanabazar inspired the foundation of two monastic sites. First, in 1639, his official residence was established under the name Örgöö at a place called Shireet tsagaan nuur, located about 80 km east of Erdene Zuu. Second, in 1647, he founded his first monastery within the Orkhon Valley, known as Baruun Khüree (Western monastery) (Pozdneev 1971 [1892], 304; Croner 2006, 14; Khatanbaatar 2019). Both monastic nodes were related to the spread of Buddhism, which in return developed into supra-local nodes.

In the perception of the Manchu rulers, the Khalkh territories were supposed to become a military buffer zone at the northern borders of the empire. However, the western Mongols intruded into the Mongolian heartlands until the Manchu army ultimately defeated them in the 1750s, thus inevitably affecting the settlement patterns and the mobility of (sacred and profane) urban sites within northern Mongol territories according to military requirements. These events also affected urban processes in the Orkhon Valley, as the monastery of Erdene Zuu was temporarily abandoned, and military garrisons were established. As it appears, military conflicts were one of the main reasons why some monastic nodes became unsettled settlements in the steppes. Monasteries, such as Örgöö and Baruun Khüree, continued to be mobile throughout this period. Örgöö moved over twenty times until it finally became a permanent settlement at the banks of the Tuul River in 1779 (Maidar 1972, 64-65). As the main residence of the Öndör Gegeen, it developed into the largest urban settlement and religious centre in Khalkh Mongolia, finally becoming the modern Mongolian capital of Ulaanbaatar.

Layout of the old monastery of the high holy

Baruun Khüree maintained its mobility and returned to the Orkhon Valley in 1787, developing into a settled monastic site near the Shankh Mountains. According to a local legend circulated by the monks, the location of the site referred to the story that

> 'a man riding by here accidentally spilled a pail of milk. Upon seeing the milk splattered on the ground a lama declared that this was a sign that the ten white virtues would flourish on this spot' (Croner 2006, 15).

Additionally, Baruun Khüree may have an even deeper connection between the monastery and its founding place, as it is mentioned that it originated from this 'nutag' (Anonymus undated, 1). The Mongolian concept of nutag, which expresses complex meanings of 'location', 'region', 'homeland', and 'birthplace', implies a sociocultural as well as a spiritual idea of belonging to a place (Bulag 1998, 175). Thus, it might not be a simple description of the place of origin, but may rather

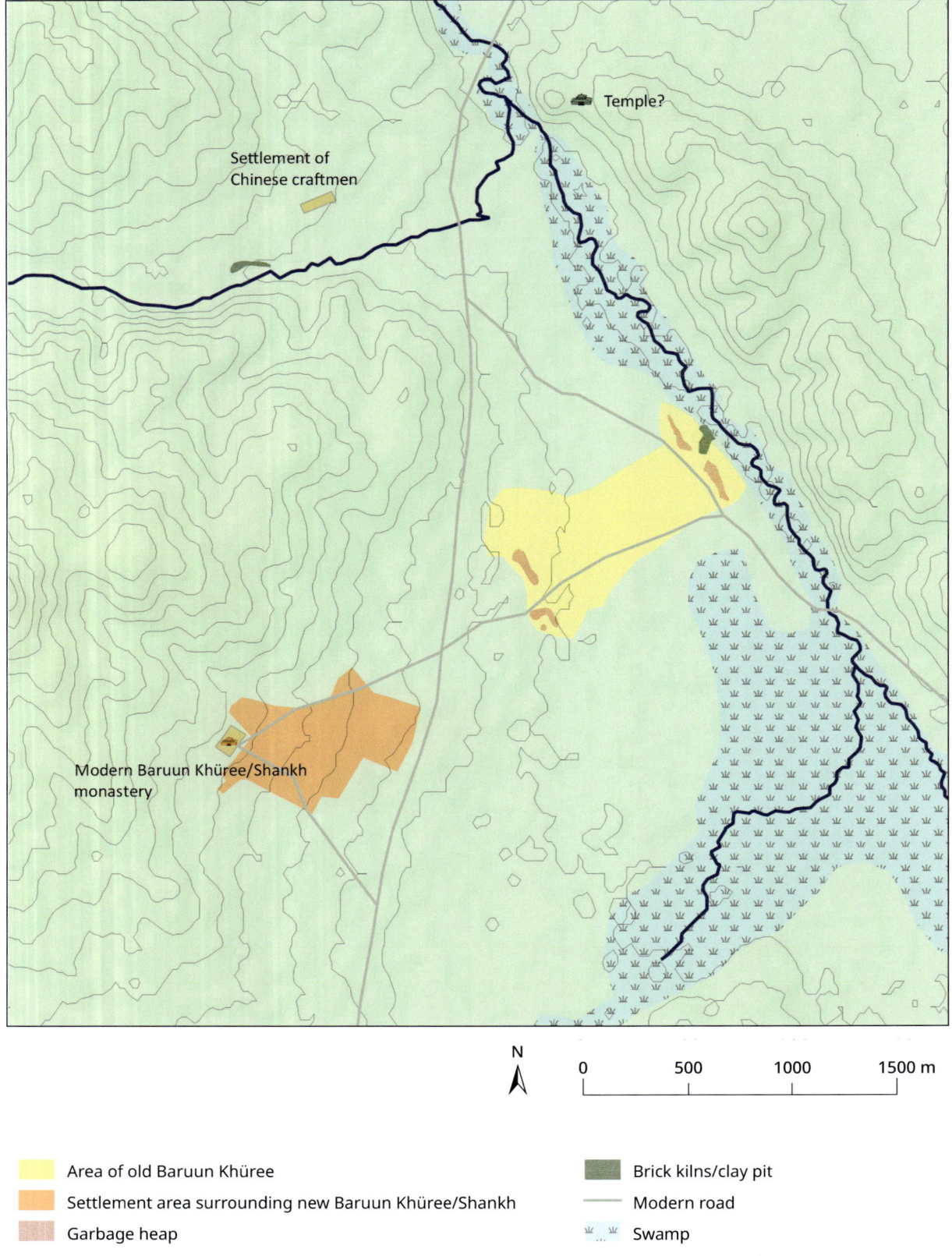

Figure 5. Baruun Khüree and modern Shankh monasteries (map: B. Ahrens).

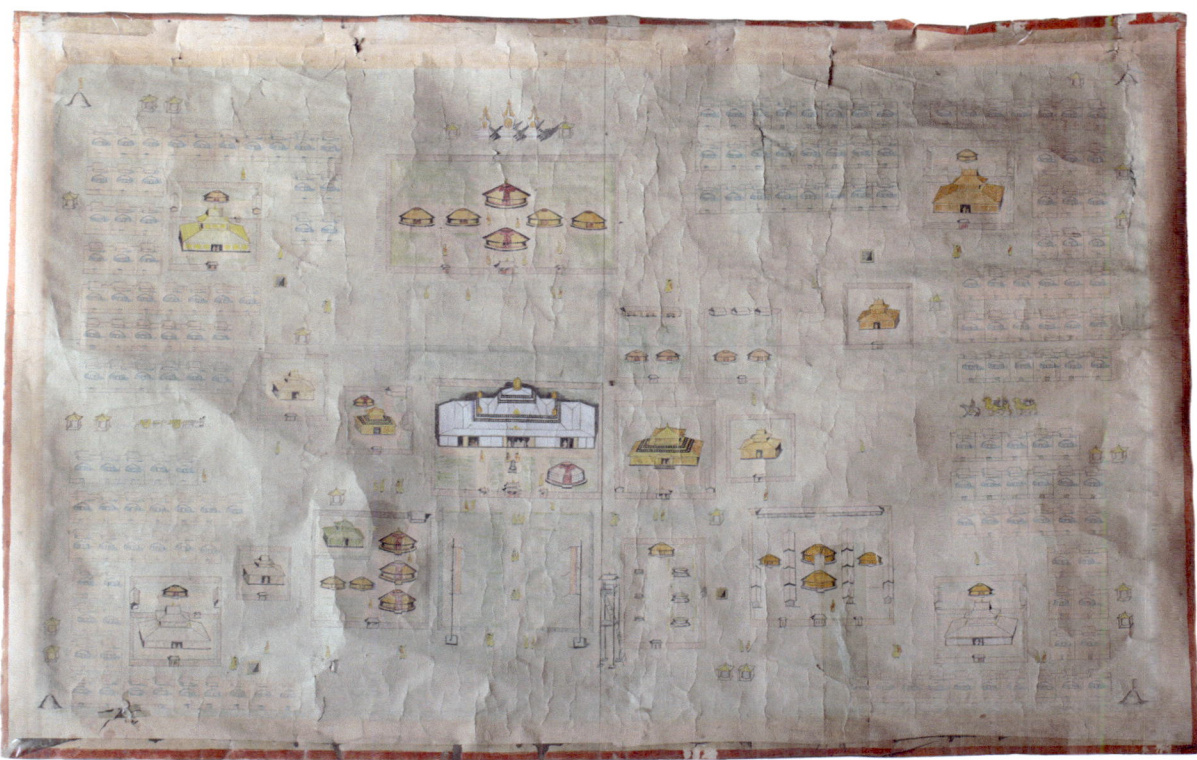

refer to underlying, symbolic connectivity that situates Baruun Khüree within the auspicious homeland of the Öndör Gegeen Zanabazar, the origin of his religious work and creation of sacred monastic space, as well as his Chinggisid descent. This is also reflected by the monastery's honorary title of 'Öndör Bogdyn Övgön Khüree' (The Old Monastery of the High Holy) (Anonymus undated).

Figure 6. Plan of Baruun Khüree. This is a replica of the city layout of Baruun Khüree, which can be found in the rebuilt Shankh monastery (photo: S. Jagiola, Kiel Univ.).

In 1787, more than 50 years after the death of Zanabazar, the construction of the permanent monastery began that constantly grew into a significant urban complex, becoming a central administrative structure in the Orkhon Valley (Pozdneev 1978 [1887], 47). Internally, a central temple (*tsogchin*) coordinated the whole community, where residents were administratively subdivided into the so-called *aimag*, with smaller temples (*dugan*) performing daily services. At the same time, religious teaching took place in the specialised colleges (*datsan*), which have been successively set up in Baruun Khüree since 1824. Among the *datsan* were the colleges of demonology (*dshud*), philosophy (*tsanid*), and astrology (*zurkhain*). At the time that Baruun Khüree was a settled monastic complex, it was comprised of only four *aimag*, but the number of lamas constantly grew. In the early 20th century, the number of lamas in Outer Mongolia (105 577) accounted for ca. 45% of the male population (Maiskii 1921, 27). According to Pozdneyev (1971 [1892], 304), the number of lamas residing in Baruun Khüree grew constantly and at the end of the 19th century even exceeded those of Erdene Zuu. At the beginning of the 20th century, Baruun Khüree included seven colleges and accommodated around 1500 lamas. An undated map of Baruun Khüree found in the current monastery (Fig. 6) shows a rectangular spatial arrangement of buildings around a central complex. The housings of the residing lamas were in the four corners, and, as the map suggests, each quarter was located around a temple building (*dugan*) that might have been assigned to one of the four *aimag*. The exterior appearance of the central building shows unique characteristics, like the shape of its roof. According to Pozdneev (1971 [1892]), the architecture of the *tsogchin* followed a design that went back to Zanabazar himself and was similar to the central building in Örgöö. According to a document from the 1860s, the overall size of the building complex of Baruun Khüree covered an area of 576 m from north to south and 627 m from west to east (Ninjbadgar 2014, 167).

Perhaps the most distinguishing feature of Baruun Khüree was its function as a site, where the 'Standard of Chinggis Khan' was kept. Stored in a building within the temple complex, it might have indicated the place as a symbol of political power in the sacred architecture of Baruun Khüree. Its previous location is nowadays commemorated by a monument (Chimiddorj 2017, 44). This may point to spatially-linked political symbolism related to the noble lineage of Zanabazar and the religious meaning of Chinggis Khan, who was later introduced into the Mongolian Buddhist pantheon. The anthropologist Jack Weatherford (2005, xvi) argues that the banner was the embodiment of Chinggis Khan's soul, and Zanabazar '*built the monastery with a special mission to fly and protect*' it. Although it is unclear when the standard became part of the inventory, it was kept in the monastery until its destruction during the socialist purges in the 1930s (Konagaya *et al.* 2008; Trapp 2015, 322).

Monastic nodes as focal points of religious, economic, and social life

Since the late 17th century, the number of Buddhist monasteries in Mongolia increased and became, as Muping Bao (2002, 221) puts it, not just religious sites '*but also the political, cultural, medical and economic hubs of the Steppes*'. As such, they represented a hierarchical organisation for religious and secular matters (*e.g.* Vreeland 1957; Pozdneev 1978 [1887]). Furthermore, nomad families were registered as subjects to a rich monastery and its leaders, such as the Jebtsundamba Khutagt. Such relationships between the monastery and registered subjects included economic and religious duties, for example, livestock herding, operating postal stations (*örtöö*), renovating temple buildings, and much more. Most families had at least one son who became a lama, establishing connectivities between the monastery and the nomadic hinterland through social ties, thus partly following a flexible settlement pattern.

In the case of the Orkhon Valley, it might be appropriate not to focus on a single monastic site, such as Baruun Khüree, but to understand the region as a kind of agglomeration of nodes. Since different group formations and settlements gradually appeared throughout the Manchu period and interacted on local and supra-local levels, the discussion of connectivity between nodes should include large monasteries like Erdene Zuu and Baruun Khüree as well as other smaller monasteries and temples within the area (cf. Maidar 1972; Gantujaa 2015), just as much as the presence of Manchu troops and Chinese settlers. At least since the 1720s, complex settlement patterns evolved in the Orkhon Valley by the presence of Manchu-Inner Mongolian troops, who erected a military garrison during the times of conflict with the Western Mongols, and by Chinese traders, who, after the Chinese-Russian Treaty of Khjakhta in 1723, took the opportunity to extend their trade networks throughout Khalkh Mongolia. According to the Mongolian historian M. Sanjdorj (1980, 28), the development of Chinese trade in the Outer Mongolian heartland began with temporary stays of Chinese merchants who camped near monastic sites like Erdene Zuu and Örgöö. Although it was forbidden by Manchu rule for a Chinese trader or craftsman to settle in the region, written sources show that the monastic elite provided parts of legitimate citizenship in their status as local Mongolian inhabitants, the settlers becoming personal serfs of the Jebtsundamba Khutagt (Tsai 2017a; 2017b). Therefore, the Chinese settlers continued trade, agriculture, and handicraft activities in the vicinity of the growing monastic nodes by selling imported goods and agricultural products, providing services, paying rental taxes, and cooperating in arrangements of long-distance transport.

As we stated above, communal bonds were created and intergroup connections were established around the sacred, monastic space. According to this, a discussion of connections between monastic nodes and mobile communities of the hinterland necessarily requires mentioning the Buddhist exertion of religious authority on certain pre-Buddhist sacred places, the so-called *ovoo* (*e.g.* Humphrey 1995; Wallace 2015). Such *ovoos* were fixed sites, usually built on mountain tops or other sacred places and around a pole that symbolised a connection between earth and sky, differing from *ovoo* stone piles used by the Manchus since the 18th century for the demarcation of administrative territories. They functioned as a kind of altar for the worship of mountain spirits, which were perceived, according to a customary 'shamanist' conception of nature (baigal'), as the most powerful entities and the 'rulers' of the land. Thus, nature was inhabited by humans, animals as well as spiritual entities as active subjects (Weiler 2002, 193), best defined by Ferdinand Lessing as *'the sum total of physical forces, agencies and processes in the external world'* (Lessing 2013, 74). Among these forces, mountain spirits were worshipped as influential agents who decided on the well-being of communities and their herds (Weiler 2002, 196).

The spread of Buddhism among the Mongol population raised conflicts with 'shamanist' beliefs and led to its suppression by lamas, as well as syncretic forms of religion (Heissig 1970, 338). Annual *ovoo* rituals, previously performed by shamans, were then taken over by lamas and, although not accepted by Buddhism as a kind of religious practice, were changed into canonised rituals in which spirits were classified as good and evil (Humphrey 1995, 140). Quite often, under the patronage of high lamas, the annual *ovoo* rituals were attended by male members of every local household and have been, according to Caroline Humphrey (1995, 148), *'a setting out of the ideologically permanently recurrent structure of society'.*

Urban sites and religion in nomadic settings: A deeper connection

Throughout history, the Mongolian cultural landscape changed according to sociocultural and politico-economic realities, yet some of its more profound transformations occurred in compliance with religious practices. Whether the local population opens their borders to a distinctive religion like Manichaeism, favours worship's freedom as a personal matter in a society free of religious ties, or supports Buddhist emancipation as a socio-political unifier, sacred spaces inherently paved the way for community formation, a sense of belonging, as well as political legitimisation. In part linked to creating and using sacred spaces, urban nodes rise and fall in a nomadic pastoral environment. In this sense, they are an integrated part of Mongolian history but do not necessarily follow conventional, settled societies' perspectives. In re-imagining urban functions in such a nomadic context and environment, Leeds' three specialisations (localities, components of technology, and institutions) offer one possible interpretation (Leeds 2017). As the specialties show forms of independence and interrelation at the same time by influencing each other, the principal actors in the process are *homo religiosus*, meaning that their actions and responses to the world are intrinsically linked to some forms of beliefs.

The Orkhon Valley presents an excellent laboratory to observe a diachronic transformation of the urbanisation process embedded in religious practices. From empire to empire, there is a continuity in using sacred spaces by acknowledging and reappropriating the past and unifying the local population through ritualisation. Sacred spaces thus guided the foundation of cities with – at their core, if not central – dedicated places to worship for community gathering and bonding. At these sites and in their vicinity, temples and shrines were built, accommodating the beliefs in place, and influencing most aspects of the community's daily life. With Altan Khan and the reborn interest in Buddhism, the later period witnessed the local practices reaching foreign interest by welcoming Chinese architects and clerical elites from Tibet. Without losing themselves in an ocean of foreign authorities, the Mongols adapted to the new conditions, incorporating outside elements in their practices by building, for example, Buddhist monasteries following Chinese, Tibetan, and Mongol techniques (Alexandre 1993; Charleux 2006). What was local was now connected on a larger scale to the political scene of Central and East Asia. Although initially reluctant, monastic centres gradually grew into urban nodes, connecting the population to a place of worship, education, arts, craftsmanship, political and economic power, and much more.

As a result, religions and sacred spaces were institutionalised, thus introducing Leeds' last specialisation. During the Uyghur period, we observe that Manichaeism was not only a part of the belief system in place but also a driving force in the economic and political affairs of the empire. Its institutionalisation connected the Sogdian with the Uyghur elite, which provided trade opportunities that extended to China. As Karakorum became the centre of the Mongolian Empire, it favoured religious freedom, a legacy of Genghis Khan, transforming the city into a cosmopolitical, urban node. The various religious elites became consultants to the Khan in power, offering advice and spiritual guidance. Towards the end of the Ming dynasty, Buddhism was proselytised on an even grander scale. As a means to legitimise the authority in place, lamas gathered immense power, which put them at the centre of economic and political life. Thus, the institutionalisation of Buddhism in Mongolia acted as an internal as well as an external connecting agent. First, locally, the people were unified under banners, an administrative and military division of the Empire, imposed by the Qing court, which monastic centres often administered. As a sacred space, the monastery was sometimes built on the remains or in the vicinity of *lieux de mémoire*. Erdene Zuu is an excellent example as it connects a new power with a glorified past and its physical iteration by constructing the temples on the ruins of Karakorum. Second, externally, lamas played a role in forming connections between China and the local elite and between the clergy and Tibet. Whether during the Uyghur era, the Mongol Empire, or the Qing dynasty, religions and sacred spaces interacted in the larger, urban dynamism.

Through the case studies discussed here, we show that religions are a dynamic force, in constant change and constantly changing their proponents that must be integrated into any discussion on the development of urbanism. As a connecting agent, religions interact at different levels, whether socially, politically, economically, historically, or naturally. This horizontal perspective renders the deeper meaning of religion in societal formations, in which they are too often seen as a passive element in a secular world. In reinforcing our understanding of past socialisation and urbanisation, one must acknowledge the actors, more often than not, as *homo religiosus*. In the formation of sacred, urban nodes in the Mongolian landscapes, major transformations occurred, leading to sociocultural and religious ramifications in an ever-growing urban context.

References

Alexandre, E., 1993. L'architecture religieuse en pays Khalkha. *In:* G. Béguin and D. Dashbaldan, eds. *Trésors de Mongolie XVIIe-XIXe siècles.* Paris: Éditions de la Réunion des musées nationaux, 82-97.

Allsen, T.T., 1996. Spiritual geography and political legitimacy in the eastern steppe. *In:* H.J.M. Claessen and J.G. Oosten, eds. *Ideology and the Formation of Early States.* Leiden: Brill, 116-135.

Anonymus, undated. *"Avral Itgel Khutagt Lamin Akhui Oron" Baruun Khüreenii Tovch Taniltsuulga [Brief Introduction to Baruun Khüree, "Domain of the faith protecting Chutagt Lama"].*

Baasansüren, K., 2011. *Enkh Tunkh Erdene Zuu (Erdene Zuu: The Jewel of Enlightenment).* Ulaanbaatar: Pozitive.

Bao, M., 2002. Study of the architecture and spatial order of the Manchu eight banners in Hohhot, Inner Mongolia, under Qing rule. *Journal of Architecture and Planning,* 67 (554), 311-316.

Bareja-Starzynska, A., 2018. Description of the Erdene Zuu Monastery Life (including čam) Based on Notes by Kotwicz. *In:* J. Tulisow, O. Inoue, A. Bareja-Starzyńska, E. Dziurzyńska, F. Majkowski, eds. *In the Heart of Mongolia. 100th Anniversary of W. Kotwicz's Expedition to Mongolia in 1912 (Studies and Selected Source Material).* Kraków: Polska Akademia Umiejętności, 131-189.

Batu, J. and Yang, H., 2005. *Aerzhai shiku – Chengjisihan de fojiao jiniantang xingshuai shi – Arjai Grotto – The Rise and Fall of a Buddhist Memorial for Chinggis Khan.* Tokyo: Fukyosha Publishing.

Bawden, C., 1961. *The Jebtsundamba Khutukhtus of Urga.* Wiesbaden: O. Harrassowitz.

Bawden, C., 1968. *The Modern History of Mongolia.* London: Weidenfeld and Nicholson.

Bayar, D. and Voitov, V.E., 2010. Excavation in the Islamic Cemetery of Karakorum. *In:* J. Bemman, U. Erdenebat, E. Pohl, eds. *Mongolian-German Karakorum Expedition – Vol 1: Excavations in the Craftsman Quarter at the Main Road.* Wiesbaden: Reichert Verlag, 289-306.

Becker, E., 2007. *Die altmongolische Hauptstadt Karakorum: Forschungsgeschichte nach historischen Aussagen und archäologischen Quellen.* Rahden, Westf.: Verlag Marie Leidorf.

Bemmann, J., 2014. Archäologische Forschungen in der Mongolei: Ein Rückblick auf ein erfolgreiches Kapitel Deutsch-Mongolischer Kooperation. *Mongolische Notizen,* 22, 9-34.

Bemmann, J. and Reichert, S., 2020. Karakorum, the first capital of the Mongol world empire: an imperial city in a non-urban society. *Asian Archaeology,* 4 (2), 121-143.

Bemmann, J., Ahrens, B., Grützner, C., Klinger, R., Klitzsch, N., Lehmann, F., Linzen, S.P., Munkhbayar, L., Nomguunsuren, G., Oczipka, M., Piezonka, H., Schütt, B., Saran, S., 2011a. Geoarchaeology in the Steppe: First results of the multidisciplinary Mongolian-German survey project in the Orkhon Valley, Central

Mongolia. *Studia Archaeologica Instituti Archaeologici Academiae Scientiarum Mongolicae*, XXX (Fasc. 5), 69-97.

Bemmann, J., Höllmann, T.O., Ahrens, B., Kaiser, T., Müller, S., 2011b. A stone quarry in the hinterland of Karakorum, Mongolia, with evidence of Chinese stonemasons. *Journal of Inner Asian Art and Archaeology*, 6, 101-136.

Bemmann, J., Lehndorff, E., Klinger, R., Linzen, S., Munkhbayar, L., Oczipka, M., Piezonka, H., Reichert, S., 2014. Biomarkers in Archaeology – Land use around the Uyghur Capital Karabalgasun, Orkhon Valley, Mongolia. *Prähistorische Zeitschrift*, 89 (2), 337-370.

Bemmann, J., Munkhbayar, L., Enkhtur, A., 2020. A Uyghur Fortified Palace in Central Mongolia Predating the Actual Empire? *In:* S. Chuluun and G. Eregzen, G., eds. Нүүдэлчид Ба Хот Суурин 2018 оны 8 дугаар сарын 24-25 ны өдөр. ШУА-ийн Тэргүүлэгчдийн газрын Их чуулганы танхим [Nomads and Urban Settlements. August 24-25, 2018. General Assembly Hall of the Presidium of the Mongolian Academy of Sciences]. Ulaanbaatar: Soëmbo Printing, 116-126.

Bernbeck, R., 2008. An Archaeology of Multisited Communities. *In:* H. Barnard and W. Wendrich, eds. *The Archaeology of Mobility: Old World and New World Nomadism.* Los Angeles, CA: Costen Institute of Archaeology at UCLA, 43-77.

Bulag, U.E., 1998. *Nationalism and Hybridity in Mongolia.* Oxford: Clarendon Press.

Charleux, I., 2006. *Temples et monastères de Mongolie-intérieure.* Paris: Éditions du Comité des travaux historiques et scientifiques: Institut national d'histoire de l'art.

Chidester, D. and Linenthal, E.T., 1995. *American Sacred Space.* Bloomington and Indianapolis: Indiana University Press.

Childe, V.G., 1936. *Man makes himself.* London: Watts & Co.

Childe, V.G., 1942. *What happened in history.* Harmondsworth, Middlesex: Penguin Books.

Childe, V.G., 1950. The Urban Revolution. *The Town Planning Review*, 21 (1), 3-17.

Chimiddorj, N., 2017. *Delkhiin Öv-Orkhoni Khöndiin Soyolin Dursgalt Gazar Dakhi Ayalal Juulchlal [Sights of cultural memorials of the World Heritage Orchon Valley].* Ulaanbaatar: Arildal KhKhK.

Cho, F. and Squier, R., 2013. Religion as a Complex and Dynamic System. *Journal of the American Academy of Religion*, 81, 357-398.

Christaller, W., 1966. *Central Places in Southern Germany.* Englewood Cliffs, NJ: Prentice-Hall.

Cleaves, F.W., 1952. The Sino-Mongolian Inscription of 1346. *Harvard Journal of Asiatic Studies*, 15 (1/2), 1-123.

Cowgill, G.L., 2004. Origins and development of urbanism: Archaeological approaches. *Annual Review of Anthropology*, 33, 525-549.

Croner, D., 2006. *Guidebook to Locales Connected with the Life of Zanabazar: First Bogd Gegeen of Mongolia.* Ulaanbaatar: Polar Star Press.

Dähne, B., 2015. *Die archäologischen Ausgrabungen der uigurischen Hauptstadt Karabalgasun im Kontext der Siedlungsforschung spätnomadischer Stämme im östlichen Zentralasien.* (Dissertation: Universität Leipzig).

de la Vaissière, É., 2018. *Sogdian Traders: A History.* Leiden, Boston: Brill.

de Rachewiltz, I., Chan, H.-L., Hsiao, C.-C., Geier, P.W., Wang, M., eds., 1993. *In the Service of the Khan: Eminent personalities of the early Mongol-Yüan period (1200-1300).* Wiesbaden: Harrassowitz.

Di Cosmo, N., 2014/15. Why Qara Qorum? Climate and geography in the early Mongol empire. *Archivum Eurasiae Medii*, 21, 67-78.

Eliade, M., 1957. *Das Heilige und das Profane: vom Wesen des Religiosen.* Hamburg: Rowohlt.

Eliade, M., 1995. *Handbuch der Religionen*. Frankfurt am Main: Suhrkamp.

Eliade, M., 2002. *Geschichte der religiösen Ideen. Band 2: von Gautama Buddha bis zu den Anfängen des Christentums*. Freiburg: Herder.

Eliade, M., 2004 [1968]. *The Sacred and the Profane: The Nature of Religion*. San Diego, London: Harvest House Publishers.

Erdenebat, U. and Pohl, E., 2009. The crossroads in Khara Khorum: Excavations at the center of the Mongol empire. In: W.W. Fitzhigh, M. Rossabi, W. Honeychurch, eds. *Genghis Khan and the Mongol Empire*. Seattle: University of Washington Press, 137-145.

Erdenebat, U., Batsaikhan, Z., Dashdorj, B., Amarbileg, Ch., 2011. Архангай аймгийн Хотонт сумын нутаг Олон дов хэмээх газар 2010 онд хийсэн археологийн шинжилгээ [Archaeological Excavation in 2010 in Olon Dov, K hotont soum, Arkhangai aimag]. *Studia Archaeologica*, XXX (Fasc. 9), 146-185.

Fletcher, R., 2019. Trajectories to low-density settlements past and present: paradox and outcomes. *Frontiers in Digital Humanities* [online]. Available at: https://doi.org/10.3389/fdigh.2019.00014.

Fox, R.G., 1977. *Urban Anthropology: Cities in their Cultural Settings*. Englewood Cliffs, NJ: Prentice-Hall.

Franken, C., 2014. Karabalgasun und Karakorum, Mongolei. Die Arbeiten der Jahre 2012 und 2013. *Online Report of the German Archaeological Institute (DAI) 2014* [online], 93-99. Available at: http://nbn-resolving.de/urn:nbn:de:0048-journals.efb-2014-1-p93-99-v4421.9 or https://publications.dainst.org/journals/efb/17/4421.

Franken, C., 2015. *Die "Große Halle" von Karakorum: Zur archäologischen Untersuchung des ersten buddhistischen Tempels der alten mongolischen Hauptstadt*. Wiesbaden: Reichert.

Franken, C., Erdenebat, U., Batbayar, T., 2014. Erste Ergebnisse der Grabungen des Jahres 2013 in Karabalgasun und Karakorum/Mongolei. *Zeitschrift für Archäologie Außereuropäischer Kulturen*, 6, 355-372.

Franken, C., Rohland, H., Block-Berlitz, M., Batbayar, T., Erdenebat, U., 2020. Remote Sensing of Large-Scale Areas at the Urban Sites of the Mongolian Orkhon Valley Using Low-Cost Drones. Preliminary Results and Some Thoughts on the Urban Layout of the Uyghur Capital Qara Balğasun. *Journal of Global Archaeology*, 1-28.

Gantujaa, N., 2015. *XVI-XX zuuni Mongolin süm khiid, erdemt merged [XVI-XX century Mongolian monastries and scholars]*. Ulaanbaatar: Soyombo Printing KhKhK.

Gatto, M., 2011. The Nubian pastoral culture as link between Egypt and Africa: A view from the archaeological record. In: K. Exell, ed. *Egypt in Its African Context*. Proceedings of the Conference Held at the Manchester Museum, University of Manchester, 2-4 October 2009. Oxford: Archaeopress, 21-29.

Golden, P., 2013. Courts and Court Culture in the Proto-Urban and Urban Developments among the Pre-Chinggisid Turkic Peoples. *In:* D. Durand-Guédy, ed. *Turko-Mongol Rulers, Cities and City Life*. Leiden, Boston: Brill's Inner Asian Library, 21-73.

Gutschow, N. and Brandt, A., 2005. Die Baugeschichte der Klosteranlage von Erdeni Joo (Erdene zuu). *In:* C. Müller and E. Pleiger, eds. *Dschingis Khan und seine Erben. Das Weltreich der Mongolen*. München: Hirmer Verlag, 352-356.

Hahn, H.P., 2017. Cities between De-Territorialization and Networking: On the Dynamics of Urbanization in the Global Context. *In:* D. Krausse and M. Fernández-Götz, eds. *Eurasia at the Dawn of History: Urbanization and Social Change*. Cambridge: Cambridge University Press, 169-180.

Hammer, E. and Arbuckle, B., 2017. 10,000 Years of Pastoralism in Anatolia: A Review of Evidence for Variability in Pastoral Lifeways. *Nomadic Peoples,* 21, 214-267.

Heissig, W., 1970. Die Religionen der Mongolei. *In:* G. Tucci and W. Heissig, eds. *Die Religionen Tibets und der Mongolei.* Stuttgart: Kohlhammer, 297-427.

Hoffman, D.R., 2010. *Seeking the sacred in contemporary religious architecture.* Kent, Ohio: Kent State University Press in cooperation with Cleveland State University's College of Liberal Arts and Social Sciences.

Honeychurch, W. and Makarewicz, C.A., 2016. The Archaeology of Pastoral Nomadism. *Annual Review of Anthropology,* 45 (1), 341-359.

Humphrey, C., 1995. Chiefly and Shamanist Landscapes in Mongolia. *In:* E. Hirsch and M. O'Hanlon, eds. *The Anthropology of Landscape: Perspectives on Place and Space.* Oxford: Clarendon Press, 135-162.

Humphrey, C. and Sneath, D., 1999. *The End of Nomadism?: Society, State and the Environment in Inner Asia.* Cambridge: White Horse Press.

Hüttel, H.-G., 2005. Karakorum – Eine historische Skizze. *In:* Kunst- und Ausstellungshalle der Bundesrepublik Deutschland and Staatliches Museum für Völkerkunde München, eds. *Dschingis Khan und seine Erben. Das Weltreich der Mongolen.* Munich: Eine Austellung der Kunst- und Austellungshalle der Bunderepublik Deutschland, 133-137.

Hüttel, H.-G., 2007. Die Stadt des Čingis Chaan. Zum Gründungsmythos von Karakorum. *In:* U.B. Barkmann, ed. *Čingis Chaan und sein Erbe: Das Weltreich der Mongolen.* Ulaanbaatar: Centre for Mongol Studies, National University of Mongolia, 284-296.

Hüttel, H.-G., 2012. Berichte für die Jahre 2009-2010 der Projekte der Kommission für Archäologie Außereuropäischer Kulturen des Deutschen Archäologischen Instituts: Karakorum, Nordstadt – Grabung 2009. *Zeitschrift für Archäologie Außereuropäischer Kulturen,* 4, 412-415.

Hüttel, H.-G. and Erdenebat, U., 2010. *Karabalgasun and Karakorum – Two late nomadic urban settlements in the Orkhon Valley: Archaeological excavation and Research of the German Archaeological Institute (DAI) and the Mongolian Academy of Sciences 2000-2009.* Ulaanbaatar: Ulaanbaatar Botschaft der Bundesrepublik Deutschland.

Jagchid, S., 1979. The Mongol Khans and Chinese Buddhism and Taoism. *Journal of the International Association of Buddhist Studies,* 2 (1), 7-28.

Jisl, L., 1960. Výzkum Külteginova památníku v Mongolské lidové republice. *Archeologické rozhledy,* 12, 86-113.

Kaplonski, C., 2004. *Truth, History and Politics in Mongolia.* London, New York: Routledge Curzon.

Kasai, Y., 2020. Uyghur Legitimation and the Role of Buddhism. *In:* C. Meinert and H. Sørensen, eds. *Buddhism in Central Asia.* Leiden, Boston: Brill, 61-90.

Khatanbaatar, N., 2019. *Mongolin khüree khiid, lam nar. XVI-XX zuuni ekhen [Mongolian temples and lamas. From XVI-early XX Centuries].* Ulaanbaatar: Mönkhiin Üseg KhKhK.

Khazanov, A.M., 2005. Nomads and Cities in the Eurasian Steppe Region and Adjacent Countries: A Historical Overview. *In:* S. Lederer and B. Streck, eds. *Shifts and Drifts in Nomad-Sedentary Relations.* Wiesbaden: Dr. Ludwig Reichert Press, 163-178.

Knott, K., 2005. Spatial Theory and Method for the Study of Religion. *Temenos,* 41, 153-184.

Knott, K., 2015. *The Location of Religion: A Spatial Analysis.* London: Taylor & Francis.

Kolbas, J., 2005. Khukh Ordung, A Uighur Palace Complex of the Seventh Century. *Journal of the Royal Asiatic Society,* 15 (3), 303-327.

Konagaya, Y., Bayaraa, S., Lkhagvasuren, I., 2008. *A. D. Simukov. Works about Mongolia and for Mongolia, Vol. 3 (part 1)*. Osaka: National Museum of Ethnology.

Kovalev, R.K., 2016. *Uyghur Khaganate* [online]. Wiley Online Library. Available at: https://doi.org/10.1002/9781118455074.wbeoe093.

Latour, B., 2005. *Reassembling the Social: An Introduction to Actor-network-theory*. Oxford, New York: Oxford University Press.

Leeds, A., 1979. Forms of Urban Integration: "Social Urbanisation" in Comparative Perspective. *Urban Anthropology,* 8 (3/4), 227-247.

Leeds, A., 1980. Towns and Villages in Society: Hierarchies of Order and Cause. *In:* T. Collins, ed. *Cities in a Larger Context.* Athens: University of Georgia Press.

Leeds, A., 2017. *Cities, Classes, and the Social Order.* Ithica, NY: Cornell University Press.

Lefebvre, H., 1992. La révolution urbaine. *Espace Temps,* 181-187.

Lehmkuhl, F., Hilgers, A., Fries, S., Hülle, D., Schlütz, F., Shumilovskikh, L., Felauer, T., Protze, J., 2011. Holocene geomorphological processes and soil development as indicator for environmental change around Karakorum, Upper Orkhon Valley (Central Mongolia). *CATENA,* 87 (1), 31-44.

Lessing, F.D., 2013. *Mongolian-English Dictionary.* Hoboken: Taylor & Francis.

Maidar, D., 1972. *Mongolin Arkhitektur Ba Khot Baiguulalt* [Mongolian Architecture and City Structure]. Ulaanbaatar: ShUA-ijn Khevlel.

Maiskii, I., 1921. *Sovremennaya Mongoliya* [Contemporary Mongolia]. Irkutsk.

Marcus, J., 1983. On the nature of the Mesoamerican city. *In:* E.Z. Vogt and R.M. Leventhal, eds. *Prehistoric Settlement Patterns: Essays in Honor of Gordon R. Willey.* Albuquerque: University of New Mexico Press, 195-242.

Marcus, J. and Sabloff, J., 2008. *The Ancient City: New Perspectives on Urbanism in the Old and New World.* Santa Fe: School for Advanced Research Press.

Massey, D.B., 1993. Power-Geometry and a Progressive Sense of Place. *In:* J. Bird, ed. *Mapping the Futures: Local Cultures, Global Change.* London, New York: Routledge, 59-69.

Massey, D.B., 2013. *Space, Place and Gender.* Hoboken: Wiley.

Minorsky, V., 1948. Tamīm ibn Bahr's Journey to the Uyghurs. *Bulletin School Oriental African Studies,* 12 (2), 275-305.

Moriyasu, T., 2015. New Developments in the History of East Uighur Manichaeism. *Open Theology,* 1 (1), 316-333.

Moses, L.W., 1977. *The Political Role of Mongol Buddhism.* Bloomington: Indiana University Press.

Nakoinz, O., 2019. *Zentralität. Theorie, Methoden und Fallbeispiele zur Analyse zentraler Orte.* Berlin: Edition Topoi.

Nakoinz, O., Bilder, M., Matzig, D., 2020. Urbanity as a process and the role of relative network properties – A case study from the Early Iron Age. *Frontiers in Digital Humanities* [online], 7. Available at: https://doi.org/10.3389/fdigh.2020.00002.

Ninjbadgar, Z., 2014. *Jibtsundamba khutagtin shaviin zakhirgaa* [Administration of the subordinates of the Jibtsundamba khutagt]. Ulaanbaatar: Arvin Sudar KhKhK.

Orsi, R.A., 1999. *Gods of the City: Religion and the American Urban Landscape.* Bloomington, Indiana: Indiana University Press.

Otto, R., 1917 [2014]. *Das Heilige: über das Irrationale in der Idee des Göttlichen und sein Verhältnis zum Rationalen.* Munich: C.H. Beck.

Perdue, P.C., 2015. 1557: A Year of Some Significance. *In:* E. Tagliacozzo, H.F. Siu, P.C. Perdue, eds. *Asia Inside Out: Changing Times.* Cambridge, Mass., London: Harvard University Press, 90-111.

Pohl, E., 2010. The excavations in the Chinese craftsmen-quarter of Karakorum

(KAR-2) between 2000 and 2005 – Stratigraphy and architecture. *In:* J. Bemman, U. Erdenebat, E. Pohl, eds. *Mongolian-German Karakorum Expedition 1: Excavations in the Craftsmen Quarter at the Main Road.* Wiesbaden: Reichert, 63-113.

Pozdneev, A.M., 1971 [1892]. *Mongolia and the Mongols: The Results of the Trip to Mongolia Executed in 1892-1893.* Bloomington: The Mongolian Society.

Pozdneev, A.M., 1978 [1887]. *Religion and Ritual in Society: Lamaist Buddhism in late 19th-century Mongolia.* Bloomington: The Mongolia Society.

Reichert, S., 2019. *A layered history of Karakorum: Stratigraphy and periodization in the City Center.* Bonn: Inst. für Vor- und frühgeschichtliche Archäologie.

Riemer, M., Abb. 2. *In:* German Archaeological Institute, ed. *Karabalgasun* [online]. Copyright: License: CC-BY-NC-DD. Available at: https://www.dainst.org/projekt/-/project-display/60891.

Rogers, D.J., Erdenebat, U., Gallon, M., 2005. Urban Centres and the Emergence of Empires in Eastern Inner Asia. *Antiquity, 79,* 801-818.

Rohland, H., 2019. *Die Nordstadt von Karakorum. Archäologische Spuren der Kirche des Ostens und interkulturelle Kommunikation in der altmongolischen Hauptstadt.* (Dissertation: Kiel University).

Rossabi, M., 2012. *The Mongols: A Very Short Introduction.* Oxford: Oxford University Press.

Rüpke, J., 2020. *Urban Religion: A Historical Approach to Urban Growth and Religious Change.* Berlin, Boston: De Gruyter.

Ruysbroeck, W. van, Jackson, P., Morgan, D., 1990. *The mission of Friar William of Rubruck: his journey to the court of the Great Khan Mongke, 1253-1255.* London: Hakluyt Society.

Sagaster, K., 2005. Das Kloster Erdeni Joo (Erdene zuu). *In:* J. Frings and C. Müller, eds. *Dschingis Khan und seine Erben.* München: Hirmer, 348-351.

Sanjdorj, M., 1980. *Manchu Chinese Colonial Rule in Northern Mongolia.* London: C. Hurst and Company.

Sassen, S., 2010. *Globalization and its Discontents: Essays on the New Mobility of People and Money.* New York: New Press.

Shiraishi, N., 2004. Seasonal migrations of the Mongol emperors and the peri-urban area of Kharakhorum. *International Journal of Asian Studies, 1* (1), 105-119.

Shiraishi, N., 2013. Avraga Site: The 'Great Ordu' of Genghis Khan. *In:* L. Komaroff, ed. *Beyond the Legacy of Genghis Khan.* Leiden: Brill, 83-93.

Shiraishi, N. and Tsogtbaatar, B., 2007. A Preliminary Report on the Japanese-Mongolian Joint Archaeological Excavation at Avraga Site: The Great Ordu of Chinggis Khan. *In:* J. Bemmann, ed. *Current Archaeological Research in Mongolia. Papers from the first International Conference on "Archaeological Research in Mongolia" held in Ulaanbaatar, August 19th-23rd 2007.* Bonn: Vor- und Frühgeschichtliche Archäologie, Rheinische Friedrich-Wilhelms-Universität Bonn, 549-562.

Sklebitz, A., 2018. *Glazed Ceramics from Karakorum. The Distribution and Use of Chinese Ceramics in the Craftsmen Quarter of the Old-Mongolian Capital During the 13th-14th Century A. D.* (Dissertation: Rheinische Friedrich-Wilhelms-Universität Bonn).

Smith, J.Z., 1978. *Map is not territory: studies in the history of religions.* Chicago, London: University of Chicago Press.

Smith, J.Z., 1987. *To take place: toward theory in ritual.* Chicago, London: University of Chicago Press.

Smith, M.E., 2016. How can Archaeologists Identify Early Cities? Definitions, Types, and Attributes. *In:* M. Fernández-Götz and D. Krausse, eds. *Eurasia at the Dawn of History: Urbanization and Social Change.* Cambridge: Cambridge University Press, 153-168.

Stark, S., 2008. *Die Alttürkenzeit in Mittel- und Zentralasien. Archäologische und historische Studien.* Wiesbaden: Dr. Ludwig Reichert Verlag.

Tilley, C.Y., 1994. *A phenomenology of landscape: places, paths, and monuments.* Oxford, Providence: Berg.

Tobler, J., 2000. 'Home is Where the Heart is?': Gendered Sacred Space in South Africa. *Journal for the Study of Religion,* 13, 69-98.

Trapp, R., 2015. *Religionspolitik in der Äußeren Mongolei (1920-1939): Die "Lama- und Klösterfrage".* (Dissertation: Humbolt-Universität zu Berlin).

Trigger, B.G., 1972. Determinants of urban growth in pre-industrial societies. *In:* P.J. Ucko, R. Tringham, G.W. Dimbleby, eds. *Man, Settlement, and Urbanism.* Cambridge: Schenkman, 575-599.

Tsai, W.-c., 2017a. *Mongolization of Han Chinese and Manchu Settlers in Qing Mongolia, 1700-1911.* (Dissertation: Indiana University).

Tsai, W.-c. 2017b. 居國中以避國——大沙畢與清代移民外蒙古之漢人及其後裔的蒙古化 （1768-1830) *[Evading the State within the State: The Great Shabi and Mongolization of Han Chinese Settlers and Their Descendants in Qing Outer Mongolia, 1768-1830].* *Journal of History and Anthropology,* 15 (2), 129-167.

Tsultem, N., 1982. *G. Zanabazar.* Ulaanbaatar: State Publishing House Ulan-Bator.

Uranchimeg, T., 2020. *A Monastery on the Move: Art and Politics in Later Buddhist Mongolia.* Honululu: University of Hawaʼi Press.

Vreeland, H.H., 1957. *Mongol Community and Kinship Structure.* New Haven: Human Relation Area Files.

Wallace, V.A., 2015. Buddhist Sacred Mountains, Auspicious Landscapes, and their Agency. *In:* V.A. Wallace, ed. *Buddhism in Mongolian History, Culture, and Society.* Oxford: Oxford University Press, 221-242.

Wang, D., Batu, J., Zhang, W., 1994. Baiyanyao shiku de yingjian niandai ji bihua zhuyao neirong chulun [First discussion on the content of wall paintings and the occupation period of the cave sites of Baiyanyao (Arjai)]. *In:* Y. Li, ed. *Nei Menggu wenwu kaogu wenji.* Beijing: Zhongguo da baike quanshu chubanshe, 566-578.

Wasilewski, J., 1976. Space in nomadic cultures: A spatial analysis of the Mongol yurts. *In:* W. Hessig, ed. *Altaica Collecta: Berichte und Vorträge der XVII. Permanent International Altaistic Conference 3-8. Juni 1974 in Bonn/Bad Honnef.* Wiesbaden: Harrassowitz, 345-360.

Waugh, D.C. 2010. Nomads and Settlement: New perspectives in the Archaeology of Mongolia. *Silk Road,* 8, 97-124.

Weatherford, J., 2005. *Genghis Khan and the Making of the Modern World.* Ulaanbaatar: Three Rivers Press.

Weeks, J., 2008. *Population: an introduction to concepts and issues, 10th ed.* Belmond, Ca: Wadsworth Thomson Learning.

Weeks, J., 2010. Defining Urban Areas. *In:* T. Rashed and C. Jürgens, eds. *Remote Sensing of Urban and Suburban Areas.* Dordrecht: Springer Netherlands, 33-45.

Weiler, A., 2002. Zum Naturverständnis nomadischer Viehzüchter in der Mongolei: alte Traditionen mit neuen Werten? *In:* U. Luig and H.-D. Schultz, eds. *Natur in der Moderne: Interdisziplinäre Ansichten.* Berlin: Berliner Geographische Arbeiten, Humboldt-Universität, 187-202.

Wirth, L., 1938. Urbanism as a way of life. *American Journal of Sociology,* 44, 1-24.

Yoshida, Y., 2020. Studies of the Karabalgasun Inscription: Edition of the Sogdian Version. 新たなアジア研究に向けて = *Modern Asian Studies Review,* 11, 1-140.

Water supply, settlement organisation and social connectivity

Annette Haug and Ulrich Müller

Abstract

In this contribution, common features and differences in the provision of water and its disposal during two different epochs – antiquity and the Middle Ages – are thematised. Thereby, reflections are made about the relationship between the city and its natural conditions, on the one hand, and the social circumstances as well as cultural needs on the other. It becomes apparent that "water art" (*Wasserkunst*) of antique and medieval cities may be understood as a manifestation of the negotiation of individual and collective needs. The connectivity between the city and the environment as well as the social connectivity within a city is reflected in the relationship of the individual households to the city as a whole.

Introduction

Permanent access to clean, drinkable water is one of the most important prerequisites for the establishment of a successful and lasting settlement. Water can therefore be seen as the basic and constitutive urban resource. It can be easily accessible in the form of open waters, such as rivers, lakes and spring water, or in the form of precipitation (rain and snow). In these cases, the collection of water is relatively easy. If water is not available in sufficient quality and quantity, artificial

Annette Haug
Institute of Classical Studies
/ Classical Archaeology
Kiel University
Johanna-Mestorf-Str. 5
24118 Kiel, Germany
ahaug@klassarch.uni-kiel.de

Ulrich Müller
Institute of Prehistoric and
Protohistoric Archaeology
Kiel University
Johanna-Mestorf-Str. 2-6
24118 Kiel, Germany
umueller@ufg.uni-kiel.de

constructions (wells, water pipes, aqueducts) are needed. The effort that is or has to be made to obtain fresh water thus depends on the prevailing environmental conditions, on the one hand, and on socio-cultural factors on the other. The social demand for fresh water can vary significantly depending on social needs: Beyond the basic need of drinking water, cities may additionally need clean water for bodily hygiene purposes (depending on culturally specific concepts of hygiene), economic uses and aesthetic display.

The following article focuses on forms of water provision and collection such as cisterns, wells/fountains, water pipes, and aqueducts. The starting point of our considerations is that the management of a resource, which has vital relevance for the inhabitants, is particularly meaningful for social connectivity within a city. In particular, the degree and forms of social organisation of a community become directly tangible with respect to water supply. We will show that water is a central factor of any urbanisation process. In the first years after the emergence of a settlement or sometimes even after decades or centuries, water supply was often organised by individual property units. With a progressive process of collectivisation and social organisation, water management frequently becomes a field of public action. This processuality will be demonstrated in the following by comparing cities in two different periods: Antiquity[1] and the Middle Ages.

Antiquity: Rome

Rome is located at a bend of the Tiber River, about 25 km from the sea. The early settlers of the 8th century BCE chose the hills surrounding a marshy hollow – the later forum area – to build their huts. In early times, the Tiber was used as a source of freshwater (Frontin. aqu. strat. 4,1). Beyond this, a spring in the forum area (the Lacus Juturnae, see Longfellow 2011, 13) and wells (Taylor 2000, 39-40) were used for freshwater. In this period, it was more the abundance of water than its lack, which was problematic. Consequently, the building of an open drainage channel, the so-called *Cloaca maxima*, around 600 BCE constituted one important step towards urbanity (Bianchi 2015). It is attributed to the fifth king of Rome, Tarquinius Priscus (Liv. 1, 38, 6; 56, 2; Dion. 3, 76, 5; 4, 44, 1; Strabo 5, 3, 8; Plin. HN 36, 104). The measure thus falls into a time when Rome was ruled by kings – perhaps comparable to the clan-based rule of the Athenian tyrants. These rulers obviously had the means of power to implement a large-scale infrastructural measure that benefited the community as a whole. The *Cloaca maxima*, however, had another consequence: it discharged waste water and with it the dirt of the urban area into the Tiber, which in the following centuries was no longer considered a source of drinking water (Thüry 2001, 46-48).

Soon, public springs and wells were no longer sufficient to meet the demand for fresh water. The provision of a collective water supply was now the responsibility of municipal officials. From the 4th century BCE onwards, they responded to the increased demand for water by building aqueducts that brought water from the mountains in the hinterland to the capital (Fig. 1). These pipelines required highly specialised hydraulic and technological knowledge, such as the use of arcades, concrete and waterproof cement, since the water flow had to be guar-

---

1   With regard to antiquity, the literature is endless. Here, reference is only made to very few, but significant contributions, a comprehensive research history is beyond the scope of this article. For this, see Rogers 2018.

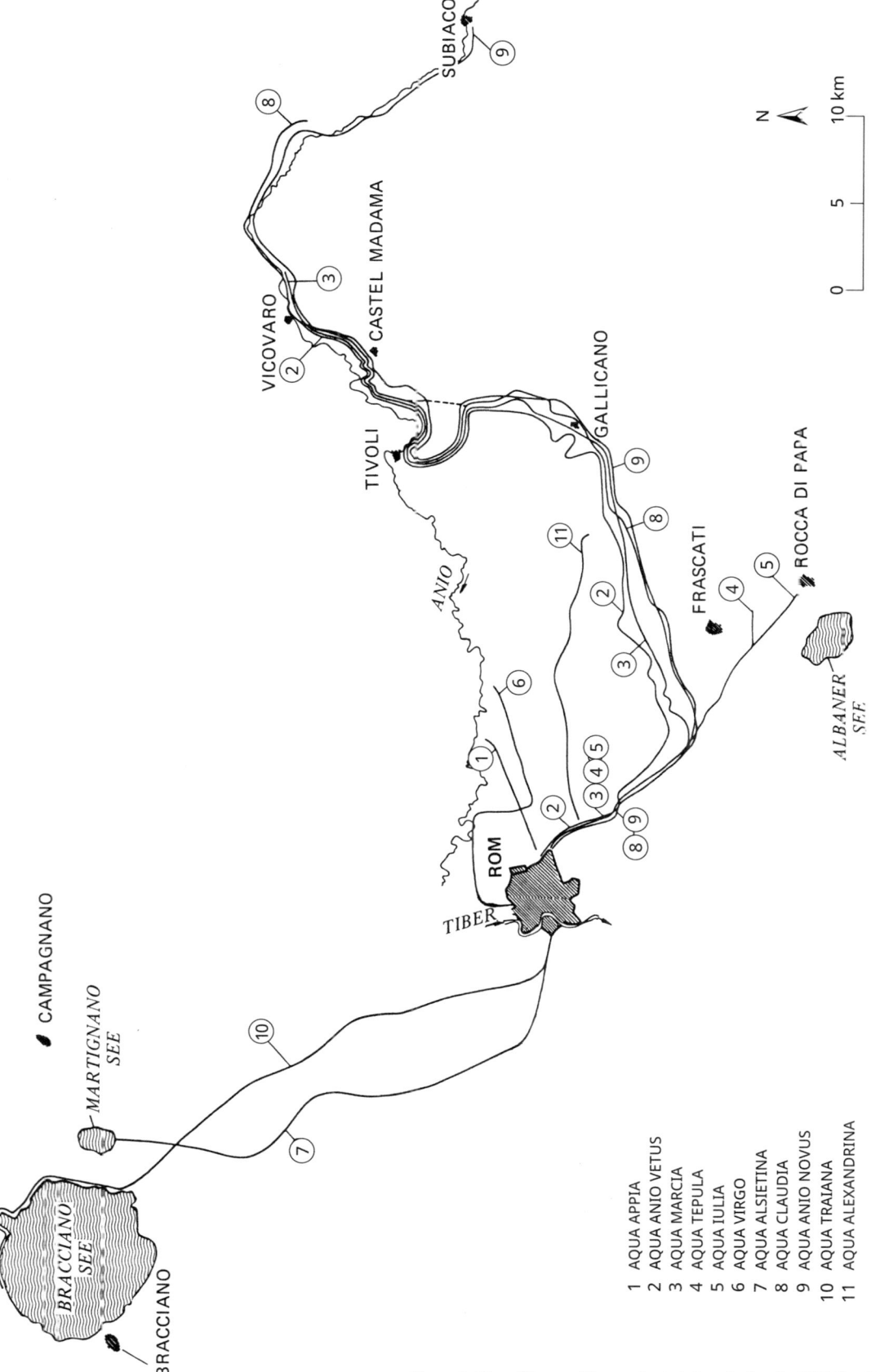

Figure 1. Map of Rome with aqueducts (after: Garbrecht 1984, fig. 4).

anteed by an appropriate gradient and by pressure pipes (Hodge 1992, 93-105, 126-170; Taylor 2000, 23-39).

The first aqueduct was the Aqua Appia, built in 312 BCE by the censor Appius Claudius Caecus, which carried water from the Anio Valley to Rome. This was followed by the Aqua Anio Vetus, inaugurated in 269 BCE. In 140 BCE, the Aqua Marcia was built by the praetor Q. Marcius Rex (144-140 BCE), followed by the Aqua Tepula in 126/25 BCE. The water was made accessible to the population through public pools. Private water connections, however, were a privilege of the upper class. With the transition to the Imperial era, the imperial court took over the water supply of the capital. Under Augustus, Agrippa undertook the construction of the Aqua Iulia (40-33 BCE) and the realisation of the Aqua Virgo (21-19 BCE) (Evans 1994, 65-128; Aicher 1995, 31-45; Taylor 2000; De Kleijn 2001, 9-29; Bianco 2007, 19-67). According to Pliny (HN 36, 121), in the course of the reorganisation of the water supply he installed 700 water basins, 500 fountains and 130 water containers (Longfellow 2011, 19-25). The high cultural value of this measure is manifested in the fact that he equipped these water installations with 300 bronze or marble statues and 400 marble columns. Such public fountains ostentatiously wasted water (Rogers 2018, 48), but precisely because of this, water obtained a decorative function. In the following centuries, the visual and aesthetic staging of water took on ever new forms (Longfellow 2011). In the Imperial era, freshwater was not only used as drinking water but also for the provision of clean water to large public thermal baths. As an example, the Augustan Aqua Virgo was (amongst other purposes) erected to supply the Thermae Agrippae and the Stagnum in the Campus Martius (Coleman 1993, 50-51; Evans 1994, 108-109). The abundant availability of water, its public staging and use were at the heart of the Roman urban lifestyle. The provision of water thus became a central means of Imperial 'propaganda' (Haug 2016).

At the time of the Twelve Tables in the fifth century BCE, water legislation was already in existence – but was further developed over the following centuries (Bannon 2009, 14-23). This implied a distinction between public and private waters sources – public sources included oceans, rivers, seas, and aqueducts, whereas private ones were comprised of wells, springs, and streams (Bannon 2009, 13; Bruun 2015, 133-135; Rogers 2018, 10). In this logic, private water was the water available on one's own land. Legislation regulated the access to the private water supply of a person other than oneself, for which a contract was needed – the *servitus aquae ductus* (the ability to channel water) and the *servitus aquae haustus* (the ability to draw water) (Bannon 2009, 13; Bruun 2015, 145-149; Rogers 2018, 17). Equally, private access to public sources was legally regulated (Bruun 2015, 136-149). In the time of Augustus, the increasing importance of the provision of an adequate water supply for the imperial regime led to growing imperial control (Ellis 1997) and to the introduction of new offices: the *curator aquarum* and the *curatores riparum et alvei Tiberis* (curators of the banks and the channel of the Tiber) (Rogers 2018, 11-12).

Apparently, the increasing demand for water, the establishment of an enormous water supply network and the increasingly complex legal and administrative organisation went hand in hand. The availability of fresh water thus became a hallmark of Roman civilisation and *urbanitas* (Longfellow 2011; Dessales 2008, 30), its visual staging an expression of a cultural habitus. This is clearly expressed by Pliny (HN 36, 123):

'If we take into careful consideration the abundant supplies of water in public buildings, baths, pools, open channels, private houses, gardens and country estates near the city; if we consider the distances traversed by the water before it arrives, the raising of arches, the tunnelling of mountains and the building of level routes across deep valleys, we shall readily admit that there has never been anything more remarkable in the whole world'.

However, as the capital of an empire, Rome is a special case. In the following, we will thus focus on a small Italian country town, Pompeii.

Antiquity: Pompeii

Before the siltation of the coastal area, Pompeii was located directly on a plateau sloping in the direction of the sea and the Sarno River. This location allowed for a disposal of rain water and waste water along the streets. The low water table allowed for the installation of cesspits in private houses. Nevertheless, the city possessed at least a rudimentary sewage system (Jansen 2000a, 38-42; Poehler in press). However, the low water table also had a problematic consequence: It made the digging of wells difficult (Dessales 2013, 181).

Nonetheless, we know of at least some public deep wells – one near Porta Vesuvio (VI 16, 21-24), one on the street leading to Porta Ercolano (VI 1, here: Fig. 2), one to the north of the forum (VII 4,7), two along the Vicolo dei Soprastanti, one within the sacred precinct of the Foro Triangolare, all dating to the 4th and 3rd centuries BCE, as well as wells providing water to the Forum Baths and the Stabian Baths (Maiuri 1931, 551-555; Dessales 2008, 29; Schmölder-Veit 2009, 118-119 with a complete list and map of deep wells). This hints to the fact that such deep wells were installed in strategically important nodes within the urban texture (Fig. 3). One would thus assume a certain level of city planning (and collective control). Parallelly, some single private houses also possessed deep wells (Maiuri 1931, 553-554; Schmölder-Veit 2009, 118-119 with a list and a map; Dessales 2013, 180-181).

In the course of increasing urbanisation in the later 3rd and then especially in the 2nd century BCE, numerous (larger) dwellings were built as atrium houses (Wallace-Hadrill 1994, 72-82). They had a courtyard with a tapped roof, which led water into an impluvium in the centre. From there, it was fed into a cistern (or several cisterns) located underneath the courtyard (Dessales 2008, 29; 2013, 55-58; Schmölder-Veit 2009, 51-52, 132-133). The individual residential units were thus largely self-sufficient in their water supply.

The situation changes significantly in Augustan times when the Serino aqueduct (*Aqua Augusta*) was built.[2] At the entrance to the city, located at the highest point (near the Porta Vesuvio), it was led into a *castellum aquae* (for its Augustan date, see Adam and Varène 2008, 48-49) and from there distributed water throughout the city via lead pipes. For this purpose, water towers were erected at various junctions of the city (Fig. 4) in order to keep the water pressure high. From here, the water was then distributed to the newly constructed fountains in the street space, to the thermal baths, which were provided with their own water supply, and to individual private houses with water con-

---

2   Even if Pompeii possessed an earlier Republican aqueduct leading from Avella to Pompeii (Ohlig 2001, 58-75; critically Schmölder-Veit 2009, 125-126; see also Keenan-Jones 2016, 783), it did not have an important effect on the water supply of public and private buildings (Haug 2020, 408 with references).

Figure 2. Pompeii. A deep well at a street junction (photo: A. Haug).

nections.[3] To what extent the *officinae* (workshops) and *tabernae* (stores), which dominated the visual appearance of the main streets from the 2nd century BCE onwards (Ellis 2018), also benefited from an individual supply has not yet been systematically investigated.[4] However, it has been observed that especially water-intensive industries, such as tanneries and laundries, were located along major road axes even though they were not very dependent on walk-in clientele (Flohr 2013, 231-232). Their location can at least partially be explained by their proximity next to a public water supply. As an example, *fullonica* V 1,2 and the dyeing workshops V 1,4 and V 1,5 in the immediate neighbourhood seem to have shared a public fountain (Flohr 2013, 81-82 fig. 12).

---

3   On several aspects of water distribution, see De Haan and Jansen 1996; Jansen 2000b, 112-113; Dessales 2008, 32; Schmölder-Veit 2009, 120-137; Dessales 2013, 216-221; Trümper 2018, 99.

4   For preliminary remarks on the industrial use of water, see Wilson 2000; for a discussion of Pompeian bakeries and the provision of water for them, see Monteix 2009, *e.g.,* bakery VII 12, 13.

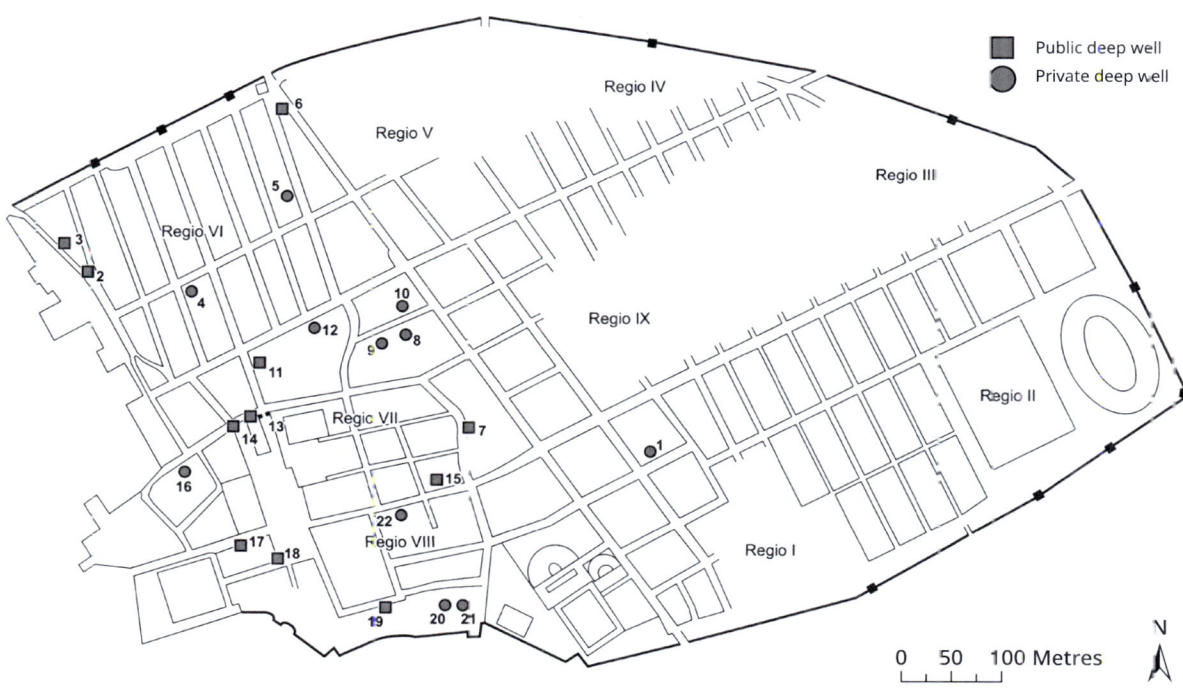

Figure 3. Pompeii. Mapping of public and private deep wells (after: A. Schmölder-Veit 2009, 117 fig. 12).

Figure 4. Pompeii. Water tower at the crossing of Via dell'Abbondanza and Via Stabiana (photo: A. Haug).

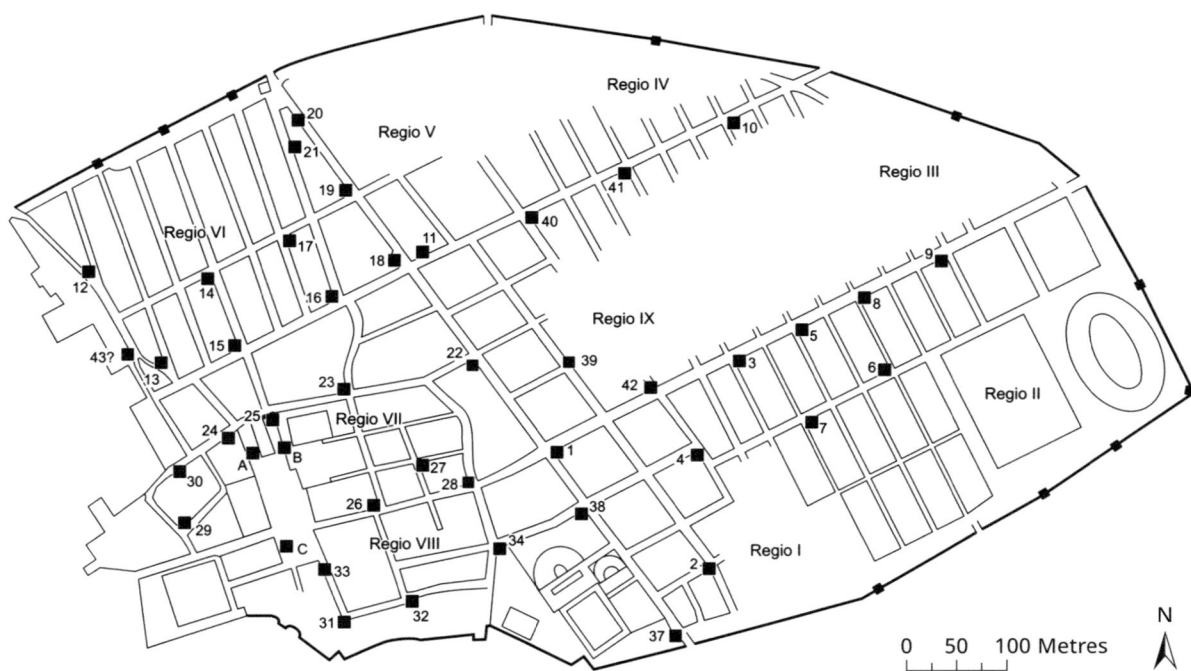

Figure 5. Pompeii. Mapping of fountains (cf. Lotta Böttcher; after: A. Schmölder-Veit 2009).

While the overland aqueduct was initiated by the emperor (De Feo and Napoli 2007), the inner-city water system of Pompeii was probably in communal hands. This is expressed not only in the location of the water towers but also in the regular placement of the new flow fountains in the urban space (Fig. 5). Especially along the main roads, there were now fountains at regular intervals, each covering a radius of about 80 m (Laurence 1994). Against this background, it is particularly noticeable that the fountains differ greatly in terms of material, technology and decoration. In our opinion, Jeremy Hartnett explained this correctly by the fact that the respective street residents were responsible for their realisation (Hartnett 2008, 84). From then on, these wells were available to supply water to the majority of the urban population. Only about 30 percent of the houses had a private water connection (Jones and Robinson 2005, 697-699). In most cases, the older cisterns still remained in operation – also in houses with a connection to the pipe system. The water pipes were alternatively used to improve the living quality. Private baths received their own water inflow (Dessales 2008, 34), and equally important: For the first time, the new pressure pipes allowed a completely new aesthetic staging of water. In the course of the 1st century CE, increasingly more house owners used public water to install magnificent fountains and nymphaea in the centre of their courtyards (Fig. 6). Water display became an important element of elegant townhouses (Dessales 2013, 275-285). This went hand in hand with a new culture of gardening – and staging of 'nature' within townhouses (Rogers 2013; Haug 2020, 407-408). This enormous demand for water even made it necessary to limit the use of the pipeline system in terms of time (Dessales 2013, 247-248). However, the flowing water was only very rarely used for household activities, as there were usually no water connections in kitchens. Consequently, the cisterns continued to provide drinking water for the houses (Andersson 1994, 31; Dessales 2008, 33-34; Schmölder-Veit 2009, 135; Dessales 2013, 289-316).

To sum up, the city of Pompeii adds further significant information to an understanding of the history of water provision in Roman times. While Rome

already had aqueducts in the 4th century BCE, the small country town only first received a water pipe in Augustan times. The example of Pompeii, however, is a good illustration of the direct effects that the construction of a pipeline had, not only on public thermal baths but also on housing culture: Water became an aesthetic element.

Figure 6. Pompeii. Casa del Toro (V 1,7) with an atrium fountain in the foreground and a peristyle nymphaeum in the background (photo: A. Haug)

Middle Ages: Lübeck

The city of Lübeck, founded in 1142/3 CE, lies between the Trave River in the west and the Wakenitz in the east on a north-south oriented moraine knoll. This rises sharply in the east and west and reaches a height of up to 13 m at the apex. In order to be supplied with enough drinking and industrial water, it appeared only at first glance that there was the possibility to obtain water from the rivers. However, water from the Trave River was hardly suitable due to its salinity, and to extract water from both rivers, height differences of up to 5 m had to be overcome. This presupposes, comparable to ancient measures, appropriate techniques for extraction or storage as well as the distribution of the water. To extract water from the groundwater area, the groundwater level in the lower sand layer had to be reached or rainwater had to be drained off and stored without contamination, if possible. These private and public wells were an important source of drinking water well into the premodern era.

Until the late 12th century CE, the inhabitants seem to have met their needs for drinking water with river water from the Wakenitz, rainfall and occasional

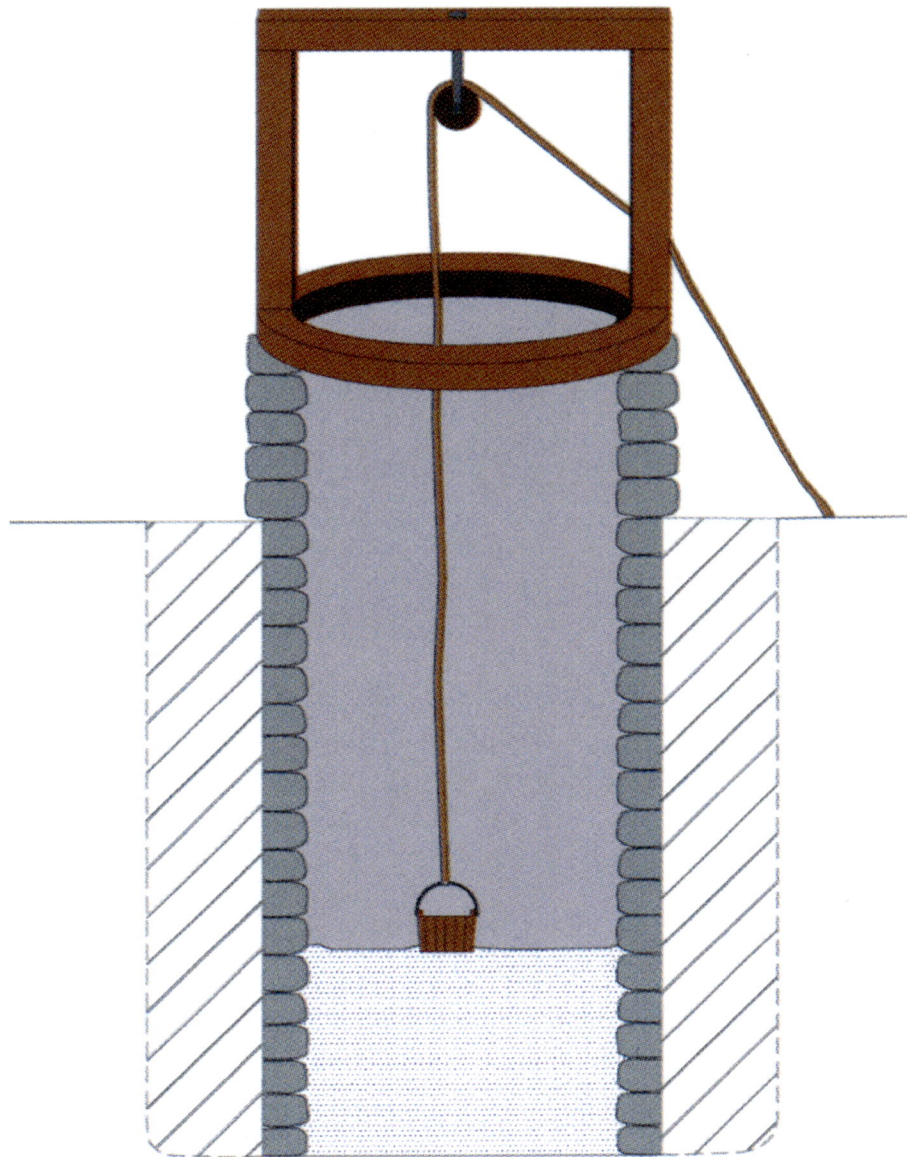

Figure 7. Lübeck. Reconstruction of a well with a jack (after: J. Harder 2019, 372 fig. 29).

springs within the city limits. It is unclear to what extent these were accessible to all or water withdrawal was regulated. We also do not know whether each household took care of its own water needs or if communal efforts were undertaken in order to secure the water supply. Water that was brought in was probably transported on foot or with wagons and it is also conceivable that rainfall was collected from roofs and courtyards.

While the wooden well (dated to 1156/57 CE) from the sovereign castle, which almost reached 11 m into the ground, is singular and can be attributed to the manorial sphere (Gläser 2004, 183), wells of various construction are only first verifiable in large numbers in Lübeck from the last quarter of the 12th century CE (Fig. 7).

In terms of construction, wooden wells, stone wells, and cisterns can be distinguished (Harder 2019, 617-619). Such systems are detectable on the properties in the so-called *Gründungsviertel* and the *Kaufleuteviertel* (Harder 2019; Legant 2010). It can be assumed that the houses and the wells were aspects of uniform, spatial planning activities. They indicate property-related, private water pumping, which

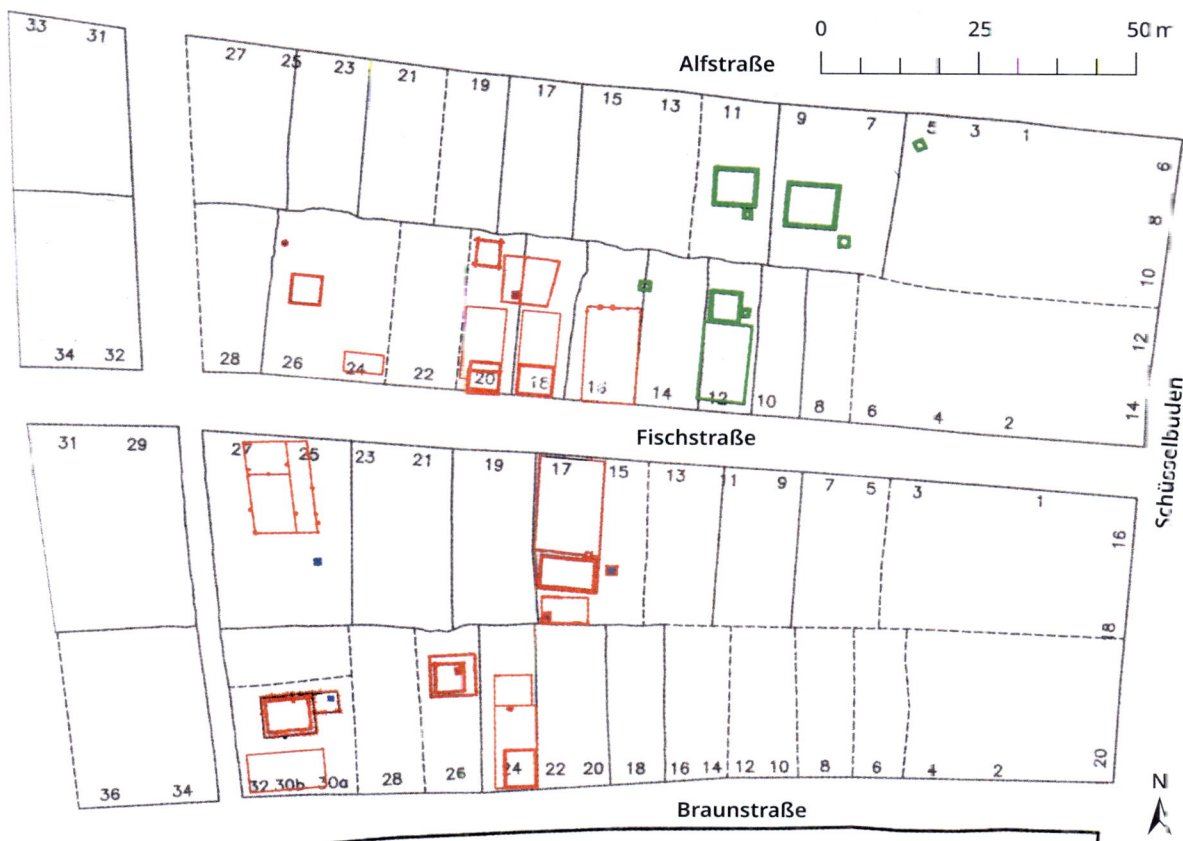

Figure 8. Lübeck. Wooden buildings and wooden wells in period IV (ca. 1176-1215). Red: wooden buildings; blue: water supply features; green: wells and house structures from excavation HL 70 (after: J. Harder 2019, 375 fig. 33).

is also verifiable elsewhere (Sydow 1981; Röber 2016). The wooden wells were sunk to the ground water level exactly where they were needed; their installation usually occurred before the construction of a main building (Fig. 8).

The few wooden wells that were in use from 1168 into the first quarter of the 13th century CE functionally served the economic needs of the nearby wooden buildings and not primarily the independent provision of drinking water. Communal use by several neighbours is improbable. However, simultaneously organised measures by several owners for the provision of drinking water prior to property division can be assumed, since there are clearly verifiable utilisation units associated with the wooden houses and box wells (Legant 2010, 163; Gläser 2004, 184).

First with the beginning of brick construction at the outset of the 13th century CE, a general change occurred. Stone wells were designed as permanent facilities. Furthermore, a new sinking technique with small-area construction pits enabled a more flexible choice of location on the now narrow rectangular plots. The wooden wells were given up within a few years. In this context, the functional connection with the wooden buildings was terminated. The few newly constructed stone wells were obviously only used in the courtyards and no longer had functional relevance for the stone front buildings.

Two further aspects are associated with well construction in the private sphere: the question concerning space requirements and the dug-out material as well as the relationship between wells and cesspits. The proximity of wells and cesspits in the narrow courtyards and the associated deterioration of the water quality up to the abandonment of the wells has been repeatedly reported (Schütte

1986). This has been ascribed to the unawareness of medieval people regarding bacteriological relationships (Sturm 2014). In the meanwhile, however, it has been shown that well and cesspit shafts – such as those in Lübeck – were deliberately designed and isolated to different depths (Arndt 2020). Thus, a direct connection cannot be generally assumed. Additionally, the spatial and temporal (bacterial) contamination of the ground, for example, depends on the flow direction of the groundwater and the possibility of the pollutants to migrate in the soil. For the plots in the *Gründungsviertel* in Lübeck, it can be verified that cesspits were located in the rearmost courtyard areas of the properties, while the wells were sunk more centrally on the plots (Harder 2019, 633-635). This solution followed the potential flow direction of the groundwater from east to west, so that there was no overlap in the extraction of water and the seepage of the liquid components of the faeces into the lower sand layer. From this, it can be assumed that individual property owners could access common know-how in the construction of their wells and cesspits.

For the construction of wooden wells, areas between 70 and 120 m² were necessary, depending on the construction method and the depth of a well (Harder 2019, 641-645). The area for a construction pit first had to be available on the property. Moreover, the question arises whether the dug-out material could be temporarily stored on the property or elsewhere. This presupposes concepts for the division of the area of the individual properties as well as logistics for the entire construction process and thus corresponding social and political-administrative structures, about which little is known for the 12th and 13th centuries CE.

The small number of wells that are mentioned in writing and have been archaeologically verified for private areas is surprising in light of the expanding city with its steadily growing consumers and households. Thus, it is assumed that rainwater was still stored or that water was supplied by carters. Commonly used wells in public spaces are also conceivable, which have not yet been archaeologically proven (Grabowski 2009). Commonly used facilities, which were reserved for certain groups, have been substantiated (Gläser 2004, 187) with the large cisterns of the Heiligen-Geist-Hospital and the Fronerei on the Schrangen.

The reason for a stronger communal organisation of water provision is based on a new economic need: The outset of a water pipe system is a result of (beer) brewers, who could no longer meet their water needs since the end of the 13th century CE through groundwater from the wells (Frontzek 2005). Furthermore, well water was unsuitable as brewing water due to the large amounts of gypsum and lime carbonate in it.

An early attempt at building a pipeline was made by the monks of the Benedictine monastery of St. Johannis, who built an underground canal at ca. 1214. By means of a bucket wheel, this led water from the Wakenitz into the monastery grounds and back again (Gläser 2004, 187). But a change was first introduced at the end of the 13th century CE by hydraulic engineering measures, such as the damming of the Wakenitz (up to one metre), documented in 1291 (Schalies 2009). In 1294, the 'art of brewing water' is referred to when "*van deme watere dat mit raden in de stat gehelet is*" is mentioned (Grabowski 2009, 65). As the first 'German' city, Lübeck had a system with artificial water lifting. Water was pumped by means of a scoop wheel with numerous scoops into an elevated tank (Fig. 9) and pressed from there into an underground pipe network in the southeastern part of the city.

The significance of the water supply for the brewers and further inhabitants can be realised in the rapid expansion of the pipeline system. A network of ca. 3000 m length was created, which supplied ca. 1800 households (Gläser 2004, 190). Until 1302, six further waterworks were built, the network of which extended to ca. 10 km in length (Fig. 10).

All of these waterworks were, however, gravity flow lines, which merely used the difference in height between the contact point in the dammed Wakenitz and the tapping points in the city as working power. The houses at the highest points of the city around the town hall and St. Mary's Church were still excluded from the meanwhile widely spread out water system with fresh artificial water from the Wakenitz. These inhabitants, in particular the influential citizens and merchants, were first supplied with water by the *Bürger- oder Kaufleute-Wasserkunst*. The 17.5 m high water tower, completed in 1533, secured the water supply via the so-called *Haussode*. The supply network, which has been verified both archaeologically and in written records, ran underground in the middle of the streets and consisted of several individual lines, which were neither technically connected with each other nor had an organisational operator. Each one was repaired, renewed and expanded individually.

The example of Lübeck shows that the provision of water for the early settlement lay first primarily in the hands of the property owners. The extent to which self-supply was supplemented by public-collective wells cannot be determined with certainty. A significant change resulted from the new 'industrial' water demand in the 13th century CE, which made extensive measures necessary that exceeded the possibilities of individuals: the damming of the river and the design and construction of a water system. It is not a coincidence that this development is termed here – as in the ancient context – as 'water art' (*Wasserkunst*).

Figure 9. Lübeck. Reconstruction of the waterworks ca. 1291/94 CE (after: M. Gläser 2004, 184 fig. 10).

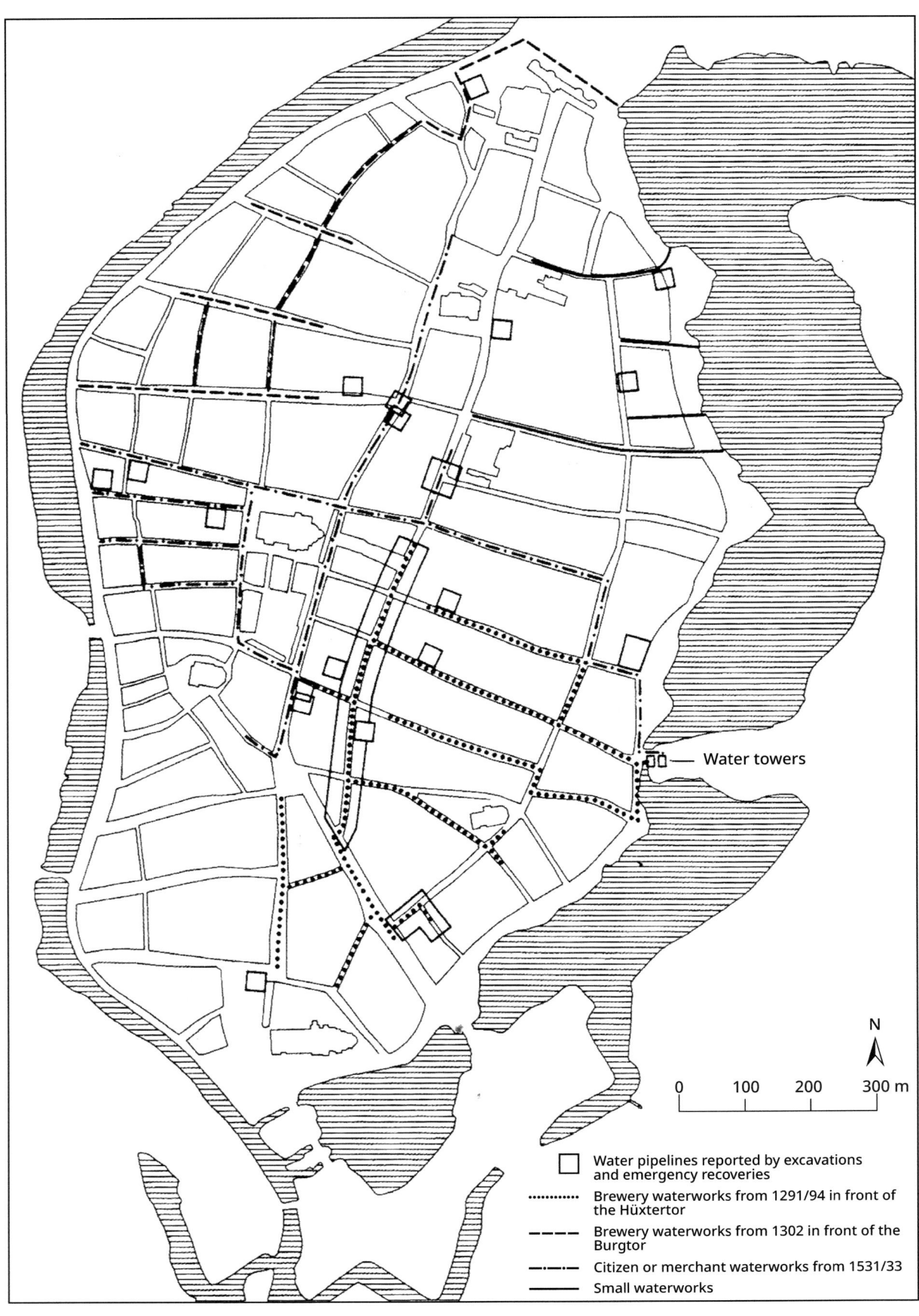

Water towers

0   100   200   300 m

N

☐ Water pipelines reported by excavations
   and emergency recoveries

········· Brewery waterworks from 1291/94 in front of
   the Hüxtertor

‐ ‐ ‐ Brewery waterworks from 1302 in front of the
   Burgtor

‐·‐·‐ Citizen or merchant waterworks from 1531/33

——— Small waterworks

While with Lübeck we became acquainted with a particularly prominent Hanseatic city, in the following, the developments observed here will be compared with a smaller Hanseatic city in order to check whether similar tendencies can be detected.

Middle Ages: Greifswald

The city of Greifswald lies on the Ryck River, which is connected to the Baltic Sea across the Greifswald Bodden. The city received its town charter (*Lübcker Stadtrecht*) in 1250/64 CE. Generally, the water supply was provided by the Ryck River and stratified water wells, which due to the low elevation of the old town (max. 5 m) quickly penetrated into groundwater-bearing levels (Schäfer 2004, 267-268). The wells were usually located, as in Lübeck, on the rear property areas and appear to have been mainly built between 1250 and 1280 CE. This falls in the early city phase. At the end of the 13th century CE, the archaeologically verifiable "private" wells decrease, which correlates with a now available public water supply. Flowing wells, which were fed from water of the Ryck or the city moat and functioned according to the principle of gradient pressure, which have been archaeologically recorded at various points, replaced the stratified water wells. The construction of this pipeline system was not only in public hands but was also financed by private sources. In 1302, Hermann Moysalle committed himself to create an "*aqueductum pro utilitate civitatis in longitudine dicte hereditatis usque ad suos terminus*" (Igel 2010, 134). Archaeological investigations, information in city registers for the 14th and 15th centuries CE as well as a plan from 1704 yield information about the position of the wells in the public sphere and the possible course of water pipes (Fig. 11).

Further sources, such as the Treasury Book (*Kämmereibuch*), recorded payments that the city made for the maintenance of the wells and that were disbursed to persons, who rented municipal buildings in the vicinity of the involved wells. This indicates that the neighbours were obliged to maintain the wells (Igel 2010, 135).

A commercial district at the western edge of the city, which was merged with the town in 1264, provides us with a view of the spatial behaviour of the various actors (Enzenberger 2007; Müller 2018). From the 1260s, red and white tanneries were located in this quarter. This trade with intensive water consumption fed its need for water from the so-called city moats and the Ryck. The 5 m wide canal with wooden stiffeners on the sides served to provide the technical systems with water, but it was also used as a channel for smaller boats as well as waste disposal. Between the leather-producing and processing workshops in the south and north, there was a bathhouse, which was built in 1270 and disposed of its waste water via a channel into the canal. Due to the frequent change of owners, Doris Bulach (2013, 228) suspects that the building was an investment. While the tanners initially met their water needs from the city channel and stratified water wells, fundamental changes occurred "around 1300". These were initiated by the acquisition of the city moat by the Greifswald council, which then pursued a larger urban planning concept – the fusion of the old and the new towns as well as the provision of building land. This appears to have gone hand in hand with the "commercialisation" of water provision and disposal. The underground water pipeline (dated to 1302) in the former ditch displayed connections to the individual parcels with their technical facilities (Fig. 12). Water disposal was ensured by pits and gutters.

Figure 10 (opposite page). Waterworks and infrastructures 13th-15th century CE (after: M. Gläser 2004, 185 fig. 11).

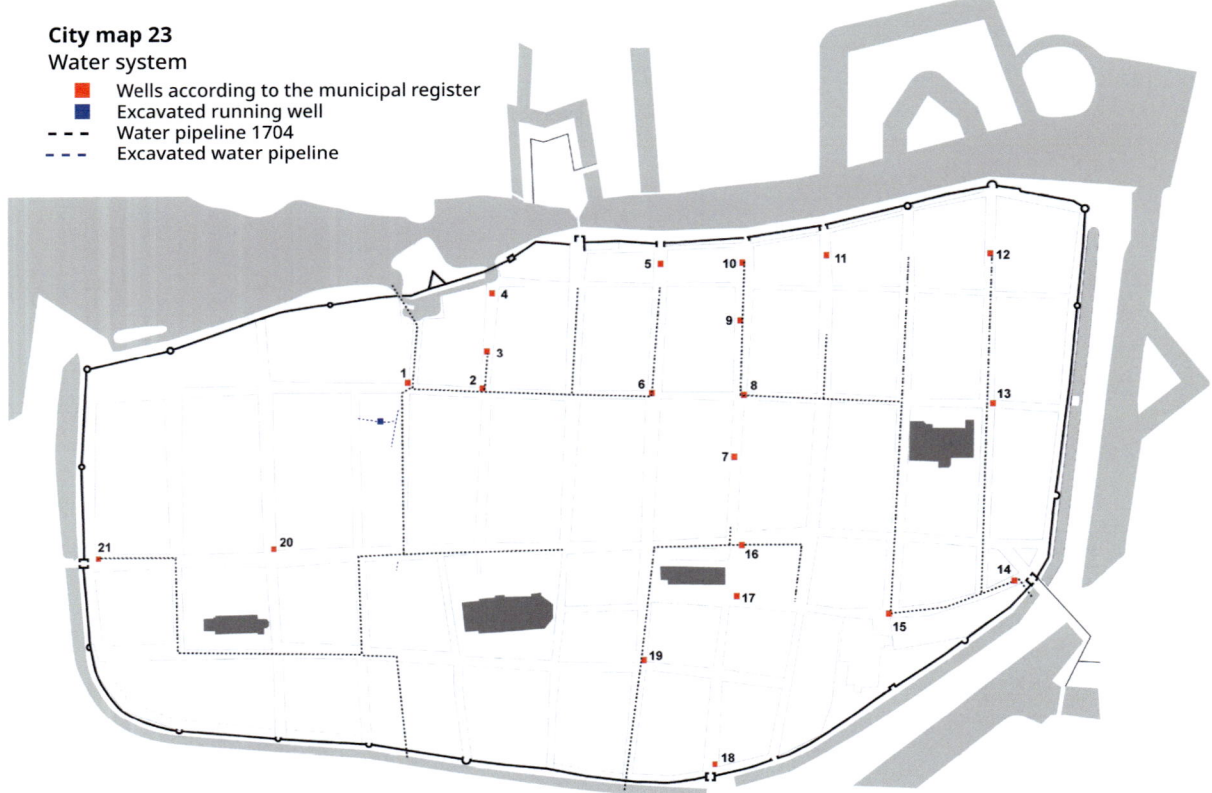

City map 23
Water system

■ Wells according to the municipal register
■ Excavated running well
- - - Water pipeline 1704
- - - Excavated water pipeline

Figure 11. Greifswald. Wells and water pipes based on written and archaeological sources (after: K. Igel 2010, 136 fig. 19; 138 plan 20).

Despite some restructuring, the tannery district persisted until ca. 1400. The redesign of the "commercial stream" did not represent an infringement for the tanners and the crafts associated with them. Rather, a stabilisation can be observed. The presence of tanners first dissipated at the end of the Middle Ages and the beginning of the modern era. These structural changes were possibly initiated by the city fire in 1461. Not only did numerous buildings in the "tanners' quarters" fall victim to the fire. Instead of a restructuring, an immediate relocation on the Ryck was preferred. Both archaeological evidence and written sources are relatively scarce from the end of the 15th century to the 17th century CE, so that only little information is available on the redesign of the urban space. A map of the water pipes and wells from 1704 shows us that access to fresh water via house connections was a luxury until the end of the pre-modern era. Thus, Greifswald had a well and a pipeline system that hardly differed technically from that of Lübeck and points similarly to a public-collective organisation of the water supply. In this city, the impetus that stood behind the public measures is well tangible, since beyond an economical use concept, the expansion was essentially pursued due to the strategic aim of urban expansion and land reclamation.

Conclusion

The comparison of water supply (and sewage) in two very different periods, antiquity and the Middle Ages, enables some fundamental considerations. On the one hand, they concern the relationship between the city and its natural conditions and, on the other hand, they shed light on specific social contexts and cultural needs.

Figure 12 (opposite page). Greifswald. Tanner's quarter. Features of the late 13th and early 14th centuries CE (after: U. Müller 2018, 245 fig. 10).

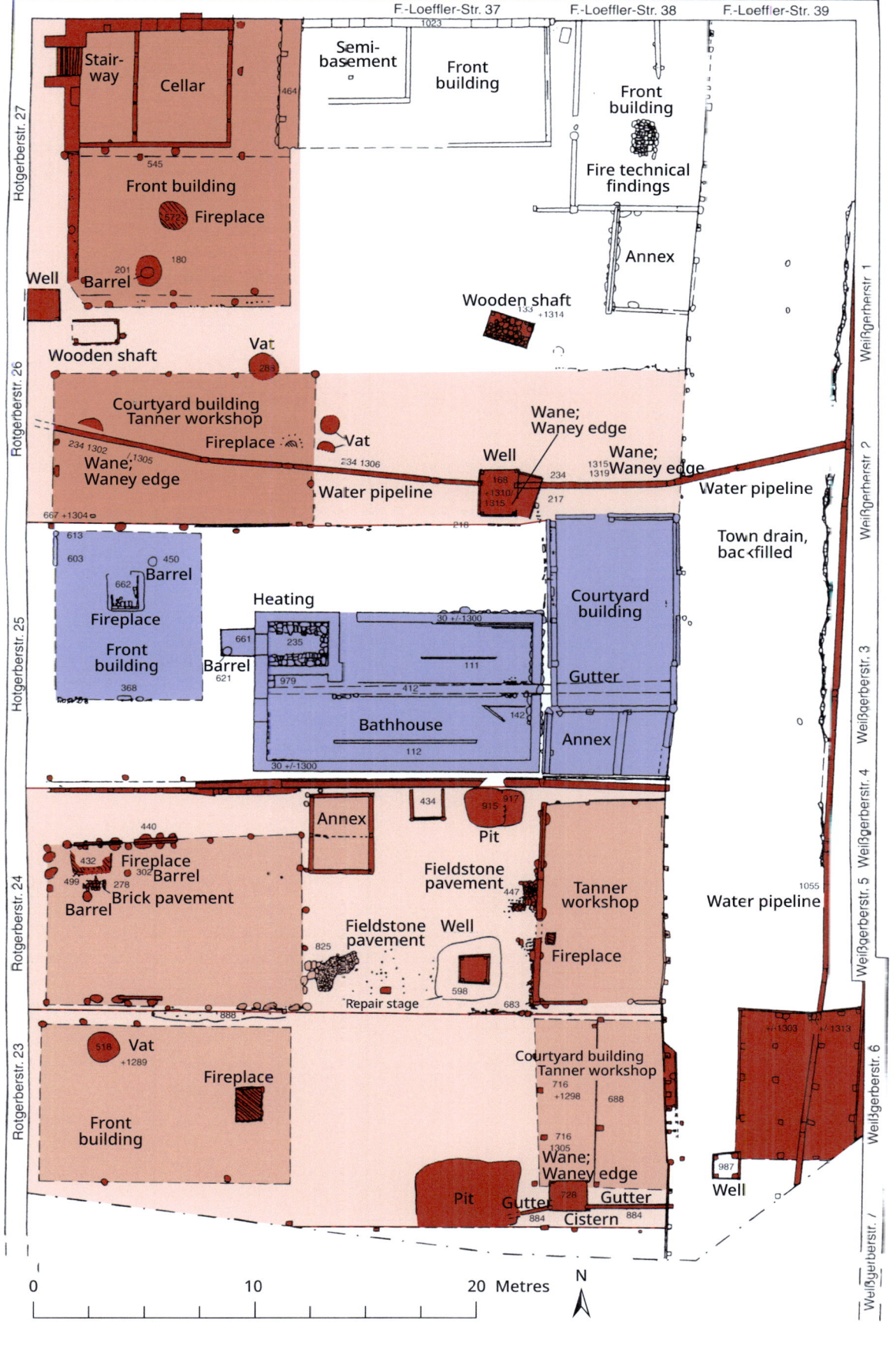

F.-Loeffler-Str. 37
F.-Loeffler-Str. 38
F.-Loeffler-Str. 39

Rotgerberstr. 27

Stair-way
Cellar
Front building
Fireplace
Well
Barrel

Semi-basement
Front building
Front building
Fire technical findings
Annex

Weißgerberstr. 1

Rotgerberstr. 26

Wooden shaft
Vat
Courtyard building
Tanner workshop
Fireplace
Vat
Wane, Waney edge
Water pipeline

Wooden shaft
Well
Wane; Waney edge
Wane; Waney edge
Water pipeline

Weißgerberstr. 2

Rotgerberstr. 25

Barrel
Fireplace
Front building
Barrel

Heating
Bathhouse

Courtyard building
Gutter
Annex

Town drain, backfilled

Weißgerberstr. 3

Rotgerberstr. 24

Fireplace
Barrel
Brick pavement
Barrel

Annex
Fieldstone pavement
Fieldstone pavement
Repair stage
Well
Pit
Tanner workshop
Fireplace
Water pipeline

Weißgerberstr. 4
Weißgerberstr. 5

Rotgerberstr. 23

Vat
Fireplace
Front building

Courtyard building
Tanner workshop
Wane; Waney edge
Pit
Gutter
Cistern
Gutter
Well

Weißgerberstr. 6
Weißgerberstr. 7

0   10   20 Metres

N

The basic prerequisite for the development of a settlement is the availability of water on site. With increasing urbanisation, however, garbage and sewage increasingly accumulate, so that open water points were no longer used for drinking water supply or only to a limited extent. As a result, technical know-how was developed that enabled the development of clean water resources: the installation of (waterproof) cisterns to collect rainwater and the construction of wells. As different as the solutions are according to the regional and historical context: In an early phase of urbanisation, such artificial strategies of water extraction are predominantly – though presumably not exclusively – a task for individual households. Water extraction is thus primarily decentralised. With advancing urbanisation, there are changes in two different but interdependent fields.

(1) Urbanisation goes hand in hand with the formation of urban authorities that make collectively organised action possible. In the ancient Mediterranean, these can be monarchic regimes (kings and emperors), but also democratic institutions; in the late medieval Hanseatic cities these are town councils and the citizenry. For the early period (12th century CE), we should also expect an individual organisational system with regulations by the authorities. All these more organised forms of rule, however, have in common that they are capable of organising collective interests. In terms of water needs, this is reflected in drainage systems and water supply systems (well houses, municipal wells, canals, and water pipes) from which the entire urban population benefits.

(2) A collective organisation of water supply is a response to the increasing demand for water which is characteristic of more urbanised settlements. On the one hand, the increasing demand for water is a consequence of the steady population growth – even though specific numbers cannot be provided for any of the case studies. On the other hand, it results from new urban needs – beyond the basic need for drinking water. The comparison between antiquity and the Middle Ages has shown that these needs can have very different reasons. In ancient urban contexts, a significant portion of fresh water was used for facilities that were at the centre of cultural self-understanding: for thermal baths, aesthetically pleasing water features and nymphaea. In ancient terms, the use of water refers, both in public and private contexts, to the categories of *utilitas* (utility), *usus* (consumption), *salubritas* (cleanliness), *salus* (health), *voluptas/amoenitas* (beauty) (Schmölder-Veit 2009, 23; Rogers 2018, 20). It may be part of the Roman self-understanding that literary sources hardly refer to the economic uses of urban water. In the medieval cities, however, elaborate waterworks were primarily motivated by economic needs – in the case of Lübeck the production of beer and in the case of Greifswald tanneries.

Against this background, the "water art" of ancient and medieval cities can be understood as an expression of the negotiation of individual and collective needs. It reflects – at least to a certain extent – the social connectivity within a city: the relationship of individual households to the city as a whole.

References

Adam, J.-P. and Varène, P., 2008. La castellum aquae de Pompéi. Étude architecturale. *Revue Archéologique*, 45, 37-72.

Aicher, P.J., 1995. *Guide to the Aqueducts of Ancient Rome*. Wauconda, IL: Bolchazy-Carducci Publishers.

Andersson, E.B., 1994. Urban Water Supply in Pompeii and the Private Water

Consumption. *In*: X. Dupré i Raventós, ed. *La ciutat en el món romà = La ciudad en el mundo romano. Actes XIV Congrés Internacional d'Arqueologia Clàssica 2, Tarragona, 5. – 11.9.1993.* Tarragona: Comitè Organitzador del XIV C.I.A.C [*et al.*], 29-31.

Arndt, B., 2020. Medieval and Post-Medieval Urban Water Supply and Sanitation. Archaeological Evidence from Göttingen and North German Towns. *In*: N. Chiarenza, A. Haug, U. Müller, eds. *The Power of Urban Water. Studies in Premodern Urbanism.* Berlin, Boston: De Gruyter, 213-228.

Bannon, C.J., 2009. *Gardens and Neighbors: Private Water Rights in Roman Italy.* Ann Arbor: University of Michigan Press.

Bianchi, E., ed., 2015. *La Cloaca Maxima e i sistemi fognari di Roma dall'antichità ad oggi.* Rome: Palombi Editori.

Bianco, A.D., 2007. *Aqua ducta, aqua distributa: La gestione delle risorse idriche in età romana.* Torino: Silvio Zamorani Editore.

Bruun, C., 2015. Water Use and Productivity in Roman Agriculture: Selling, Sharing, Servitudes. *In*: P. Erdkamp, K. Verboven, A. Zuiderhoek, eds. *Ownership and Exploitation of Land and Natural Resources in the Roman World.* Oxford: Oxford University Press, 132-151.

Bulach, D., 2013. *Handwerk im Staatraum: Das Ledergewerbe in den Hansestädten der südwestlichen Ostseeküste vom 13. bis 16. Jahrhundert.* Köln: Böhlau Verlag.

Coleman, K.M., 1993. Launching into History: Aquatic Displays in the Early Empire. *Journal of Roman Studies*, 83, 48-74.

De Feo, G. and Napoli, R.M.A., 2007. Historical Development of the Augustan Aqueduct in Southern Italy: Twenty Centuries of Works from Serino to Naples, Water Science & Technology. *Water Supply*, 7 (1), 131-138.

De Haan, N. and Jansen, G.C.M., eds., 1996. *Cura Aquarum in Campania, Proceedings of the Ninth International Congress on the History of Water Management and Hydraulic Engineering in the Mediterranean Region, Pompeii.* Leiden: Stichting Babesch.

De Kleijn, G., 2001. *The Water Supply of Ancient Rome: City Area, Water, and Population.* Amsterdam: J.C. Gieben.

Dessales, H., 2008. Des usages de l'eau aux évaluations démographiques: L'exemple de Pompéi, Maison des Sciences de l'Homme. *Histoire urbaine*, 22 (2), 27-41 [online]. Available at: <http://www.cairn.info/article.php?ID_REVUE=RHU&ID_NUMPUB-LIE=RHU_022&ID_ARTICLE=RHU_022_0027 > [Accessed: 18 December 2020].

Dessales, H., 2013. *Le partage de l'eau: Fontaines et distribution hydraulique dans l'habitat urbain de l'Italie romaine.* Bibliothèque des Écoles Françaises d'Athènes et de Rome 351. Rome: École Française de Rome.

Ellis, S.P., 1997. Pooling Resources: The Use of Water for Social Control in the Roman Empire. *In*: K. Meadows, ed. *TRAC 96: Proceedings of the Sixth Annual Theoretical Roman Archaeology Conference.* Oxford: Oxbow Books, 144-150.

Ellis, S.R., 2018. *The Roman Retail Revolution: the Socio-Economic World of the Taberna.* Oxford: Oxford University Press.

Enzenberger, P., 2007. *Handwerk im mittelalterlichen Greifswald: Ein Beitrag zur Darstellung der Siedlungs- und Produktionsweise in einem spätmittelalterlichen Handwerkerviertel am Übergang vom 13. zum 14. Jahrhundert.* Schwerin: Landesamt für Kultur und Denkmalpflege.

Evans, H.B., 1994. *Water Distribution in Ancient Rome: The Evidence of Frontinus.* Ann Arbor: Univ. of Michigan Press.

Flohr, M., 2013. *The World of the Fullo.* Oxford: Oxford University Press.

Frontzek, W., 2005. *Das städtische Braugewerbe und seine Bauten vom Mittelalter bis zur* frühen Neuzeit. Untersuchungen zur Entwicklung, Ausstattung und Topographie der Brauhäuser in der Hansestadt Lübeck. Häuser und Höfe in Lübeck 7. Neumünster: Wachholtz.

Garbrecht, G., 1984. Die antiken Wasserleitungen Roms. Antike Welt, 15 (2), 2-13.

Gläser, M., 2004. Die Infrastrukturen der Stadt Lübeck im Mittelalter und in der frühen Neuzeit. In: M. Gläser, ed. Lübecker Kolloquium zur Stadtarchäologie im Hanseraum IV, Die Infrastruktur. Lübeck: Schmidt-Römhild, 173-196.

Grabowski, M., 2009. Kunstwasser für Lübeck: Technische und organisatorische Innovation der städtischen Wasserversorgung an Lübecks Beispiel. Mitteilungen der Deutschen Gesellschaft für Archäologie des Mittelalters und der Neuzeit, 21, 65-72.

Harder, J., 2019. Aspekte der Infrastruktur. In: J. Harder, D. Mührenberg, I. Sudhoff, H. Kräling, U. Radis, D. Rieger, M. Schneider, eds. Die Ausgrabungen im Lübecker Gründungsviertel I. Die Siedlungsgeschichte. Lübeck: Schmidt-Römhild, 614-781.

Hartnett, J., 2008. Fountains at Herculaneum. Sacred History, Topography, and Civic Identity. Rivista di Studi Pompeiani, 19, 77-89.

Haug, A., 2016. Unterwegs im antiken Rom. Spektrum der Wissenschaft Spezial Archäologie – Geschichte – Kultur, 1, 48-53.

Haug, A., 2020. Decor-Räume in pompejanischen Stadthäusern. Ausstattungsstrategien und Rezeptionsformen [online]. Berlin: De Gruyter. Available at: https://doi.org/10.1515/9783110702705.

Hodge, A.T., 1992. Roman Aqueducts & Water Supply. London: Duckworth.

Igel, K., 2010. Zwischen Bürgerhaus und Frauenhaus: Stadtgestalt, Grundbesitz und Sozialstruktur im spätmittelalterlichen Greifswald. Städteforschung A 71. Köln: Böhlau Verlag.

Jansen, G.C.M., 2000a. Systems for the Disposal of Waste and Excreta in Roman Cities: The Situation in Pompeii, Herculaneum, and Ostia. In: X.D. Raventós and J.A. Remolà Vallverdú, eds. Sordes Urbis: La eliminación de residuos en la ciudad romana. Rome: "L'Erma" di Bretschneider, 37-49.

Jansen, G.C.M., 2000b. Urban Water Transport and Distribution. In: Ö. Wikander, ed. Handbook of Ancient Water Technology. Leiden: Brill, 103-125.

Jones, R. and Robinson, D., 2005. Water, Wealth, and Social Status at Pompeii: The House of the Vestals in the First Century. American Journal of Archaeology, 109 (4), 695-710.

Keenan-Jones, D.C., 2016. Fountains, Lead Pipes and Water Systems in Pompeii, Rome, and the Roman West. Journal of Roman Archaeology, 29 (2), 778-85.

Laurence, R., 1994. Roman Pompeii: Space and Society. London: Routledge.

Legant, G., 2010. Zur Siedlungsgeschichte des ehemaligen Lübecker Kaufleuteviertels im 12. und frühen 13. Jahrhundert. Nach den ältesten Befunden der Grabung Alfstraße – Fischstraße – Schüsselbuden, 1985-1990. Lübecker Schriften zur Archäologie und Kulturgeschichte 27. Rahden/Westf.: Verlag Marie Leidorf.

Longfellow, B., 2011. Roman Imperialism and Civic Patronage: Form, Meaning, and Ideology in Monumental Fountain Complexes. Cambridge: Cambridge University Press.

Maiuri, A., 1931. Pozzi e condotture d'acqua nell'antica cittá: Scoperta di un antico pozzo presso Porta Vesuvio. Notizie degli Scavi di Antichità, 546-557.

Monteix, N., 2009. Pompéi, Pistrina: recherches sur les boulangeries de l'Italie préromaine. Mélanges de l'École française de Rome [online], 121 (1), 322-335. Available at: https://doi.org/10.3406/mefr.2009.10542 [Accessed: 18.12.2020].

Müller, U., 2018. Gerberei im späten Mittelalter. Überlegungen zur Anwendung der Theorien sozialer Praktiken für die Erforschung handwerklicher Tätigkeiten. In: M. Bentz and T. Helms, eds. Craft Production Systems in a Cross-cultural Perspective.

Bonn: Verlag Dr. Rudolf Habelt GmbH, 233-259.

Ohlig, C.P.J., 2001. *De aquis Pompeiorum: Das Castellum Aquae in Pompeji. Herkunft, Zuleitung und Verteilung des Wassers.* Norderstedt: Books on Demand.

Pliny 1962. Natural History, Volume X: Books 36-37. Translated by D. E. Eichholz. Loeb Classical Library 419. Cambridge, MA: Harvard University Press.

Poehler, E., in press. Urban Infrastructure and the Perception of Neighborhood, In: A. Haug, A. Hielscher, A.-L. Krüger, eds. *The Social Patterning of Urban Space. City Quarters and Neighbourhoods.* Leiden: Sidestone Press.

Röber, R., 2016. Die Belastung von Wasser und Boden in der mittelalterlichen Stadt – Einzelfall oder Paradigma? *Mitteilungen der Deutschen Gesellschaft für Archäologie des Mittelalters und der Neuzeit,* 29, 21-36.

Rogers, D., 2013. Il piacere dell'acqua: i ninfei di Pompei. In: V. Gheller, ed. *Ricerche a confront. Dialoghi di Antichità Classiche e del Vicino Oriente.* Milano: Edizioni Saecula – Weirdstudio, 154-166.

Rogers, D., 2018. Water Culture in Roman Society. *Ancient History,* 1 (1), 1-118.

Schäfer, H., 2004. Öffentliche Bautätigkeiten und Einrichtungen in Greifswald unter besonderer Berücksichtigung der archäologischen Quellen des 13. bis 15. Jahrhunderts. In: M. Gläser, ed. *Lübecker Kolloquium zur Stadtarchäologie im Hanseraum: IV, Die Infrastruktur.* Lübeck: Schmidt-Römhild, 263-274.

Schalies, I., 2009. Wasserbaumaßnahmen im mittelalterlichen und neuzeitlichen Lübeck. *Mitteilungen der Deutschen Gesellschaft für Archäologie des Mittelalters und der Neuzeit,* 21, 2009, 73-86.

Schmölder-Veit, A., 2009. *Brunnen in den Städten des westlichen Römischen Reichs.* Palilia 19. Wiesbaden: Dr. Ludwig Reichert Verlag.

Schütte, S., 1986. Brunnen und Kloaken auf innerstädtischen Grundstücken im ausgehenden Hoch- und Spätmittelalter. In: H. Steuer, ed. *Zur Lebensweise in der Stadt um 1200.* Zeitschrift für Archäologie des Mittelalters, Beiheft 4. Köln, Bonn: Verlag Dr. Rudolf Habelt GmbH, 237-255.

Sturm, P., 2014. „sagen all natürlich arczet, der mensch, der von bösem gestanck kranck wirdet, dem sey nit ze helffen" – Fäkalien in der Seuchentheorie und -bekämpfung an der Wende vom Mittelalter zur Frühneuzeit. In: O. Wagener, ed. *Aborte im Mittelalter und der Frühen Neuzeit (Bauforschung – Archäologie – Kulturgeschichte.* Studien zur internationalen Architektur- und Kunstgeschichte 117. Petersberg: Michael Imhof Verlag, 219-227.

Sydow, J., 1981. *Städtische Versorgung und Entsorgung im Wandel der Geschichte.* Stadt in der Geschichte 8. Sigmaringen: Thorbecke.

Taylor, R., 2000. *Public Needs and Private Pleasures: Water Distribution, the Tiber River, and the Urban Development of Ancient Rome.* Studia Archaeologica 109. Rome: "L'Erma" di Bretschneider.

Thüry, G.E., 2001. *Müll und Marmorsäulen: Siedlungshygiene in der römischen Antike.* Mainz: Philipp von Zabern.

Trümper, M., 2018. Gymnasium, Palaestra, Campus and Bathing in Late Hellenistic Pompeii. A Reassessment of the Urban Context of the Republican Baths (VIII 5, 36). In: U. Mania and M. Trümper, eds. *Development of Gymnasia and Graeco-Roman Cityscapes.* Berlin Studies of the Ancient World 58. Berlin: Humboldt-Universität zu Berlin, 87-113.

Wallace-Hadrill, A., 1994. *Houses and society in Pompeii and Herculaneum.* Princeton, NJ: Princeton Univ. Press.

Wilson, A.I., 2000. Industrial Uses of Water. In: Ö. Wikander, ed. *Handbook of Ancient Water Technology.* Leiden: Brill, 127-149.

An archaeological perspective on social structure, connectivity and the measurements of social inequality

Tim Kerig, Johannes Bröcker (†), René Ohlrau, Tanja Schreiber, Henry Skorna, Fynn Wilkes

Tim Kerig
Cluster of Excellence ROOTS
Kiel University
Olshausenstr. 80h
24118 Kiel, Germany
tkerig@roots.uni-kiel.de

Johannes Bröcker (†)

René Ohlrau
Cluster of Excellence ROOTS
Kiel University
Olshausenstr. 80h
24118 Kiel, Germany
rohlrau@roots.uni-kiel.de

Tanja Schreiber
Cluster of Excellence ROOTS
Kiel University
Olshausenstr. 80h
24118 Kiel, Germany
tschreiber@roots.uni-kiel.de

Henry Skorna
Cluster of Excellence ROOTS
Kiel University
Olshausenstr. 80h
24118 Kiel, Germany
hskorna@roots.uni-kiel.de

Fynn Wilkes
Cluster of Excellence ROOTS
Kiel University
Olshausenstr. 80h
24118 Kiel, Germany
fwilkes@roots.uni-kiel.de

Abstract

Social differentiation and connectivity are obviously connected to social inequality, but this relation needs further investigation. We start from a historical positioning of the term 'social inequality' within the current archaeological discussion. Here we focus on households as the principal units of decision-making. In accordance with current research and for the time being, we accept differences in house floor areas as wealth differences. To describe wealth or income inequality in archaeology, the well-known Gini coefficient has been used several times since the 1980s. Here, the Gini coefficient is explained and, for the first time, the concepts of the inequality frontier and the inequality extraction ratio (which are based on the Gini coefficient) are introduced into archaeology. As a case study, the development of inequality is investigated for household sizes in two important sites of the Bulgarian Aeneolithic – the tell sites of Poljanica and Ovčarovo, respectively. Finally, an important unresolved problem can be identified and discussed: where is the fundamental place of social inequalities within past societies, especially within what has been denoted as segmentary societies?

Introduction

How were past social inequalities and societal connectivity interrelated? Does high social inequality always cause lesser connectivity in society or does increasing economic inequality force different parts of societies, such as families, households, and lineages, to strengthen their fitness by increasing group-internal connectivity? In general, and especially for vertically described feudal and class societies, increasing economic inequalities can be expected to result directly in widening the differences and contradictions between classes – those differences may pull societies apart. In societies described as segmentary, social inequalities can be assumed to arise *between* as well as *within* those segments – it can be presumed that both of these forms of inequality have different effects. In a wider perspective: will inequality between segments lead to dominantly vertically organised societies such as feudal or class societies?

Over the last decade, archaeologists have not only adopted concepts of social inequality but some have also successfully contributed to interdisciplinary social inequality studies implementing impressive time series (*e.g.* Flannery and Marcus 2012; Kohler *et al.* 2017; Kohler and Smith 2018; Scheidel 2017; Turchin 2015). To this growing field, archaeology has the potential to contribute a wide range of examples from all over the world: for societies which can be arranged, in principle, in time series of arbitrary length. In the following, we will not stress this obvious need for archaeology in social research, but will take a short look at how social inequality can be measured in the archaeological realm. Moreover, we will explain standard methods for the measurement of social inequality in sociology and economics. We will then apply these methods to briefly examine an archaeological case study: A comparison of two important settlements of the Aeneolithic of Bulgaria, which represents a classic textbook example of emerging inequalities. We will briefly discuss where we expect to find added value of the recorded measurements to explain the relation between connectivity and social inequality. Finally, we will ask where to find social inequality within hierarchical and within non-stratified past societies.

Social inequality, social structure and societal connectivity

In the following, we use the term *social inequality* as the degree of uneven access to resources which are available to the society in total. *Social structure* describes the interplay of societal institutions which form society. *Societal connectivity* may not be confused with social cohesion: the term connectivity comes from graph theory and describes the degree of stability of a network when certain agents – in network terms: nodes – were hypothetically removed (Diestel 2016, 59-87). Inequality and connectivity can directly be measured in theory and by proxy in practice, while social structure is much more open to purely qualitative interpretations.

In contrast to the term social structure, which has been used in archaeology for a long time, social inequality can be seen as a newer concept pushing the focus from social order to social dysfunction. Since the very term "social structure" was coined by the Kiel sociologist Ferdinand Tönnies (1905), it has been a central concept of most of the school-building sociologists of the twentieth century. From there, it diffused into archaeology for which the concept helped to identify past social order. From the sixties onwards, identifying signs of social distinction, ranking combinations of grave-goods into classes, and computing indices of wealth and rank became common, especially in burial archaeology.

Even if this approach to social structure does not necessarily assume a fixed set of social relations of some permanence, such a perspective poses the danger of connoting social stability, whereas actually a high dynamic development may have taken place, or it also might mask motives, internal contradictions, strategic action, *etc*. Almost every archaeological reconstruction assumes a functioning system of some stability that lasts at least one archaeological phase – these systems, in reality, may have often been short-lived and maladaptive.

In the functionalist social structure perspective as well as in evolutionary studies, all kinds of social differentiation can be seen as answers to challenges: In early New Archaeology (and in some US Marxist archaeological interpretations), the main challenges were environmental factors, such as climate change, available food resources, and population densities (*e.g.* Binford 1968). Slightly later, Colin Renfrew (1972) argued for a principal conservatism of all cultures but identified driving forces in the effects between challenged, co-occurring subsystems of a society leading to what he called multiplier effects. In parts of post-processual archaeology of the eighties and nineties as well as in some of the more recent interpretative approaches, social structure is no longer an issue, while in other branches of interpretative archaeology the concept of social structure lives on again. Some authors, *e.g.*, in a structuralist tradition, maintain the idea of structure, sometimes even harmony in society. At the same time, it is obvious that radical, critical and activist approaches do not need the concept of social order but might profit from investigations into dysfunctions and maladjustments. The general perspective on social inequality is rooted in the social movements of the nineteenth and twentieth centuries, where it grew out of claims for distributive justice: A focus on social inequality counteracts the perspective on the societal benefits of social structure and rather asks about the costs of social differentiation (in sociology, *e.g.*, Therborn 2013; cf. Schwinn 2019). Especially in Marxist thinking, the instability of any social order due to steady contradictions between economic and societal development is seen as history's major driver.

A perspective on instability in itself could also be understood as a processual heritage. It is vital in current evolutionary studies, where social differentiation is, *e.g.*, explained in terms of niche construction (Shennan 2011), which increases the sustainability of the individual as well as of the total system, leading to growing complexity. In functionalist approaches, including resilience theory of the last years, higher complexity is explained by adaptive loops in subsystems with complexity as an outcome. Since Leslie A. White (1959), complex social structures can be described quantitatively, first as being of higher order in terms of potential energy and, *e.g.*, more recently as being more skilful (Henrich 2004). In general, *social complexity* has replaced social structure to avoid the dangers of essentialism. Complexity is mostly seen as the outcome of an adaptive advantage of a kind that drives societal evolution. In continental sociology, the term *social differentiation* is preferred (Schwinn 2004; 2019), which refers rather to a historical and sociological tradition than to natural history. In this framework of current critical and evolutionary archaeology, including activism as well as complexity science, an archaeological concept of social inequality has to find its place.

Households as actors

When interpreting graves, social inequality seems obvious: funerary archaeology deals with individuals, burial practices and grave goods, all within their burial society, promising to infer the living individual's position within a living society from the rank of the deceased. In the following, however, we will turn to households as actors: The household is the very place *'where ecology, economy, society and culture met'* (Ames 1996, 131). In micro-economics, a *household* is often seen as the principal unit of decision-making, regardless of its internal social structure. We will apply a comparable analytical concept of the household below.

For most archaeologists, households are first and foremost connected to dwelling remains (Ames 1996, 132) from which house units need to be reconstructed in order to constitute households as social entities (Wilk and Rathje 1982, 618). The house forms the basic common perception of a household, the physical frame for residential activities, which, though varying through time and space, in all cases represent co-resident groups (Blanton 1994; 1995). Nevertheless, houses did not only serve as residences but also as working spaces, and were used for storage, for rituals and gatherings as well as for distribution and consumption (Coupland and Banning 1996). Due to this and by reason of being intermediate social entities between individuals and entire communities (Hammel 1984), households may be suitable to represent small-scale models of the social organisation of inequality within human societies. They are therefore widely acknowledged as indicators for the status and wealth of their occupants in archaeological and ethnographic research (*e.g.* Forrest and Murie 1995; Kamp 2000; Byrd 2000, see also Netting 1982). The house floor area is frequently used as a standardised, inter- and cross-culturally applicable proxy for wealth (Ames and Grier 2020, 1042; Basri and Lawrence 2020; Kohler and Smith 2018; Kohler *et al.* 2017; Porčić 2019; Smith *et al.* 2014).

Though the reasons for the variety of house sizes are diverse, the presence of exceptionally big houses among many smaller-sized ones hints at special conditions under which the necessity to build such structures arises, irrespective of the size of the household. Big houses may not only give shelter to more occupants but also to more extensive storage. In this way, they display the success of their occupants and their ability to gather further labour forces (Ames 2006, 21; Vaneeckhout 2010, 18), which in turn may increase the prestige of the house owner. Gary Coupland and Edward B. Banning (1996) claim that bigger buildings often provide a material correlate of wealth and complexity, since they are linked to larger households, in which the foundation of social stratification predominates, linking large house structures inevitably with social and economic inequality.

Many researchers see the emergence of enduring inequality as well as political hierarchies in household production (*e.g.* Pauketat 1996; Diehl 2000). Both inequality and political hierarchies are central in the process of the redistribution of goods, whereby consumption is dependent on social and demographic stratification. Households are essential elements in the study of social inequality (Curtis 1986, 168). Moreover, social relations, especially gender- and age-specific factors, are reproduced and legitimised through everyday practices as well as through ritualised domestic behaviour. Members of a household may tacitly acknowledge but also oppose them.

Marshall Sahlins emphasises the significance of what he once called the household mode of production. He now sees the domestic relations within the household as *'principal relations of production in [a tribal] society'* (Sahlins 2017, 69), since decisions of labour expenditure and its conditions and outcomes are made on the domestic level and usually for the benefit of the household residents. In some economic-anthropological theories, however, household production is stated to be based on subsistence needs and the distribution of goods on equity and not on efficiency (Graeber 2017, xv). Alexander Chayanov (1966), in his classic study, claims that households produce until a balance between labour investment and its desired output is reached, thus retaining a constant level of well-being. Thus, household production only increases if it satisfies household consumption. For Sahlins (2017), it is the political elite that forces further surplus production. In pre-state societies, the amount of surplus extraction is not only limited by ecological and technological restraints but also by social levelling mechanisms that counteract the agglomeration of wealth (see below).

Measuring social inequality by the distribution of wealth

Measuring social inequality has long been an issue in sociology and economics (*e.g.* Gini 1912; Ceriani and Verme 2012; for an overview Requate 2021a). Economic inequality analysis mainly deals with three ingredients, the *subjects* of analysis collected in a set called the *population*, and the *objects*. The subjects are individuals or groups of individuals, such as families or households. The population may be a geographically, culturally or institutionally delineated social entity. The object is either a single indicator (the univariate case) or a list of indicators (the multivariate case) associated with each subject, quantifying its respective wealth. The term "wealth" is obviously problematic, because it suggests a monetary dimension, although even in modern societies there is no way to translate the many facets of humans' capabilities in a society into a single monetary indicator. This is even more the case for ancient societies lacking developed markets, where one item of well-being was exchanged against another at a certain relative price. Nonetheless, we typically have access to only a very small number of proxies roughly correlating with the subjects' economic position in a society, including house sizes, burial mounds, indicators of nutrition and health, and some more. Here, to keep things simple, we assume to be able to associate a unidimensional indicator that we call wealth with each subject.

An *indicator* is assumed to be comparable between subjects on a ratio scale implying that ratios of these indicators have meaning. Given a unidimensional indicator of wealth for each subject, one cannot only order them in terms of more or less wealth – "richer" or "poorer". In the following, it is also sensible to denote a subject X as double, triple or half as rich as subject Y. The unit of measurement is arbitrary, but the zero point is not. Any conclusion we draw from the data is unaffected by the choice of units. Note, however, that measuring, for example, the sizes of burial mounds in terms of diameters, ground areas or volumes does affect conclusions, because these measures are not related to each other just by the choice of units.

To compare inequalities between different populations across space and time, we use unequal distributions of certain indicators of wealth in the population. The first and most obvious question to ask is whether inequality has decreased or increased in a geographical area between certain points in time. Was inequality in one group larger than in another group? To achieve an answer, we need an operational criterion, which at least orders societies in terms of the degree of inequality. This leads to the concept of an ordinal measurement of inequality. An ordering criterion should be transitive and complete, the former meaning that if society A is more equal than society B and society B more equal than society C, then the criterion should also declare society A to be more unequal than society C. The latter, completeness, means that, for any pair of societies, A and B, the

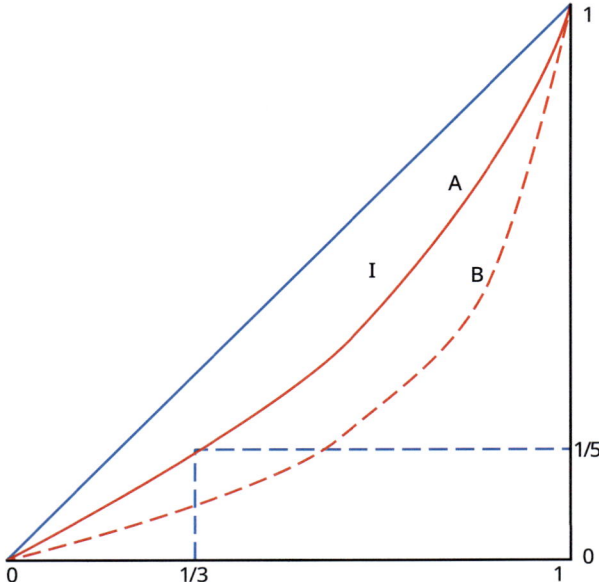

Figure 1. Lorenz curves. Two non-intersecting Lorenz curves A and B (red) (diagram: the authors).

criterion should classify A as more unequal than B, or the reverse (or, by coincidence, they are just equally unequal), but it should not be inconclusive for any possible pair of societies.

For the unidimensional measurement case, a fairly convincing criterion can be constructed that is transitive, but unfortunately often incomplete. This is the criterion of Lorenz dominance, based on the famous und intuitive concept of the Lorenz curve (Fig. 1 and 2). To construct the Lorenz curve, we let subjects line up from the poorest to the richest from left to right. Points on the abscissa are marked by the percentage of subjects poorer than or just as poor as the one standing at the respective point, itself included (its left side). The point on the curve shows the total wealth accruing to all left side subjects jointly. For example, at the point marked in the figure, the left side covers one third of the population owning jointly one fifth of total wealth (distribution A, the solid line on Fig. 1).

Hence, four fifths of total wealth accrue to the right side corresponding to two thirds of the population. The average wealth of those on the right side is thus double the average wealth of those on the left side. The lower the point on the curve, the bigger the right side to left side ratio. A more sagging Lorenz curve, like the dashed one (distribution B), thus represents a more unequal distribution.

What is meant by a *more sagging* curve is clear as long as the curves do not intersect (cf. Fig. 2).

This case is called *Lorenz dominance*. With Lorenz dominance, the interpretation seems to be convincing also in light of further theoretical arguments. Let, for example, distributions A and B refer to one and the same population in two different situations, such that the distribution of wealth among the subjects differs between the two situations. Starting from distribution B, we can get to the distribution A by a series of transfers of wealth, keeping the total constant, from a richer to a poorer subject each. Such an equalising sequence of transfers is always possible in case of Lorenz dominance. Interestingly, the reverse also holds: If such a series of transfers is possible, then Lorenz dominance holds or, in other words, the respective Lorenz curves do not intersect.

Another compelling argument is the following: Let us assign a utility of wealth to each subject, a number that goes up with increasing wealth, but it goes

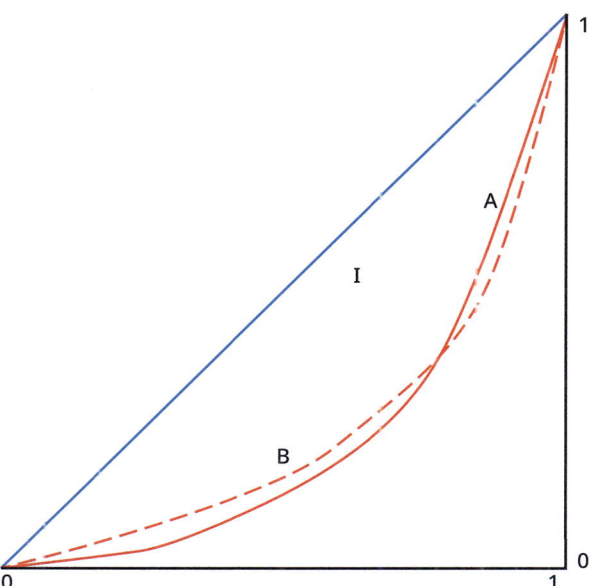

Figure 2. Lorenz curves. Intersecting Lorenz curves (red) (diagram: the authors).

up less and less the more the subject already has. Summing these numbers up across the population, we obtain a number that we might call *social welfare*. It turns out that this social welfare is larger for distribution A than for distribution B for *any* such social welfare index. Whenever an extra unit of wealth for a richer subject is socially valued higher than an extra unit for a poorer subject, distribution A is socially valued higher than distribution B.

Unfortunately, in figure 2 with intersecting Lorenz curves the situation is less clear. B is more equal than A in the lower range of wealth and less so in the upper range. Moreover, the two arguments supporting our interpretation in the case of non-intersecting curves, questions them in the case of intersecting curves. Getting from B to A by a series of redistributions always requires some transfers from rich to poor and some from poor to rich. How to trade off the former against the latter? Without arbitrary value judgements, it is hard to know. Furthermore, in the intersecting case of figure 2, we can always construct a social welfare function of the kind described above, the values A higher than B and another one that does the reverse. Again, which one we prefer is impossible to say without further value judgements that are hard to justify.

To avoid ambiguity, it is common practice to associate a single number with the extent to which the Lorenz curve sags and to call a distribution more unequal, if the number is higher. An obvious number is just twice the area G, the famous Gini index (for formulas and references cf. Requate 2021b). One chooses twice the area G rather than G because this restricts the Gini to numbers between zero (perfect equality) and one meaning maximal inequality, although the latter interpretation is a problem, see below. Obviously, in case of Lorenz dominance, the Gini is always larger for the more unequal distribution. But conversely, a higher Gini does not imply higher inequality in the Lorenz dominance sense. Ordering distributions from more to less unequal by the Gini index in case of intersecting Lorenz curves is no more than common practice without deeper theoretical justification.

Beyond this and many other issues related to the exclusive use of Gini co-efficients in inequality analysis, here we will focus on a different aspect called the inequality frontier by Milanovic (Milanovic *et al.* 2007; Milanovic *et al.* 2011; cf. Milanovic 2013). As mentioned, a Gini equal to one is regarded as indicating

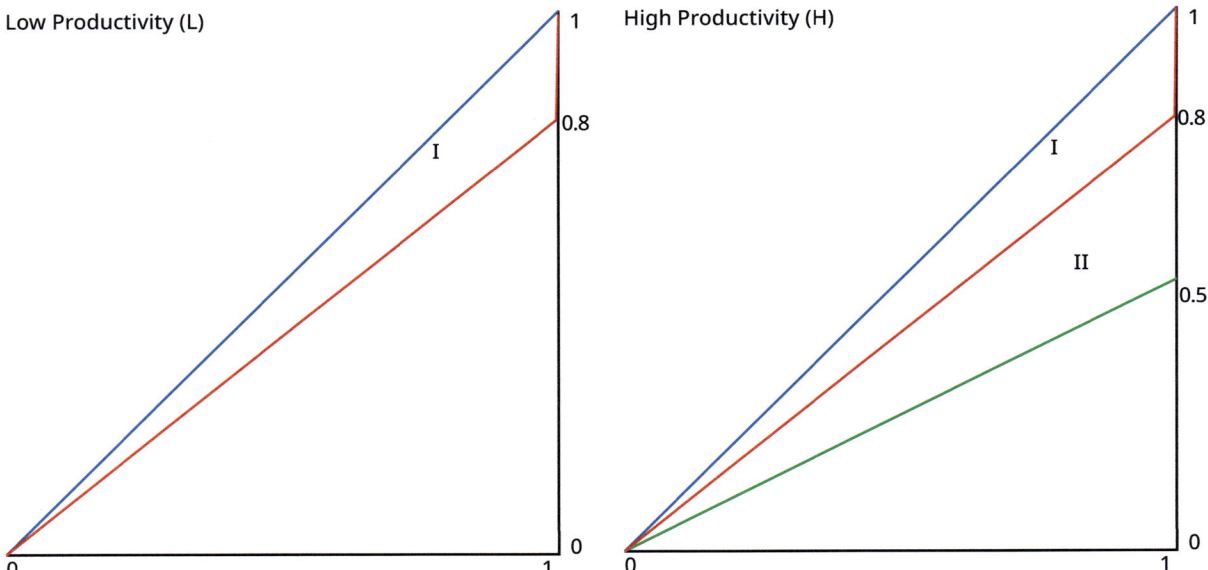

Figure 3. Lorenz curves. Left: Lorenz curves (red) equal the inequality frontier, low productivity society L; Right: Lorenz curve (red) above inequality frontier (green), high productivity society H (diagram: the authors).

maximal inequality. If the population is finite, and if one member takes it all and all others have nothing, the Gini is strictly speaking a bit smaller than one and approaches one if the population is increasing and the weight of the single subject taking it all approaches zero. Abstracting from this nuisance, we assume this single subject to have a negligible weight epsilon, a number arbitrarily close to zero. Call this subject the epsilon-subject. It is a metaphor for a powerful elite able to appropriate wealth but being very small in number as compared to the entire population under study.

Hence, the theoretical upper limit of the Gini is one, and we can understand any observed Gini intuitively as the share of the actual degree of inequality in the maximal degree of inequality. The problem with this interpretation is not that the upper bound of one is not literally attained in a finite population, but that a deeper difficulty arises: it neglects a key aspect when comparing different societies or different time slices, namely the fact that the maximal degree of inequality depends on the productivity of a society. Inequality is bounded above by the necessity of the deprived part of the population to survive. The maximal inequality in a population subject to the constraint of survival is called the *inequality frontier*. When applying inequality measures to compare societies and to infer on social structures and stratifications, one should control for productivity and the differential inducing different inequality frontiers.

Let us compare a low productivity society L with a high productivity society H. In L, subjects are unable to survive with less than 80% of the average wealth per subject, while in H the respective border line is 50%. Furthermore, every subject except the epsilon-subject receives 80% of the average wealth per subject, while the epsilon-subject takes the rest. The Lorenz curves are the straight lines from the origin cutting the abscissa on the right at 0.8, and the traditional Gini is 0.2 in both L and H (Fig. 3).

In L, the Lorenz curve is at the same time the inequality frontier, *i.e.*, the Lorenz curve represents the maximal inequality subject to survival. In L, the ratio of the Gini to the maximal Gini subject to survival is one. Milanovic *et al.* (2011) call this ratio the inequality extraction ratio.

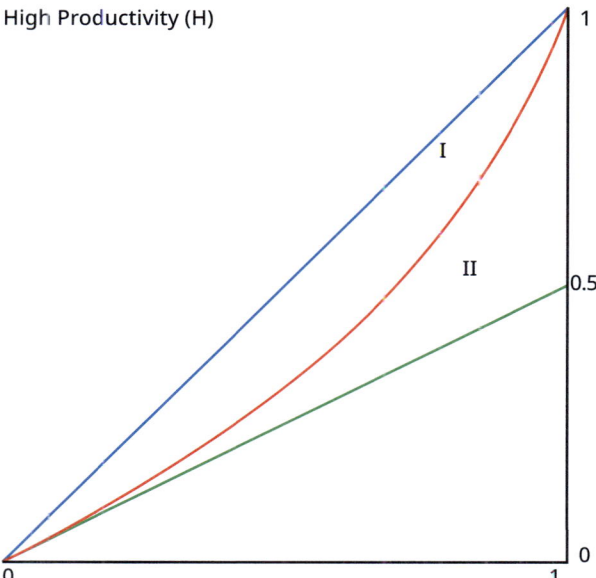

High Productivity (H)

Figure 4. Lorenz curve (red) and inequality frontier (green) for the high productivity society H in case of a curved Lorenz curve (diagram: the authors).

In H, to the contrary, the Lorenz curve lies well above the inequality frontier. The deprived part of the society receives 80% of the average, while 50% would suffice to survive. In other words, their respective wealth exceeds the subsistence level by 60%. Even though the Gini indices are the same in L and H (0.2 in both cases), the inequality extraction ratio is one in L, but only one fifth in H. As a general definition, the inequality extraction ratio is the ratio of the Gini over the hypothetical maximal Gini that would prevail if the entire population lived on the level of subsistence, while a very small elite (the epsilon-subject) got the rest.

To put it differently, we may call the difference between the total wealth of a society and the minimal wealth required for survival the social or *societal surplus*. The surplus ratio is the ratio of the societal surplus over the total wealth, and the ratio of the traditional Gini (twice area I) over the surplus ratio (twice areas I plus II) is the inequality extraction ratio (the ratio of area I over areas I plus II, 0.4 in our case). Figure 4 repeats the definition in case of a typical curved form of a Lorenz curve.

Although H and L exhibit identical traditional Ginis, the inequality extraction ratio is much smaller in H than in L. We may conclude that the elites in H command over less power to extract wealth from the economy in H than in L.

A tale of two tells: Case study Poljanica and Ovčarovo

Over the last decades, multiple prehistoric settlement sites in the Bulgarian Vrana Valley have been subject to intensive archaeological research (Todorova 1982; Krauß and Schneider 2014). Especially the two case study sites, in which the mounded sites of Poljanica and Ovčarovo were investigated, have been part of previous studies addressing inequality (Porčić 2012; 2019). In the following, this ongoing research is not discussed in detail, nor are significances calculated for the described changes in social inequality. This contribution rather focuses on a comparison between the trajectories of the Gini coefficient over time, the inequality frontier and the inequality extraction ratio. Both tell sites are part of the same microregion with a total of nine Aeneolithic tell settlements (Fig. 5) and both are characterised by houses erected using posts with walls constructed with wattle and daub.

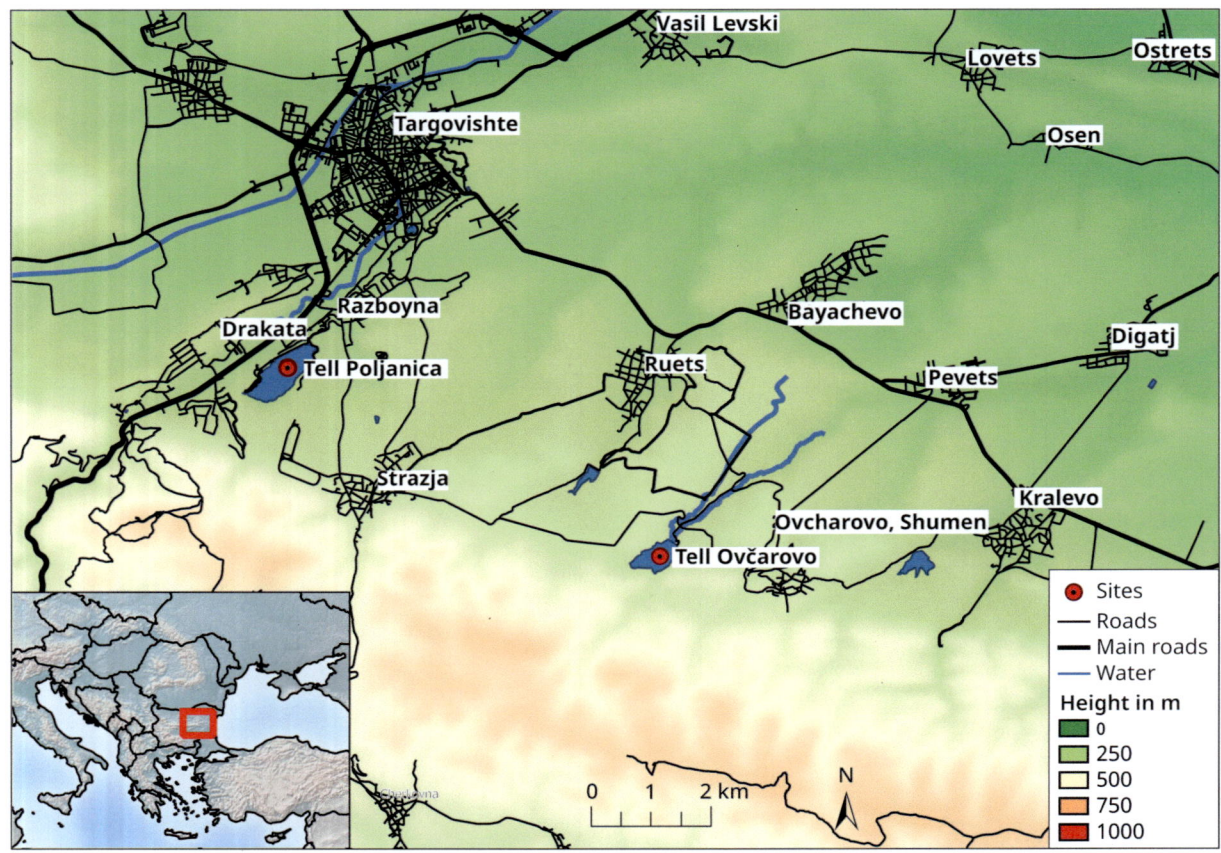

Figure 5. Targovishte province (Bulgaria). Location of Poljanica and Ovčarovo (map: F. Wilkes).

Generally, the interior was divided into one to four rooms (Todorova 1982). From Poljanica, a total of 136 clearly distinguishable houses from 8 layers and from Ovčarovo, 95 houses from 12 layers, are known. The number of contemporaneous houses documented in the settlement layers has been criticised by Clemens Lichter (1993) as having been calculated on a weak basis. However, for the purpose of this investigation, we will rely on the initial numbers provided by Todorova (1982). The settlements were dated to the Aeneolithic, corresponding to chronological phase II of the Poljanica culture and chronological phase III of the Kodžadermen-Gumel-niţa-Karanovo VI (KGK VI) culture (Todorova 1982). In absolute terms, the settlement activity spans from 4850 to 4000 BC (Fig. 6; Todorova 1978).

The Poljanica fortified tell settlement (Fig. 7) was located on a small elevation between two stream valleys. It was fully excavated prior to the construction of a water reservoir. The excavations were carried out in 1971 and from 1973-75 by Todorova. The settlement mound had eight layers with a preserved height of 2.7 m. While layers I to VII were well-preserved, the youngest layer was damaged by flooding and was later disturbed by a medieval burial site. Tell Poljanica, with its settlement layers spanning from chronological phases Poljanica II to IV, is the eponymous site of the Poljanica culture (Table 1).

A transition period was observed between layers IV and V, where mixed material from the chronological phases Poljanica III and IV is present. The youngest settlement layer VIII, which ended in a burning event and led to the abandonment of the settlement, corresponds to the first stage of the Kodzadermen-Gumel-nitza-Karanovo-VI (KGK VI) culture. During the initial three layers, the settlement was divided into four quarters formed by two alleys along the N-S and E-W axes

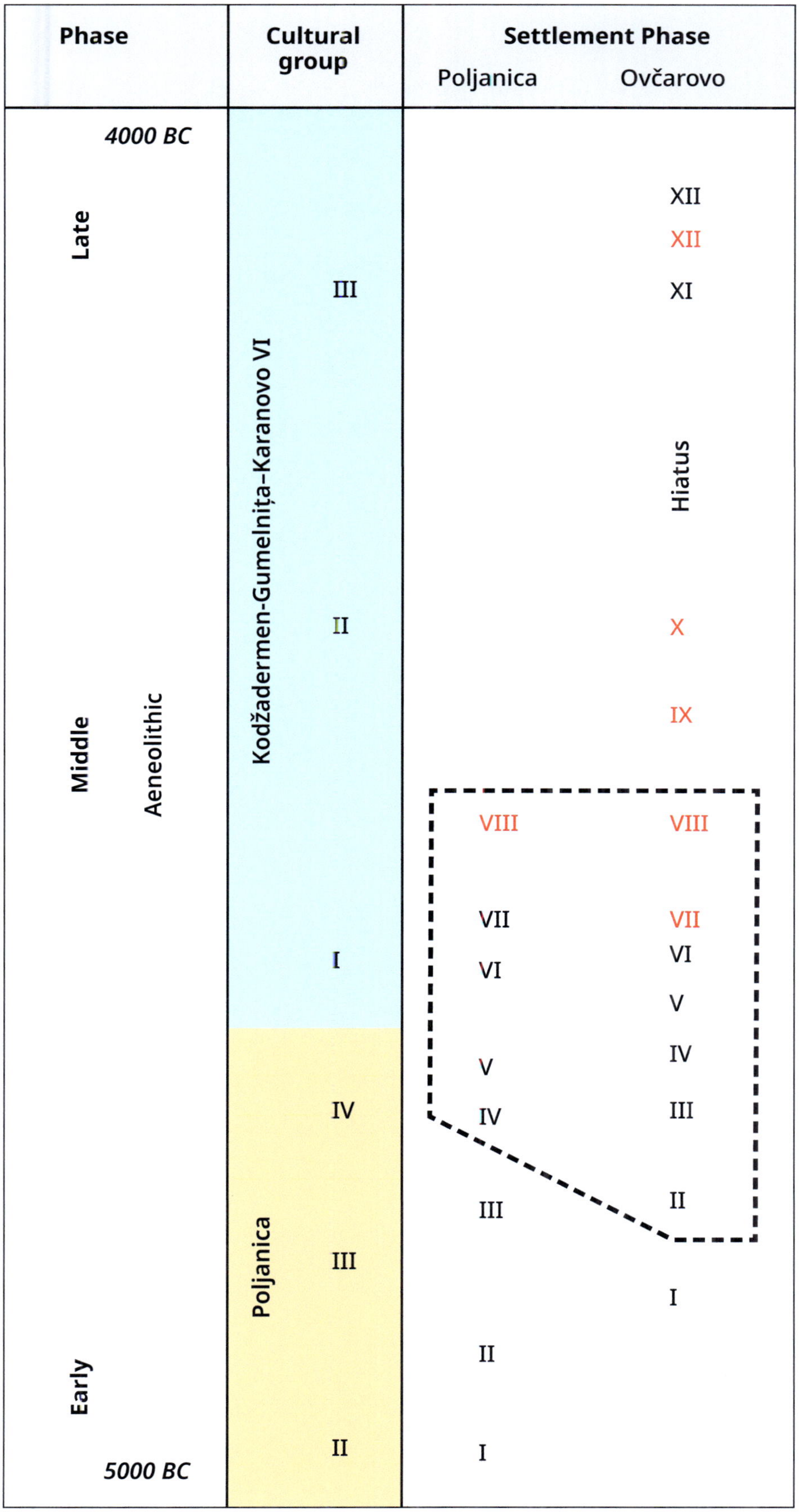

Phase		Cultural group	Settlement Phase	
			Poljanica	Ovčarovo
Late	Aeneolithic	Kodžadermen-Gumelnița-Karanovo VI — III		XII
				XII
				XI
Middle		II		Hiatus
				X
				IX
		I	VIII	VIII
			VII	VII
			VI	VI
				V
			V	IV
			IV	III
			III	II
Early	Poljanica — IV			I
		III	III	
			II	
		II	I	

4000 BC

5000 BC

Figure 6. Aeneolithic chronology of the Targovishte microregion (Bulgaria): cultural phases and settlement layers of Poljanica and Ovčarovo. Settlement phases written in red ended with a burning event, simultaneous settlement phases on both tells are indicated with a dotted box (chart: the authors)

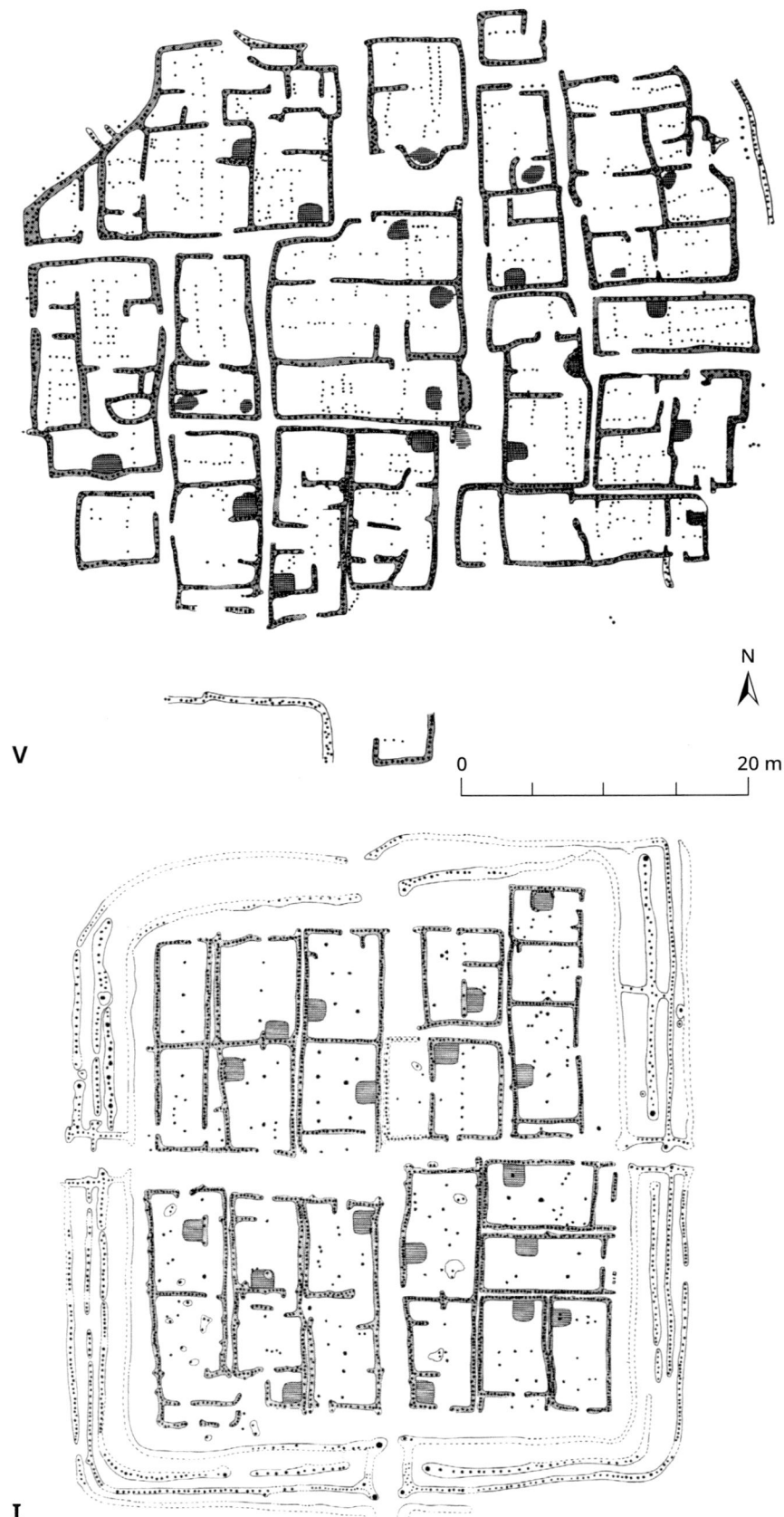

Figure 7. Tell Poljanica (Bulgaria): General plan of households in settlement phases I and V, respectively. Hearths are shaded (modified after Todorova 1982).

Phase	n	Minimal house size (m²)	Average house size (m²)	GC	IF	IER
I	14	33.92	63.61	0.2	0.467	0.428
II	16	34.97	60.39	0.183	0.421	0.435
III	15	46.86	82.46	0.193	0.432	0.447
IV	30	15	49.93	0.263	0.700	0.376
V	18	16.6	84.44	0.37	0.803	0.461
VI	22	7.28	65.25	0.344	0.888	0.387
VII	21	26.1	78.51	0.318	0.668	0.476
VIII	23	17.42	78.68	0.271	0.779	0.348

Table 1. Poljanica. Share of house areas, results of the analyses: GC: Gini coefficient IF: inequality frontier, IER: inequality extraction ratio.

connecting the four entrances. Due to an increase in construction activities, this division was less visible in layer IV before completely disappearing in layer V. In the subsequent layers VI-VIII, the settlement organisation, while continuing to grow, turned back to its "traditional" quarter structure. Generally, the settlement size increased in time with a small plateau during layer V. Three to four palisades/emplecton walls surrounded the settlement throughout its history. The palisades were plastered with a mixture of wattle and daub (Todorova 1982). In layer III, clay bastions at the edges and entrances of the settlement were added to the fortification. Additionally, a ditch secured the more accessible south side of the tell. The fortifications were enlarged, repaired, rebuilt and more elements were added throughout the settlement history.

The Ovčarovo fortified tell settlement was located on a small elevation above a small stream. The settlement mound was 4.5 m high and had a diameter of 60 m (Lichter 1993). Due to the construction of a water reservoir close to the village of Ovčarovo, the site was also fully excavated by Tordorova from 1971-73 (Todorova 1982; 1983). The settlement layers were distinguishable due to the use of wooden fundament plates for the construction of the houses. The rotten wooden remnants, as well as several burning events, were well-visible in the archaeological context. In total, 13 different settlement layers were identified and divided into four different settlement stages (Todorova 1982). The settlement is dated to Poljanica III (layers I-III), Poljanica IV (layers V-VII), KGV VI phase I (layers VIII-X) and KGK VI phases II/III (layers XI-XIII). Settlement layer IV is interpreted as a transition period (Table 2).

The Ovčarovo tell site, in contrast to Poljanica, did not have a quarter-like settlement structure. The density of household construction inside the fortified area was persistently documented throughout most of the settlement stages. During the first half of its occupation, the Ovčarovo tell was characterised by a broad alley, which was documented along the E-W axis. Afterwards, the size of the settlement increased twofold. A series of burning events were observed, marking the final occupation of layers VIII, IX, and X. A big fire in layer X led to the temporal abandonment of the settlement. After a short hiatus, a much smaller settlement was re-established (layer XI), followed by a slightly enlarged settlement (layer XII) both ending with a burning event. Due to erosion and building activity related to the construction of the water reservoir, the youngest layer XIII was disturbed and no settlement plan could be documented.

Phase	n	Minimal house size (m²)	Average house size (m²)	GC	IF	IER
I	6	43.66	46.43	0.022	0.060	0.369
II	8	40.89	80.79	0.221	0.494	0.447
III	9	44.13	71.64	0.214	0.384	0.557
IV	8	54.27	104.64	0.299	0.481	0.621
V	7	17.81	96.31	0.341	0.815	0.418
VI	10	32.94	78.79	0.307	0.582	0.528
VII	10	27.36	81.92	0.275	0.666	0.413
VIII	8	64.19	79.70	0.105	0.195	0.540
IX	9	24.64	61.92	0.273	0.602	0.453
X	8	34.10	73.65	0.166	0.537	0.309
XI	6	23.92	37.01	0.104	0.354	0.294
XII	6	33.35	54.97	0.235	0.393	0.598
XIII			Destroyed			

Table 2. Ovčarovo. Share of house areas, results of the analyses: GC: Gini coefficient, IF: inequality frontier, IER: inequality extraction ratio.

The fortifications of the site included a ditch and one to three palisades. Additionally, layers V and VI showed the presence of a clay/gravel rampart. Moreover, an emplecton wall was found in layer IV. Throughout its history, the fortifications underwent constant changes: similar to Poljanica, they were enlarged, repaired, and rebuilt, while new elements were added.

As mentioned above, living spaces measured from house sizes are frequently used as a proxy in archaeological inequality measurements. Here, this established proxy is used, too. Three values are calculated for each settlement layer: (1) the Gini coefficient, (2) the inequality frontier, and the (3) inequality extraction ratio. For the time being, the following assumptions apply for the area of the study:

▸ The dataset pictures an entire society. Both analysed settlements are fully excavated.

▸ A house represents a household, which is formed by all inhabitants of the building. The analysis is conducted on the household level.

▸ The share of the floor area of a house within the total area of the settlement corresponds directly to the share of the associated household within the societal wealth.

▸ All houses serve the same purposes and there are no significant functional differences between buildings.

▸ The subsistence minimum equals the size of the smallest house of a settlement layer.

▸ The mean house size of a settlement phase equals the average share of wealth.

▸ The share of wealth of a possible elite is of infinitesimal size and therefore not of interest for the calculations.

House sizes have been measured by digitalising the published settlement maps. The house floor area was measured by using Datinf (Available at: https://datinf.de; accessed: 20 July 2021). The house sizes have been assigned to settlement phases and a normalised Gini coefficient, whereas the inequality frontier and the inequality extraction ratio have been calculated for each settlement phase, the latter two by using the formulas from Branko Milanovic *et al.* (2007). Gini coefficients have been calculated and plotted using R (packages ineq and ggplot2: Zeileis and Kleiber 2015; Wickham *et al.* 2021).

At Poljanica, an initial slight decrease of the Gini coefficient between layers I and II is followed by a strong increase of the Gini value from the second to the fifth settlement layer. From the fifth layer onwards, the Gini coefficient moderately decreases until the end of the settlement activity. Looking at the inequality frontier, it can be observed that after an initial decline between layers I and II, the inequality frontier rises strongly between layers III and VI. Towards layer VII, it declines again, but stays on a higher level than in the first three layers. In layer VIII – the last settlement layer – the inequality frontier increases again. The inequality extraction ratio slightly increases over the course of the first three layers. In layers IV to VIII, the inequality extraction ratio falls and rises alternately. In the last settlement layer, the inequality extraction ratio has the lowest value of the total settlement activity on Poljanica, well under the initial inequality extraction ratio. The development of the Gini coefficient of house sizes at Poljanica indicates an increase in inequality between households over time. With a peak in layer V and a slow decline of Gini coefficient towards the end of the settlement activity, this might be interpreted as follows: After a first stable period, the layers I to III, the settlement grew and the number of houses doubled. A possible inflow of wealth might have caused changes in wealth distribution among the inhabitants of Poljanica, resulting in a lower Gini coefficient. Growing inequality might have forced households to move away, resulting in a shrinkage of the settlement towards layer V. It might be possible that households of intermediate wealth moved, which resulted in a further increase of the Gini coefficient. Over the last three settlement layers, the number of houses indicated no bigger changes in settlement and population size. The slowly declining Gini coefficient might be seen as a result of inner-societal dynamics, such as marriage between households that lead to an alignment of wealth. However, this naive interpretation changes when the inequality frontier and the inequality extraction ratio are taken into consideration (Table 1). First of all, the inequality frontier indicates a growing potential of high inequality within the settlement population of Poljanica. Looking at the inequality extraction ratio, it appears that the potential maximum inequality was not exploited. Nevertheless, the extraction of surplus by one or several societal groups remains at a quite stable and moderate level. The impact of the extraction of surplus can be best seen in layers IV and V. It is obvious that population growth needs accessible resources (Milanovic *et al.* 2011). The doubling of the settlement size in layer IV is correlated in time with a decline of the inequality extraction ratio. This means more economic surplus may enable settlement growth. In layer V, this development turns around: a higher share of the surplus is extracted from the society as a whole by individuals, households, or societal groups, which might have led to a reduction of the settlement size.

At Ovčarovo, the results are different: During the first five settlement phases, Gini coefficients constantly rise with a steep increase from layer I to layer II. After decreasing in layer VI and VII, the Gini coefficient drops in layer VIII considerably to the lowest value since the start of the settlement, before rising again in layer IX to roughly the former level. Characterised by a decrease of the Gini coefficients are layers X and XI. The last settlement layer XII again shows a steep increase. The inequality frontier also starts off with a very steep increase from layer I to layer II followed by a decrease to layer III. After a slight increase in layer IV, it reaches its highest value within the settlement's history. The inequality frontier declines again towards layer VI with a slight incline in layer VII. A rapid increase to the lowest value can be observed in layer VIII since the beginning of the settlement. Layers XI to XII are characterised by a general downward trend, while a slight increase is visible from layer XI to XII. Major trends and events can be observed in the course of the inequality extraction ratio development: At the beginning, a period of steady incline from layer I to IV is followed by a sharp decline in layer V. The following layers VI to IX are characterised by stability and only minor ups and downs. The downward trend, already visible in layer IX, continues in layers X to XI, which exhibit the lowest values since the beginning of the settlement. The second major event is a steep incline in layer XII. For the settlement's final layer XII, no data is available due to conservation conditions. With only the Gini coefficient at hand, one would interpret that Ovčarovo starts off as a more egalitarian society with low social inequality represented by a very low Gini coefficient. After establishing the settlement site, social inequality seems to rise and reach its peak in settlement layer V and stays roughly the same until layers VIII. At this point, the level of social inequality seems to drop considerably. The end of the settlement is characterised by a more dynamic development with increases and decreases of social inequality and a steeper rise in the last stage of the inhabitation. This narrative changes, in parts drastically, when the inequality frontier and the inequality extraction ratio are considered. The inequality frontier is constantly way below the settlement maximum value of 0.81, indicating that the values of the Gini coefficient have to be interpreted differently. In settlement layer I, the seemingly low Gini coefficient indicates a rather low level of social inequality, which is also accompanied by a very low inequality frontier. Combined with the inequality extraction ratio, this shows that the existing potential for social inequality was considerably exploited. In short, the social inequality within the starting settlement was higher than the Gini coefficient alone indicates. In general, a clear trend of rising social inequality in the first four phases is observable. While an economic surplus is still available to allow the growth of the settlement, it is increasingly consumed by a certain societal group as indicated by a rising inequality extraction ratio. In layer IV, the inequality extraction ratio shows that the economic surplus was exploited to the highest degree in the settlement's history. This is also reflected in a decline of the settlement size in layers IV to V. This only can be seen through the inequality extraction ratio – it is not reflected in the Gini coefficient. In layer V, the need for the inequality extraction ratio and the calculation of the inequality frontier becomes visible. While the Gini coefficient again suggests a peak of social inequality, the inequality extraction ratio and inequality frontier show a different picture. During this phase, the potential for inequality is the highest in the history of the settlement, but the inequality extraction ratio decreases considerably, indicating that the potential for social inequality was not exploited. While the Gini coefficient alone indicates increasing inequality, the inequality extraction ratio and the inequality frontier exhibit a different pattern of exploitation as compared to the foregoing phases, *i.e.* the economic surplus of the society is less extracted by a certain group. Which social factors led to this decrease of surplus exploitation are unknown. Here, the strength of the inequality extraction ratio and inequality frontier is clearly visible. From layers VII onwards, a series of burning events could be interpreted – taking monocausality to the extreme and excluding other factors for the time being – as the result of societal contradictions. These events could explain the decrease in measurable inequality (as evident in Gini coefficients), settlement size and the exploitation of surplus (the inequality extraction ratio). This development could have led to a hiatus in settlement activity between layers X and XI. Towards the end of the settlement activity in Ovčarovo, layers XI to XII, an increase of the Gini coefficient as well as the extracted surplus (inequality extraction ratio) can be observed. This comparatively steep increase of social inequality ends with the destruction of the settlement in layer XII. In this case, the inequality extraction ratio strengthens the interpretation of rising social inequality as indicated by the Gini coefficient. The increasing Gini coefficient and inequality extraction ratio probably show that a substantial part of the surplus was extracted which may be suspected to have led to social conflict. This may have ultimately resulted in the abandonment sometime after the last burning event.

Between social differentiation and connectivity: Finding a place for social inequalities

The case study shows how social inequality can be successfully measured even for prehistoric times. Economic concepts can be transferred from economics and integrated into archaeology. Such a transition causes slight changes in the meaning from the original context to new archaeological concepts. In the case study, the economic question about measuring a share of modern income or property inspired the archaeological investigation about the share of communal space which is thought to represent a kind of social inequality in itself. A necessary starting point is a clear concept of what can serve as a proxy and where the proxy's restrictions are. The Gini coefficient in combination with the calculation of the inequality frontier and the inequality extraction ratio can be used as powerful tools. In combination with a formal concept of significance levels – not presented here – the tool box allows quantitative assessable and justifiable conclusions to be drawn about wealth distribution in an archaeologically explored population.

One major problem remains unsolved: It is possible to compare archaeological entities (Fig. 7), but exactly where is the position of social inequality within the population?

As emphasised in the beginning, a general social structure in the form of a pyramid is no longer to be expected when non-stratified or hardly stratified societies are studied. Not only if a segmentation – in the sense of Émile Durkheim (1893; cf. Sigrist 2004) – exists, one is compelled to inquire about the very position of social inequalities within society: In the case study here, inequality in the share of communal space could be analysed on the level of households. The household conceptualised as a decision-making agent makes sense in larger parts of ecological and economic archaeology, but also may mask many possible inter- and intra-household inequalities. The total economic performance of a household may be based on its accessibility to natural resources, the labour gathered under its roof, on its connections to exchange partners, or on special services offered by its members. The share of a household's wealth remains crucial: it makes a difference to be the *pater familias* or a slave, even if both are members of the same household.

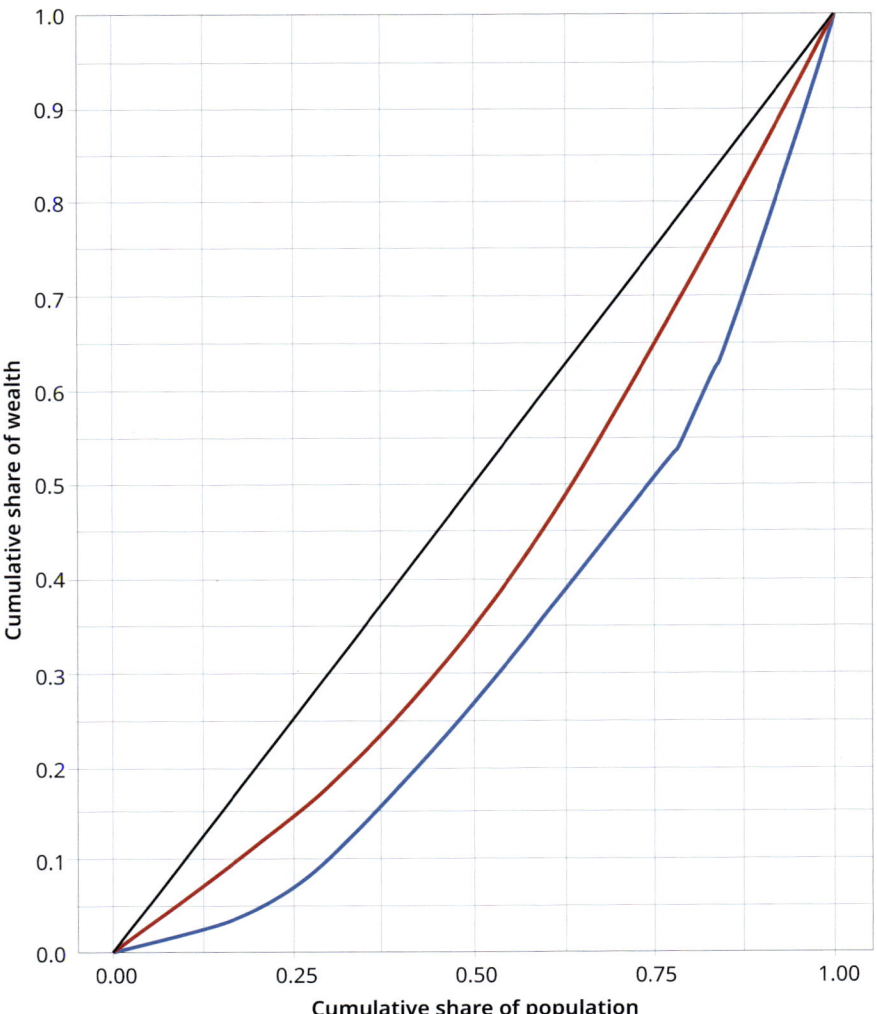

Figure 8. Poljanica. A comparison between two layers using non-intersecting Lorenz curves. Black: line of equality, red: layer I (Gini: 0.2), blue: layer V (Gini: 0.37) (diagram: the authors).

Taking this into account, the relation between social inequality and connectivity (in the strict sense of the definition quoted at the beginning) can never be simple. In the perspective of a single agent, the connectivity of a richer household or a richer individual can be expected to be much higher than the connectivity of a poorer agent – such connectivity is a source of resilience in times of change or crisis where connections become looser or are cut off. Maintaining more ties secures relative economic success even under worsening conditions, whereas those with fewer ties fail. In such a situation, the richer household's share increases just by upholding the previous standard.

Another perspective – taken by most of the ROOTS members in this volume – focuses on intra-group connectivity and on a group's success in relation to connectivity. Again, in predominantly stratified societies, social inequalities between strata may pull the society apart. Therefore, in predominantly stratified societies, low social inequality and high connectivity can be expected to contribute to secure the society's stability. But does this also apply for non-predominantly stratified societies? Within a segmentary society with ranked positions within the segments (in archaeology, *e.g.*, Kurz 2007; 2010), several perspectives on connectivity become possible: not only the individual perspective and the perspective concerning the entire society but also the connectivity between segments and between individuals or sub-groups crossing the segments' borders. It is probably much easier to measure social inequalities in known segmentary societies – *e.g.* on different graveyards or for collective burials belonging to different segments – than to recognise segmentary societies in the archaeological record. It must not be forgotten that ideal-typical constructions, such as that of the segmentary society, probably always exist in reality as mixed forms (Meeker 2004). Identified structural aspects – such as connectivity – must therefore be presented in quantitatively weighted forms, which then can be related to measurements of social inequality. Therefore, measuring social inequalities from archaeological remains first requires qualitative as well as subsequent quantitative studies on societal differentiation – obviously, the question on order or maladaptation was wrongly posed.

Acknowledgements

The preparation of this paper has benefited greatly from the contributions of Johannes Bröcker, who has since passed away. This article is dedicated to his memory. The authors thank Johannes Marzian for additional help with economic questions. Work on this paper was funded by the Deutsche Forschungsgemeinschaft (DFG, German Research Foundation) under Germany´s Excellence Strategy – EXC 2150 – 390870439.

References

Ames, K.M., 1996. Life in the Big House: Household Labor and Dwelling Size on the Northwest Coast. *In:* G. Coupland and E.B. Banning, eds. *People Who Lived in Big Houses: Archaeological Perspectives on Large Domestic Structures.* Monographs in World Archaeology 27. Madison: Prehistory Press, 131-150.

Ames, K.M., 2006. Thinking About Household Archaeology on the Northwest Coast. *In:* E.A. Sobel, D. Ann Trieu Gahr, K.M. Ames, eds. *Household Archaeology on the Northwest Coast.* Archaeological Series 16. International Monographs in Prehistory. Ann Arbor, Michigan: Berghahn Books, 16-36.

Ames, K.M. and Grier, C., 2020. Inequality on the Pacific Northwest Coast of North America Measured by House-Floor Area and Storage Capacity. *Antiquity,* 94 (376), 1042-1059.

Basri, P. and Lawrence, D., 2020. Wealth Inequality in the Ancient Near East: A Preliminary Assessment Using Gini Coefficients and Household Size. *Cambridge Archaeological Journal,* 30 (4), 689-704.

Binford, L.R., 1968. Post Pleistocene adaptations. *In:* S.R. Binford and L.R. Binford, eds. *New perspectives in archaeology.* Chicago: Aldine Publishing Company, 313-342.

Blanton, R.E., 1994. *Houses and Households: A Comparative Study.* New York: Plenum Press.

Blanton, R.E., 1995. The Cultural Foundations of Inequality in Households. *In:* T.D. Price and G.M. Feinman, eds. *Foundations of Social Inequality.* New York: Plenum Press, 105-128.

Byrd, B.F., 2000. Households in Transition. Neolithic Social Organization within Southwest Asia. *In:* I. Kuijt, ed. *Life in Neolithic Farming Communities. Social Organization, Identity, and Differentiation.* New York: Kluwer Academic, 63-102.

Ceriani, L. and Verme, P., 1912. The origins of the Gini index: extracts from Variabilità e Mutabilità (1912) by Corrado Gini. *The Journal of Economic Inequality,* 10, 421-443.

Chayanov, A.V., 1966. The Theory of Peasant Economy. *In:* D. Thorner, B. Kerblay,

R.E.F. Smith, eds. *The American Economic Association Translation Series.* Homewood: Irwin.

Coupland, G. and Banning, E.B., 1996. Introduction: The Archaeology of Big Houses. *In:* G. Coupland and E.B. Banning, eds. *People Who Lived in Big Houses: Archaeological Perspectives on Large Domestic Structures.* Monographs in World Archaeology 27. Madison: Prehistory Press, 1-9.

Curtis, R.F., 1986. Households and Family in Theory on Inequality. *American Sociological Review,* 51, 168-183.

Diehl, M.W., 2000. Some Thoughts on the Study of Hierarchies. *In:* M.W. Diehl, ed. *Hierarchies in Action: Cui Bono?* Center for Archaeological Investigations Occasional Paper 27. Carbondale: Southern Illinois University, 11-30.

Diestel, R., 2016. Graph Theory [online]. 5th Electronic Edition. Available at: https://www.math.uni-hamburg.de/home/diestel/books/graph.theory/preview/Ch3.pdf [Accessed 23 July 2021].

Durkheim, E., 1893. *De la division du travail social.* Paris: Les Presses universitaires de France.

Flannery, K. and Marcus, J., 2012. *The Creation of Inequality: How our Prehistoric Ancestors set the Stage for Monarchy, Slavery and Empire.* Cambridge: Harvard University Press.

Forrest, J.G. and Murie, A., eds., 1995. *Housing and Family Wealth: Comparative International Perspectives.* London: Routledge.

Gini, C., 1912. *Variabilità e Mutabilità. Contributo allo Studio delle Distribuzioni e delle Relazioni Statistiche.* Bologna: C. Cuppini.

Graeber, D., 2017. Foreword to the Routledge Classics Edition. *In:* M. Sahlins, *Stone Age Economics.* 3rd edition. London, New York: Routledge Classics, IX-XIX.

Hammel, E.A., 1984. On the *** of Studying Household Form and Function. *In:* R. McC. Netting, R.R. Wilk, E.J. Arnold, eds. *Households: Comparative and Historical Studies of the Domestic Group.* Berkeley, Los Angeles, London: University of California Press, 29-43.

Henrich, J., 2004. Demography and Cultural Evolution: How Adaptive Cultural Processes can Produce Maladaptive Losses – The Tasmanian Case. *American Antiquity,* 69 (2) April 2004, 197-214.

Kamp, K., 2000. From Village to Tell. Household Ethnoarchaeology in Syria. *Near Eastern Archaeology,* 63 (2), 84-93.

Kohler, T.A. and Smith, M.E., eds., 2018. *Ten thousand years of inequality. The archaeology of wealth differences.* Amerind Studies in Archaeology. Tucson: University of Arizona Press.

Kohler, T.A., Smith, M.E., Bogaard, A., Feinman, G.M., Peterson, Ch.E., Betzenhauser, A., Pailes, M., Stone, E.C., Prentiss, A.M., Dennehy, T.J., Ellyson, L.J., Nicholas, L.M., Faulseit, R.K., Styring, A., Whitlam, J., Fochesato, M., Foor, T.A., Bowles, S., 2017. Greater Post-Neolithic Wealth Disparities in Eurasia than in North and Mesoamerica. *Nature,* 551, 619-623.

Krauß, R. and Schneider, G., 2014. *Ovčarovo-Gorata. Eine frühneolithische Siedlung in Nordostbulgarien.* Archäologie in Eurasien 29. Bonn: Habelt.

Kurz, S., 2007. *Untersuchungen zur Entstehung der Heuneburg in der späten Hallstattzeit.* Forschungen und Berichte zur Vor- und Frühgeschichte in Baden-Württemberg 105. Stuttgart: Theiss.

Kurz, S., 2010. Zur Genese und Entwicklung der Heuneburg in der späten Hallstattzeit. *In:* D. Krausse, ed. *"Fürstensitze" und Zentralorte der frühen Kelten, Abschlusskolloquium des DFG–Schwerpunktprogramms 1171 in Stuttgart, 12.–15. Oktober 2009.*

Forschungen und Berichte zur Vor- und Frühgeschichte in Baden-Württemberg 120. Stuttgart: Theiss, 239-256.

Lichter, C., 1993. *Untersuchungen zu den Bauten des südosteuropäischen Neolithikums und Chalkolithikums.* Internationale Archäologie 18. Buch am Erlbach: Leidorf.

Meeker, M.E., 2004. Magritte on the Bedouins: Ce n'est pas une société segmentaire. *In:* B. Streck, ed. *Segmentation und Komplementarität. Organisatorische, ökonomische und kulturelle Aspekte der Interaktion von Nomaden und Sesshaften. Beiträge der Kolloquia am 25.10.2002 und 27.06.2003.* Orientwissenschaftliche Hefte 14. (Mitteilungen des SFB 'Differenz und Integration" 6). Halle: Orientwiss. Zentrum der Martin-Luther-Univ. Halle-Wittenberg, 33-55.

Milanovic, B., 2013. *The Inequality Possibility Frontier: The Extensions and new Applications.* Comparative Institutional Analysis Working Paper Series. Lund: University Press.

Milanovic, B., Lindert, P.H., Williamson, J.G., 2011. Pre-Industrial Inequalities. *The Economic Journal,* 121, 255-272.

Milanovic, B., Williamson, J.G., Lindert, P.H., 2007. *Measuring ancient inequality.* NBER working paper series working paper 13550. Cambridge, MA: NBER.

Netting, R. McC., 1982. Some Home Truths on Household Size and Wealth. *American Behavioral Scientist,* 25, 641-662.

Pauketat, T.R., 1996. The Foundations of Inequality within a Simulated Shan Community. *Journal of Anthropological Archaeology,* 15, 219-236.

Porčić M., 2012. Social complexity and inequality in the Late Neolithic of the Central Balkans. Reviewing the evidence. *Documenta Praehistorica,* 39, 167-184.

Porčić M., 2019. Evaluating Social Complexity and Inequality in the Balkans between 6500 and 4200 BC. *Journal of Archaeological Research,* 27, 335-390.

Renfrew, C., 1972. *The Emergence of Civilisation: the Cyclades and the Aegean in the Third Millennium BC.* Studies in prehistory. London: Methuen.

Requate, T., 2021a. [Lemma] Measures of Inequality. *In:* Kerig, T., ed. *An ABC of Past Social Inequality* [online], forthcoming.

Requate, T., 2021b. [Lemma] Gini coefficient. *In:* Kerig, T. ed. *An ABC of Past Social Inequality* [online], forthcoming.

Sahlins, M., 2017. *Stone Age Economics.* 3rd edition. London, New York: Routledge Classics.

Scheidel, W., 2017. *The Great Leveler. Violence and the History of Inequality from the Stone Age to the Twenty-First Century.* The Princeton Economic History of the Western World Series. Princeton: Princeton University Press.

Schwinn, T., ed., 2004. *Differenzierung und soziale Ungleichheit – Die zwei Soziologien und ihre Verknüpfung.* Frankfurt am Main: Humanities Online.

Schwinn, T., 2019. *Soziale Ungleichheit in differenzierten Ordnungen – Zur Wechselwirkung zweier Strukturprinzipien.* Tübingen: Mohr Siebeck.

Shennan, S., 2011. Property and wealth inequality as cultural niche construction. *Philosophical Transactions of the Royal Society, B: Biological Sciences,* 366 (1566), 918-926.

Sigrist, C., 2004. Segmentary Societies: The Evolution and Actual Relevance of an Interdisciplinary Conception. *In:* B. Streck, ed. *Segmentation Komplementarität. Organisatorische, ökonomische und kulturelle Aspekte der Interaktion von Nomaden und Sesshaften. Beiträge der Kolloquia am 25.10.2002 und 27.06.2003.* Orientwissenschaftliche Hefte 14. Mitteilungen des SFB "Differenz und Integration" 6. Halle: Orientwiss. Zentrum der Martin-Luther-Univ. Halle-Wittenberg, 3-31.

Smith, M.E., Dennehy, T., Kamp-Whittaker, A., Colon, E., Harkness, R., 2014. Quantitative Measures of Wealth Inequality in Ancient Central Mexican Communities. *Advances in Archaeological Practice*, 2 (4), 311-323.

Therborn, G., 2013. *The Killing Fields of Inequality*. Cambridge: Polity Press.

Todorova, H., 1978. *The Eneolithic period in Bulgaria in the fifth millennium B.C.* BAR International series 49. Oxford: BAR.

Todorova, H., 1982. *Kupferzeitliche Siedlungen in Nordostbulgarien*. Materialien zur allgemeinen und vergleichenden Archäologie 13. München: Verlag C.H. Beck.

Todorova, H., 1983. *Ovčarovo – Razkopi I proučvanija*. Sofia: Archeologičeski Institut i Muzej.

Tönnies, F., 1905. The Present Problems of Social Structure. *The American Journal of Sociology*, 10 März 1905 (5), 569-588.

Turchin, P., 2015. *Ultrasociety: How 10,000 Years of War made Humans the Greatest Cooperators on Earth*. Chaplin: Beresta.

Vaneeckhout, S., 2010. House Societies among Coastal Hunter-Gatherers: A Case Study of Stone Age Ostrobothnia, Finland. *Norwegian Archaeology Review,* 43 (1), 12-25.

White, L.A., 1959. *The Evolution of Culture. The Development of Civilization to the Fall of Rome*. New York: McGraw-Hill.

Wickham, H.W., Chang, L. Henry, T., Lin Pedersen, K., Takahashi, C., Wilke, K., Woo, H., Yutani, D. Dunnington/RStudio, 2021. Package "ggplot2" [online]. Available at: https://cran.r-project.org/web/packages/ggplot2/ggplot2.pdf [Accessed: 22 June 2021].

Wilk, R. and Rathje, W.L., 1982. Household Archaeology. *The American Behavioral Scientist*, 25 (6), 617-639.

Zeileis, A. and Kleiber, C., 2015. Package "ineq." [online]. Available at: https://cran.r-project.org/web/packages/ineq/ineq.pdf [Accessed: 22 June 2021].

Oliver Nakoinz
Institute of Prehistoric and
Protohistoric Archaeology
Kiel University
Johanna-Mestorf-Straße 2-6
24118 Kiel, Germany
oliver.nakoinz@ufg.uni-kiel.de

Anna K. Loy
Cluster of Excellence ROOTS
Kiel University
Olshausenstr. 80h
24118 Kiel, Germany
aloy@roots.uni-kiel.de

Christoph Rinne
Institute of Prehistoric and
Protohistoric Archaeology
Kiel University
Johanna-Mestorf-Straße 2-6
24118 Kiel, Germany
crinne@ufg.uni-kiel.de

Jutta Kneisel
Institute of Prehistoric and
Protohistoric Archaeology
Kiel University
Johanna-Mestorf-Straße 2-6
24118 Kiel, Germany
jutta.kneisel@ufg.uni-kiel.de

Tanja Schreiber
Cluster of Excellence ROOTS
Kiel University
Olshausenstr. 80h
24118 Kiel, Germany
tschreiber@roots.uni-kiel.de

Maria Wunderlich
Institute of Prehistoric and
Protohistoric Archaeology
Kiel University
Johanna-Mestorf-Straße 2-6
24118 Kiel, Germany
m.wunderlich@ufg.uni-kiel.de

Nicole Taylor
Institute of Prehistoric and
Protohistoric Archaeology
Kiel University
Johanna-Mestorf-Straße 2-6
24118 Kiel, Germany
ntaylor@sfb1266.uni-kiel.de

Connectivity and fortifications

Oliver Nakoinz, Anna K. Loy, Christoph Rinne, Jutta Kneisel, Tanja Schreiber, Maria Wunderlich, Nicole Taylor

Abstract

Connectivity is a buzzword used for the description of the change of the current world in the context of globalisation, social media, and digitalisation. Furthermore, connectivity also appears to be a useful concept in order to understand ancient developments. This article clarifies the term 'connectivity' and discusses the two associated facets 'interaction potential' and 'interaction intensity'. In addition, different kinds of connectivity, positive and negative aspects of connectivity, and the relevance of interaction group sizes are discussed. Subsequently, the basic concept of connectivity is applied to fortifications, which appear to have been a certain type of archaeological site with specific influence on connectivity. Finally, connectivity diagrams are proposed as a tool in order to reflect on connectivity and to compare different sites.

Introduction

The current world – a world of globalisation – is usually characterised by fast growing connectivity (*e.g.* Tomlinson 1999). This process started with developments in transport technologies in previous centuries and accelerated considerably in the previous decades due to social media and other forms of digital communication. Although not wrong, this perspective conceals the general role of connectivity, which is a central focus of ROOTS and requires a much more differentiated conceptualisation as well as a diachronic perspective. From this point of view, connectivity is interpreted as a key factor in the performance and the success of communities and individuals in general.

This paper explores the concepts and meanings of connectivity and investigates the relationship between connectivity, conflict and the role of interaction. Afterwards, we apply these ideas to some case studies to obtain a deeper understanding of connectivity in past societies.

Concepts and terminology

Definition of connectivity

At first, we need to define connectivity. Obviously, in the case of connectivity, things are somehow connected or have the ability to be connected. This means that there are at least two meanings of 'connectivity'. For formal definitions of the different kinds of connectivity, the following statements are proposed:

1. Connectivity is a metaphor for phenomena where things are connected in some way.

2. Connectivity is a generalised measure of interaction. In this case, we can distinguish between:

    2.1. Connectivity as a measure of potential interaction. This kind of connectivity refers to the ability to interact with interaction partners. For example, two settlements are connected in this way, if there is a road or pathway between them. Contemporarily, social connectivity of this kind could refer to having a phone number of people, who might help me solve my problems or, more up to date, being part of a social network.

    2.2. Connectivity as a measure of the intensity of interaction. This kind of connectivity refers to actual interactions, which can be measured. Interaction, here, is not only possible but actually occurs to a certain amount. For instance: How many people are travelling on the road? How many phone calls do we have or messages do we exchange?

Our differentiation between two kinds of non-metaphoric connectivity types corresponds with the two aspects of connectivity – the structural aspect (network) and the process aspect (flow) described by Andreas Hepp *et al.* (2006, 47) and refers to a structural research paradigm, on the one hand, and a system-oriented research paradigm on the other. We have to be aware that in different contexts different connectivity terms are used. It is not always clear which term is in use and a certain degree of fuzziness and confusion has to be assumed when applying the term 'connectivity' without a specific definition. This is particularly problematic because the term 'connectivity' seems to link different disciplines and fields of research, but this broad connection is partly superficial due to the usage of two different terms (potential interaction and intensity of interaction) and further obscured by the metaphoric use of the term 'connectivity'. Nonetheless, both kinds of connectivity or even three kinds of connectivity, if we acknowledge the metaphoric term to be an independent one, link different research fields and are even entangled.

Both types of connectivity, the structural and the processual, are tightly linked to the term 'interaction'. Both represent an aspect of interaction and form a perspective on a system or structure of multiple interactions. The one views the chance to interact and the other the degree of actual interaction. In both cases, we need to know what interaction is and which kinds of interaction are addressed within the connectivity definitions. Thus, we turn to the term 'interaction'.

Interaction

While connectivity can be considered a key factor in the performance and the success of communities and individuals, as mentioned before, interaction is considered to be one of the main drivers of cultural, social, economic, and historical processes (Nakoinz 2013b). Interaction is important in archaeology and other disciplines because humans possess a natural desire and need to interact socially (Knappett 2011, 4-6), as many other species do as well. These interactions add another level of reality to mere existence and metabolism. This additional level provides both sound factors of life, including good quality and conditions of life, and a new kind of world perception. This new perception is known as social space, which is a relative space constituted by social action and interaction (Löw 2001).

Social space is the conceptual frame of our behaviour. In contrast to absolute physical space, social space depends on our behaviour, conceptualisation, and perception. Since social space is constituted by social interaction, the latter is the strongest means to change it. In the context of globalisation and connectivity, two spatial transformations are known, both leading to a rescaling of a specific space (Tomlinson 1999; Harvey 1989). The first transformation is the contraction of geographical space caused by developments of transport technology in the previous centuries. The other is the contraction of social space caused by social media in the previous decades. The transformations of both geographical and social space show how different aspects of interaction have severe influences on our behaviour and even more on our perception, which then loops back to the interaction aspect.

The role of interaction, in general, clarifies why this term is a key word in archaeology and why Kristian Kristiansen (2014, fig. 1) places the terms 'interaction' and 'network' in the centre of his theory wheel and considers them as an axis for theorising. But what is interaction? Let us turn to the definition of this key term, which is used in many disciplines.

Georg C. Homans (1950), for instance, understands interaction as common participation in social processes. This is a specific definition focused on social processes. Michael Argyle's (1969, 166) definition: *'interaction is a series of alternating responses'* focusses on the discrete nature of actions in interaction processes. It becomes obvious that there are many available definitions and that it is difficult to agree on one as Joshua D. Englehardt and Michael D. Carrasco (2019) stress. However, we can use a rather simple and formal definition, focussing on the actions and the outcomes of interaction processes (Nakoinz 2013b; Nakoinz *et al.* 2020a), which is perhaps no all-encompassing, general definition of interaction, since it excludes only some aspects, but it serves our purpose in the context of connectivity research. We can define interaction as joint action of at least two interaction partners.

This definition is rather abstract and open to any content. An interaction may be positive, *e.g.,* trade and cooperation, or negative, *e.g.,* violence. An interaction can be physical or just communication. In the case of human interaction partners, communication is always involved, but interaction cannot be reduced to communication. Nonetheless, the communication aspect is important because it defines the nature and perception of the interaction process.

The possible interaction partners also cover a wide range. They can be humans or animals, individuals or groups and even objects if we consider agency. In case of human nature or human-environment interaction, we would need to substitute the action facet in our definition with reaction because a common action of humans and environment is not defined. Our definition is also inappropriate for the interaction between particles as analysed in physics. This fact is acceptable for us because we exclude human-environment and particle-particle interaction from our considerations in the context of connectivity.

Our definition also allows interaction to be an event or a process. Both are possible and, in general, it depends on the scale. Chronologically zoomed into the details, any interaction appears as a process, while zoomed out many interaction processes appear as events. Therefore, it rather depends on the kind of interaction model we are using. But at this point, we return to connectivity and the usage of interaction in the context of connectivity research. From the perspective of interaction intensity, sometimes a simplification of the process to a focus on an event makes sense and the associated decisions depend on the available measures of interaction intensity. From the perspective of an interaction potential, the distinction of an event or process is irrelevant because the potential is neither process nor event, but rather a condition or infrastructure.

Requirements and effects of connectivity

Turning back from interaction to connectivity, which represents a kind of interaction system, we have to give thought to the effects of connectivity. Generally, a positive effect is assumed, but we also have to consider negative ones. We also need to consider the requirements of connectivity and will start with this issue.

Requirements of connectivity

There are three main requirements of connectivity. First, a certain number of individuals (population), who can interact, are required. Second, the distance between the potential interaction partners needs to be small enough to enable interaction (proximity). Third, the interaction partners need to know how to establish and perform connections (knowledge). If one precondition is missing, a system of individuals cannot be connected. The specific thresholds depend on the kind of systems we are looking at and their internal mechanisms.

Connectivity as a precondition

Understood as interaction potential, connectivity is a precondition for actual interaction. If interaction is just not possible, *e.g.,* due to complete isolation, interaction cannot take place. This is a trivial consideration, but if we turn to the understanding of connectivity as intensity of interaction, it becomes interesting. Not only an interaction potential but also actual interaction is required to establish social structures because they are negotiated through communication processes and hence, interaction. Connectivity is even assumed to be a precondition of democracy (Krotz 2006, 25).

Connectivity can also be assumed to be a precondition of culture. Here, we are referring, in particular, to the concept of culture by Klaus Peter Hansen (2003). He states that

> '[c]ulture covers standardisations that are valid in collectives' (Hansen 2003, 39, translated by the authors).

The standardisations are ideas, knowledge and values that people have in common, whereby the collective is the group of people, who shares these standardisations. This culture concept is very useful for archaeology because it solves many issues associated with the traditional interpretation of archaeological cultures (Nakoinz 2013a) and makes the role of interaction for culture rather clear. The standardisations, i.e. the things in common, can only be in common if they are negotiated or transmitted within a certain group of people and hence, cultures are constituted by interaction. Furthermore, culture can be considered a specific kind of connectivity. Collectives are emphasised by their internal connectivity in contrast to other groups of individuals.

In order to underline the full power of this aspect, we should mention some implications of Hansen's culture concept. This kind of culture not only allows multiple memberships in contrast to traditional archaeological cultures but also assumes a very high number of cultures in which individuals participate. This culture concept does not assume crisp spatial borders and even no spatial definition at all. It becomes clear that Hansen's cultures connect society to a full extent with the knowledge, ideas and values of the individuals. Culture in this sense is a concept of mapping the complex relationship of individual-cognitive entities with a polyhierarchy of groups, which complements network approaches (Nakoinz 2017a). In other words, culture maps the connectivity of a society. Obviously, there are also many other things, which require actual interaction.

Connectivity as opportunity

Connectivity opens the door to some completely new objects. These objects emerge with a certain degree of interaction or a certain state of interaction systems. The balance of interests, for instance in the form of trade, requires interaction to be initiated and a certain interaction potential to be implemented.

Collaborative creativity, where ideas are developed in dialogue, requires a sound understanding of each other, of course, as the result of previous communication and actual interaction when ideas are exchanged and assembled. Not every potential interaction partner is a decent partner for such creative processes, so that we can assume a certain critical mass of potential interaction partners or interaction potential to exist. The division of labour, the emergence of political entities, and centrality also can be mentioned as phenomena, which require a certain critical mass.

With these examples, we did not differentiate between interaction potential and interaction intensity. The reason for this is that in the case of connectivity as opportunity, both aspects are tightly entangled. Urbanity may serve as an example to clarify this. First, we need a settlement of a certain size, i.e. population, as the nucleus of urban development. Such a site needs to exceed the critical population threshold, which means that a certain interaction potential is required. Furthermore, a certain degree of actual interaction also has to be exceeded. Then, the emergence of an urban lifestyle with specific practices and rituals can follow and produce new interaction potentials, which in turn trigger new interactions.

Connectivity as a threat

Connectivity also has a dark side. The interaction potential also includes a potential for conflicts, whereby the higher the number of interactions the higher the likeliness of conflicts. Apart from this rather statistical observation, perception and behaviour play an important role in how connectivity works. If we perceive others mainly as a threat, it is likely that our behaviour is not particularly welcoming and that we tend to minimise connectivity (Copland 1996). In this case, interaction potential is read as a threat and interaction intensity might correspond with the amount of conflicts. In contrast, we might perceive others not as a threat and in this case, we tend to increase connectivity. A third solution would be to perceive some people as a threat, while perceiving others rather as support or protection. In this case, we tend to develop a differentiated connectivity landscape by increasing connectivity in our vicinity with rather protective individuals and decreasing connectivity with the outer world comprised of potentially dangerous individuals. Based on these assumptions, we can read the proximity of individuals and settlements as a map of preferred and avoided connectivity and interpret the results in terms of perception.

Another threatening aspect of connectivity is the fact that increasing connectivity leads to increasing complexity. This is a problem because it is difficult to handle complexity. A popular observation, known as Dunbar's number (Dunbar 1993; 2002; 2010), proposes that communities tend not to exceed 150 members, at least communities of primates and groups under certain conditions. Similar size thresholds can be observed for human communities. Thresholds of 175 and 375 members, for instance, are mentioned (Feinman 2011; MacSweeny 2004).

The reason for such thresholds is rooted in a cognitive phenomenon. It is difficult to manage a number of contacts exceeding 150. We might forget agreements, appear not to be able to comply with all demands and have some other issues. This is called scalar stress (Alberti 2014). If such issues emerge, communities become unstable.

In the case of communities, which exceed these size thresholds, measures for complexity reduction take effect. These measures consist of rules, which reduce effective interactions. People who might interact can still say 'hello' but they are not supposed to conclude arrangements. Valid connections are limited to small numbers and ensure that interactions fall below the thresholds. Defining groups or hierarchies are part of such complexity reduction measures (Nakoinz 2017b).

Hence, the aforementioned contraction of space, leading to increasing complexity, requires mechanisms of complexity reduction. In other words, an increase of connectivity has to go hand in hand with complexity reduction and the usually observed geometries of power (Massey 1994). Corresponding social differentiation is a natural side effect, which cannot be avoided although it causes other problems.

At this point, we might ask how the network society (Castells 1996) with a number of members considerably exceeding the size thresholds can function without obvious complexity reduction. The answer is that most of the connections are weak in the sense that they do not require a high management capacity and do not allow dependable agreements.

Connectivity balance

So far, we have seen that connectivity has both negative and positive effects and that it is definitely necessary to balance them. In the case of interaction intensity, we need to find a balance, which allows as much connectivity as possible, but limits it to a size where the drawbacks do not outweigh the advantages. This equilibrium of advantages and disadvantages, *i.e.* the balance of connectivity, depends on certain parameters and is specific for each historical situation.

In the case of the interaction potential, there do not seem to be 'too many opportunities to interact' at a first glance, but too extensive possibilities to interact require increasing time and perhaps even resource-consuming decision processes. Furthermore, the requirement to limit actual interaction can only be met on a structural level. We need structural mechanisms, which restrict possible interaction. These tools need to filter the desired interactions and prevent the other ones. The selection depends on cultural, social and economic factors as well as specific conditions.

Concepts for finding a connectivity balance are essential for societies to be successful. Too much connectivity can cause a collapse of the system and too little connectivity can cause unsuccessfulness in competition between communities.

Urbanity is a reinforcing system of finding a connectivity balance, while democracy requires more determination and activity in doing so. Currently, social media with all its side effects, such as alternative facts, can be understood as a big experiment aiming at finding the balance. Successful as well as unsuccessful examples of increased connectivity in the past might help us reflect on and understand current processes.

Fortifications

Obviously, fortifications can help in reducing unwanted connectivity, but they play, in fact, a more complex role in balancing connectivity. Before we start exploring this role, we have to clarify the meaning of the term 'fortification'. Although many publications concerned with fortifications abstain from providing or even referring to a definition of the term 'fortification', those that do deal with a clarification of the term cover a wide range of different definitions. This is not the place to discuss the term fully, so we just refer to a definition from another paper:

> 'A fortification is an artificially modified place in the landscape. The transformation of this place is suitable to strengthen the place against any kind of threat scaling from human attacks and the action of natural forces to the mere feeling of a threat. The place can scale from a small spot enough for one person up to regions and includes enclosing structures as well as linear structures' (Nakoinz and Loy in print).

This is deliberately a broad definition, which does not make any claims concerning the function of fortifications. We prefer that basic archaeological terms should not be defined using assumed functions and other interpretations, but that they should rather focus on descriptions of the observations. The term 'suitable to strengthen the place' represents such observations and uses the function 'strengthening' not as an assumed function of the defined objects, but in order to deliver an open reference to possible observations. A list, such as ramparts, ditches and dykes, would limit the accepted observations to a certain set. Nonetheless, with this definition we particularly refer to ringforts, hillforts, palisades, fences, linear dykes and ditches, but also accept other, perhaps less frequent kinds of categories.

Linear fortifications

Let us start with considering simple linear fortifications. We could mention the Limes (Schallmayer 2011), the Limes Saxoniae (Auge 2019), the Danevirke (Andersen 2004; Schleswig-Holstein, Germany), the Olgerdiget (Neumann 1982; Dyddanmark, Denmark), the Leese (Hegewisch 2012; Lower Saxony, Germany), and the linear pit zone fortifications, the so-called Hulbælter (Eriksen and Rindel 2018), in Denmark. These lines delimit two areas from each other and usually face towards one side. The first effect of such fortifications is to symbolise power and the ability to defend oneself and, hence, to frighten off potential enemies. This effect decreases interaction intensity. The next effect is to provide the defending party with an advantage. In this case, the actual interaction is influenced, but not the intensity of the violent conflict at the frontier. The outcome of the interaction event or process is influenced. The fortification reduces the likeliness of having unwanted interaction after the battle at the frontier to some degree, for instance, plundering and enslaving the defending party by spatially focussing the interaction at the border. Furthermore, this effect directs the border crossing movements to a corridor or passageway and represents an additional movement friction. Thus, the second effect rather influences the interaction potential.

For a full evaluation of the connectivity-related effects of linear fortifications, we need to step back and take a more abstract perspective. The lines in the landscape, representing borders (Paasi 1998) and establishing territories (Van-Valkenburgh and Osborne 2013), are connected with some interesting phenomena (see also Kneisel *et al.* in print). First, they can be considered spatial structures, which serve to support, if not create, social facts (Löw 2001; Werlen 2008). The social border, existing or imagined, between two groups of people is mapped by a spatial border, which in turn supports or legitimates the social border. The spatial border is associated with certain practices, *e.g.,* preventing certain people from crossing the border, verifying the identity of people intending to cross the border, and patrolling along the border. These practices, in fact, reproduce the assumed or pre-existing social borders. These practices change both the landscape of interaction potentials and the actual interaction intensity.

Such borders also establish territories. These territories lead to a new perception of space. The areas inside the territories are perceived as rather homogeneous areas, which in turn highlight the borders. This phenomenon is called the 'purification of space' (Sibley 1988). The borders can be completely artificial or random, but as soon as the territories are defined, we tend to perceive internal homogeneity and external heterogeneity. Different communities might perceive different features characterising the territories. Since different groups can have different imaginations, desires and cognitive maps, the perception of social and spatial organisation can be completely different, creating new conflict potentials. The phenomenon of the territorial trap (Agnew 1994) describes that once territories are defined we cannot turn back time and act as if they never existed. It is clear that the purification of space is the reason for this strange effect, but the territorial trap goes further. It does not only assume a certain persistence of territories but also accounts for the partly irrational political behaviour, which is connected with the idea of territories. Territorial traps and the purification of space, in particular, change interaction potentials considerably.

The purification of space also leads us to another phenomenon. Borders and territories provide us with a much simpler model of reality than some others. We just need to consider the two sides of the border, and we begin to identify 'good' and 'bad' people just by considering their position in relation to the border. Even if this description is oversimplified, it makes clear how much simpler the world looks after establishing borders and territories. These elements of spatial organisation lead to a considerable reduction of complexity. A complex world, as discussed in the context of Dunbar's number, requires time-consuming and complicated, even knowledge-demanding decision processes and, hence, complexity reduction is usually warmly welcomed. Since the effort of making decent decisions grows exponentially with the population, these complexity reduction effects are thus roughly correlated with the population. We have to be aware that the mechanisms of complexity reduction sometimes produce oversimplifications and, hence, wrong decisions. All the same, they also simplify the complex world of interaction potentials and potentially change connectivity.

Finally, we should also address the circumstance that the collective effort of building a fortification and facing a real or imagined enemy forms or strengthens a collective identity. It is obvious that this collective identity or imagined community (Anderson 1993) modifies the interaction potential and thus strengthens internal connectivity.

Circular fortifications

Nearly all aspects of linear fortifications can be applied to circular and semi-circular ones also. There are three differences. First, in the case of a circular fortification, the 'in front' of and 'behind' become inside and outside. Second, these fortifications, hillforts, *etc.*, are sometimes nested or are comprised of a more or less complicated combination of different parts. Third, while linear fortifications usually represent a kind of frontier or border, the circular ones serve multiple purposes. Now, we will consider the specific aspects of some of these fortifications and we start with small, fortified refuges (German: *Fluchtburgen*). For such a place, we do not discuss if the interpretation is right, we just assume that such fortifications exist without traces of permanent usage and that they might have existed at rather hidden locations. Such a hidden location is, in fact, the point that we need to discuss here. This feature reduces the interaction potential very effectively. Complete communities disappear for a while for people without knowledge of the local topography. For this time, inter-community interaction is very unlikely because the probability of the spatio-temporal coincidence of the presence of both communities is rather low. Obviously, this solution is used, when (a) violent conflict escalations are assumed, (b) de-escalation strategies are unknown or unlikely to work and (c) it is assumed that the costs of further escalation and of fighting back are not acceptable, be it fearing complete defeat or just a painful number of victims. In some cases, it is assumed that people from some or many open villages move to the fortified place. In this case, an increase of the internal community interaction potential is likely. This has a positive and a negative aspect. The positive aspect is the chance to support each other in light of practical problems or as violent conflicts increase. The negative aspect is the chance of disagreeing with others and the chance of increasing internal conflicts. In any case, internal community interaction intensity increases. The increased interaction intensity creates a potential of unifying or splitting the community, of forming one or multiple collective identities.

Let us move to permanent community centres of a small scale such as the Öland fortresses of the Roman Iron Age (Edgren and Herschend 1999; Herschend 2009; Öland, Sweden) or rather large-scale fortresses such as the *oppida* of the late Pre-Roman Iron Age (Collis 1984). At least for the *oppida*, written sources confirm the political nature of the sites. Here, we have already mentioned the creation or support of one or multiple collective identities, but on a different level and with sites such as Bibracte (Bourgogne-Franche-Comté, France), as meeting places for multiple tribes (Goudineau and Peyre 1993) and communities on a spatial range which exceeds the hinterland or territory. The important point is that such sites provide an opportunity for very effective and efficient meetings and hence of a very substantial increase of the interaction potential on a community level. The increased interaction potential and, in fact, increased interaction intensity on the personal level as well, could be considered side effects. However, perhaps these 'side effects' are part of the explanation why and how political centres work. It would be worth exploring the interrelations of personal and community level interactions in such cases.

Ritual centres with sacrificial pits, such as Lossow (Beilke-Voigt 2014; Brandenburg, Germany), the fortified cemetery Odensala, Prästgård (Olausson 1995; Uppland, Sweden), or Cuxhaven-Duhnen (Mennenga 2019; Lower Saxony, Germany), all from the Bronze Age, have a focus on group interaction and the formation of identities in a similar way as community centres or political centres. The group size of such centres may vary, and rites and practices form specific mechanisms to organise and canalise interaction. They shape a connectivity pattern, which can complement or support the political structures.

Trading centres, such as Hedeby from the Viking Age (Jankuhn 1986; Schleswig-Holstein, Germany), have the main purpose of creating a space of increased interaction potential. In contrast to political centres, the focus is rather on small interaction groups since trade is mainly done between individuals or small groups and, in particular, on economic transactions between two people.

A particular kind of centre is represented by the so-called Trelleborgen, a set of circular fortifications from 10th century Denmark CE (Roesdahl 1977; Runge 2018). While many interpretations have been proposed, their connections to royal power seem to be common sense. The interpretation of the Trelleborgen as military training camps or boot camps is especially associated with connectivity. Certain people were concentrated at these sites and trained to go on raids to England. Here, we find a highly increased, internal interaction intensity of a medium-sized group, which serves the main purpose of increasing the external connectivity potential. As a side effect, the interaction of the 'inhabitants' with their original communities might have been reduced for a while.

With these different kinds of specialised centres, we touch on the phenomenon of centrality. Centrality intensity can be defined as a relative concentration of interaction and central places, hence as places of high relative interaction node density (Nakoinz 2019, 53-56). From the perspective of connectivity research, a central place is a place with a relative concentration of interaction potential (= interaction node density), which leads to an increased interaction intensity. This definition does claim specific structures, which implement the concentration of interaction such as that of Christaller's models (Christaller 1933) or network centrality (Koschützki *et al.* 2005). What we gain from Christaller is the term 'relative', which is very important and refers to the fact that centrality is not just a lot of people (potential interaction nodes) but also a certain surplus of interaction, which emerges and is above the interaction intensity predicted by the population. Therefore, centrality is a phenomenon, which works on the basis of connectivity that is higher than we would assume based on the population or the size of a place. On the first page of this contribution, we claimed that connectivity is an important factor of success and centrality points straight in this direction by enabling increased connectivity.

The frequent and uncritical usage of the term 'centrality' somehow hides the fact that it has different dimensions and hence, can be described as a centrality vector rather than a centrality value (Nakoinz 2019, 56). This centrality vector is comprised of the dimension's intensity, reach, hierarchy levels and interaction control. We already discussed intensity. The reach dimension refers to the spatial extent of the organisation structure and network of the interaction contacts and directly refers to the spatial component of connectivity. The number of hierarchy levels refers to the structure, which constrains the interaction potential. In fact, hierarchies define certain access points for each member so that not all possible connections are allowed and thus need not to be considered. In the framework of centrality research, this leads to an optimised system and, in the case of Christaller, to a minimisation of transport costs and in the framework of complexity research to a reduction of complexity. The connectivity concept bridges these research concepts. Finally, interaction control also constrains the interaction potential. This is concerned with the question of how interaction can be canalised by concentrating interaction at certain sites or transport routes. This can be perceived as gaining synergies or as reducing complexity. The centrality vector highlights the fact that centrality concentrates and increases connectivity, but not at any cost. Centrality can be interpreted as a mechanism of balancing connectivity.

Connected fortifications

We also need to address the phenomenon of connected fortifications (Beilke-Voigt and Nakoinz 2017). The term 'connected fortifications' is chosen because a specific kind of connectivity plays a central role for these sites. We can define that

> '[c]onnected fortifications are two or more fortifications, which refer or are related to each other in some way' (Nakoinz and Loy in print).

The kind of relationship is not defined. They can oppose or complement each other. An indicator for a strong connection is the fact that one fortification cannot fulfil its purpose to a full extent without the other(s).

We can distinguish three major classes of fortifications: (a) directly opposing ones such as counter-castles, (b) fortification chains securing a border or similar line, and (c) complementary fortifications such as poly-centres. We will start our discussion with the directly opposing fortifications and use the example of a pair of counter-castles (Nowakowski 2017). The main purpose of these fortifications is to stand against each other. They create an interaction potential just because of their military presence at a short distance from each other, which constitutes a pure threat. The interaction intensity has two main levels. First, a continuous interaction by permanently maintaining the communication process with the castle as a strong symbol. In addition to the permanent semiotic interaction, occasional assaults or attacks may occur. These processes involve the permanent garrison of both sides but can also involve reinforcement troops. Thus, the group size of the two interaction partners is usually rather symmetrical but occasionally asymmetric events may occur. The asymmetric case is rather the standard with siege castles, which usually are supported by additional troops.

Lines or chains of fortifications are comprised of fortifications with the same function for one side of the assumed conflict partners. The chain of fortifications is intended to secure a certain line by providing a control point, troop base or stronghold at certain distances. The Limes castles can be mentioned as a well-known example. Fortifications lining along borders have a similar effect as linear fortifications. The difference is particularly the clusters of people of the garrison, which form interaction groups primarily placed at a fixed location that carry out the specific interactions between the forts. The kind of communication between the sites, which is an important feature of fortification lines, is the increase of a very specific interaction potential leading to the occurrence of a very targeted interaction intensity. The interaction intensity can vary between contact in case of attacks and permanent communication and even movement. The Maginot Line (Grand Est, France), which includes supply and communication tunnels/tubes, is an example for rather intensive interaction. In prehistory, we rather assume less intense communication. To verify fortification lines and similar fortification geometries for this period is rather challenging, as the discussion of a possible fortification system in the Eifel (Rhineland Palatinate, Germany) shows (Koch 1988). While we usually assume that all sites of a fortification line belong to one political unit – whatever this might be in a certain period – fortifications securing trade routes also are lined up along a line, but are more likely to belong to different political units (e.g. Early Bronze Age fortified settlements in East Central Europe, Kneisel et al. in print). In this case, the communication between the sites that is organised by the crew of the fortifications is perhaps less intense than the communication initiated by the travelling merchants, which decreases the effect of the fortification line to act as one 'organism'. This reduced effectiveness applies for certain situations only, e.g., for situations of a concerted attack. Everyday effectiveness can be judged rather high, in particular, if we also consider the function of linear fortifications as a customs office.

Finally, complementary fortifications should be mentioned. In this case, the sites fulfil different functions and contribute to the functionality of the whole. Sanctuaries are just one example. From different case studies, it is known that sanctuaries are sometimes located rather at the border than at the centre of a territory (Polignac 1995). In the case of the Bronze Age fortifications of Lossow and Lebus (Beilke-Voigt 2017; both Brandenburg, Germany), it is likely that they represented a sanctuary or some type of ritual place at two entrances to a common territory (Nakoinz 2017c). Two medieval castles, Oldenburg and Möweninsel (Nakoinz 2005; both Schleswig-Holstein, Germany), located at the two ends of the then extremely intensively used waterway of the Schlei, also complemented each other as a customs office to collect toll and to secure the waterway in different contexts. Such complementary fortifications control access to specific functions and hence, canalise interactions. This is perhaps done by applying specific practices at certain key locations. Success of these practices then increases the interaction potential for specific interaction partners. This process focusses the actual interaction at the key locations and canalises any other interaction.

Urbanity

Literature provides many definitions of urbanity. Some definitions that are based on feature lists include a fortification as one of the features of an urban place (Irsigler 2010). There are many more approaches to define urbanity, *e.g.,* simple quantitative approaches using size or density thresholds, functional approaches referring to economic functions, structural approaches making use of aspects such as centrality, qualitative approaches pointing to a specific urban lifestyle, and system approaches understanding urbanity as a complex system (Nakoinz 2017b). Most of these concepts fail to cover all aspects of urbanity and appear to be too inflexible to map a highly dynamic phenomenon such as urbanity. However, the system approach seems to be a decent starting point because it is the most flexible approach. Urbanity, being rather a process than a feature or status of a place, can be defined as the search for opportunities and the attempt to cope with highly connected and unpredictable environments (Nakoinz *et al.* 2020b).

We already acknowledged that connectivity can be understood as both opportunities and threats. In the case of urban places, as for some fortified places, connectivity offers opportunities by enabling trade, the distribution of labour and by offering an environment of creativity and the free exchange of ideas. Threats include exceeding a size larger than the community size threshold, which influences complexity reduction mechanisms at work, but also the challenge caused by the specific requirements of knowledge of the specific urban environments. Opportunities can be understood as centripetal forces, while threats represent centrifugal forces. People are attracted and rejected by urban places at the same time and it is important to find a balance. Otherwise, urban places collapse or stagnate.

The urban process is a somehow self-reinforcing system that guarantees the balance at large, as the extraordinary large number of successful cities and towns testifies. The urban process starts with an increased interaction potential, which enables actual interaction and attracts people. This growth increases the interaction potential further, but complexity also increases at the same time. Hierarchies, groups, sub-communities, rules, rituals, and specific practices are developed step by step and also ensure the limitation and canalisation of interaction and the attraction of people. Which rural person would not be attracted by the urban opportunities and practices on a Saturday night or even by the religious rituals on a Sunday morning? The urban process is two-sided. On the one hand, it decreases interaction intensity by limiting specific interaction potentials and, on the other hand, it increases the general interaction opportunities. At a first glance, a city is open to all newcomers and offers all kinds of interaction opportunities. However, even superficial urban experiences make it clear that there are many opportunities, but that there are even more limitations. Access to certain individuals, communities and many kinds of interaction is limited by certain rituals and practices.

Knowledge about how to find and use interaction opportunities, on the one hand, and to focus on beneficial interaction and reject the less useful interaction attempts and temptations, on the other, becomes a central competence in the urban jungle. We need to know how to recognise helpful interaction opportunities and how to act as interaction partners in certain situations. We need to know the different roles of interaction partners and the behaviour rules for successful transactions. Furthermore, we need to recognise the risks and perils of the buffet of interaction opportunities.

Urban life can be interpreted as a semiotic puzzle for which we have to know the encoding of the messages of different communities and different contexts. The semiotic dimension is tightly intertwined with the aspect of perception and visibility. How are organisational structures, individual roles, and ambitions indicated in the urban information overload? How are certain practices and behaviour rules associated with certain roles, contexts and institutions? The anecdotes about the inappropriate behaviour of rural people in urban contexts are numerous and very telling about the extent, importance and power of urban knowledge. A lack of urban knowledge leads to exclusion and the deception of persons without such knowledge as well as a substantial limitation of the interaction potential. Urban life in the field of tension of sprawling possibilities and restrictive limitations has to be learned.

In particular, knowledge is important in the social context. Social interactions in urban environments are multifaceted and heterogeneous because each individual plays numerous roles with different statuses. The question of power is double-sided. On the one hand, the adaptation of the dynamic urban system is unlikely to be successful with total and absolute power, which explains the strong role of citizens in urban contexts. On the other hand, the need to apply complexity reduction mechanisms, such as hierarchies and sub-communities, simplifies the gain of power for some key persons. The size of groups involved in interaction processes and events, scaled between pairs of interaction partners and extremely large groups, is an organisational challenge but also an opportunity to implement political ideas very fast because the entire population is involved as well as each sub-community with a focus on specific aspects. The sub-communities overlap and are tightly interlinked. This model represents a highly dynamic, quick responding and complex system with the ability of self-recreation and the emergence of previously unseen phenomena.

Although a certain degree of central control can be assumed in most cases, the urban system appears to be a self-organising network, which adapts the different interaction opportunities and restrictions to each other and to the whole. This appears to be the self-reinforcing factor of urbanity and is the reason why most definitions of urbanity are insufficient. Each site develops a specific path-dependant urban profile. Some profiles might be similar but each is nonetheless unique and is comprised of a specific set of practices, institutions and symbols.

Now, we can modify the above given definition. Urbanity is a process of finding the balance between centripetal and centrifugal forces of connectivity. This process consists of specific practices and structures ensuring a dynamic development. Urbanity appears to be a prime example of multiple facets of connectivity and of the immense influence of connectivity on our lives.

Site location

With urbanity, we addressed an important facet and an extraordinary meaningful example of connectivity. While the intersection of fortified and urban places includes some very important sites, urbanity is a more general aspect and cannot be limited to fortifications. This is even truer for the last aspect to be discussed: site location. In the context of connectivity, site location is mainly concerned with other sites and we are interested in factors influencing the interaction between sites. According to Tobler's first law of geography, distance is an important parameter:

'Everything is related to everything else, but near things are more related than distant things' (Tobler 1970).

This means that interaction becomes less likely and intense with a growing distance between the interaction partners. Hence, distance is a factor of the interaction potential. In other words, settlement patterns with short distances between the sites have a higher interaction potential than settlement patterns with long distances.

The mathematical field of research dedicated to this kind of question is called point pattern analysis (Baddeley *et al.* 2016). The relationship of a point to other points belongs to the category of second order effects. While many second order point processes are known in point pattern analysis, there are only three major classes: random point processes, clustered point processes and regular point processes. Random point processes do not consider other points and hence are in fact no proper second order effects. However, they play a central role in point pattern analysis because testing if a random point process is given allows one to conclude the existence of proper second order effects. If a random process is likely, we cannot assume second order effects and the relevance of other points for the location of new points. If random processes are not likely, the relevance of other points can be assumed and interaction between the sites seems to be important. In this case, we can distinguish between regular and clustered point processes.

The distance between the sites is used not only for testing random point processes but also for differentiation between the other two categories. Clustered point processes show smaller average distances to the nearest other point (nearest neighbour) than random point processes and in case of regular points, the distance is larger. Hence, we assume the prevention of interaction for regular point patterns and the search for interaction in the case of clustered point patterns. Before we continue with considerations of the interpretation of point patterns and point processes, a short introduction to methods used in point pattern analysis is presented.

The methods to test complete spatial randomness are based on the idea that specific point pattern types possess specific distances between the points (Knitter and Nakoinz 2018; Nakoinz and Knitter 2016). The G-function is an accumulative function of nearest neighbour distances, which counts the number of distances to other points up to a certain threshold. The result is mapped with a graph where the x-axis represents the threshold and the y-axis the number of cases. A large number of small distances leads to high y-values for small x-values. For random processes in a certain area, a theoretical G-curve can be calculated. If the empirical curve fits the theoretical curve, a random process is assumed. But how good must the fit be to assume random processes? In practice, using Monte-Carlo simulations of random processes and looking if the empirical curve is covered by the area of the simulations is much more suitable and even applicable for complicated point processes. The F-function works in the same way. The difference is that the F-function does not use nearest neighbour distances, but rather the distances from the points of the provided data to the nearest point of a set of random points. This results in a different interpretation of the curves because now, disproportionately many short distances indicate a regular distribution. The chance to capture a random point within a certain distance is higher from a regular than from a clustered point pattern. The advantage of the F-function is that the focus is switched from the clusters of data to the empty areas in between and hence, the F-function is also called empty space function. The K-function, also known as Ripley's K, works like the G-function with distances between the data points, but it is not restricted to the nearest neighbours. The different functions are sensitive for different aspects of the point pattern and complement each other. All these functions are only concerned with second order effects. If a cluster is produced by favourable soil in a certain area and not by attraction to other sites, it still appears as a cluster. Second order point pattern analyses need either to exclude all first order effects, such as soil preferences, or to include them into the point processes.

The interpretation of the point pattern analysis is guided by the idea of physical interaction. The attraction of points to each other leads to clusters, while rejections produce regular point patterns. This also works in a social context and as said before, clusters of settlements can be perceived as the vicinity of either supporting people or of threatening people. If we trust the other people in our surroundings, we tend towards the first interpretation and we are happy with the cluster. In this case, we prefer small distances and high interaction potentials within our community. But there are some contradicting effects. First, the community size threshold sets limits to the clustering and second, the requirements of space, for example, for agriculture also limit the clustering effect. The other perception, in which we distrust other people, leads to a preference for long distances, rather regular point patterns and a small interaction potential. We try to stay separate from other people and avoid any unnecessary interaction, which might be dangerous. Processes, which require interaction or intervention such as a division of labour, support in the case of catastrophes, or gene mixture for completely isolated groups, set a limit to this solution.

Moving from a focus on community internal interaction to external interaction, things might change. Even if we distrust our own people up to a certain degree, they might be a certain support against external threats. The bigger our own community, the more difficult it is for others to defeat us. In this case, clusters appear to be a certain protection against external forces and offer a high interaction potential, which needs not to be used in practice. Mistrust and fear can lead to low interaction intensity in settlement clusters, although providing a high interaction potential. In this case, clusters provide the potential of a very specific interaction against external forces. External threats can also lead to a different result, even in cases of high internal attraction and trust. For example, if we assume not to be able to withstand the enemy and that a dispersed distribution makes it more difficult for the enemy to defeat us due to a lack of local knowledge and guerrilla tactics, a regular point pattern with a small interaction potential might be the right choice.

Now it is obvious that the interpretation is not as straight forward as the mathematical approaches might suggest and that perceptions about security issues are a dominant factor of settlement patterns. Each point pattern represents a specific balance between attracting and rejecting forces, but the internal mechanisms also need to be considered. Point pattern analyses are still a very promising approach for connectivity research.

Visualising connectivity: Connectivity graphs

Description of connectivity graphs

Thus far, we discussed many aspects of connectivity in general and specific aspects of the connectivity of fortifications. It appears that this topic is rather complicated and a certain simplification would be very helpful as a starting point for further discussions. We would like to conclude this article with the proposal of a visual connectivity model, which we denote as a connectivity graph. This semi-quantitative visualisation bundles and simplifies many of the aspects we have discussed before. Although these graphs cannot cover all aspects and information, they provide the opportunity to communicate diverse information and to reflect on what information is provided, what information is not supplied and if the simplifications are adequate for certain purposes. These connectivity graphs are not intended to perfectly describe connectivity for certain case studies, but to communicate some important aspects.

A connectivity graph consists of two halves centred at a red vertical line. The left side is dedicated to the interaction potential, while the right one is dedicated to the interaction intensity. The x-axis is a logarithmic scale of the size of interacting groups with zero in the centre and growth in both directions. The y-axis maps the change of connectivity ranging between 0 = no change, 1 = small change, 2 = medium change and 3 = substantial change. Positive values indicate an increase of connectivity, while negative values indicate a decrease.

In this frame, points and areas are plotted. The areas represent the assumed range of connectivity change induced by a certain site. Blue areas refer to group internal interaction, while red areas refer to external interaction. The points indicate certain events such as the foundation of a site or certain modifications. The grey value indicates if the effect is a primary one (black) or secondary ones (grey shades). The secondary effects are side effects of some kind as discussed above.

Usually, the community size is guessed rather than measured and the same goes for the connectivity change. Optimal case studies may enable the involvement of measures of network connectivity and the degree of interaction.

Examples of connectivity graphs

Some examples, shown here as four different selected sites (Fig. 1), illustrate the proposed connectivity graphs without going into details.

The diagrams show the relative connectivity difference caused by the sites and the assumed practice of using them. Zero values indicate that the sites cause no difference in connectivity. The Olgerdiget (Neumann 1982; Ethelberg et al. 2003), a linear rampart in Jutland with a palisade on top from the Roman Iron Age, is the first example (Fig. 2.1). The deterrence of potential attackers decreases the external interaction potential and intensity. The decrease is particularly high for the interaction potential of big groups, respectively, the entire communities of the territories of both sides. The corresponding values for interaction intensity are much smaller because even without a linear fortification, the actual interaction can be assumed to be a realisation of just a small part of the interaction potential. For small groups or pairwise interaction, the effect is also much smaller because the deterrence is partly compensated for or even overcompensated by the control mechanisms at the border. Internal interaction is mainly increased by

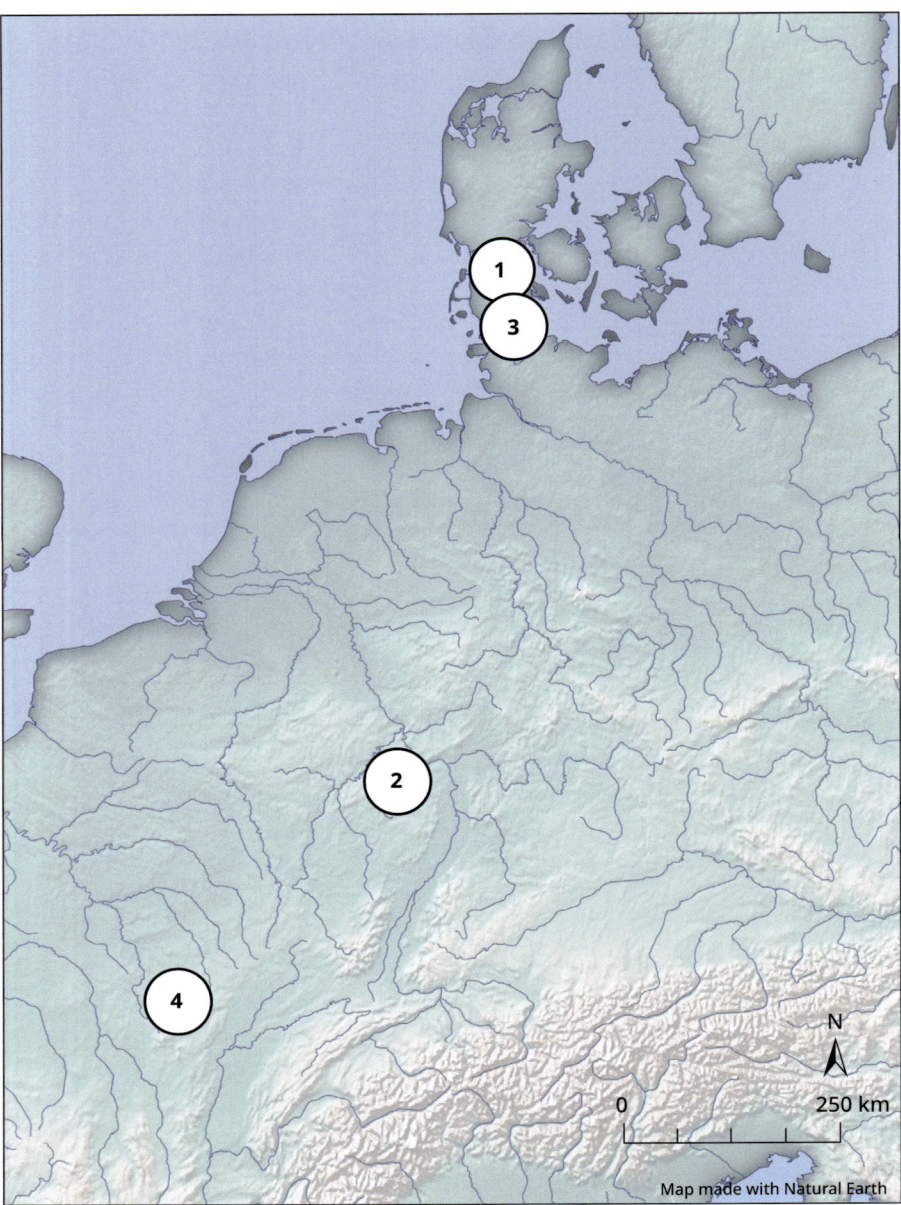

Figure 1. Selected sites. 1: Olgerdiget, 2: Bundenbach, 3: Hedeby and 4: Bibracte (map: the authors; source: map made with Natural Earth).

strengthening the collective identities, which effects small groups but big groups even more. Collective identities are imagined communities and, hence, particularly increase the interaction potential, which entails a certain but moderate interaction intensity. The impact on interaction intensity depends on specific historical situations and political contexts.

The next example is the small Latène hillfort Bundenbach from Hunsrück (Rhineland Palatinate, Germany) (Schindler 1977; Fig. 2.2). The hillfort belongs to a group of fortifications, which are contemporaneous with the well-known *oppida*, but the hillforts are much smaller and rather represent village sites than protourban or urban sites. The Bundenbach site was excavated completely in the 1970s, which makes it an outstanding monument. We focus on the middle period, which corresponds roughly with Latène C. The main function of such a site is to secure the settlement inside the ramparts, causing both a reduction of external interaction potential and interaction intensity. The effects on internal connec-

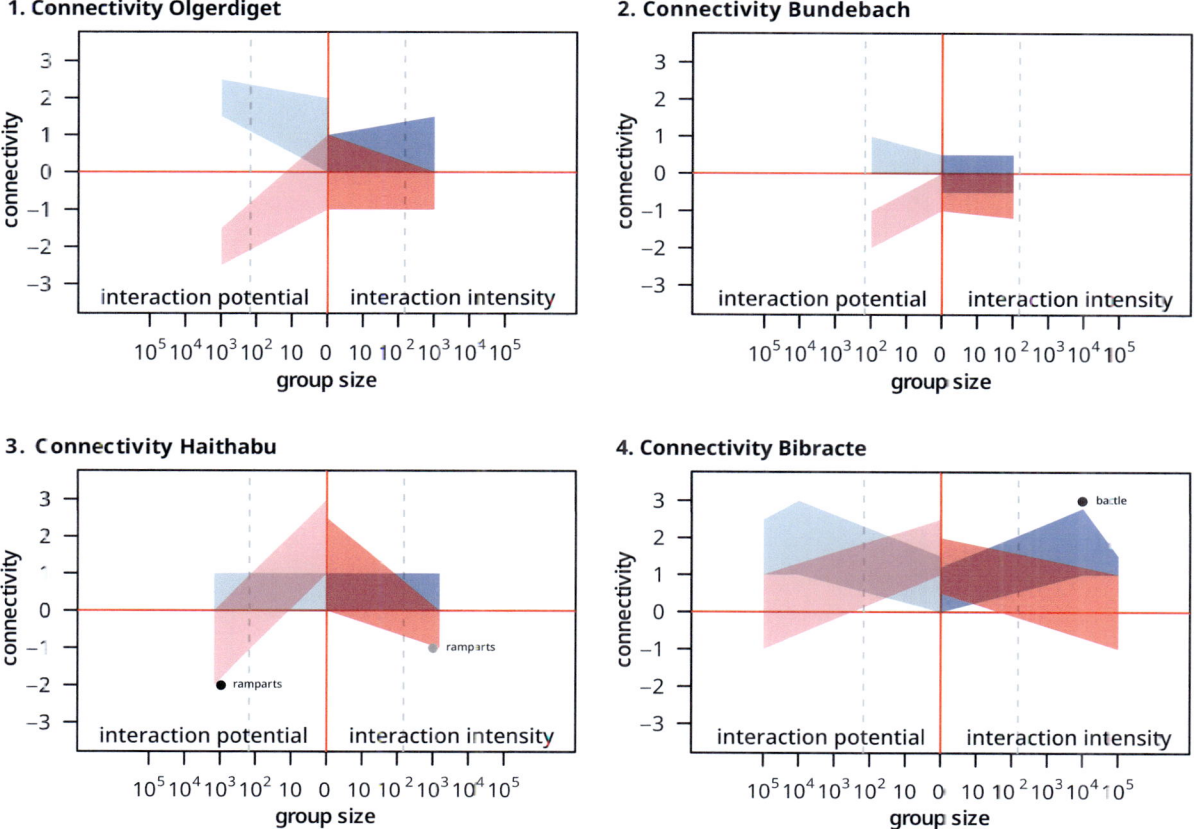

Figure 2. Connectivity graphs of selected sites (graphs: O. Nakoinz).

tivity are very moderate. A minimal unifying effect by building the fortification increases the internal interaction potential slightly. This assertion is backed up by the fact that the site is assumed to be an ordinary village furnished with ramparts.

Now, we turn to Hedeby, a multi-ethnic Viking Age trading centre located at the southern border of the Danish empire and the southern shore of the narrow Schlei Fjord (Jankuhn 1986; Fig. 2.3). The settlement emerged in the 8th century CE and it was furnished with ramparts in the 10th century. The site was abandoned in the 12th century in favour of Schleswig (Schleswig-Holstein, Germany), just at the northern shore of the Schlei Fjord. We have to be aware that not the complete effect described in the connectivity diagram can be attributed to the fortification and we have to admit that the ramparts have, in fact, a rather minor connectivity impact. For our diagram, we focus on the time around 1000 CE.

The internal interaction potential is slightly increased by trade and community formation, but the effect on the external interaction potential is rather substantial because we have to assume that most trade is done with small groups of external people and the ramparts still have a deterrence effect on troops. The effect on the interaction intensity side is similar but less pronounced because just a certain part of the interaction potential is turned into actual interaction. The primary effect of ramparts is the reduction of the interaction potential for possible external attackers, which is marked as a point in the diagram. This also causes a reduced interaction intensity, marked by a grey point.

Bibracte, an oppidum from the late Latène period, is not only well-known from archaeological excavations of the 19th century but also from Caesar's *De bello Gallico* (Goudineau and Peyre 1993, fig. 2.4). Bibracte was the political centre, *i.e.*

the capital of the Gaulish tribe of the Aedui. Bibracte has the same connectivity effects as the other sites, such as deterrence, but the outstanding feature is its function as a political centre, which causes a substantial increase of internal interaction potential and even intensity. Concerning the internal interaction intensity, we should consider that, in particular, the opportunities for tribe meetings are perhaps less frequent than possible. In addition, we plot the event of the Battle of Bibracte from 58 BC, which was a substantial increase of actual interaction intensity.

Conclusion

Combining the topic of connectivity and fortifications has many advantages. Most fortifications are rather substantial monuments in and of themselves, still existing in the landscapes known in archaeological records. Hence, we obtain a rather complete picture of this particular site category, which is a circumstance that enables founded interpretations that are much better than less complete site categories. In contrast to simple settlements, fortifications represent a rather complex site category, which makes them a diverse and powerful indicator of social, economic and historical processes, which stresses their important role even more.

In addition to the general advantage of fortifications, they are sites, which appear to influence, canalise, enhance and limit connectivity and, all the more, they seem to be intended for exactly this purpose.

The discussion of fortifications with respect to connectivity revealed that processes similar to recent globalisation are not new. They were already relevant in prehistory. Even then, technical developments, such as the domestication of horses, the invention of wheels and the construction of complex ships, anticipated some technical innovations of the 19th and 20th centuries. Archaeological complexity research shows that connectivity is and always was a key factor of cultural development in a broad sense.

The discussion of fortifications with respect to connectivity also revealed that an undifferentiated use of the term 'connectivity' is not appropriate and that more is concealed behind the term. The discussion showed the relevance of group size, of a differentiation between interaction potential and interaction intensity, of group internal and external interaction and some further aspects. Furthermore, the entanglement of different aspects and phenomena has become evident. This makes connectivity a very challenging field of research, which is not adequately covered by buzzwords such as globalisation and social media. It requires much deeper investigations of present and past processes.

This article rather sketched archaeological connectivity research, focussing on fortifications but without being limited to fortified sites. This kind of connectivity research promises to clarify the role of connectivity for human societies far beyond globalisation, social media and other forms of digital communication.

Acknowledgements

We would like to thank Anna-Theres Andersen for proofreading and technical support.

Funded by the Deutsche Forschungsgemeinschaft (DFG, German Research Foundation) under Germany's Excellence Strategy – EXC 2150 – 390870439.

References

Agnew, J., 1994. The Territorial Trap: The Geographical Assumptions of International Relations Theory. *Review of International Political Economy*, 1 (1), 53-80.

Alberti, G., 2014. Modeling Group Size and Scalar Stress by Logistic Regression from an Archaeological Perspective. *PLOS ONE* [online], 9 (3). Available at: <https://doi.org/10.1371/journal.pone.0091510> [Accessed 22 June 2021].

Andersen, H.H., 2004. *Til hele rigets værn. Danevirkes arkæologi og historie.* Højbjerg: Moesgård & Wormianum.

Anderson, B.R., 1993. *Imagined Communities: Reflections on the Origin and Spread of Nationalism.* London and New York: Verso books.

Argyle, M., 1969. *Social Interaction.* Piscataway: Transaction Publishers.

Auge, O., ed., 2019. *Der Limes Saxoniae: Fiktion oder Realität? Beiträge des interdisziplinären Symposiums in Oldenburg/Holstein am 21. Oktober 2017.* Kieler Werkstücke 53. Berlin: Peter Lang.

Baddeley, A., Rubak, E., Turner, R., 2016. *Spatial Point Patterns: Methodology and Applications with R.* Chapman & Hall/CRC Interdisciplinary Statistics Series 17. Boca Raton, London, New York: CRC Press.

Beilke-Voigt, I., 2014. *Das jungbronze- und früheisenzeitliche Burgzentrum von Lossow. Ergebnisse der Ausgrabungen 2008 und 2009.* Materialien zur Archäologie in Brandenburg 8. Rahden/Westf.: Marie Leidorf.

Beilke-Voigt, I., 2017. Lossow und Lebus. Ein Burgenpaar an der Oder? *In:* I. Beilke-Voigt and O. Nakoinz, eds. *Enge Nachbarn: Doppel- und Mehrfachburgen in der Bronzezeit und im Mittelalter.* Berlin Studies of the Ancient World 47. Berlin: Edition Topoi, 91-123.

Beilke-Voigt, I. and Nakoinz, O., eds., 2017. *Enge Nachbarn: Doppel- und Mehrfachburgen in der Bronzezeit und im Mittelalter.* Berlin Studies of the Ancient World 47. Berlin: Edition Topoi.

Castells, M., 1996. *The Rise of the Network Society. The Information Age: Economy, Society and Culture 1.* Oxford: Blackwell.

Christaller, W., 1933. *Die zentralen Orte in Süddeutschland: Eine ökonomisch-geographische Untersuchung über die Gesetzmäßigkeit der Verbreitung und Entwicklung der Siedlungen mit städtischen Funktionen.* Jena: Fischer.

Collis, J., 1984. *Oppida: Earliest Towns North of the Alps.* Sheffield: Academic Press.

Copeland, D.C., 1996. Economic Interdependence and War. A Theory of Trade Expectations. *International Security*, 20 (4), 5-41.

Dunbar, R.I.M., 1993. Coevolution of Neocortical Size, Group Size and Language in Humans. *Behavioral and Brain Sciences*, 16 (4), 681-694.

Dunbar, R.I.M., 2002. The Social Brain Hypothesis. *In:* J.T. Cacioppo, G.G. Berntson, R. Adolphs, C.S. Carter, R.J. Davidson, M. McClintock, B.S. McEwen, M. Meaney, D.L. Schacter, E.M. Sternberg, S. Suomi, S.E. Taylor, eds. *Foundations in Social Neuroscience.* Social Neuroscience Series XII. Cambridge, Mass: MIT Press, 69-87.

Dunbar, R.I.M., 2010. *How Many Friends Does One Person Need? Dunbar's Number and Other Evolutionary Quirks.* London: Faber and Faber.

Edgren, B. and Herschend, F., 1999. *Eketorp: The fortified village on the island of Öland.* Stockholm: Riksantikvarieämbetet.

Englehardt, J.D. and Carrasco, M.D., 2019. Introduction: Interaction and the Making of Ancient Mesoamerica. *In:* J.D. Englehardt and M.D. Carrasco, eds. *Interregional Interaction in Ancient Mesoamerica.* Louisville: University Press of Colorado, 1-33.

Eriksen, P. and Rindel, P.O., 2018. *Lange linjer i landskabet: hulbælter fra jernalderen.*

Jysk arkæologisk selskabs skrifter 104. Højbjerg: Jutland Archaeological Society.

Ethelberg, P., Hardt, N., Poulsen, B., Sørensen, A.B., 2003. *Det sønderjyske landbrugs historie: jernalder, vikingetid og middelalder*. Skrifter udgivet af Historisk Samfund for Sønderjylland 82. Haderslev: Haderslev Museum.

Feinmann, G.M., 2011. Size, Complexity, and Organizational Variation: A Comparative Approach. *Cross-Cultural Research*, 45 (1), 37-58.

Goudineau, Ch. and Peyre, Ch., 1993. *Bibracte et les Éduens: à la découverte d'un peuple gaulois*. Paris: Éditions Errance.

Hansen, K.P., 2003. *Kultur und Kulturwissenschaft: eine Einführung*. UTB für Wissenschaft 1846. Tübingen, Basel: A. Francke.

Harvey, D., 1989. *The Condition of Postmodernity: An Enquiry into the Origins of Cultural Change*. Oxford: Blackwell.

Hegewisch, M., 2012. Von Leese nach Kalkriese? Ein Deutungsversuch zur Geschichte zweier linearer Erdwerke. *In:* E. Baltrusch, M. Hegewisch, M. Meyer, U. Puschner, Ch. Wendt, eds. *2000 Jahre Varusschlacht: Geschichte, Archäologie, Legenden*. Berlin Studies of the Ancient World 7. Berlin, Boston: De Gruyter, 177-209.

Hepp, A., 2006. Translokale Medienkulturen: Netzwerke der Medien und Globalisierung. *In:* A. Hepp, F. Krotz, S. Moores, C. Winter, eds. *Konnektivität, Netzwerk und Fluss. Konzepte gegenwärtiger Medien-, Kommunikations- und Kulturtheorie*. Wiesbaden: Verlag für Sozialwissenschaften, 43-68.

Hepp, A., Krotz, F., Moores, S., Winter, C., 2006. Konnektivität, Netzwerk und Fluss. *In:* A. Hepp, F. Krotz, S. Moores, C. Winter, eds. *Konnektivität, Netzwerk und Fluss. Konzepte gegenwärtiger Medien-, Kommunikations- und Kulturtheorie*. Wiesbaden: Verlag für Sozialwissenschaften, 7-20.

Herschend, F., 2009. *The Early Iron Age in South Scandinavia: Social Order in Settlement and Landscape*. Occasional Papers in Archaeology 46. Uppsala: Uppsala University.

Homans, G.C., 1950. *The Human Group*. New York: Harcourt, Brace and Co.

Irsigler, F., 2010. Annäherungen an den Stadtbegriff. *In:* F. Opll and Ch. Sonnlechner, eds. *Europäische Städte im Mittelalter*. Forschungen und Beiträge zur Wiener Stadtgeschichte 52. Innsbruck, Wien: Studienverlag, 15-30.

Jankuhn, H., 1986. *Haithabu: ein Handelsplatz der Wikingerzeit*. Neumünster: Wachholtz.

Knappett, C., 2011. *An Archaeology of Interaction: Network Perspectives on Material Culture and Society*. Oxford: Oxford University Press.

Kneisel, J., Nakoinz, O., Beilke-Voigt, I., in print. Interpreting Bronze and Iron Age enclosed spaces, fortifications and boundaries in the western Baltic. *In:* D. Hofmann, F. Nikulka, and R. Schumann, eds. The Baltic in the Bronze Age. Regional patterns, interactions and boundaries. Amsterdam: Sidestone Press.

Knitter, D. and Nakoinz, O., 2018. Point Pattern Analysis as Tool for Digital Geoarchaeology: A Case Study of Megalithic Graves in Schleswig-Holstein, Germany. *In:* C. Siart, M. Forbriger, O. Bubenzer, eds. *Digital Geoarchaeology: New Techniques for Interdisciplinary Human-Environmental Research*. Natural Science in Archaeology. Cham: Springer, 45-64.

Koch, K.H., 1988. Existierte ein eisenzeitliches Befestigungssystem im Gebiet der Treverer? *Archäologisches Korrespondenzblatt*, 18 (2), 169-182.

Koschützki, D., Lehmann, K.A., Peeters, L., Richter, S., Tenfelde-Podehl, D., Zlotowski, O., 2005. Centrality Indices. *In:* U. Brandes and T. Erlebach, eds. *Network Analysis: Methodological Foundations*. Lecture Notes in Computer Science 3418. Berlin, Heidelberg: Springer, 16-61.

Kristiansen, K., 2014. Towards a New Paradigm? The Third Science Revolution and its Possible Consequences in Archaeology. *Current Swedish Archaeology*, 22 (4), 11-34.

Krotz, F., 2006. Konnektivität der Medien: Konzepte, Bedingungen und Konsequenzen. *In*: A. Hepp, F. Krotz, S. Moores, C. Winter, eds. *Konnektivität, Netzwerk und Fluss. Konzepte gegenwärtiger Medien-, Kommunikations- und Kulturtheorie*. Wiesbaden: Verlag für Sozialwissenschaften, 21-42.

Löw, M., 2001. *Raumsoziologie*. Suhrkamp-Taschenbuch Wissenschaft 1506. Frankfurt am Main: Suhrkamp.

MacSweeney, N., 2004. Social Complexity and Population: A Study in the Early Bronze Age Aegean. *Papers of the Institute of Archaeology*, 15, 53-66.

Massey, D.B., 1994. *Space, Place and Gender*. Cambridge: Polity Press.

Mennenga, M., 2019. Die rituelle Landschaft von Cuxhaven-Duhnen, Ldkr. Cuxhaven – neue Ergebnisse aus dem Umfeld des Ringwalles. *Siedlungs- und Küstenforschung im südlichen Nordseegebiet* 42, 23-41.

Nakoinz, O., 2005. Burgen und Befestigungen an der Schlei. *Archäologische Nachrichten Schleswig-Holstein*, 13, 91-131.

Nakoinz, O., 2013a. *Archäologische Kulturgeographie der ältereisenzeitlichen Zentralorte Südwestdeutschlands*. Universitätsforschungen zur prähistorischen Archäologie 224. Bonn: Habelt.

Nakoinz, O., 2013b. Räumliche Interaktionsmodelle. *Prähistorische Zeitschrift*, 88 (1-2), 226-257.

Nakoinz, O., 2017a. Kollektive und Netzwerke als komplementäre Ansätze in der Eisenzeitforschung. *Zeitschrift für Kultur- und Kollektivwissenschaft*, 3 (2), 61-82.

Nakoinz, O., 2017b. Quantifying Iron Age Urbanism (Density and Distance). *In*: S. Stoddart, ed. *Delicate Urbanism in Context: Settlement Nucleation in pre-Roman Germany. (The DAAD Cambridge Symposium)*. Cambridge: McDonald Institute, 87-95.

Nakoinz, O., 2017c. Modelle der Polyzentralität. *In*: I. Beilke-Voigt and O. Nakoinz, eds. *Enge Nachbarn: Doppel- und Mehrfachburgen in der Bronzezeit und im Mittelalter*. Berlin Studies of the Ancient World 47. Berlin: Edition Topoi, 125-144.

Nakoinz, O., 2019. *Zentralität: Theorie, Methoden und Fallbeispiele zur Analyse zentraler Orte*. Berlin Studies of the Ancient World 55. Berlin: Edition Topoi.

Nakoinz, O. and Knitter, D., eds., 2016. *Modelling Human Behaviour in Landscapes – Basic Concepts and Modelling Elements*. Quantitative Archaeology and Archaeological Modelling. New York: Springer.

Nakoinz, O., Bilger, M., Matzig, D., 2020a. Urbanity as a Process and the Role of Relative Network Properties – A Case Study from the Early Iron Age. *Frontiers in Digital Humanities*, 7 (2), 1-16.

Nakoinz, O., Knitter, D., Faupel, F., Nykamp, M., 2020b. Modelling Interaction in Landscapes. *In*: P. Łuczkiewicz, ed. *Landschaft und Siedlungen: archäologische Studien zur vorrömischen Eisenzeit- und älteren Kaiserzeit im Mittel- und Südost Europa*. Lublin: Uniwersytet Marii Curie-Skłodowskiej, 12-45.

Nakoinz, O. and Loy, A., in print. The Location of Connected Fortifications. *In*: T. Ibsen, K. Ilves, B. Maixner, S. Messal, J. Schneeweiß, eds. *The Setting of Fortifications in the Natural and Cultural Landscape*. Hamburg, Kiel: Wachholtz.

Neumann, H., 1982. *Olgerdiget – et bidrag til Danmarks tidligste historie*. Skrifter fra Museumsrådet for Sønderjyllands Amt 1. Haderslev: Haderslev Museum.

Nowakowski, D., 2017. Mittelalterliche Doppelburgen in Polen. Einleitung zur Forschungsproblematik anhand ausgewählter Beispiele aus Pommern,

Schlesien, Groß- und Kleinpolen. *In*: I. Beilke-Voigt and O. Nakoinz, eds. *Enge Nachbarn: Doppel- und Mehrfachburgen in der Bronzezeit und im Mittelalter*. Berlin Studies of the Ancient World 47. Berlin: Edition Topoi, 247-281.

Olausson, M., 1995. *Det inneslutna rummet – om kultiska hägnader, fornborgar och befästa gårdar i Uppland från 1300 f. Kr. til Kristi födelse*. Arkeologiska undersökningar 9. Stockholm: Riksantikvarieämbetet.

Paasi, A., 1998. Boundaries as Social Processes: Territoriality in the World of Flows. *Geopolitics,* 3 (1), 69-88.

Polignac, F. de, 1995. *Cults, Territory, and the Origins of the Greek City-state*. Chicago: University of Chicago Press.

Roesdahl, E., 1977. *Fyrkat. En jysk vikingeborg. II. Oldsagerne og gravpladsen*. Nordiske Fortidsminder 4. København: Andelsbogtrykkeriet.

Runge, M., 2018. New Archaeological Investigations at Nonnebakken, a Viking Age Fortress in Odense. *In*: J. Hansen and M. Bruus, eds. *The Fortified Viking Age. 36th Interdisciplinary Viking Symposium, in Odense, May 17th, 2017*. Kulturhistoriske Studier i Centralitet 3. Odense: Syddansk Universitetsforlag, 44-59.

Schallmayer, E., 2011. *Der Limes: Geschichte einer Grenze*. München: C.H. Beck.

Schindler, R., 1977. *Die Altburg von Bundenbach: eine befestigte Höhensiedlung des 2./1. Jh. v. Chr. im Hunsrück*. Trierer Grabungen und Forschungen 10. Mainz: von Zabern.

Sibley, D., 1988. Survey 13: Purification of space. *Environment and Planning D: Society and Space,* 6 (4), 409-421.

Tobler, W., 1970. A Computer Movie Simulating Urban Growth in the Detroit Region. *Economic Geography,* 46 (2), 234-240.

Tomlinson, J., 1999. *Globalization and Culture*. Chicago: University of Chicago Press.

VanValkenburgh, P. and Osborne, J.F., 2013. Home Turf: Archaeology, Territoriality, and Politics. *In*: J.F. Osborne and P. VanValkenburgh, eds. *Territoriality in Archaeology*. Archaeological Papers of the American Anthropological Association 22. Arlington, Virgina: American Anthropological Association, 1-27.

Werlen, B., 2008. *Sozialgeographie: Eine Einführung*. UTB 1911. Bern, Stuttgart, Wien: Haupt.

Connecting linguistics and archaeology in the study of identity: A first exploration

John Peterson, Nicole Taylor, Ilja A. Seržant, Henny Piezonka, Ariba Hidayet Khan, Norbert Nübler

Abstract

In this study, we discuss the ways in which linguistics and archaeology approach and investigate identity, focusing on potential areas of overlap between the two disciplines as a possible research program for future collaborative studies. Although the two disciplines may appear quite removed from one another at first sight, both deal with cultural items – whether material or linguistic – which are intrinsic to what it means to be human and which have an inherent function both as a means of communication and in their symbolic dimensions. Our ultimate goal here is to develop an interdisciplinary approach to identity as a specific field of human connectivity which can yield deeper insights into the topic than those achieved within the individual disciplines thus far and for which such a joint approach could be especially fruitful.

Introduction: Identity as a platform of social and cultural connectivity

Identity is an inherently relational concept, as someone or something can only be similar to or different from someone or something else (Assmann 1992). As such,

John Peterson
Institute of Scandinavian Studies, Frisian Studies, and General Linguistics (ISFAS)
Kiel University
Leibnizstr. 10
24118 Kiel, Germany
jpeterson@isfas.uni-kiel.de

Nicole Taylor
Institute of Prehistoric and Protohistoric Archaeology
Kiel University
Johanna-Mestorf-Str. 2-6
24118 Kiel, Germany
nicole.taylor@ufg.uni-kiel.de

Ilja Seržant
Institute of Slavic Studies
Kiel University
Leibnizstr. 10
24118 Kiel, Germany
serzant@slav.uni-kiel.de

Henny Piezonka
Institute of Prehistoric and Protohistoric Archaeology
Kiel University
Johanna-Mestorf-Str. 2-6
24118 Kiel, Germany
hpiezonka@ufg.uni-kiel.de

Ariba Hidayet Khan
Cluster of Excellence ROOTS
Kiel University
Olshausenstr. 80a
24118 Kiel, Germany
akhan@roots.uni-kiel.de

Norbert Nübler
Institute of Slavic Studies
Kiel University
Leibnizstr. 10
24118 Kiel, Germany
nuebler@slav.uni-kiel.de

it is a showcase example of *connectivity*, as it can be seen as an interaction or interrelation between two or more entities. All humans possess personal as well as collective identities, and through them they are situated in a multi-dimensional and dynamic mesh of relations construed by identifications, alterities, and the spaces and thresholds in between. Identity requires human and "beyond-human" connectivities to develop, to be constructed, performed, maintained and changed, and at the same time it is, in itself, a platform of connectivity spanning individuals, social groups, and imagined communities.

Identity is thus a constituting element of what it means to be human, reaching back through time to the beginning of our species, and it remains highly relevant socially and politically in the post-modern, increasingly globalised world. Personal or self-identity can reflect the integration of a person with their experiences, internal and external expectations, and pre-ascribed social roles into a society based on stable social and metaphysical structures (*e.g.* cosmic order, religious world view, *etc.*), but it can also be situated at a more unstable intersection of various concurrent systems of meaning (Glomb 2013). Collective or group identity needs internal strengthening through common culture, *e.g.*, language, rituals, unifying symbols and myths as well as through the construct of alterity in order to justify the group's own superiority (Assmann 1992; Horatschek 2013) and it is connected to the development of group-specific cultural forms. Post-colonial discourses, in particular, have been increasingly focusing on the intermediate area between identities, tracing strategies and phenomena such as mimicry and cultural hybridity (Bhabha 2016), and going so far as to even denying the existence of cultural identity in favour of the more fluid and plastic category of cultural distances (Jullien 2017). Thus, negotiation, translation and plural "communities of being" with their fuzzy edges (Bird-David 2017) are taken into view in order to understand the flexible and situational character that identities can take along temporal, spatial and trans-cultural trajectories.

Research on identity is conducted in a number of disciplines, including anthropology, sociology, philosophy, politics, psychology, archaeology and linguistics, among others. In this paper, we examine the ways in which linguistics and archaeology approach and investigate identity, focusing, in particular, on determining areas of potential epistemological overlap and of mutual reinforcement between the two disciplines as a possible research program for future collaborative studies. While linguistics and archaeology as scholarly fields may appear far removed from one another at first sight, language, material items, and embodied structures and features are all cultural artefacts, which are intrinsic to what it means to be human, and they have an inherent function both as means of communication and in their symbolic dimensions. Language and material items, in particular, are connected to each other in complex relationships: Only through the mediation of language do "things" as realia receive a cultural and historic context and are embedded into narratives, thus becoming *telling objects* that are recognisable in their meaning (Bal 1994). One and the same object can develop different meanings and significances in different contexts, whereby language is the major factor that constitutes the readability of things (Vedder 2014). Structurally, both language and material culture are comparable in certain respects, *e.g.*, concerning grammar in language, and *chaînes opératoires* in the production of material items.

While there has been some collaboration between the disciplines of archaeology and linguistics at a more general level (for example the Archaeology and

Language book series by Blench and Spriggs 1997; 1998; 1999a; 1999b; or Anthony 2007), in our cross-disciplinary discussion we strive to determine whether an interdisciplinary approach to identity as a specific field of human connectivity could yield deeper insights into the topic than those achieved within the individual disciplines thus far, and for which questions, aspects and scientific prospects such a joint approach can be especially fruitful.

Approaches to identity in archaeology and linguistics

In order to identify research areas in which a collaborative archaeological and linguistic approach to identity could be fruitful, we first very briefly review the state-of-the-art within each discipline.

Approaches to identity in archaeology

Archaeology, as the study of humanity in the past, has always been concerned with identity. The earliest archaeological studies appeared to be more interested in the material culture created by past people than in the people themselves, judging from the distribution maps of artefacts marching seemingly autonomously across the landscape. In time, these artefact assemblages were mapped, this time in a metaphorical sense and seemingly uncritically, onto the humans who made and used them, creating the concept of archaeological cultures which drew on the older ethnological concept of the *Kulturkreislehre* with its key fields culture, language, people, and race (Brather 2004). Within the frames of an "ethnic interpretation", these archaeological cultures were equated with monolithic and invariable social groups with names directly linked to their material culture such as the 'Beaker people' or the 'Linearbandkeramiker' (Kossinna 1912). It was assumed that these material culture assemblages were the result of a common set of norms and values shared by a community and such a community would, in turn, have to be understood as an ethnic community/population with shared ancestry (Childe 1929). Such simplistic presumptions have been widely criticised in archaeology for many decades now (*e.g.* Brather 2004; Jones 1997; Gramsch 2015), although they have gained ground again over the last few years in the wake of palaeogenetic studies (*e.g.* Haak *et al.* 2015; Kristiansen *et al.* 2017). For certain time periods and constellations, language is also added to the equation (in the sense of "pots equal people equal shared language", see, *e.g.*, Kristiansen *et al.* 2017). Such suggestions have triggered controversial discussions and strong reactions, especially from anthropologically-informed archaeology (*e.g.* Furholt 2018; Heyd 2017; Hofmann 2015).

Over time, archaeologists have become more reflexive and critical in the way they apply their knowledge about artefacts to what it means in terms of the people of the past. The first major shift occurred in the mid-twentieth century, when the focus of much research became the "people behind the pots". However, this again often meant applying ethnic labels to the same monolithic groups that had previously been defined by the material culture. With the rise of post-processual archaeology in the later twentieth century, increasingly critical approaches (*e.g.* feminist and gender archaeology, post-colonial archaeology, ethnoarchaeology and archaeologies of age, to name but a few) expanded the ways in which the identities of past peoples were studied and interpreted (*e.g.* Hodder 1982; Conkey and Spector 1984; Gero and Conkey 1991; Brather 2004; Gosden 2004; Díaz-Andreu *et al.* 2005; Burmeister and Müller-Scheeßel 2006; Appleby 2010). The agency of past humans was acknowledged as well as the ways in which not only artefacts but also people and ideas moved between groups over distances. Additionally, archaeologists are now more aware of the role that their own socio-political contexts play in shaping how they interpret the past, which is likely to have been far removed from the version of the world in which we currently exist and our own life experiences (Taylor 2013).

In current archaeological approaches to identity, it is widely accepted that we can never know for certain how individuals identified themselves; this inner life is highly inaccessible, even to disciplines that study it in living people. From an anthropological point of view, it is understood that identity tends to be both multifaceted and processual (*e.g.* Barth 1969). Identity is componential, its major facets being those termed as ethnic, social, cultural, religious and linguistic (Banks 1996). Semiotic approaches to material culture styles have taken into view the various types of "stylistic messages" in communicating and enhancing personal as well as group identities (Furholt and Stockhammer 2008; Zeeb-Lanz 2006; Wobst 1977). In archaeology, a focus on practice and agency over the last years has led to more dynamic and fluid concepts of identity, emphasising the multi-faceted arena of continuity and change, of performativity and (re)negotiation, and of the already mentioned hybrid communities, the members of which might express identities differently, depending on situation and addressee (Gramsch 2015).

In terms of which aspects of identities archaeologists are able to access, the focus has primarily been on *groups*; whether cultural groups, social roles, or age or sex-based groups, among others. However, where the data permits, archaeologists also aim to study individual identities: Natural scientific methods can provide detailed insights into aspects of a person's biography that may have been relevant to their identities. For example, aDNA can provide kinship relationships or information on pathogens carried, stable isotopic analyses can determine dietary inputs and probable geographic origins, and osteological analyses can determine whether an individual suffered from particular illnesses, injuries and disabilities or performed certain repetitive tasks that left traces on their skeleton.

Thus, when using evidence from prehistoric settlements and mortuary sites as a whole, the focus has traditionally been on what can be said about group identities and their dynamics; often of one community versus a neighbouring one, since identities are most pertinent, visible and actively communicated in situations of contact or opposition, although emphasis is increasingly being given to individuals' identities.

Approaches to identity in linguistics

As with the study of identity in archaeology, discussed in the previous section, identity in linguistic research is likewise understood to be both multifaceted and processual and shares many other features in common with the discussion of identity in archaeology. However, identity in linguistics, with its concentration on the use of linguistic forms as expressions of identity, differs in subtle ways from its counterpart in archaeology. The following therefore provides a very brief overview of the main components of identity in linguistics.

Similar to material objects, certain linguistic signs – *i.e.* particular choices of linguistic words, grammatical items or pronunciation patterns – are associated with specific social and cultural subdomains, while other linguistic signs are much more frequent, occur across domains and, thus, represent a weaker signal of identity. While this is by its very nature essentialist, a "trap" which most researchers go to great lengths to avoid, linguistic researchers must acknowledge the fact that speakers themselves strongly link specific words, speech patterns and pronunciations with certain social groups and identities, allowing them to creatively exploit variations in their speech to express or even create a projection of their self-identities, which in turn allows linguists to study this phenomenon more easily than other expressions of human culture might allow.

The two most prominent subfields of linguistics which deal with identity, each with its own assumptions and methodology, are sociolinguistics and linguistic anthropology.[1] In both of these traditions, the notion of *indexicality* plays a central role. The classical example used to illustrate indexicality in introductory linguistic courses is that of a footprint; although, *e.g.*, a bear's footprint is not the same as a bear, it is uniquely connected to a bear in an essentialist manner, *i.e.*, it inherently points to the (earlier) presence of a bear, and only of a bear, at a particular location. When speaking, speakers exploit these conventionalised associations to equate a certain pronunciation or the use of certain words or grammatical constructions with a particular social identity. These so-called *shibboleths* are sometimes restricted to a few highly emblematic items, which serve to show one's own membership in this group or to identify someone else as belonging to a particular group. This reliance on the essentialist nature of indices is thus not to be understood as meaning that these sociolinguistic studies take an essentialist stance. Rather, linguists productively exploit speakers' essentialist associations, since lay conceptions of identity are themselves predominantly essentialist (Bucholtz and Hall 2004, 375-376).[2]

Most sociolinguistic studies thus tend to focus on the use of language to signal the speaker's desire to be viewed as belonging to a particular socially recognised / recognisable group, for which these indexical markers are key, allowing them to express or even quite literally create their identity through speech. This corresponds to what Penelope Eckert (2012) refers to as the third wave of sociolinguistic studies, in which the emphasis on stylistic practice views speakers

'[...] *not as passive and stable carriers of dialect, but as stylistic agents, tailoring linguistic styles in ongoing and lifelong projects of self-construction and differentiation' (Eckert 2012, 97-98).*

The assumption of a conventional norm also holds for language use in multilingual situations, where the use of one language instead of another – whether as the preferred language of the entire conversation, of a particular sentence or even of a single word – is perceived to be a "contextualisation cue" and used in multilingual speech in many ways similarly to intonation in monolingual speech (Gumperz 1982, 98). More central to our discussion here is that it is often employed to signal

---

1   Or "anthropological linguistics", depending on one's perspective.

2   Indexicality plays a central role in one recent, highly influential school of sociolinguistics, following Silverstein's (2003) theoretical discussion of this concept. It has been used to describe, *e.g.*, the processes involved in the re-interpretation of the pronunciation of highly emblematic words in what was once a working-class pronunciation in Pittsburgh as a means of self-identification with that city, including those who had left the area to look for work elsewhere (*e.g.* Johnstone *et al.* 2006). It is also productively used to describe the elevation of the status of a particular dialect to that of a standardised national language, which plays a central role in modern societies with respect to identification with a nation state, such as the enregisterment of Received Pronunciation in Great Britain (Agha 2003) or of Putonghua in the People's Republic of China (Dong 2010).

identity, *e.g.*, with a local ethnic minority and its traditional language, with the vernacular of a larger region, or with a national language, among others. For example, Cantonese-English code-switching, *i.e.*, the use of morphemes or words from two different languages in a sentence or conversation (cf. Swiss *Herr Müller et les enfants*), at the University of Hong Kong serves both to express one's own perceived identity with the local, Cantonese community but at the same time also as a part of the educated, English-speaking university (Trudgill 2000, 106).

In contrast to the emphasis in sociolinguistics on the expression of identity discussed above, linguistic anthropology is much more concerned with the conceptual notions involved in understanding identity as a whole. An overview of this topic is presented in Mary Bucholtz and Kira Hall (2004), in which the authors also outline their approach to the topic, which they refer to as the "tactics of inter-subjectivity". Here, in addition to the mechanisms through which identities are produced, such as *practice, performance, indexicality* and *ideology*, these tactics are claimed to

> *'[...] illuminate the motivations for identity work, in the same way that research on the semiotic processes of practice, indexicality, ideology, and performance helps to account for the mechanisms where identities are produced' (Bucholtz and Hall 2004, 387).*

Unlike archaeology, which by definition deals with (the remains and traces of) earlier societies, specialists in synchronic sociolinguistics and linguistic anthropology work with actual speakers and can, at least to a certain point, determine to what extent linguistic reflection is *conscious* or *subconscious*. This has important consequences, as language is often viewed – and spoken of – as an emblem of ethnic or some other social identity. For example, Papua New Guinea has one of the highest degrees of linguistic diversity in the world, with ca. 760 languages in a territory comparable in size to Sweden. It has often been reported in the literature that, in addition to possible environmental factors, this high language density is due to the local attitude toward languages as a highly salient marker of ethnic group-identity (*e.g.* Kulick 1992, 2). For example, Don Kulick (1992, 2-3) reported that a village in Papua New Guinea (Huon Valley) decided by committee that the word for 'no' (*bia*) was to be changed to *buŋɛ* in order for their language (Selepet) to be different from the otherwise identical language in the next village. Another example of emblematicity is the non-Mandarin-like word order pattern in Cantonese with respect to the adverb *sin* 'first', which follows and does not precede the verb. This emblematic feature is consciously identified by Cantonese speakers as authentic in the context of otherwise similar word-order patterns in Cantonese and Mandarin (Aikhenvald 2007, 41).

Identity in archaeology and linguistics: Definitions and concepts

As we have seen, the study of identity involves many similar concepts in linguistics and archaeology, despite all differences. This is not unexpected, since the objects of study of both disciplines emerge as the result of the cultural evolution of the human species (cf. Dediu *et al.* 2013 on language) and, unavoidably, both are subject to social constraints. What is more, in both cases they emerge primarily for practical purposes of everyday life that are not restricted to identity issues. Thus, most material objects (tools, dress, buildings, *etc.*) serve diverse practical

Identity targets	*self*-identity vs. *group*-identity
Types of acts-of-identity	*conscious* vs. *subconscious*
Direction of identification	*projected* vs. *perceived*
Identity domains	*language, ethnicity, religion, social status, gender, kinship, teacher-student relations, etc.*
Modes of identification	*relational* vs. *categorical*
Identity parameters	*performativity, regulatory ideals, individuals* vs. *dividuals*

Table 1. Constructing identity.

purposes and needs. Likewise, language is designed for the transfer of information from one individual to another, but at the same time, in its phatic function, it serves as a social instrument to form and maintain bonds with others in a group. Identity thus emerges as a kind of by-product, *i.e.*, as a blueprint of human socialisation while speaking, acting, and creating as well as using objects.

Both material and linguistic strategies of constructing identity build upon the pragmatic principle of "tacit alternatives". Thus, there are always alternative ways of achieving the same practical goal. For example, a winter jacket may potentially have very different designs and all of these could perhaps fulfil the primary function equally well. Likewise, language inventories are abundant and provide a number of alternative means and circumventions for expressing largely the same state of affairs (cf. Labov 1972). The particular means selected often does not come "for free", but – in addition to its purely semantic content – brings in socially relevant effects. As a result, linguistic production is always individualised and each particular choice among possible alternatives brings about an *act of identity* (a term coined by Le Page and Tabouret-Keller 1985). This makes languages simultaneously social institutions in addition to being individual cognitive representations and dispositions (Evans 2013, 236-237). Likewise, in the production and use of material artefacts, especially in non-industrial conditions, individual choices and opportunities are inherent. This is also the case in other realms of human life, *e.g.*, concerning mobility, diets and subsistence occupations, some of which are traceable via archaeological methods.

In what follows, we present our conceptual apparatus for describing and investigating identity, which we anticipate in Table 1 by way of overview.

Before we take a closer look at these categories, we emphasise that, in most real-life situations, we encounter complex combinations of these categories simultaneously, with particular categories being more salient than others in specific contexts (Meyerhoff 2006, 71-72, quoting Tajfel 1978).

Identity targets

We begin with the following two definitions, which describe what is arguably the primary distinction with respect to identity:

(1) *Self-identity* embraces various acts-of-identity (linguistic, material, dietary, *etc.*) that make an individual a unique entity within their community.[3] It is important to note, however, that self-identity is located at the intersection of

---

3   Also referred to as "personal identity" (*e.g.* Glomb 2013; Meyerhoff 2006).

the various group-identities held by an individual, plus a certain additional, unknowable, factor related to a person's inexpressible inner world, as mentioned above.

(2) *Group-identity* embraces various acts-of-identity (linguistic, material, dietary, *etc.*) that make a particular social group inwardly cohesive and outwardly distinct within its larger social field.

Ethnic identity is a special case of group identities. It is characterised by a belief in commonality, most often also entailing a common origin. In trying to elucidate the different aspects of identity, people may cluster into discrete units, reducing the complexity of their self-identity and intersecting group identities to their ethnic identity. According to Fredrik Barth (1969), ethnicities are categories of ascription and identification as well as a means of distinguishing (social) groups. Taking a more dynamic view, it can be said that

> '[e]*thnic groups rarely exist as structurally distinct isomorphs. Instead, there often tend to be overlapping sets, groupings that encompass other groupings'* (Williams, cited in Banks 1996, 45).

It is a truism in linguistics that there is no one-to-one relationship between "ethnic groups" and a particular language; for as long as we have records, (perceived) ethnic groups have been documented "abandoning" their traditional languages at some point in time in order to only pass a more prestigious or useful language on to their offspring, usually a language of administration, trade, or some other supra-regional variety, which holds the promise of social and material advancement, but which also eventually leads to the "death" of the respective traditional language. Nevertheless, the essentialist view of the relation between ethnicity and language is, at least at present, almost universally accepted, with many ethnic groups claiming that only those who speak the traditional language associated with their group are "real" members of that group. This can even go so far that perceived ethnic groups in which no one still speaks the traditional language are said to no longer have a "native language" or "mother tongue".

Types of acts-of-identity

Acts-of-identity may be either *conscious* or *subconscious* (Meyerhoff 2006, 23). For example, it is entirely impossible for us not to interpret speech as a marker of identity. Consider John E. Joseph's (2004, 2) example of a group of strangers waiting at a taxi stand when an empty taxi drives by without stopping, with the following reactions of those waiting:

A. Out*rage*ous.

B. I say.

C. Fuckin hell.

As Joseph notes, it is highly likely that we all have a very clear picture in our head of what speakers A, B and C look like, how they are dressed, what backgrounds they come from and even whether or not we would like them, although these pictures will likely vary from speaker to speaker. While this clearly involves the "over-reading" of a speaker's words "since the data on which it is based is (nearly) always inadequate to support the inferences made" (Joseph, 2004, 38), it is – for better or worse – an integral part of the human experience. Much of this happens *subconsciously* during speech production to such an extent that it is nearly impossible to suppress one's group- and/or self-identity while producing language. Similarly, the instinctive or habitual use of certain material objects in specific ways related to identity-based habits or cultural learning can be very difficult to change. For example, residue analyses of imported Mediterranean drinking and serving vessels – designed for wine and specific feasting ceremonies – in Early Iron Age (Celtic) France showed that these were used in local practices of beer consumption (Rageot *et al.* 2019). Archaeology can also investigate subconscious markers of embodied identities. For example, certain social roles or occupations – such as grinding grain by hand or regularly wielding a weapon with one arm – would have caused pathologies marking the individual as holding a specific identity through the way in which their bodies and movements were affected. During the Bronze Age in Central Europe, some women were buried wearing bronze leg spirals joined by chains, which would have caused a very specific gait. Use-wear analysis shows that these spirals were intensely worn during life and had not been produced merely for inclusion in the graves (Sørensen 1997; Rebay-Salisbury 2017).

The distinction between *conscious* and *subconscious* acts-of-identity is orthogonal to the distinction between self- and group-identity made above. With respect to language, the conscious construction of identity requires an awareness of the linguistic items in question, whereas the subconscious identity applies to linguistic items that speakers are less aware of. Thus, tangible foreign elements, such as loanwords, can become the focus of discussion and be frowned upon, while in structural convergence patterns often go unnoticed. Thus, language planning, language cleansing and language ideology primarily target lexical elements of which speakers tend to be conscious, while structural patterns of which speakers are not conscious are more amenable to adaptation. Similarly, a language which is no longer spoken but which an ethnic group considers to be an integral part of its heritage, and therefore of its identity, can be consciously revived and integrated into the group's daily lives. Subconscious acts of identity can also often be found in the opposition between dialect and standard variety (cf. Labov 1966; 1969), while conscious identity strategies lead to *language ideology* and *language engineering*, i.e., creating linguistic norms and standards, often based on a supposedly stereotypical variety.

Similarly, material culture in archaeology is among the most widely used physical markers of conscious acts-of-identity, with examples ranging from clothing and ornaments to building styles and everyday items such as pottery vessels. From an archaeological point of view, *conscious* vs. *subconscious* acts-of-identity can be reflected in the types of stylistic messages that are carried by material items, constituting non-verbal means of communication (Furholt and Stockhammer 2008, 62-65).

Linguistic and material conscious identities need not coincide. For example, in the Middle Ob region of Western Siberia, Yugan Khanty women wear their ethnic costumes during trips to the Russian town market in the knowledge that they will be perceived as members of a small indigenous group not so familiar with the modern Russian market economy, in the hope that the Russian salespersons will not cheat them (pers. comm. Stephan Dudeck). At the same time, many of these Yugan Khanty communities do not teach their children their ethnic group's traditional language in order to provide them with better future chances as fluent Russian speakers. In contrast, Taz Selkup communities, while no longer wearing ethnic costumes in everyday life, take great care to teach their children their "own" language, which is directed at the preservation of the internal cohesion of the community (Piezonka *et al.* 2020, 540).

Based on a model developed by the anthropologist Polly Wiessner (1983), the so-called *emblemic style* aims at transmitting a clearly defined meaning to a consciously selected addressee. Emblemic style, in its discursive function, can be employed, *e.g.*, for emphasising group identity while at the same time demarcating the boundary to neighbouring groups. In archaeological contexts, such conscious emblematic identity markers have been preserved, *e.g.*, as personal ornaments and parts of costume. The *assertive style*, on the other hand, would not have a clearly defined addressee, it would be directed more towards the producers and users themselves, directed internally at the group, thereby strengthening the common identity. The assertive style can be subconsciously employed and perceived and is thus situated more on a habitual rather than on a discursive level. In the archaeological record, assertive style might, for example, manifest itself in building traditions, decorative schemes, *etc*. However, due to the patchy character of archaeological sources, it is generally very difficult to distinguish between these two stylistic modes of communicating and constituting identities (Furholt and Stockhammer 2008).

The notions of conscious vs. subconscious aspects of identity are intricately interwoven with those of individual or self-identity vs. group-identity. For example, the complex nature of relations between languages in multilingual and multi-ethnic settings can favour various conscious group-identity activities. These kinds of settings are often found, *e.g.*, in exogamic societies where language can become the main source of ethnic self-identity. By way of example, in Vaupés (Northwest Central Amazonia), it is the father's language that is a badge of individual identity (Aikhenvald 2003, 2; 2013). Thus, despite the traditionally highly multilingual settings in Vaupés, all members of a particular village identify with just one language, while being proficient in at least one or more other languages. Despite highly multilingual settings even within one family in this community, there is a strong inhibition against code-switching to maintain this symbol of identity and, with the exception of some very restricted contexts, code-mixing and code-switching are considered inappropriate in Vaupés. Depending on the source language, the subject may be interpreted as sloppy or even slightly foolish (Aikhenvald 2003, 17).

Other multilingual situations can be quite different, however, with the respective speakers much less or even not at all concerned with language mixing. For example, Evgeniy V. Golovko (2003) provides a number of examples from Russia: Sakha and Russian (Sakha, Russia), Karelian and Russian (Karelia), Komi and Russian (Komi), *etc*. Here, the "mixed" language resulting from code-switching has become an identity marker of the group (Golovko 2003, 187), quite the opposite of the Vaupés case.

In cases such as these, if the source languages are dialects or closely related languages, this can result in various types of *koiné*, *i.e.*, a common language. Peter Trudgill (2020) provides a number of examples of koiné that have developed into nation-state languages: Hellenistic Koiné (the common language of Alexander the Great's empire), Arabic (the basis of modern Arabic dialects, which spread during the Islamic expansion), Icelandic (new settlers from various dialects of the Scandinavian homeland), Russian (due to the merger of Moscow Russian and Church Slavic), and different European dialects of Spanish in Latin America, *etc*.

When the respective language varieties are not closely related, a very different situation results. With increased use of code-switching above and beyond its local functions (*e.g.* to express a new concept, mark something as focused, change of speech partner, signaling membership to two ethnic groups, *etc.*), continued extensive use can eventually lead to a new group identity, where not the individual changes themselves but rather the constant use of the two languages together in virtually every sentence becomes the new norm, referred to as "language mixing" (*e.g.* Auer 1999).

As new generations of speakers grow up with this constant code-switching of their parents' generation as the default, they may not be able to fully reconstruct the original languages being mixed in the speech of their parents. Instead, they may identify with the new "mixed" language, referred to in linguistics as a "fused lect" (*e.g.* Auer 1999), which is no longer mutually intelligible with the two original languages and hence must be viewed as a language in its own right. Oversimplifying a bit, these fused lects can consist, *e.g.*, of the grammar of one of the original languages together with the lexicon of the other, *e.g.*, Media Lengua (Spanish and Quechua) in Ecuador or Anglo-Romani in Great Britain, or they can be structures as Mitchif (French and Cree) in Canada, where the noun phrase is largely from French while verb morphology is largely from Cree, *etc.* (cf. Winford 2003, 19 for further discussion).

In situations of superdiversity, *polylanguaging* can also result as a marker of identity. Polylanguaging is

'the way in which speakers use features associated with different 'languages' – even when they know very little of these 'languages'' (Jørgensen et al. 2011, 1)

and is particularly popular among urban youths, especially those from ethnic minorities. For example, Jørgensen *et al.* (2011, 2) depicts a brief Facebook conversation between three Danish girls combining linguistic elements from standard and colloquial Danish, English, Arabic, Turkish, and Spanish as a signal of membership by the speakers (or in this case, writers) to this young, international urban and predominantly Muslim group (Jørgensen *et al.* 2011, 3-5), all within the space of a few lines.

Direction of identification

It is of course impossible to know how a person sees themselves: we can only construct our own ideas about another person's "identity", as we do not have direct access to their self-perception. As such, all of us will have different "versions" of ourselves and those around us (Joseph 2004, 8). This means that while we construct an "identity" of ourselves, this is not necessarily the identity that our counterpart constructs of us or we construct of them. For example, upper-middle class white youths of German descent from well-to-do neighbourhoods often use language from rappers' songs from the "Kiez" in Berlin; while this may make them "cool" in their own minds, it may just as well have an entirely unintended comical effect on those with whom they are interacting at the moment of utterance.

In archaeology, while we can never know how important the use of particular objects was to the identity of prehistoric peoples, we can at least infer projected identities as archaeological concepts and as a way to understand the patterns within our evidence. When looking specifically at burial evidence, we can also gain insights into the perceived identities of individuals, that is, how their identities were perceived by others, since they were interred by their community rather than being actively involved in the deposition of their own mortal remains and grave goods.[4] Prehistorians usually assume that "personal" items (jewellery or costume items that appear to have been worn in life or well-used tools or weapons, *etc.*, as opposed to new items made for the burial) are part of the communication of personal identity during life which was carried over into the grave. To this can be added the additional evidence from natural scientific methods regarding the diet, everyday activities, illnesses or injuries, and geographical origins of individuals, which can also contribute to how someone chooses to identify themselves or how their identity is communicated in death.

But whether projected or perceived, stereotypical associations with the social structure as well as identities (on which they are based) are inherently *dynamic*. Acts-of-identity change and develop with time and life experiences, adapting to changes in the social structure. In linguistics, this realisation has only recently been fully appreciated. According to Eckert (2012), sociolinguistic studies on variation in the 20th and 21st centuries can largely be assigned to one of three different "waves", generally in chronological order and differing markedly with respect to the approach taken. In the "first wave", speakers are considered to be primarily "passive" members of large, static categories such as "class", "sex", *etc.*, that is, classes to which they "belong" as a result of which they speak in one fashion or another. By contrast, in the "second wave", researchers make use of ethnographic methods to locate local meaningful categories, concentrating largely on social networks whose members strongly tend to accommodate their own speech to that of the other members of the network. In addition, speakers can, and often do, belong to several networks, and can accordingly modify their speech to the appropriate register for each network, which we could associate here with "different identities".

Although this "second wave" of studies has the virtue of moving away from monolithic – and highly problematic – categories such as "class", *etc.*, it is still largely concerned with static categories, whose speakers speak the way they do because of the group(s) they associate with. In contrast, the third – and to date final – "wave" sees speakers as agents in a creative and dynamic process:

> 'The emphasis on stylistic practice in the third wave places speakers not as passive and stable carriers of dialect, but as stylistic agents, tailoring linguistic styles in ongoing and lifelong projects of self-construction and differentiation' (Eckert 2012, 97).

In this third wave, variation is viewed as an essential characteristic of language, reminiscent of Joseph's (2004, 192) view:

> 'Linguistic diversity is something much more unassailable than a 'human right' – it is a tautology'.

Identity domains and modes of identification

The next two points from Table 1, identity domains and modes of identification, while conceptually distinct, are so closely interrelated that they are discussed together in this section.

---

4   Although one could of course argue that there may have been some participation in the choice of objects, just as is possible in the modern world through discussions with family members and requests in last wills and testaments.

Stereotypical associations can be established in different *identity domains*. These domains reflect two different *modes of identification*: relational and categorical (Brubaker and Cooper 2000, 15). Among the domains associated with relational webs are, for example, kinship, friendship, social status, but also asymmetrical relations such as teacher-student relations or patron-client ties. On the other hand, categorical attributes characterise identity domains such as ethnicity, language, gender, nationality, or political identity.

Different identity strategies seem to favour some of these domains over others. Thus, as we have already seen, language is an important and often the major defining marker of ethnic group-identity (Trudgill 2000, 45). While this is the most frequent situation, there are exceptions in which language is not part of the ethnic identity (Fishman 1997; Mumm 2018, 77). For example, the Tsalka Greeks of the Republic of Georgia speak Turkish as their native language, as they emigrated from Turkey in the 19th century, although they do not consciously identify with this language. What is more, they may even express a negative attitude towards it and explain that it was forced upon them in Turkey (Jeloeva 1995, 4-6). Moreover, they may even refer to their native language as the *musulman dil* – 'Muslims' language' – while they themselves strongly identify with Christianity.

Thus, as noted above, language is not inherently connected to any clear notion of ethnicity, but may rather be connected to any number of factors, such as gender (*e.g.* in exogamous communities), nation (*i.e.* political identity, *e.g.*, Russian), religion (*e.g.* Pāli, the language of the Theravada-Buddhist canon), social status (*e.g.* Latin in the Middle Ages), or some combination of these factors.

In archaeologies of identity, the study of different identity domains is often restricted by the visible remnants available. For example, age and gender categories are most clearly visible in the archaeological record in combination with human remains for which age or sex can be determined. Hence, there is a focus on costume elements, such as jewellery, or differences in burials between males, females and other diverse individuals when it comes to these domains. However, archaeologists can also address less obvious domains of identity. For example, with the aid of ancient DNA analyses it was possible to determine that four people buried together in a single grave at Eulau in Saxony-Anhalt were genetically a nuclear family consisting of the mother, the father and their two sons (Meyer *et al.* 2012).

Identity parameters

Stereotypical associations thus play an important role within the dynamics of conscious and subconscious acts-of-identity. Connected to this, and mainly drawing on concepts developed in anthropology, feminist thought, and queer theory, the idea of bounded individual identity based on the physical biological entity of a (human) person has been increasingly contested over the last decades. An important concept introduced by Judith Butler in her works on gender is that of the *performativity* of identities (Butler 1990). *Regulatory ideals* inherent in a group or society put down the baseline for how identity operates. These can, *e.g.*, encompass basic concepts of what is appropriate and/or typical for certain groups, *e.g.*, dress codes for women and men, haircuts, and social behaviours, for example, of children vs. adults.

As the application of these ideas is performative, it not only marks identities but also creates and reinforces them. For example, a specific burial rite in which the deceased is furnished and interred in an appropriate way for all of their roles and functions reinforces the stereotypical associations by performing and thus recreating them. This, in turn, means that identities can be seen as the outcome of the dynamic interplay of regulatory ideals and the related stereotypical associations, and not of (biological) individual predispositions.

A specific effect of the performativity of identities is their embodied dimension: Physical structures of the body can be shaped by the actions and practices performed by it, which in turn are influenced by the regulatory ideals that streamline actions (Soafer 2006). For example, this can encompass physical effects of constant hard work, of regular horse riding, of food cultures and dietary rules, and of mobilities. Thus, the history of the body itself is closely interconnected with the performativity of identities, and this is a field that is at least partially accessible to archaeology.

Drawing on anthropological cross-cultural comparison, the concept of people as bounded individuals has been identified as a stereotype in western perception, and it has been placed into a wider and more diverse context by numerous examples of differently constructed self- and group-identities from ethnography. Diverse alternative understandings of personhood are possible, especially with respect to the relational aspects of identity (*e.g.* Fowler 2004). For example, in her study of contemporary Melanesian society, Marilyn Strathern shows that persons are not first and foremost indivisible *individuals*, but in many respects divisible *dividuals*, emerging and constantly developing and changing through dynamic relationships with other people and also with the non-human world, *e.g.*, through gifts to others, such as breast milk, valuable artefacts, *etc.* (Strathern 1988). In this sense, people and their self-identities are defined by their relationships with others (Harris and Cipolla 2017, 63). An important though contested concept promoted by Strathern based on these studies is that personhood, according to such an understanding, is actually not limited to humans but can be expanded to other things and beings.

Thus, these concepts of the performativity of identity, of the role of regulatory ideals in it, and of the connected complex notions of what personhood can be, are highly relevant for archaeological interpretations of identity and its material footprint. They open up alternative conceptual backgrounds in order to assess past foreign societies, which were different from our current individualistic understanding of person and society, rooted in dualisms such as nature-culture and human-environment and which is – as a specific historical situation – progressively dominating our increasingly globalised world.

Case studies

The following three case studies from the authors' own research – one linguistic case study, one primarily archaeological case study and one which combines these two fields – illustrate some of the categories discussed in the previous sections in somewhat more detail.

Case study 1: Socio-linguistic dynamics and identities in Central and Eastern Europe

The present case study serves to highlight two examples of conscious acts-of-identity within and for groups in which language is used to project a specific identity within specific domains.

The first example deals with German, which was officially introduced by Habsburg rulers in 1626 into the Czech part of their empire. In the 17th and 18th centuries, Czech receded and became primarily the language of the rural population, servants and craftsmen in certain cities in some areas, while other areas became completely German-speaking. Self-identification had a primarily political or geographical basis in terms of being a citizen of the Habsburg Empire or – in a narrower sense – a citizen of the Bohemian part of it. The mother tongue of the inhabitants was not insignificant, but certainly a secondary feature of self-identification, mostly connected to the lower social status in contrast to the upper classes who spoke German. It is only towards the end of the 18th century and the first half of the 19th century that interest in the Czech language began to resurface. The most important event leading up to this resurgent interest was the publication of a Czech grammar by J. Dobrovský in 1809 written in German with the title *Ausführliches Lehrgebäude der böhmischen Sprache zur gründlichen Erlernung derselben für Deutsche, zur vollkommenern Kenntniß für Böhmen* (Dobrovský 1809/1940), which served as the foundation of a large (and successful) revitalisation effort. Since a learned grammar alone, even if composed by a scholar of European reputation at the time, was not sufficient to revitalise a language, a group of influential patriots popularised Dobrovský's grammar and accompanied it with "patriotic" propaganda, *e.g.*, the foundation of a Bohemian national museum (in 1818), the publication of forged, supposedly medieval Czech manuscripts (discovered in 1817 and 1818), scientific journals in Czech (*e.g.* Journal of the National Museum starting in 1827), *etc*. These efforts resulted in a vast improvement in the standing of the Czech language and loosened its ties to a particular social status. At the same time, language was reinterpreted as a political and "ethnic" or "national" symbol, distinguishing speakers of Czech as the "real" or "original" inhabitants from speakers of German as foreign intruders. But it was not until the late 19th and the early 20th century that Czech replaced German completely as the marker of political (and "ethnic" in the sense of "national") identity.

Another example is the change of the linguistic marker of the group identity of the social "elite" in East Slavic areas (modern Russia, Belarus and Ukraine) from (Old) Church Slavic, also known as "(Old) Church Slavonic", or German and French to Standard Russian. The Christianisation of the early East Slavic population in the 11th century brought Old Church Slavic – genealogically a South Slavic language – as the language of the church and, later, the language of the East Slavic elite from the Balkans. Initially, Old Church Slavic may have been rather strange or foreign for Eastern Slavs, although to a certain extent intelligible. Over the following centuries, different changes in both languages made them become more distinct from one another. Mutual intelligibility decreased despite a large number of lexical and grammatical borrowings from Old Church Slavic into East Slavic and penetrations of East Slavic features into the Church Slavic of the east. The originally religious language developed into the group-identity marker of the local church and secular elites. This situation of *diglossia* lasted until around 1700 CE (Uspenskij 1987, 20-21), when Tsar Peter the Great brought the idea of a written vernacular back from his journey through Western Europe. The tsar himself restricted the use of Church Slavic to religious affairs and ordered the use of Russian in all "worldly" matters.

Since secular elites had used Church Slavic as their "status language", Peter the Great's restriction of Church Slavic to the religious realm created a kind of linguistic vacuum in his empire which was consequently filled by foreign languages:

The educated chose to speak (and write) German (especially in the administration and the military) and/or French (with respect to "high culture"). There are also quite a few cases of Russian nobility not being able to speak Russian well during the 18th and 19th centuries – cf. Fleckenstein's remark about French being the cultivated everyday language of the Russian nobility by the end of the 18th century in Eckert *et al.* (1983, 217). After a period of experiments with secular literature, it was not until the end of the 18th / the beginning of the 19th century that several writers (N. M. Karamzin, A. S. Puškin)[5] managed to create a "new" Russian. This form of Russian was clearly a compromise between the Moscow vernacular (East Slavic) and Church Slavic (South Slavic), which was also influenced by western languages (especially French and German), although standardising grammars did not yet appear at this time. A general system of education (which established a standard variety of Russian) was not set up until after the communist takeover in the 1920's. This development illustrates the formation of modern Russian as a koiné language (cf. the discussion above). The two source languages functioned as social markers of identity, with the resulting "new" Russian language being a new marker of a "national" identity encompassing all social layers.

Case study 2: Mortuary rites, geographic origins and identities in Bronze Age Slovakia

At the Early Bronze Age cemetery of Jelšovce, Slovakia, individual burials presented a connection with other, *e.g.*, non-local groups in a number of different ways from body position within the grave to grave goods. When looking solely at the burials, there appear to be mainly traditional local burials and a few divergent burials with elements from more distant groups that first suggested that these individuals were foreigners and that this element of their identity was highlighted in their graves. However, a strontium isotope study, which was able to determine whether the deceased were born, raised or died geographically close to the area of the cemetery, revealed that these local vs. foreign identities are far more complex than they first appeared (Reiter and Frei 2015). It thus appears that a person's "true" origins were less important to their identity in death than we might have assumed.

For example, the man in grave 444 was buried in a 'frog' position (supine with knees splayed and feet together), more common in the Ukrainian Steppe region at the time, in contrast to the traditional position (a crouched position lying on one side) for graves of the Nitra period to which he dates (Reiter and Frei 2015, 126). Archaeologically speaking, this man could be considered to have had a foreign identity at death. Yet, a strontium isotope analysis of his bones revealed that for the final 15-20 years of his life, this man lived in an area local to the burial ground; therefore, in his case this link to a foreign group either harks back to his earlier life or his "foreign" burial position holds a different significance.

One sign that a non-local burial identity at this site might not be directly related to expressing a foreign identity based on geographical origins is that there are also two burials where foreigners (isotopically) were buried with foreign goods from a region that was not that of their geographical origins. The women in graves 110 and 190A were each buried with an obsidian blade; objects foreign to the site, yet also to the areas indicated by their strontium ratios (Reiter and Frei 2015, 126).

---

5   In this paper, we transliterate Cyrillic according to the DIN norm.

Why might a foreign identity be highlighted, outside of being part of how a person defined themselves? For the case of the woman from grave 80, whose strontium ratio from tooth enamel shows that she had been living in an area local to the site since her childhood but was buried with non-local ceramics from the area of modern-day Hungary, it has been argued that the use of exotic goods is a marker of status rather than geographic origins (Reiter and Frei 2015, 126). Access to foreign goods was apparently considered to have been an element of this woman's life that was important enough to be displayed in her burial.

This is likely related to the fact that communities across the Eurasian continent became more connected during the European Bronze Age, allowing individuals to more frequently come into contact with other, non-local individuals and even wider networks of material culture. Burials, in particular, allow archaeologists to see how these new contacts affected individual (if not necessarily self-) identities as well as wider social reactions to this opening of social worlds.

The processes of cultural synthesis and adoption were at work when isotopically local individuals were buried with non-local objects (in the merging of local and non-local cultures or the acceptance of non-local traditions/material culture by locals, respectively), whereas sublimation (in the sense of transformation into an idealised form) occurred when an isotopically non-local individual was buried in the local manner with no indication of their differing geographical origin (Reiter 2014, 18). These represent insights into identities that were in use within the community of the deceased.

Both individual and group identities can be seen in prehistoric burials, but through the lens of how the deceased individuals were perceived by the community that buried them. In this particular cemetery, joining the community later in their life was not necessarily important for how that individual was presented in death. Being local or foreign may have been a more performative element of identity than a category assigned based on one's geographical origins.

Case study 3: Maintaining Taz Selkup identity in Western Siberia

Contrasting roles of material culture and language in the negotiation and expression of identity are demonstrated by the Samoyed group of the Taz Selkup in Western Siberia. As a mobile hunter-fisher-reindeer herder community, the Selkup migrated from the southern to the northern taiga in the 17th and 18th centuries CE (Golovnev 1995). This relocation history enables us to trace socio-economic adaptations to the new region and their recursive effects on the further development of the Selkup ethnic identity within the framework of material culture, language and toponyms, self-perception, and inter-group relations (Piezonka et al. 2020).

There are a few main family groups based on totemic clan structures that are historically associated with different tributary catchments of the upper Taz area. Exogamy with other ethnic groups (e.g. Evenks, Kets, Russians, Khanty) have led to "terribly international, almost cosmopolitan conditions", as the Finnish scholar Kai Donner observed in 1912. As an example, Donner describes a man, whose mother was an Evenki woman, his father a Khant, and his wife a Ket, who spoke Selkup at home but was also fluent in all these other languages (Donner 1926, 152). This inter-ethnic ambiguity continues today, as many people who consider themselves Selkup have a parent or one or more grandparents from other ethnic communities. Thus, (personal) ethnic identity among the Taz Selkup forms a continuum between Selkup self-perception and trans-ethnic kinship relations; it is influenced by factors such as family background, marriage relations and language use. The Selkup identity is sometimes only developed after childhood and adolescence when returning to the taiga and adopting a mobile hunter-herder way of life within the Selkup extended family group and, in connection with this, a more intense relationship with and command of the Selkup language (field recordings by Vladimir Adayev and Henny Piezonka 2017). In the case of the Taz Selkup, language forms a major means in maintaining, enacting and consciously strengthening ethnic identity. While children are mainly taught in Russian at boarding school, in several Taz Selkup families conscious efforts are now made to teach the children the Selkup language in order to preserve their Selkup identity.

While language continues to play a central role in consciously upholding Selkup identity (Tučkova *et al.* 2013, 281), other aspects which were formerly linked to a specific Selkup identity, including cosmology and associated rituals (including burial rites, but also fairy tales and stories), have changed in the north under the influence of neighbouring groups to a more general Arctic culture (Donner 1926, 152). Material culture has increasingly lost its function as a (conscious) identity marker; among the Northern Selkup, ethnic costumes and ornaments have now virtually disappeared from everyday life and are only worn on festive occasions. Also, typologies and technologies of functional items, such as sledges, show the influence of other northern peoples, *e.g.,* the Nenets, and have lost all stylistic connections to the forms used by the Southern Selkup in their former, southern homeland.

The temporary dwellings used by the mobile Selkup hunter-fisher-herders in the upper Taz region until today are interesting as they point out the dangers of interpreting structures and boundaries of social groups based solely upon the remains of their material culture. Stylistically, these dwellings reflect the combination of habitual persistence of assertive stylistic elements with the pragmatic adoption of new, northern forms. A hybrid type that developed in the north is the earthen winter house that combines southern Selkup/Khanty house building traditions with features of northern Samoyed conical tents. The Entsy and forest Nenets, who settled the wider region before the arrival of the Selkup migrants, used only tipi-like tents but no winter earth houses. Earth houses with sunken floors, on the other hand, were a wide-spread dwelling type of the Southern Selkup, and also of the Khanty settling the middle Ob' region between the southern and northern Selkup areas.

The Selkup newcomers to the Taz brought this southern earth house building tradition with them when they migrated northwards and continued to erect such houses at their winter stations (Adayev and Zimina 2016). However, due to an increased mobility that is connected to the uptake of reindeer husbandry in the north, the winter houses developed into simpler and easier-to-build forms. The sunken floors were lost altogether and the interior layout changed from the complex southern style, with a clay oven by the wall and asymmetrically arranged earthen sleeping benches along the walls, to a simple symmetrical ground-level layout resembling that of the symmetrical tent.

This has two main implications concerning identity and its archaeological recognisability: (1) In contrast to the observation that migrant newcomers would often adapt the external domain to the common ways in the immigration area, while preserving assertive, habitual styles in the interior (Burmeister 2000, 542; Burmeister 2017), the contrary seems to be the case with the Northern Selkup. Here, the interior is adjusted pragmatically and modelled on what is common in the immigration area, while the imported architectural form itself, the earthen dwelling that is alien to the north, is preserved and continued. (2) From an archaeological point of view, the importation of the Selkup earth house as a distinct southern dwelling type into the north, as well as its further stylistic development, would be recognisable archaeologically, given the necessary data density.

Unlike in the south, where kurgan burials dominated, burial customs among the Northern Selkup became rather diverse and included surface, below-ground, and air burials; the practice of cremation is also documented (Poshekhonova *et al.* 2018). Nowadays, Russian-style burials in grave pits are the most common type, albeit with the specific custom of placing the possessions of the deceased on the ground beside the grave, where they are henceforth left untouched. Some of the above-ground structures find parallels in Khanty burial customs further south. Air burials represent an element which is especially widespread among the Nenets, Evenki and other northern groups.

In summary, with regards to the materials and methods available to archaeologists, the territorially distinct and strongly developed ethnic self-identification of the Taz Selkup community, which is expressed, *e.g.*, by the conscious maintenance of the language, would be more or less invisible archaeologically. The material culture has evolved further in their new northern home, adapting to the new environmental and economic conditions by adopting suitable styles and types from other northern groups, no longer containing any clear, conscious material identity markers. This also concerns the hybrid character of the burial customs. Due to the lack of further material, emblematic identity markers, and the archaeological invisibility of the main field of northern Selkup identity enactment – the language itself – it is questionable whether the Selkup migration and the persistence and further development of a distinct northern Selkup ethnic identity could be recognised, or even suspected, on the basis of archaeological evidence alone. Instead, this ethnic community would most probably not be recognised as a distinct group, but would be archaeologically diluted in a material continuum of regional styles, hybrid items, and adaptive solutions.

Discussion and outlook

This paper is a first attempt by the present group of authors – and to our knowledge the first of its kind – to compare and contrast the notion of *identity* and its various components in the fields of archaeology and linguistics with the hope that this can serve as a springboard for future interdisciplinary collaboration on this topic. It has therefore raised many more questions and potential avenues for investigation than it has provided answers. As such, we would like to suggest some commonalities and interfaces between the study of identity in linguistics and archaeology that our discussion has brought to light.

Synthesising the cross-disciplinary account above, we have seen that identity expression can be conscious or subconscious (Fig. 1). Expressions of identity can also be enacted (verbally and non-verbally), embodied, and materialised. Linguistics and archaeology have different access to these realms of identity expression: Linguistics has access to the verbal part of enacted identities. Archaeology, on the other hand, has access to material expressions and, through a collaboration with physical anthropology and archaeometrics, also to certain embodied expressions (conscious: *e.g.* skull flattening; subconscious: *e.g.* health status, access to certain foods/food tabus, *etc.*).

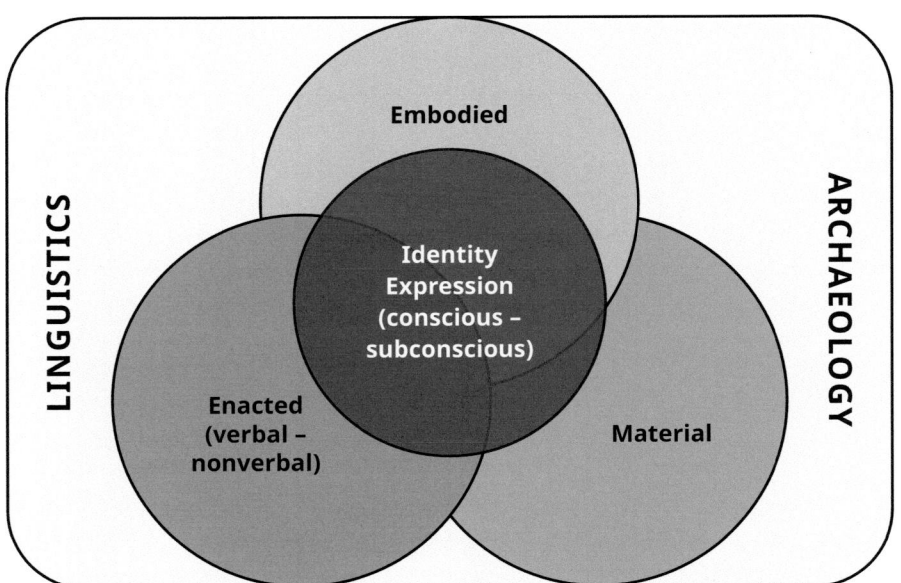

Figure 1. Scientific access to enacted, embodied and material identity expressions through linguistics and archaeology (diagram: the authors).

Archaeologists have a long tradition of co-opting concepts from other disciplines in order to increase the potential ways in which they can fill gaps in the archaeological record and interpretative limitations. When it comes to the topics discussed here, emblematicity and code-switching have already been touched upon in archaeological inquiry. A number of other concepts discussed here relating to group identities have also already been incorporated by archaeologists in their work, especially in the fields of ethnoarchaeology and historical archaeology, where some element of language is accessible to archaeologists (in addition to the examples in this paper, see also, *e.g.*, Hodder 1982, Blench and Spriggs 1997; 1998; 1999a; 1999b; Anthony 2007; Blench 2017). Direct collaborations between linguists and ethnoarchaeologists could thus expand upon this theme, potentially identifying interlinked linguistic and material patterns that could perhaps be applied to archaeological research even in the absence of any knowledge of the contemporary language. The direction of identification in the examples and case studies discussed here is more inwardly focused and linked to projected identity, but given the communicative role of language and the visual nature of artefacts related to costume or style, it is likely the case that there are aspects of how such emblematicity is perceived by other groups.

Code-switching has also been applied to material culture, especially from the ancient Mediterranean area, where information about language use of the time is available (*e.g.* Wallace-Hadrill 2008 on Roman cultural identity; Winther-Jacobsen 2013 on the similarity between a conversation and a burial as acts of identity; Revell 2013 on performative Roman and pre-Roman ethnic identities). The notion of switching between different "assemblages" or "repertoires" available to an individual (whether material or linguistic) to fit the current context and the most appropriate identity in that moment is certainly an interesting element of human behaviour, past or present (Schneeweiß 2020, 46-47). Future collaboration here could, *e.g.*, focus on similar aspects of "switching", "fused lects" or "polylanguaging" with respect to material culture, for example, possible group identity defined through the acceptance of material culture associated with two or perhaps several different social groups as a possible expression of a new, unique, perhaps even cosmopolitan identity.

Further potential areas of collaboration could include possible material parallels to linguistic ideology, language planning and notions of linguistic purity, *i.e.*, well-known, conscious attempts found throughout the world today to make language fit into a pre-defined identity which does not yet exist but is propagated as necessary, correct, or "pure", and attempts are made to enact it to make reality fit the aspired identity.

Linguistics as a field also has much to gain through collaboration with archaeologists working on aspects of identity in pre-modern societies. The most obvious benefits would certainly be in the field of historical linguistics, in which, *e.g.*, the traditional comparative method is highly constrained by the time-depth of the oldest extent texts for a particular language family or region. Although language typologists can go back somewhat further in time, in the end we are merely left with data for structural features of various languages and their geographical spread which await further context from other fields – such as archaeology.

Knowledge of the way members of earlier societies identified themselves can also help historical linguists avoid potential pitfalls. For example, although the abrupt, widespread introduction of a new style of pottery into a region could be due to the arrival of a new ethnic group with a new language in a particular region, this could also be a false conclusion with serious consequences. Here, more informed studies of the potential material expression, or the lack thereof, of identities of the members of such societies by archaeologists ethnoarchaeologists could provide linguists, for example, those working within the newly formed field of sociolinguistic typology (*e.g.* Trudgill 2011), with critical information about the social make-up of these earlier societies, their likely degree of multilingualism or relative isolation based on their material culture, *etc*. Sociolinguistic typologists would then be in the position to interpret this societal information more cautiously with respect to potentially related linguistic developments, which could then possibly lead to an identification of the respective language(s).

A related field of inquiry, which would strongly benefit from intensified interdisciplinary dialogue between linguistics and archaeology, concerns the identification and localisation of "protolanguages" with the reconstruction of subsequent language developments and dispersals. The above-mentioned pitfall of indiscriminately equating language groups with groups of ethnic self-identification and extrapolating such presumed associations onto patterns in material culture as expected expressions of such postulated groups ("pots equal people") can thus be avoided and replaced with better-informed, more comprehensive discussions of this multi-facetted field. Novel multi-disciplinary studies on bio-cultural co-evolution that integrate studies in linguistic, cultural and biological trajectories (*e.g.* DFG Center for Advanced Studies 'Words, Bones, Genes, Tools', Tübingen) are a positive step in this direction. For example, we would expect to find a slow, gradual complexification of a language's phonological and/or morphological systems to result from a situation of relative isolation of a small ethnic group speaking a single language, whereas a language with a large number of adult second-language learners in a highly cosmopolitan society would likely result in a strong simplification in these two areas of the grammar. Such information, which would otherwise likely remain undetected, could be of great value in identifying with at least some degree of certainty the respective language(s) from among any later languages of this region for which such grammatical information is known.

While this may seem somewhat abstract at the moment, as the present cross-disciplinary research program progresses one thing seems certain: the benefits for both linguists and archaeologists will soon exceed the short list mentioned here, extending beyond the intrinsic potential of a better understanding of just what constitutes *identity* and thereby allowing us to find simplicity and meaning in a complex world.

References

Adayev, V.N. and Zimina, O.Y., 2016. Above-Ground Frame Buildings in Western Siberia: Archaeological and Ethnographic Parallels. *Archaeology, Ethnology and Anthropology of Eurasia,* 44 (3), 63-71.

Agha, A., 2003. The social life of cultural value. *Language and Communication,* 23, 231-273.

Aikhenvald, A.Y., 2003. Multilingualism and ethnic stereotypes: The Tariana of northwest Amazonia. *Language in Society,* 32, 1-21.

Aikhenvald, A.Y., 2007. Grammars in contact: a cross-linguistic perspective. *In:* A.Y. Aikhenvald and R.M.W. Dixon, eds. *Grammars in Contact: a cross-linguistic typology.* Explorations in Linguistic Typology 4. Oxford: Oxford University Press, 1-66.

Aikhenvald, A.Y., 2013. The value of language and the language of value. A view from Amazonia. *Journal of Ethnographic Theory,* 3 (2), 53-77.

Anthony, D.W., 2007. *The Horse, the Wheel and Language. How Bronze-Age Riders from the Eurasian Steppes shaped the Modern World.* Oxford: Princeton University Press.

Appleby, J.E.P., 2010. Why we need an archaeology of old age, and a suggested approach. *Norwegian Archaeological Review,* 43, 145-168.

Assmann, J., 1992. *Das kulturelle Gedächtnis. Schrift, Erinnerung und politische Identität in frühen Hochkulturen.* München: Beck.

Auer, P., 1999. From code-switching via language mixing to fused lects: Towards a dynamic typology of bilingual speech. *The International Journal of Bilingualism,* 3 (4), 309-332.

Bal, M., 1994. Telling Objects: Narrative Perspective on Collecting. *In:* J. Elsner and R. Cardinal, eds. *The Cultures of Collecting.* London: Reaktion Books.

Banks, M., 1996. *Ethnicity: Anthropological Constructions.* London: Routledge.

Barth, F., 1969. *Ethnic Groups and Boundaries. The Social Organization of Culture Difference.* Boston: Little, Brown and Company.

Bhabha, H., 2016. *Über kulturelle Hybridität. Tradition und Übersetzung.* Herausgegeben und eingeleitet von Anna Babka und Gerald Posselt. Wien and Berlin: Turia + Kant.

Bird-David, N., 2017. *Us, Relatives: Scaling and Plural Life in a Forager World.* Oakland, California: University of California Press.

Blench, R., 2017. Ethnographic and archaeological correlates for a Mainland Southeast Asia linguistic area. *In: A. Acri, R. Blench, A. Landmann, eds. Spirits and Ships. Cultural Transfers in Early Monsoon Asia.* Singapore: ISEAS, 207-238.

Blench, R. and Spriggs, M., eds., 1997. *Archaeology and Language I: Theoretical and Methodological Orientations.* London: Routledge.

Blench, R. and Spriggs, M., eds., 1998. *Archaeology and Language II: Archaeological Data and Linguistic Hypotheses.* London: Routledge.

Blench, R. and Spriggs, M., eds., 1999a. *Archaeology and Language III: Artefacts, Languages and Texts.* London: Routledge.

Blench, R. and Spriggs, M., eds., 1999b. *Archaeology and Language IV: Language Change and Cultural Transformation.* London: Routledge.

Brather, S., 2004. *Ethnische Interpretationen in der frühgeschichtlichen Archäologie.*

Geschichte, Grundlagen und Alternativen. Reallexikon der Germanischen Altertumskunde, Ergänzungsband. Berlin and New York: Verlag Walther de Gruyter.

Brubaker, R. and Cooper, M., 2000. Beyond "Identity". *Theory and Society,* 29 (1), 1-47.

Bucholtz, M. and Hall, K., 2004. Language and identity. *In:* A. Duranti, ed. *A companion to linguistic anthropology.* Malden, Oxford, Carlton, Victoria: Blackwell Publishing.

Burmeister, St., 2000. Archaeology and Migration. *Current Anthropology,* 41 (4), 539-567.

Burmeister, St., 2017. The archaeology of migration: what can and should it accomplish? *In:* H. Meller, F. Daim, J. Krause, R. Risch, eds. *Migration und Integration von der Urgeschichte bis zum Mittelalter/Migration and Integration from Prehistory to the Middle Ages.* Tagungen des Landesmuseums für Vorgeschichte Halle 17. Halle/Saale 2017. Halle (Saale): Landesamt für Denkmalpflege und Archäologie Sachsen-Anhalt, Landesmuseum für Vorgeschichte, 57-68.

Burmeister, S. and Müller-Scheeßel, N., 2006. *Soziale Gruppen – kulturelle Grenzen. Die Interpretation sozialer Identitäten in der Prähistorischen Archäologie.* Tübinger Archäologische Taschenbücher 5. Münster, New York, München, Berlin: Waxmann.

Butler, J., 1990. *Gender Trouble: Feminism and the Subversion of Identity.* London: Routledge.

Childe, V.G., 1929. *The Danube in Prehistory.* Oxford: The Clarendon Press.

Conkey, M.W. and Spector, J.D., 1984. Archaeology and the study of gender. *In:* M.B. Schiffer, ed. *Advances in archaeological method and theory.* Vol. 7. Orlando: Academic Press. 1-38.

Dediu, D., Cysouw, M., Levinson, St.C., Baronchelli, A., Christiansen, M.H., Croft, W., Evans, N., Russel, S.G., Gray, D., Kandler, A., Lieven, E., 2013. Cultural Evolution of Language. *In:* P.J. Richerson and M.H. Christiansen, eds. *Cultural Evolution: Society, Technology, Language, and Religion.* Cambridge, MA and London: MIT Press, 303-332.

Díaz-Andreu, Lucy, M.S., Babić, S., Edwards, D.N., 2005. *The Archaeology of Identity. Approaches to gender, age, status, ethnicity and religion.* Abingdon: Routledge.

Dobrovský, J., 1809/1940. *Podrobná mluvnice jazyka českého v redakcích z roku 1809 a 1819.* Praha: Melantrich.

Dong, J., 2010. The enregisterment of Putonghua. *Language and Communication,* 30, 265-275.

Donner, K., 1926. *Bei den Samojeden in Sibirien.* Stuttgart: Strecker und Schröder.

Eckert, P., 2012. Three waves of variation study: The emergence of meaning in the study of sociolinguistic variation. *Annual Review of Anthropology,* 41, 87-100.

Eckert, R., Crome, E., Fleckenstein, Ch., 1983. *Geschichte der russischen Sprache.* Leipzig: VEB Verlag Enzyklopädie.

Evans, N., 2013. Language Diversity as a Resource for Understanding Cultural Evolution. *In:* P.J. Richerson and M.H. Christiansen, eds. *Cultural Evolution: Society, Technology, Language, and Religion.* Cambridge, MA and London: MIT Press, 233-268.

Fishman J.A., 1997. Language and ethnicity: the view from within. *In:* F. Coulmas, ed. *The Handbook of Sociolinguistics.* Oxford: Blackwell, 327-343.

Fowler, C., 2004. *The Archaeology of Personhood: An Anthropological Approach.* London: Routledge.

Furholt, M., 2018. Massive Migrations? The Impact of Recent aDNA Studies on our View of Third Millennium Europe. *European Journal of Archaeology,* 21 (02), 159-191.

Furholt, M. and Stockhammer, Ph.W., 2008. Wenn stumme Dinge sprechen sollen – Gedanken zu semiotischen Ansätzen in der Prähistorischen Archäologie. *In:* M. Butter, R. Grundmann, C. Sanchez, eds. *Zeichen der Zeit – Interdisziplinäre*

Perspektiven zur Semiotik. Frankfurt a.M.: Verlag P. Lang, 59-71.

Gero, J.M. and Conkey, M.W., 1991. *Engendering Archaeology: Women and Prehistory.* Cambridge, Mass.: Basil Blackwell.

Glomb, St., 2013. Identität, persönliche. *In:* A. Nünning, ed. *Metzler Lexikon Literatur- und Kulturtheorie. Ansätze – Personen – Grundbegriffe.* Stuttgart, Weimar: Verlag J. B. Metzler, 324.

Golovko, E.V., 2003. Language contact and group identity: the role of "folk" linguistic engineering. *In:* Y. Matras and P. Bakker, eds. *The Mixed Language Debate. Theoretical and Empirical Advances.* Trends in Linguistics Studies and Monographs 145. Berlin, New York: DeGruyter, 177-208.

Golovnev, A.V., 1995. *Govorjaščie kul'tury: tradicii samodijcev i ugrov.* Ekaterinburg: UrO RAN.

Gosden, C., 2004. *Archaeology and Colonialism: Cultural Contact from 5000 BC to the Present.* Cambridge: Cambridge University Press.

Gramsch, A., 2015. Culture, change, identity – Approaches to the interpretation of cultural change. *Anthropologie,* 53 (3), 341-349.

Gumperz, J.J., 1982. *Discourse strategies.* Studies in Interactional Sociolinguistics 1. Cambridge, New York: Cambridge University Press.

Haak, W., Lazaridis, I., Patterson, N., Rohland, N., Mallick, S., Llamas, B., Brandt, G., Nordenfelt, S., Harney, E., Stewardson, K., Fu, Q., Mittnik, A., Bánffy, E., Economou, C. Francken, M., Friederich, S., Pena, R.G., Hallgren, F., Khartanovich, V., Khokhlov, A., Kunst, M., Kuznetsov, P., Meller, H., Mochalov, O., Moiseyev, V., Nicklisch, N., Pichler, S.L. Risch, R., Rojo Guerra, M.A., Roth, C., Szécsényi-Nagy, A., Wahl, J., Meyer, M., Krause, J., Brown, D., Anthony, D., Cooper, A., Alt, A.W., Reich, D., 2015. Massive migration from the steppe was a source for Indo-European languages in Europe. *Nature,* 522/7555, 207-211.

Harris, O.J.T. and Cipolla, C., 2017. *Archaeological Theory in the New Millennium: Introducing Current Perspectives.* Abingdon: Routledge.

Heyd, V., 2017. Kossinna's smile. *Antiquity,* 91 (356), 348-359.

Hodder, I., 1982. *Symbols in Action: Ethnoarchaeological studies of material culture.* Cambridge: Cambridge University Press.

Hofmann, D., 2015. What Have Genetics Ever Done for Us? The Implications of aDNA Data for Interpreting Identity in Early Neolithic Central Europe. *European Journal of Archaeology,* 18 (3), 454-476.

Horatschek, A.-M., 2013. Identität, kollektive. *In:* A. Nünning, ed. *Metzler Lexikon Literatur- und Kulturtheorie. Ansätze – Personen – Grundbegriffe.* Stuttgart, Weimar: Verlag J. B. Metzler, 323-24.

Jeloeva, F.A., 1995. *Tjurkojazyčnye pravoslavnye greki Vostočnoj Gruzii (Calkinskij i Tetricikaroisskij rajony).* Saint Petersburg: Saint Petersburg State University.

Johnstone, B., Andrus, J., Danielson, A.E., 2006. Mobility, indexicality, and the enregisterment of "Pittsburghese". *Journal of English Linguistics,* 34, 77-104.

Jones, S., 1997. *The Archaeology of Ethnicity. Constructing identities in the past and present.* London: Routledge.

Jørgensen, J.N., Karrebæk, M.S., Madsen, L.M., Møller, J.S., 2011. Polylanguaging in superdiversity. *Diversities,* 13 (2), 23-38.

Joseph, J.E., 2004. *Language and Identity. National, ethnic, religious.* Basingstoke, Hamphsire, New York: Palgrave Macmillan.

Jullien, F., 2017. *Es gibt keine kulturelle Identität.* Berlin: Suhrkamp.

Kossinna, G.. 1912. *Die deutsche Vorgeschichte – eine hervorragend nationale Wissenschaft.* Würzburg: Kabitzsch.

Kristiansen, K., Allentoft, M.E., Frei, K.M., Iversen, R., Johannsen, N.N., Kroonen, G., Pospieszny, Ł., Price, T.D., Rasmussen, S., Sjögren, K.-G., Sikora, M., Willerslev, E., 2017. Re-theorising mobility and the formation of culture and language among the Corded Ware Culture in Europe. *Antiquity,* 91 (356), 334-347.

Kulick, D., 1992. *Language Shift and Cultural Reproduction: Socialization, Syncretism and Self in a Papua New Guinean Village.* Cambridge: Cambridge University Press.

Labov, W., 1966. *The Social Stratification of English in New York City.* Washington, D.C.: Center for Applied Linguistics. Cambridge: Cambridge University Press.

Labov, W., 1969. *The Study of Nonstandard English.* Washington, DC: National Council of Teachers of English.

Labov, W., 1972. *Sociolinguistic Patterns.* Philadelphia: University of Pennsylvania Press.

Le Page, R.B. and Tabouret-Keller, A., 1985. *Acts of identity: Creole-based approaches to language and ethnicity.* Cambridge: Cambridge University Press.

Meyer, C., Ganslmeier, R., Dresely, V., Alt, K.W., 2012. New Approaches to the Reconstruction of Kinship and Social Structure Based on Bioarchaeological Analysis of Neolithic Multiple and Collective Graves. *In:* J. Kolář and F. Trampota, eds. *Theoretical and Methodological Considerations in Central European Neolithic Archaeology.* BAR International Series 2325. Oxford: Archaeopress, 11-23.

Meyerhoff, M., 2006. *Introducing Sociolinguistics.* London, New York: Routledge.

Mumm, P.-A., 2018. Sprachgemeinschaft, Ethnizität, Identität. *In:* P.-A. Mumm, ed. *Sprachen, Völker und Phantome. Sprach- und kulturwissenschaftliche Studien zur Ethnizität.* Berlin: De Gruyter.

Piezonka, H., Poshekhonova, O., Adayev, V., Rud, A., 2020. Migration and its effects on life ways and subsistence strategies of boreal hunter-fishers: Ethnoarchaeological research among the Selkup, Siberia. *Quaternary International,* 541, 189-203.

Poshekhonova, O.E., Kisagulov, A.V., Gimranov, D.O., Nekrasov, A.E., Afonin, A.S., 2018. Transformation of Upper Taz Selkup funeral rites according to paleoecological data. *Journal of Archaeological Science: Reports,* 22, 132-141.

Rageot, M.S. Cafisso, Fries-Knoblach, J., Krausse, D., Hoppe, Th., Stockhammer, Ph., Spiteri, C., 2019. New insights into Early Celtic consumption practices: Organic residue analyses of local and imported pottery from Vix-Mont Lassois. *PLoS ONE* 14 (6), e0218001. Available at: https://doi.org/10.1371/journal.pone.0218001.

Rebay-Salisbury, K., 2017. Bronze Age Beginnings: The Conceptualization of Motherhood in Prehistoric Europe. *In:* C.D. and C. Phelan, eds. *Motherhood in Antiquity.* Cham: Springer Nature, 169-196.

Reiter, S.S., 2014. A Choreography of Place. Globalisation and Identity in the Bronze Age. *In:* S.S. Reiter, H.W. Norgaard, Z. Kolcze, C. Rassmann, eds. *Rooted in Movement. Aspects of Mobility in Bronze Age Europe.* Jutland Archaeological Society Publications 83. Aarhus: Jutland Archaeological Society, 15-22.

Reiter, S.S. and Frei, K.M., 2015. Migration and Identity at the Early Bronze Age Cemetery of Jelšovce, Southwest Slovakia: The strontium evidence. *In:* P. Suchowska-Ducke, S. Reiter, H. Vandkilde, eds. *Forging Identities. The Mobility of Culture in Bronze Age Europe. Report from a Marie Curie Project 2009-2012 with Concluding Conference at Aarhus University, Moesgaard 2012.* BAR International Series S2771. Oxford: BAR, 121-130.

Revell, L., 2013. Code-switching and identity in the Western Provinces. *HEROM* 2, 123-141.

Schneeweiß, J., 2020. *Zwischen den Welten. Archäologie einer europäischen Grenzregion zwischen Sachsen, Slawen, Franken und Dänen.* Kiel, Hamburg: Wachholtz.

Silverstein, M., 2003. Indexical order and the dialectics of sociolinguistic life. *Language and Communication*, 23 (3-4), 193-229.

Soafer, J., 2006. *The Body as Material Culture: A Theoretical Osteoarchaeology.* Cambridge: Cambridge University Press.

Sørensen, M.L.S., 1997. Reading Dress: The Construction of Social Categories and Identities in Bronze Age Europe. *Journal of European Archaeology,* 5 (1), 93-114.

Strathern, M., 1988. *The Gender of the Gift: Problems with Women and Problems with Society in Melanesia.* Cambridge: Cambridge University Press.

Tajfel, H., 1978. Interindividual behaviour and intergroup behaviour. *In:* H. Tajfel, ed. *Differentiation between Social Groups: Studies in the Social Psychology of Intergroup Relations.* London, New York: Academic Press, 27-60.

Taylor, N., 2013. Broken Mirrors? Archaeological Reflections of Identity. *In:* V. Ginn, R. Enlander, R. Crozier, eds. *Exploring Prehistoric Identity in Europe. Our Constructs or Theirs?* Oxford: Oxbow, 175-185.

Trudgill, P., 2000. *Sociolinguistics. An introduction to language and society.* 4th Edition. London: Penguin Books.

Trudgill, P., 2011. *Sociolinguistic typology. Social determinants of linguistic complexity.* Oxford Linguistics. Oxford: Oxford University Press.

Trudgill, P., 2020. *Millennia of Language Change. Sociolinguistic Studies in Deep Historical Linguistics.* Cambridge: Cambridge University Press.

Tučkova, N.A., Gluškov, S.V., Košeleva, E.Ju, Golovnev, A.V., Bajdak, A.V., Maksimova, N.P., 2013. *Sel'kupy. Očerki tradicionnoj kul'tury i sel'kupskogo jazyka.* Tomsk: Izd-vo Tomskogo politexničeskogo universiteta.

Uspenskij, B.A., 1987. *Istorija russkogo literaturnogo jazyka (XI – XVII vv.).* Sagners Slavistische Sammlung 12. München: Otto Sagner.

Vedder, U., 2014. Sprache und Dinge. *In:* S. Samida, M.K.H. Eggert, H.P. Hahn, eds. *Handbuch Materielle Kultur. Bedeutungen, Konzepte, Disziplinen.* Stuttgart, Weimar: Metzler. 39-46.

Wallace-Hadrill, A., 2008. *Rome's Cultural Revolution.* Cambridge: Cambridge University Press.

Wiessner, P., 1983. Style and Information in Kalahari San Projectile Points. *American Antiquity,* 48, 253-76.

Winford, D., 2003. *An Introduction to Contact Linguistics.* Language in Society 33. Malden, MA: Blackwell Publishing.

Winther-Jacobsen, K., 2013. Artefact variability, assemblage differentiation, and identity negotiation. Debating code-switching in material culture: introduction. *HEROM* 2, 11-20.

Wobst, M., 1977. Stylistic Behavior and Information Exchange. *In:* Ch.E. Cleland, ed. *For the Director: Research Essays in Honor of James B. Griffin.* Ann Arbor: Museum of Anthropology, University of Michigan, 317-342.

Zeeb-Lanz, A., 2006. Überlegungen zu Sozialaspekten keramischer Gruppen. Beispiele aus dem Neolithikum Südwestdeutschland. *In:* St. Burmeister and N. Müller-Scheeßel, eds. *Soziale Gruppen – kulturelle Grenzen.* Münster: Waxmann, 81-102.

The dimensions of refuse: Discard studies as a matter of connectivity

Jens Schneeweiß

Introduction

Archaeologists work with remains and reconstruct past life on the basis of evidence acquired from these remains. Rubbish is their daily bread. The natural handling of other people's refuse and the appreciation of it as a source of information are possibly one reason that it is seldom discussed what sort of relationship existed between the refuse and those to whom it belonged. What exactly is refuse?

Natural processes on Earth can be described as material cycles. These cycles are closed on a global level; the Earth represents a closed system for substances. In physics, this fact is expressed by the energy conservation law. In the physical sense, energy is neither generated nor expended, but rather only transformed. For example, the material cycle of rocks is decisive in geology: By external influences of weathering, pressure and temperature, the igneous, metamorphic and sedimentary rocks are transformed. In ecological systems, material cycles are driven by producers, consumers and destructors. Producers make organic biomass from inorganic substances, destructors break them down again into inorganic, mineral substances. The consumers stand in between. In order to build body tissues, consumers use biomass, which they ingest from food. The rest that is not used is excreted in various ways (via faeces, breathing, *etc.*). These refuse materials – the biomass that is bound in the consumer's or-

Jens Schneeweiß
Cluster of Excellence ROOTS
Kiel University
Olshausenstraße 80h
24118 Kiel, Germany
jschneeweiss@roots.uni-kiel.de

ganism after the death of the customer – are immediately returned to the material cycle by the destructors.

From a scientific perspective, refuse material is thus closely linked to production and represents the rest that is not used by the organisms to build biomass. At the same time, this refuse is available as a raw material for the production of new material in the material cycle. We approach a scientific definition of refuse, which concentrates exclusively on the material level. But even from this perspective, it becomes clear that refuse is nothing absolute.

The material level of refuse also plays a role in the context of the humanities, particularly in connection with specific production processes. However, there are further levels that are of special importance for connectivity. It is clear that what we consider to be "refuse" and how it is dealt with are not universals. In addition to the material level, the object level is also crucial. Both levels are highly dependent on culture and closely connected with value systems.

> 'Abfall ist eine soziale bzw. kulturelle Kategorie, die Objekte relativ unabhängig von ihren intrinsischen Eigenschaften bezeichnet. Die Bezeichnung eines Objekts als Abfall repräsentiert also nicht dessen 'Wesen', sondern vielmehr das pragmatische Verhältnis, das der Bezeichnende zu seinem Objekt einnimmt' [transl. ed.: 'Refuse is a social or a cultural category that describes objects relatively independent from their intrinsic properties. The designation of an object as refuse does not represent its 'essence', but rather the pragmatic relationship that the signifier has with the object'] (Bardmann 1994, 213).

The affiliation of objects to the category 'refuse' is thus a selection process of the culture (Bardmann 1994, 190). The pointed sentence "Is that art or can it be thrown away?", which is meanwhile a commonplace, symbolises this fact. The topic of "refuse management" cannot be handled here exhaustively. Its high relevance for today's society, which faces the challenges posed by refuse problems and the exhaustion of resources in an unprecedented dimension, is obvious (cf. Windmüller 2003; 2004; Wolfram and Fansa 2003). In the following, a few topics will be highlighted that illuminate the very wide contextual field, provide food for thought, and serve as a basis for the formulation of specific research questions.

A conceptual history of refuse

The term 'refuse' (in German: Abfall) has undergone significant changes in meaning over the last 300 years, which at the same time reflects the modern development of people's relationship to rubbish (in German: Müll) and refuse. With the help of entries in encyclopaedias, Ludolf Kuchenbuch (1988; 1989) traced this development. Without going into the details,[1] the following merely represents a conceptual history of the term 'refuse' in this relatively short time span. In 1732, the first meaning for Abfall in Zedler's Grossem vollständigen Universallexikon is: 'Untreue gegen den, welchem man mit Pflichten verbunden ist' [transl. ed.: 'Unfaithfulness to whom one is bound to by duties']. As a second entry, 'Ausnahme von der Regel' [transl. ed.: 'Exception to the rule'] is noted. The third meaning denotes the difference in level, for example, in the terrain. As a forth meaning, it is expressed as a word of miners meaning a decrease in ore content and thus the yield of a mine. At that time, the idealistic meaning of the word was clearly in

---

1   For a comprehensive summary: Bardmann 1994, 162-165.

the foreground. The term was defined in a religious-political sense, including a moral and ethical component. The term *Abfall* condemned apostasy against God or an earthly ruler as unauthorised behaviour, referring to a deviation from the norm. One hundred years later, this meaning is still mentioned first in *Meyers Grossem Conversations-Lexicon für die gebildeten Stände* (1840, 64),[2] but as the second meaning of a total of eleven meanings, the following is added:

> '*Abgänge bei allerlei Fabriks- und Gewerbetätigkeiten, insbesondere, wenn sie sonst noch zu benutzen sind'.'* [transl. ed. *'Leavings from all kinds of factory and commercial activities, in particular if they still can be used'*].

Around the middle of the 19th century, however, this aspect is not yet equally represented in all encyclopaedias. In Grimm's dictionary from 1854, *Abfall* is first of all:

> '*das niederfallen oder gefallensein, des blattes vom baume, des wassers vom felsen, der späne vom hobel, der spreu vom korn' oder 'des tisches abfall (die brosamen)'* [transl. ed.: *'The failing down or having fallen, a leaf from the tree, the water from the cliffs, the shavings from the plane, the chaff from the grain' or 'the refuse from the table (the crumbs)'*],

then also to fall away '*von einem Wesen oder einer Sache*' [transl. ed.: *'from a being or a thing'*] and further, other meanings (Grimm and Grimm 1854, Col. 36). First at the end of the 19th century, material refuse prevailed over ideal refuse:

> '*die Produktion hat Politik (und Konfession) überflügelt*' [transl. ed.: *'Production has surpassed politics (and denomination)'*] (Kuchenbuch 1988, 161).

At the turn of the century, canalisation, water treatment, fertilisation, sewage fields, *etc.* belonged to the meaning of the term 'refuse'. The refuse of urban consumption was mentioned as a problem and a hazard and its safe disposal became a hygienic requirement. Around this time, in addition to different kinds of *Abfall*, refuse also appears lexically as *Müll*[3] (in the sense of 'rubbish') for the first time and is clearly associated with its elimination. In the 1930s, refuse from town and country, from production and consumption, in material, liquid, and gaseous states is finally combined under the one term – and its elimination soon lies only in the hands of the cities and municipalities (Bardmann 1994, 164). In the 1970s – a period of unrestrained refuse growth – refuse disposal became the focus of attention; refuse was then quantified according to volume and juridification was necessary. In 1972, a refuse disposal law was passed in Western Germany for the first time, the function of which is currently fulfilled by the recycling law.

With industrialisation, a one-sided, materialistic understanding of refuse gained the upper hand, whereby the original meaning of the term *Abfall*

> '*im Sinne von Apostasie (Religion) und Empörung (Politik)*' [transl. ed.: *'in the sense of apostasy (religion) and indignation (politics)'*]

---

2   "*Lossagen von einer früher ausgesprochenen Überzeugung, einer angelobten oder tatsächlich kundgetanen Ergebenheit gegen eine Person oder Sache*". [transl. ed.: "*renouncement of a previously expressed conviction, a sworn or an actually expressed loyalty to a person or a thing*"].

3   In Grimm's dictionary, *rubbish* (*das Mull or Müll*) is described as '*dust (staub), disintegrating earth (zerfallende erde) and filth (Unrat)*' and is assigned to the verb *müllen* (grind, crush). It is noted that the term was derived from the colloquial language of Lower Saxony and 'only the most recent written language uses it' (Grimm and Grimm 1885, Col. 2353-2654).

was almost completely put into the background.[4] Today, 'refuse' means only

> 'Rückstände, Nebenprodukte oder Altstoffe, die bei der Produktion, Konsum und Energiegewinnung entstehen'. [transl. ed.: 'Residues, by-products or second-hand materials that arise during production, consumption and energy production'].

The term rubbish (Müll) is

> 'häufig synonym und v. a. für Haus- und Gewerbe-Abfälle verwendet' [transl. ed.: 'often used synonymously and above all for household and commercial refuse'] (Die Zeit 2005, 29).

The meaning of the current term 'refuse' is illustrated below using the terminological spectrum of contemporary language in the form of a small "ABC of refuse" (in both German and English):[5]

> 'Abfall, Abraum, Abschaum, Abwasser, Asche, Ausschuss, Biomüll, Bockmist, Bodensatz, Dreck, Fraß, Gerümpel, Heidendreck, Jauche, Kacke, Kehricht, Kot, Klimbim, Krempel, Lumpen, Matsch, Mist, Modder, Müll, Neige, Pampe, Pfusch, Plunder, Ramsch, Rest, Rückstand, Schadstoff, Scheiße, Schmutz, Schrott, Schund, Schutt, Tand, Tinnef, Trödel, Überrest, Unding, Unflat, Ungeziefer, Unkraut, Unrat, Verunreinigung, Zeug'.

A comparable spectrum of the terms used in English is as follows:

> 'Crud, Debris, Dirt, Discard, Dregs, Drop-off, Dross, Dung, Feculence, Filth, Garbage, Gook, Grime, Grunge, Junk, Leftover, Litter, Lumber, Mire, Muck, Mud, Oddment, Offal, Ordure, Pollutant, Refuse, Rejects, Residue, Rubbish, Rummage, Scrap, Sewage, Sleaze, Slush, Smut, Sweepings, Trash, Waste'.

Some aspects of the research history

At the end of the 19th century, the dissertation of the officer and ethnologist, John Gregory Bourke, was published in the USA (1891), in which he evaluated and presented observations that he had gathered over many years among North American Indians about customs related to excrement together with similar studies on other indigenous people. His dissertation titled *Scatologic Rites of all Nations.*

---

4   Bardmann (1994, esp. 166-168) analyses the presented conceptual history in its meaning for the present-day: The one-sided materialistic, technical view means the loss of self-referentiality when thinking about refuse. The result is the attempt to represent refuse as something which is objectively definable, causally explainable, precisely measurable and thus manageable with technical means. The refuse problem is outsourced to the scientific-technical discourse and therefore detached from us as the "observers". "Observing" is meant here as the act that constitutes the world, value and refuse, which hardly plays a role in the current social discourse: the often rumoured "own actions" only refers to the practical handling of material things. However, the materialistic view is only one possible perspective. In an economically influenced culture, in which the observers orientate themselves to the exploitability and usefulness of things and calculate pragmatically, refuse becomes a worthless, useless or even annoying matter. It becomes an external thing in a world of things beyond the observers. In contrast, in a religious and moral culture, in which the observer is oriented to what is godly and good, refuse becomes evil and sinful. Refuse only arises from a culturally formed practise used by observers in differentiating between value and refuse. Thus, it is clear that our current, modern one-sided understanding of rubbish is not suitable for a comprehensive understanding of refuse management in past societies.

5   Christian Enzensberger (1968) presented an artistic textual treatment of everything that can be refuse or filth, which can be recommended as good reading for sensual stimulation.

A Dissertation upon the Employment of Excrementicious Remedial Agents in Religion, Therapeutics, Divination, Witchcraft, Love-Philters, etc., in all Parts of the Globe was labelled "Not for general perusal" and was only distributed to selected scholars. The interest in investigating how humans deal with their excretions was mainly a topic for ethnologists[6] and philosophers, whose literature Bourke had meticulously compiled. Two decades later, a German translation and revision of the book, titled *Der Unrat in Sitte, Brauch, Glauben und Gewohnheitsrecht der Völker* (Bourke 1913) was published by Leipziger Ethnologischer Verlag. However, it was also:

> *'Nur für Gelehrte, nicht für den Buchhandel bestimmt'* [transl.: *'Only for scholars, not for bookselling'*] (Bourke 1913, IV).[7]

Conventions designated this part of life a taboo zone, since there was something disreputable about it and it was at best something for people with a higher level of education. Recognised in its exclusion, this detached relationship to the body and its excrement, *i.e.* to the "dirt" produced by it (blood, faeces, urine, gases, sebum, sweat, saliva, semen, tears), determines our modern western world, although is not an ethnological constant, but rather a historical novelty (Bardmann 1994, 1987). Its development in the last 200 years is closely connected with the strengthening of the enlightened bourgeoisie and its new ideals, which combine the principle of physical purity with efficient performance (Kaschuba 1988, esp. 312). However, rubbish or refuse encompass much more than the specific human or animal excreta, which will be discussed later. Rather, the close connection of refuse to the value system in a community, including the sociological dimension of garbage and rubbish, make it interesting for us. Michael Thompson (1979) presented this connection comprehensively in his *Rubbish Theory*, in which he explicitly deals with the *'creation and destruction of values'* (German translations: Thompson 1981; 2003).

Objects can alternate between the categories of valuable, worthless, and unworthy, whereby the boundaries between these are more or less sharply delimitated by social interests. Refuse is ambivalent and has a transitory and transformative character. On the one hand, it has a constitutive effect on a social order (*Ordnung*) but, on the other hand, it can also endanger it. Theodor Bardmann (1994, here esp. 200-205) clearly worked out this ambivalence. He points to the fact that unity is formed by exclusion. In a social context, the mechanism of exclusion is thus implicit. Processes, such as marginalisation and discrimination, lead to the emergence of marginalised groups and outsiders, who deviate from the prevailing norms and values. The expulsion of people is part of an expulsive system, whereby outsiders also live in the system.[8] What is normality and what lies outside of the norm (*abfällt*), where order ends and chaos begins, is determined by the established rules of social coexistence. The more inflexible a social order system becomes, the greater the amount of generated refuse. This close connection emphasises the significance of refuse as a topic of study, because

---

6   As an example, ethnological studies from the same period are mentioned, which describe the remedies made from excrements in the folk medicine of Upper Bavaria that were still in existence at the time (cf. M. Höfler 1888).

7   Significantly, the work was published as the 6th volume of the *Beiwerke zum Studium der Anthropophyteia. Jahrbücher für folkloristische Erhebungen und Forschungen zur Entwicklungsgeschichte der geschlechtlichen Moral* and was furnished with a foreword by Sigmund Freud.

8   As an example of self-exclusion, with the symbolic "self-scrapping" as a survival strategy, punks (punk = worthless stuff, tinder wood, rubbish, scraps, trash, rejects) are cited, who pointedly exhibit their worthlessness for the prevailing utilisation contexts (Bardmann 1994, 201).

'Sicht auf den Abfall ist nur die Kehrseite der allgemeinen Sicht auf die soziale Ordnung' [transl.: *'A view of refuse is only the reverse side of a general view of the social order'*] (Bardmann 1994, 194).

The studies by Mary Douglas in the 1960s formed an important point of reference for this research. They particularly underscored the symbolic content of the different ways of dealing with refuse and dirt in different cultures (Douglas 1966; German translation: Douglas 1985). It is not only about pure moments of reason but also about the concerns of a culture to present itself and to be experienced as a unit. This can, however, only be achieved selectively. There is no order without dirt and refuse

'weil Ordnen das Verwerfen ungeeigneter Elemente einschließt' [transl.: *'because ordering includes throwing away unsuitable elements'*] (Douglas 1985, 53).

Particularly since the 1980s, as the environmental movement gained importance, scientific studies have increasingly become devoted to disposal behaviour and the handling of rubbish and refuse in different human societies. This also had an increasing impact on archaeology. The question of the origin of find contexts and the archaeological findings – the taphonomy – became increasingly important (see, *e.g.,* Schiffer 1987). Ethnoarchaeological analyses of rubbish distribution processes in preindustrial societies had a great influence on the interpretation of archaeological findings and the understanding of taphonomic processes. In these contexts, the practice of disposal was understood as a significant part of society. From the abundance of possible examples, some particularly pioneering studies have been chosen and are mentioned here: Binford 1978; Gould 1980; Murray 1980; Hodder 1982; Hayden and Cannon 1983; Binford 1984, esp. 149-204; Hodder 1987; Arnold 1991; Sommer 1991. In addition to spatial distribution patterns and categorisations of refuse, these studies benefited from the above-mentioned close sociological connection between refuse and social order. The investigations are based on the knowledge that the reconstruction and interpretation of disposal practices in past societies are a key to their world perception and values.

Some studies about disposal strategies in the Middle Ages follow a somewhat different approach. They are often based on written sources, which can be combined with archaeological findings. The body of source material involves a concentration on medieval cities with a focus on aspects of hygiene and illness (cf. Sydow 1981; Dirlmeier 1986; Grewe 1986; Hösel 1987; E. Höfler and Illi 1992; Oexle 1992; Kluge-Pinsker 2003; Meier 2008). Antiquity is comparable in terms of the source material, so that corresponding overview works are also available (cf. Thüry 2001).

Meanwhile, a multitude of research questions have been posed about dirt, rubbish and refuse; there is also a wide range of investigation methods. This reflects the great potential of rubbish as an element of historical culture studies (cf. Eggert 2006). However, there is no mutual "rubbish research". The various disciplines usually pursue their own approaches (Civis 2015). The social sciences have long focused on the social role of the current discourse about rubbish (cf. Keller 1998). Another line of research is designated as "rubbish archaeology" or "garbology", which concentrate on a comprehensive analysis of recent rubbish as part of consumer research (Church 2012; Humes 2012). This is understood as a source of data that is analysed with archaeological methods. This procedure was first used in the 1970s in the USA and is in the meanwhile established as a method of the social and cultural sciences, which is situated at the intersection of contemporary archaeology, social sciences and material culture studies (Rathje and Murphy 1992; 1994; cf. also Sosna *et al.* 2019). Anglophone rubbish research from a social science perspective was summarised a few years ago in the *Encyclopedia of Consumption and Waste: The Social Science of Garbage* (Zimring and Rathje 2012).

One aspect of disposal and deposition strategies that is particularly relevant and thus widely received in archaeology is fragmentation. John Chapman initiated the discussion two decades ago when he published his thesis stating that archaeological records mostly do not consist of rubbish of past societies (Chapmann 2000). Rather, the location of the finds is a sequence of meaningful practices (structured deposition), their broken state a product of targeted actions (deliberate fragmentation), and their incompleteness is connected with a series of mutual social relationships (enchainment). In the last two decades, further fundamental investigations on this topic have been published (Chapman and Gaydarska 2007; 2009; Garrow 2012). They make it clear that destroying and dividing things was an integral part of the ideology of past communities. These actions were often so charged with meaning that they appear to be almost ritual actions. In this discussion, the view that archaeological finds are primarily refuse is questioned, but not deconstructed. Our general relationship to refuse is not discussed, *e.g.*, why we view certain archaeological remains and not others as refuse. Chapman's approach tends to lead to confrontations with object biographies in which deliberate fragmentation has a firm position.

The special case of faeces

Humans are social and biological beings. To the latter belongs our metabolism as a basic characteristic, *i.e.* the vital absorption of nutrients and the associated excretion of refuse material. In a narrower sense, we are dealing here with nutrition and defecation. The securing of adequate food is without a doubt a fundamental driver of human action at all times. In this respect, it is understandable and justifiable that research on palaeo-nutrition and the related supply strategies receive great attention in archaeological sciences (cf. for example Ambrose 1993; Woolgar *et al.* 2006; Kosiba *et al.* 2007; Schoeninger 2010; Yoder 2010, and many more). In contrast, research on the disposal of human faeces is unjustly neglected. Admittedly, the conscious handling of it – faecal management – must first have become necessary with a sedentary lifestyle and larger numbers of people living together. But then at the latest, society was faced with challenges to which it could and had to respond to in different ways. Analyses on this topic from a historical perspective are still very rare. Overarching investigations are based on written and pictorial sources and only in exceptional cases on archaeological sources (*e.g.* Furrer 2004; Schrader 2006; Furrer 2010). The above-mentioned work by John G. Bourke (Bourke 1891; 1913), which comprehensively deals with the subject from an ethnological point of view, remains unparalleled for over a century. This is not necessarily due to the sources, but is rather an expression of the situation that the topic is largely taboo in our society or tainted with shame and thus is marked as something disreputable. This has not been the case for long. Up to the 19th century, to relieve oneself was not a taboo zone. Human excrements, like animal dung, were in demand as valuable fertiliser (Furrer 2004, 9). Faeces have first been considered as worthless refuse in our modern world. Apparently, a change is taking place here. Scientific questioning – including archaeological research – does not develop independently from the spirit of the time (*Zeitgeist*). There are always certain research fields, which are more *en vogue* in the general social discourse than others; the current decline in budget research and the simultaneous steering of various research funding instruments reinforce this effect. A headline-generating anecdote from 6 November, 2018 may underline the explosive nature and topicality that faeces management has for our globalised society: With a glass full of faeces at the lectern, Bill Gates called for a worldwide toilet revolution at the *'Reinvented Toilet Expo'* in Beijing, a trade fair for innovative toilet technology that does without sewers.[9] The aim is to combat diseases on a global scale. This is not only about hygiene and health but also about resource conservation and the preservation of valuable materials. All these concerns also had great importance for humans in the past. A research desideratum can thus be established from various perspectives. The fact that the attention-grabbing action by Gates in Peking was not much of a taboo breach – a partial removal of taboos from this topic has already set in for quite some time – is shown, among other things, by various publications that are aimed at a broad public (Laporte 1978; 1991; Werner 2011), a new edition of Bourke's work (Bourke 1992), and the thematisation of this topic in trend media.[10]

Case study: Slavs

The great potential of archaeological research in this regard can be illustrated by the case of the Slavs. The Christianisation of Northeast Europe continued in the early Middle Ages. It progressed with fundamental changes in the entire way of life of the affected population, including the property (ownership) situation, the economic system and religious as well as value perceptions/ideals, *etc*. We are poorly informed about daily life in the period before this. In particular, little is known about the Slavs. They lived for a long time far away from centres with scribality, so that archaeology plays a special role. Later, as contacts with their Christian neighbours existed, elites, who operated on a European or even global level, became recognisable. In the north, they were so closely intertwined with the Scandinavian elites, commonly known as the "Vikings", that an ethnic ascription of their archaeological remains is often not easy. This is also due to the fact that only modern perspectives assign people of that time to ethnic-national categories. Most of the population, "the people",[11] lived in simple settlements in rural areas. We have a certain idea of this, but on closer inspection, we notice that we do not have an assured knowledge of the life and economy of the Slavs in the middle and the eastern parts of the continent. However, it is striking that essential features are missing here that are known from the contemporaneous Scandinavian or the West Central European hinterland. Meant here are, for example, farmland on which agriculture or field cultivation were carried out, stables for domesticated animals, homestead structures with main and auxiliary buildings, enclosures and parcelling. The rural settlements in Scandinavia and on the Northwest European mainland had all of these features.

The settlers lived there in heath landscapes, which were kept open by grazing cattle. They tilled the different soils, the quality of which they tried to improve

---

9   URL: https://www.bbc.com/news/technology-46108083. Last access: 13 January 2021.
10   For example, the Unabhängiges Gesellschaftsmagazin "DUMMY" (Independent Society Magazine "Dummy") dedicated its 32nd issue in autumn 2011 to the subject of "shit".
11   On the term, cf. Schneeweiß 2020, 47-48.

by fertilisation, and ran a well-developed supply economy on their homesteads. Large residential stables housed the cattle. Excretions from humans and animals were mixed in the stables with straw and were used on the fields as fertiliser.

But how and where did humans relieve themselves, who at the same time inhabited the wide wooded areas southeast of the Baltic Sea that we generally associate with the Slavs? In Slavic settlement areas, there is no evidence of the stabling of cattle and arable land is unknown. Without stables, there is no manure, so there is no fertiliser either.

Archaeobotanical and archaeozoological evaluations verify that cultivated plants were used and grown, and that cattle were also kept. But we do not know exactly where and to what extent. Forest pasture and swidden agriculture are assumed, but it is difficult to prove this. How were the faeces of both animals and humans treated? Were they viewed as valuable raw material for soil amelioration? Empirically gained experience shows that it was especially typical for Slavic settlements in Eastern Middle Europe that an apparently homogeneous, mostly strongly mixed occupation layer with a deep black colour has been preserved, often on a very nutrient-poor mineral substrate. A high content of charcoal is responsible for the intense colour. This is reminiscent of the well-known *Terra preta do indio* (black Indian soil) from the Amazon region, which is considered to be a prime example of historical sustainable agriculture that formed the basis for a complex civilisation until the arrival of the Spaniards (Glaser *et al.* 2001; Lehmann *et al.* 2003; Glaser and Woods 2004; Glaser 2007). The legendary *El Dorado* was likely a farming culture. The high yield potential of the converted, actually very nutrient-poor soil was achieved there through faeces and charcoal, which were collected and then purposefully mixed in the soil (Glaser and Birk 2012; Glaser 2014). Faeces supplied the microorganisms; the large surface of the charcoal provided the necessary habitat. In contrast to fertilised soil, *Terra preta* does not leach out, but rather regenerates itself, and high fertility is maintained over the long term.

Mighty, conspicuous black occupation layers are also found in some Scandinavian contexts of the Viking Age, primarily in the trading centres of the Baltic Sea region, which were first only used seasonally, but then permanently. These were places where very many people lived close together and apparently did not use stables. Often, the necessary hinterland for sustenance was also missing. In this context, the most famous place is probably central Swedish Birka, where even the field name refers to the striking black earth: *svarta jorden* (Håkansson 1997; Ambrosiani 2013). While faeces posed no problem on the countryside and were valuable as a raw material, they could have been problematic in such early urban places[12] and required an effective management.

It has long been proven that *Terra preta* soils can also be produced in the European temperate climate zone (*Terra Preta Nova*). In Germany, the clear interest in sustainability and environmental awareness has even recently sparked enthusiasm for *Terra preta*, which is gaining importance in the context of alternative forms of economy such as urban gardening (Scheub *et al.* 2013). A historical *Terra preta* soil (Nordic Dark Earth) has only been proven for a single Slavic settlement with a deep black occupation layer from the Viking Age (Wiedner *et al.* 2015). This is due to the state of research, since there have not been any further investigations thus far. Comparable in terms of their origin and fertility could also be the so-called *Formigueren* soils in Northeastern Spain, but they are a more recent

---

12   In Lübeck, thick, humus layers were related to disposal on the street. Cf. Gläser 1999, 162-163.

phenomenon and are associated with late medieval-early modern wine and olive cultivation on mountain terrace.[13] Faeces and charcoal are wrongly underestimated and given little attention in archaeological research. The combination of the described observations suggests a link between the black occupation layers of Slavic settlements, the missing evidence of stables, arable land and homesteads, the type of cultivation and faecal management. Accordingly, an efficient management of faeces in combination with charcoal could have improved the soil so sustainably that high yields independent of the substrate could have been achieved in a small space. It is noteworthy that the old settlement areas from the Slavic era are often the most fertile areas of modern fields to this day.

The Viking Age is a period of far-reaching social, economic and ethnic change. The hypothesis of the existence of targeted faecal management with the help of charcoal for soil improvement can provide, beyond the mere findings, answers to some central research questions on the early and high medieval history of the Slavic areas by helping us to understand the soil management system that was widespread there before the high medieval land development (*Landesausbau*). In the course of the land development, the well-established techniques from the west were adopted, whereas older forms of economy were abandoned and knowledge about them was lost. But prior to this, they may have played a decisive role in the early urbanisation of the Slavic-Scandinavian contact area, because during the Viking Age, the first non-agrarian (proto-) urban settlements emerged in Northern and Northeastern Europe. The high intensity of life in these places is reflected in massive occupation layers, sometimes several metres thick, which accumulated in a relatively short period of maximally 200-300 years. Effective and sustainable faecal management with soil improvement could have helped to meet the high need for partial food self-sufficiency in concentrated areas and to ensure the disposal of residues.

It is worthwhile to pursue this hypothesis and leave the well-trodden paths that always highlight trade, exchange and the elite culture. Everyday culture, the handling of faeces and hygiene – these are all central aspects of human life in pre-industrial times that are underrepresented in research and wrongly have the reputation of being curious. Even if still on the sidelines, evidence of this can certainly be found in research literature if one applies a change of perspective.

Consumption rubbish (*Müll*)

The physical remains of past human societies have always had a fixed place in archaeology and are, in some sense, its "core business". Our reconstructions of the former daily life of humans are based to a great extent on that what they unintentionally left behind.[14] Depots, grave goods, even the dead themselves, were valuable or charged with value and were deliberately and respectfully deposited. Thus, they reflect to a certain extent an exception from daily life and are special, extraordinary moments in life. These connections form a fundament of archaeological work. Quite naturally, a distinction is made between deposited finds, loss finds and refuse deposits. For the (usually not reflected) categorisation, the context of the finds and the find material play a major role. However, the behaviour associated with refuse is rarely discussed and even more seldom is it the subject of archaeological investi-

---

13   They are currently the subject of a research project funded by the DFG. Cf. lecture by Steven Polifka *et al.* on Sept. 22, 2020 at the German Archaeology Congress.

14   Cf. Hahn 2005 for an ethnological perspective.

gations. Food remains, broken or disused vessels and other objects were likely carelessly thrown away. But we do not know this for sure. Intentionally destroyed objects, which were rendered unusable, were surely not viewed as rubbish or refuse, but had a meaning or a value (cf. Chapman 2000; Chapman and Gaydarska 2007). They were possibly even considered to have had a soul.

It is obvious that it depends on the values of humans or the human community, which objects are considered to be refuse – without a value – and which objects are not considered to be refuse and thus are given value.[15] The behaviour associated with refuse enables conclusions to be drawn about the value system of a community as already mentioned above. From an economic standpoint, the deliberate rendering of an object unusable is without a doubt a devaluing act, which places it in the vicinity of (worthless) refuse. However, values are not necessarily bound to materiality. The destruction of an object (or the killing of a subject) in connection with ritual acts can also be understood as an upgrading in that it was "chosen" from a larger, equivalent set in order to serve a higher purpose. Beyond the spiritual, symbolic level, there is also a close relationship between the value of an object and the availability of resources. The rarer a resource, the more valuable it is. The latter is particularly true from an economic perspective, which is easiest for us to comprehend from today's perspective.

A recent archaeological study focused on disposal practices and thus on an important aspect of human behaviour in rural areas of the Middle Ages (Civis 2015).[16] In this context, the archaeological material of the medieval rural settlement of Diepensee is generally viewed as refuse and then examined on the basis of spatial and statistical analyses. In the process, characteristic differences were identified concerning how the various material groups were disposed of, which Civis explains with the hazards attributed to them. She makes a subdivision between solid (ceramic, clay, stone, slag), usable (presumably all kinds of metal, but certainly iron) and ambivalent (bones) material (Civis 2015, 296). The archaeological perspective, *i.e.* the material, must speak for itself, since written sources do not provide insights into rural disposal practices. The image of medieval disposal strategies is based on written sources and relates to urban contexts. Moreover, these sources primarily deal with grievances and decrees from which general practices can only be derived indirectly.[17] With the chosen methodological approach (Civis 2013, 177), Civis follows the premises formulated by Bardmann (1994, 194) that the distinction between value and refuse as such seems to be universal and timeless, but the contents, characteristics, ordering principles and radicality of their implementation, however, is extremely variable. She attempts to approach the potential value ascriptions on the material level and differentiates between valuable (+1), worthless (0) and archaeological material with a negative value (-1) (Civis 2015, 37).[18] Moreover, she introduces a concept of contamination and confrontation, which is closely connected to the negative value category. Objects, which are included in this negative category, pose an acutely perceived social, health or aesthetic hazard, so that even a contamination

---

15   On values and the ambivalent relationship between rubbish and value, cf. Civis 2013.

16   The main focus is placed on the topics of space, hygiene and economy. Cf. also (less comprehensive) Biermann and Frey 2014.

17   In contrast, what triggered conflicts can be all the more easily assessed, and inferences to mentalities and sensitivities can be made.

18   This threefold division is also found in Bardmann (1994) as valuable, worthless, unworthy; the use of a "negative" value is based on Thompson (1979). Civis (2013, 177) still argues with the somewhat unsuitable term "anti-value".

of objects of the other categories is possible. A confrontation with this rubbish (*Müll*) in a real sense is thus avoided. Efforts are made to intentionally dispose of it. Leaving it lying on the surface means confrontation, as can be observed with "harmless" refuse (ceramics). Strong confrontation is manifested in strong fragmentation, which thus can be considered as a sort of indicator.

Spatial aspects play an important role. Rubbish marks boundaries, as it is mostly placed outside of or on the edge of immediate activity zones. No rubbish is produced without human activity, so it is always an indication of such activity zones.

The results of the investigations enable the recognition of some disposal patterns, which appear to be material specific and underpin the concept of contamination and confrontation (Civis 2015, 279-281). As the most common type of finds, ceramics exhibit the fewest patterns and the strongest fragmentation (confrontation). Physically comparable substances, such as burnt clay and (forged) slag, acted similarly in terms of confrontation; they remained at the place of their use/ origin within an activity zone.

Animal bones belong to the ambivalent material groups. They can be regarded as components of food, as a raw material and as potentially contaminated refuse (rubbish). A regular distribution of animal bones could be recognised. In contrast to the cities, bones that were preserved as a raw material were missing in the rural context. They were primarily food and slaughter refuse. They were removed from the living quarters and disposed of in the vicinity with household refuse. Metals, particularly iron, were kept for reuse and collected at certain places.[19]

In summary, the disposal behaviour in the village of Diepensee in the 13th/14th century CE is relatively easy to comprehend (Civis 2015, 286). Refuse or rubbish posed no great challenges for the village community. Living quarters were regularly swept and house refuse remained above ground in the vicinity of the farmyards until the refuse was placed in a pit or in a different feature. Value neutral refuse from which no danger arose and which could be reused (metals, iron) were collected. For the most part, such a disposal practice was likely conducted in the majority of sedentary communities (cf. Murray 1980). Changes were initiated by external events (*e.g.* village fires).

Production refuse

While refuse disposal in rural-agrarian environments usually never became a problem, because the traditional strategies in handling "dangerous" and "harmless" refuse were continually successful, these strategies were not effective when the space-refuse ratio became unfavourable. This was the case when there was a higher population density in the settlements (urbanisation processes) or if the production of goods grew way beyond the needs of the community and the "mountain of refuse" increased accordingly. With the transition from home production to handcraft, not only the market but also the development of a corresponding refuse management became a necessary challenge. The connection to the resources becomes much more obvious. A few examples are briefly noted here, which address this set of problems but do not explore it fully.

---

19   In this context, note the phrase "to belong to the scrap heap", which is applied to humans. On the use of scrap metal in early history, cf. Baumeister 2004.

Mining

It was already observed for flint mining in the Neolithic that in addition to the extracted amount of desired stone, a large amount of refuse rock accumulated for which there was no further use. Consequently, the path of least resistance was chosen and the old shafts were filled with it – the material did not have to be transported and was not in the way during the progress of further work (Fober und Weisgerber 1999, 43-44; cf. also Körlin and Weisgerber 2006, esp. 37-212). There is no danger from refuse rock, it is not contaminating, but can at most develop into a space problem. Silex mining left behind huge refuse dumps, which partially still shape the landscape today. Ore mining since the Bronze Age had a massive impact on local environments.[20] The shafts were not usually filled with the by-products or refuse. In addition to deforestation, the overburden and, above all, slag heaps led to considerable limitations and pollution of the natural vegetation and also of the waters. The older slags often still contain numerous heavy metals and other elements, so that they were sometimes important in later times as (secondary) raw materials and were smelted again. As early as the Middle Ages, slags were used as construction material, as is common practice in modern times.[21] Basically, mining introduced a new dimension of refuse, which presented new challenges for humans and the environment.

Pottery

The need of a small community for pots in households is manageable. Neither the production nor the disposal of ceramic vessels that are no longer in use present a major refuse problem. This is different in the development of the pottery handcraft. On the one hand, enough high-quality raw material must be available and, on the other hand, misfired pottery always builds up in a pottery workshop because not every firing process is successful. Misfired ceramics pose neither a risk nor can they be secondarily used in a meaningful way. In this respect, they remain on site and are often a valuable source of information for archaeologists about the production spectrum of a pottery workshop. Piles of shattered ceramic vessels and misfires can sometimes reach considerable proportions. The recycling aspect comes into play in the use of ground pottery as fireclay for tempering in the production of vessels. However, this only played a role in simple, hand-made pottery and not in the mass production in the context of pottery trade.

Tannery

The tannery handcraft gained importance in the High and Late Middle Ages. Its development was closely tied to the cities (Bulach 2013). Tanneries produced large amounts of solid, semi-liquid and liquid refuse that needed to be disposed of. Particularly (red) tannery,[22] where leather laid in the tan for several years, had

---

20 In general, the natural resources are the focus of investigations on the organisational forms of mining, which, however, are closely related to the refuse. On the sustainability and cultural ties of concepts of earlier raw material extraction and on the influence of the respective economic system on the development of a mining region, cf. Stöllner 2003.

21 Since the 19th century, slag has played an important role, particularly for paving roads and paths. A well-known example is represented by the Mansfeld copper cinder blocks, which until recently were used in large parts of Germany primarily for street paving, but also for building houses.

22 According to the tanning agents, a distinction is generally made between four processes, which lead to different leather types. Plant-based raw materials, such as oak or spruce bark, were used for (red) tannery.

a high need for water and significantly impacted water pollution. Moreover, the hides and the tannery pits stank considerably. For these reasons, the tanner's quarters were later always located at the edge of the cities on a river. The leached oak tanbark could be recycled as a refuse product in different ways. As so-called tan cheese, dried tan was used as fuel for a long time (Müller 2018, 241). In addition, it was also mixed with plaster, mortar or brick clay and was used as building and insulation material or as fertiliser (Ansorge *et al.* 2003). As one of the most important medieval and early modern handicrafts with its abundant refuse, (red) tannery makes a more detailed analysis appear worthwhile from a "refuse perspective".

Linen production

Common flax (*Linum usitatissimum*) belongs to the so-called *founder crops*. It is one of the nine plants that are included in the crop inventory of the Neolithic Euro-Asian basic crop package (Karg 2015, 27). It is used for oil extraction, for its plant fibres or the flax seeds are eaten. The production of yarn and linen from flax is a lengthy process with many intermediate steps, which particularly played a large role in rural areas during the Middle Ages and modern times. In the context of production refuse discussed here, our attention is placed on so-called flax retting.[23] In order to extract the plant fibres from the stalks of the flax, the flax straw was stored after the harvest in shallow open pits, ponds or trenches filled with water so that they "rotted". Subsequently, the fermented stalks were dried and processed.[24] The strong-smelling rotting process, also known as "roasting", polluted the waters in which the degradation products were discharged. The considerable smell is the main reason why flax digs were established outside the settlements (Karg 2015, 30).

No feast for the senses

The last examples of tan pits and flax rotting have once again made the connection between refuse and sensory perceptions clear. The stench leads to avoidance strategies by removing the stinking pits and the activities associated with them as far as possible from the living areas. Of all senses, the sense of smell plays a prominent role in connection with refuse. This is definitely the case in historical times. Odours could indicate when a danger was literally in the air. The experiences with the great epidemics and pandemics in the Late Middle Ages and modern times probably contributed significantly to the fact that the idea of "bad" miasmas (μίασμα: defilement, pollution) as the source of evil, disease and death caused fear among the people. The idea that malicious odours from the earth are distributed in the air and thus spread diseases goes back to classical antiquity, particularly to Hippocrates of Kos and his theory of the humours. In the age of the Renaissance and the Enlightenment, they again became important, especially among the educated classes of the bourgeoisie. Particularly in the cities, the stench was unbearable, whereby the disposal standards in richer

---

Tanning with minerals, above all with potassium alum (potassium aluminium sulphate), were referred to as white tanning. By chamois or fat tanning, whale oil, fats from bones or parts of the brain are worked into the leather. All smoking processes in tanning are summarised by the term aldehyde tanning.

23 The names vary regionally. Flax roast, *Rottekuhle* or *Rötelteich* are also common names.

24 The next working steps, such as *breaking* (the shredding of the wood core), *swinging* (separating the fibres from the shives, the wood residues) and *heckling* (combing), followed before the fibres could be spun.

and poorer city districts during the Middle Ages and the early modern period were very different (Dirlmeier 1986, 155). Great effort was made to eliminate the causes of malodours, which were considered to be dangerous.[25] Ideas about purity, hygiene and morality were closely linked. This also had an effect on social order and urban development measures. The measures against "miasmas" were even partially successful because the causes of bacteria and viruses were unconsciously combated. The roots of the ideas about the negative effects of bad odours reach far back before the Middle Ages to antiquity and perhaps even further. The sense of smell is the most archaic and sensitive human sense. Due to subliminal stimuli, the sense of smell can subconsciously influence thinking and acting. Neurobiology has researched its functioning quite well. Even if the human sense of smell is far inferior to that of many animals, it does provide signals for food, spoilage, and danger – familiar and strange – and can trigger the appropriate reactions (disgust, appetite, curiosity, joy, lust, aggression, *etc*).[26] In contrast to taste, the evaluation of odoriferous substances is first learned in childhood and changes in the course of life, whereby it is subject to social and cultural influences (Klinke and Silbernagl 1994, 630). In this respect, smells can be an important key for the relationship and behaviour towards certain categories of refuse. However, the difficulty to archaeologically detect this is obvious. Smells can persist in exceptional cases (manure, sewers, *etc*.) or possibly be chemically reconstructable, but the (individual or collective) reactions of people to them are not necessarily deducible.

Written sources can provide information about this for historical times. However, already for the Middle Ages, evidence is rare. For example, we do not know what the settlements and castles of the Viking Age smelled like. In this respect, the description of the Slavic city of Karentia by the Danish historian Saxo Grammaticus from the 12th century is impressive, which provides us with such a rare insight. Under Waldemar I, the Danes conquered the Arkona temple fort(ress) on Rügen in the year 1168 and destroyed the central Slavic sanctuary located there. Thereby, the last pagan stronghold in the Baltic Sea region had fallen and the Christianisation of the Slavs there could no longer be stopped. After their success, the victorious Danes marched into the near Slavic town of Karentia[27] on Rügen, which – initially to the amazement of the attackers – surrendered without a fight.

> 'The town was famous for three very notable temples that had been built there, worth visiting for the splendour of their noble architecture; the authority attaching to the local deities had won them almost as much reverence as was commanded by the powerful god of the state among the citizens of Arkona. Now this locality, though empty in the time of peace, at that period stood crammed with numerous dwellings. These were three storeys high, the lowest one providing support for the weight of the middle and highest floors. Moreover, the houses were so tightly packed together that, were boulders to be hurled into the city from ballistas, they would never strike bare earth when they fell. In addition, such a fierce stench of filth pervaded every home in the community that it tormented their bodies no less than fear racked their

---

25 For France in the 17th-19th centuries, cf. especially: Corbin 1984.

26 Cf. the German idiom of being hostile towards someone else: *not being able to smell someone*, means not being able to stand someone.

27 According to new findings, Karentia is no longer identified with Garz (Schuchhardt 1944, 377; Leube 2019, 34), but with Gingst (Ruchhöft 2019).

minds. In view of this factors it was obvious to our army that the people of Karenz could not have resisted a siege; the Danes saw no reason to be any longer amazed at the inhabitants' swift capitulation when they clearly perceived how confined they were forced to be' (Friis-Jensen 2015).

The stench in the overcrowded Slavic town, which was apparently perceived by the Danes as indecent,[28] is considered here to be decisive for the surrender. Either the sense of cleanliness of the Christian Danes and the Slavs, who were still pagan at this point in time, were very different[29] or the besieged city actually had a massive disposal problem due to dense building and the high population density.

Some final thoughts on connectivity

At places like strongholds or towns, where very many people lived together at times or permanently, and produced, consumed and disposed of their remains, the problem was acute: The people were forced to deal with each other and their refuse. The narrowness could have held a significant potential for conflict. In this regard, it was probably a bit more relaxed on the countryside. In principle, very little rubbish accumulated in agriculture, since practically all refuse was used. In grain production, of course, threshed grain was the product with various "refuse" products that accrued during the chain of production, such as straw or threshing residues (husks, *etc.*), all of which were further utilised. Everything had a function – straw and threshing residues were used for the stalled cattle and manure production as fertiliser for the fields. Particularly in agricultural production, the connection between refuse and resources is especially close. This is also true for the above-mentioned subsistence economy of the Slavs, although no stalls or fields are known. A slightly different view is provided by weeds as unwanted plants (or even animals) that are quasi co-produced, but for which there is no use. Here the designation as weeds (*Unkraut*) or vermin (*Ungeziefer*) speaks a clear language that relinquishes them to potential destruction. From a sociological perspective, the evaluation of something as refuse is not limited to physical objects, but can also be related to animals, plants, humans, their actions and experiences (Bardmann 1994, 194-195). In a very similar way as described above, evaluation or the ascription to a value category determines the relationship of humans to a certain plant or animal and makes them seem dangerous, unworthy or worthless, which in turn leads to certain behaviours in order to get rid of them. Considerations about neophytes or invasive species also belong in this context. Such neophytes have an ambivalent character, which becomes all the more apparent in their historical dimension. If one chooses large enough time periods to be considered, many species that have now become indigenous started their "careers" as neophytes,[30] but the relationship of humans to them has changed over the course of time.

Even these superficial considerations exhibit clearly that the topic of refuse and faeces management as well as the associated disposal practices overlap with

---

28   "*Super haec natus immunditiis foetor cunctos urbis penates asperserat nec minus corpora quam metus animos cruciabat.*" The stench comes from *immunditiae*. The word means uncleanliness, in Middle Latin also indecency, and is formed from *immundus* (unclean, impure, dirty, disgusting, repugnant, and indecent). Cf. Langenscheidt Latein-Deutsch Online-Wörterbuch.

29   In my opinion, it cannot be ruled out that this blatant representation is a deliberate exaggeration, which is meant to underline the blessing of Christianisation.

30   So, for example, flax (*Linum*), which is mentioned above.

numerous further topics. In order to fathom the subject, a wide interdisciplinary breadth is necessary and helpful. Social and cultural implications enable the identification of hierarchies and conflict potentials on different levels. Not only human-thing relationships but also human-human relationships play a role. Behaviour that results from the relationship to refuse can be identified from archaeological remains if they are examined from a physiological, biological, culture-anthropological and philosophical perspective.

Concepts of pureness and impureness, sacred and profane, private and public – or the lack thereof – can be developed. A separate field arises from the investigation of the formation of dark occupation layers. The possible "rediscovery" of lost early or high medieval knowledge about effective and sustainable soil management creates a clear link to current sustainable resource management as well as to current supply and disposal problems in modern areas of high population density. A multi-perspective research approach enriches the discourse by the specific approaches, questions and methods of the different disciplines: archaeology, soil science, parasitology, archaeobotany, ethnology, history (written sources), art history (image sources), linguistics, sociology, and philosophy, to mention just a few of the most important disciplines.

Mutual reflection about refuse of foreign cultures helps us to get closer to their ideas about order (and disorder) in the world and to rethink our own.

References

Ambrose, S.H., 1993. Isotopic analysis of paleodiets: methodological and interpretive considerations. *In:* M.K. Sandford, ed. *Investigations of Ancient Human Tissue: Chemical Analysis in Anthropology.* Boca Raton: CRC Press, 59-130.

Ambrosiani, J., 2013. *Excavations in the Black Earth 1990-1995. Stratigraphy* Vol. 1. Birka Studies 9. Stockholm: Birka Project at Riksantikvarieämbetet.

Ansorge, J., Stolze, S., Wiethold, J., 2003. Gerberlohe als Bau- und Dämmmaterial im mittelalterlichen Stralsunder Rathaus. *Archäologische Berichte aus Mecklenburg-Vorpommern* 10, 268-282.

Arnold III, P.J., 1991. *Domestic ceramic production and spatial organization. A Mexican case study in ethnoarchaeology.* New Studies in Archaeology. Cambridge: Cambridge University Press.

Bardmann, T.M., 1994. *Wenn aus Arbeit Abfall wird. Aufbau und Abbau organisatorischer Realitäten.* Frankfurt am Main: Suhrkamp.

Baumeister, M., 2004. *Metallrecycling in der Frühgeschichte. Untersuchungen zur technischen, wirtschaftlichen und gesellschaftlichen Rolle sekundärer Metallverwertung im 1. Jahrtausend n. Chr.* Würzburger Arbeiten zur Prähistorischen Archäologie 3. Rahden/Westf.: Verlag Marie Leidorf.

Biermann, F. and Frey, K., 2014. Wiederverwendung und Entsorgung von Dingen am uckermärkischen Kloster Seehausen im späten Mittelalter und in der frühen Neuzeit. *In:* U. Klein and M. Untermann, eds. *Vom Schicksal der Dinge. Spolie – Wiederverwendung – Recycling. Tagung in Brandenburg an der Havel, 13. und 14. Juni 2013.* Mitteilungen der Deutschen Gesellschaft für Archäologie des Mittelalters und der Neuzeit 26. Paderborn: Deutsche Gesellschaft für Archäologie des Mittelalters und der Neuzeit, 151-158.

Binford, L.R., 1978. *Nunamiut Ethnoarchaeology.* New York: Academic Press.

Binford, L.R., 1984. *Die Vorzeit war ganz anders. Methoden und Ergebnisse der Neuen Archäologie.* München: Harnack.

Bourke, J.G., 1891. *Scatologic Rites of all Nations. A Dissertation upon the Employment of Excrementicious Remedial Agents in Religion, Therapeutics, Divination, Witchcraft, Love-Philters, etc., in all Parts of the Globe.* Washington D.C.: W. H. Lowdermilk & Co.

Bourke, J.G., 1913. *Der Unrat in Sitte, Brauch, Glauben und Gewohnheitsrecht der Völker.* Beiwerke zum Studium der Anthropophyteia. Jahrbücher für folkloristische Erhebungen und Forschungen zur Entwicklungsgeschichte der geschlechtlichen Moral 6. Leipzig: Ethnologischer Verlag.

Bourke, J.G., 1992. *Das Buch des Unrats: Mit einem Geleitwort von Sigmund Freud. Aus dem Amerikanischen von Friedrich S. Krass und Hermann Ihm. Bearbeitet und mit einem Essay von Louis Kaplan.* Die Andere Bibliothek 91. Frankfurt am Main: Eichborn.

Bulach, D., 2013. *Handwerk im Stadtraum: Das Ledergewerbe in den Hansestädten der südwestlichen Ostseeküste vom 13. bis 16. Jahrhundert.* Quellen und Darstellungen zur hansischen Geschichte, N. F. 45. Köln, Weimer, Wien: Böhlau.

Chapman, J., 2000. *Fragmentation in Archaeology. People, Places and Broken Objects in the Prehistory of South Eastern Europe.* London: Routledge.

Chapman, J. and Gaydarska, B., 2007. *Parts and Wholes: Fragmentation in Prehistoric Context.* Oxford: Oxbow.

Chapman, J. and Gaydarska, B., 2009. The fragmentation premise in archaeology: from the Paleolithic to more recent times. *In:* W. Tronzo, ed. *The fragment: an incomplete history.* Los Angeles: Getty Research Institute, 131-153.

Church, J.M., 2012. Archaeology of Garbage. *In:* C.A. Zimring and W.L. Rathje, eds. *Encyclopedia of Consumption and Waste: The Social Science of Garbage.* Los Angeles, London, New Delhi, Singapore, Washington, D.C.: SAGE Publications, 31-36.

Civis, G., 2013. Wertnetze und Wertverschiebungen im mittelalterlichen Dorf Diepensee. *In:* F.X. Eder, O. Kühschelm, B. Schmidt-Lauber, P. Ther, C. Theune, eds. *Kulturen des Ökonomischen. Historisch-kulturwissenschaftliche Beiträge.* Wien: Institut für Europäische Ethnologie, 167-195.

Civis, G., 2015. *Entsorgungspraxis im mittelalterlichen Dorf. Die Abfallfunde von Diepensee.* Dissertation an der Historisch-Kulturwissenschaftlichen Fakultät der Universität Wien [online]. Available at: http://othes.univie.ac.at/38680/1/2015-04-24_0963148.pdf [Accessed 12 February 2021].

Corbin, A., 1984. *Pesthauch und Blütenduft. Eine Geschichte des Geruchs.* Berlin: Klaus Wagenbach.

Dirlmeier, U., 1986. Zu den Lebensbedingungen in der mittelalterlichen Stadt: Trinkwasserversorgung und Abfallbeseitigung. *In:* B. Herrmann, ed. *Mensch und Umwelt im Mittelalter.* Stuttgart: Deutsche Verlags-Anstalt, 150-159.

Douglas, M., 1966. *Purity and Danger. An Analysis of Concepts of Pollution and Taboo.* London: Routledge.

Douglas, M., 1985. *Reinheit und Gefährdung. Eine Studie zu Vorstellungen von Verunreinigung und Tabu.* Berlin: Dietrich Reimer.

Eggert, M.K.H., 2006. *Archäologie. Grundzüge einer Historischen Kulturwissenschaft.* Tübingen, Basel: Verlag A. Francke.

Enzensberger, C., 1968. *Größerer Versuch über den Schmutz.* München: Carl Hanser Verlag.

Fober, L. and Weisgerber, G., [3]1999. Feuersteinbergbau – Typen und Techniken. *In:* Deutsches Bergbau-Museum Bochum, ed. *5000 Jahre Feuersteinbergbau. Die Suche nach dem Stahl der Steinzeit. Ausstellung im Deutschen Bergbau-Museum Bochum vom 25. Oktober 1980 bis 31. Januar 1981.* Veröffentlichungen aus den Deutschen Bergbau-Museum Bochum 77. Saarbrücken: SDV, 32-47.

Friis-Jensen, K., ed., 2015. *Saxo Grammaticus, Gesta Danorum – The History of the Danes XIV, 39, 38*. Vol. II. Translated by Peter Fisher (Oxford Medieval Texts). Oxford: Oxford University Press, 1305.

Furrer, D., 2004. *Wasserthron und Donnerbalken. Eine Kulturgeschichte des stillen Örtchens*. Darmstadt: Primus.

Furrer, D., 2010. *Geschichte des stillen Örtchens*. Darmstadt: Primus.

Garrow, D., 2012. Odd deposits and average practice. A critical history of the concept of structured deposition. *Archaeological Dialogues* 19 (2), 85-115.

Gläser, M., 1999. Umweltnutzung und Umweltprobleme im mittelalterlichen Lübeck. *Offa* 56, 149-164.

Glaser, B., 2007. Prehistorically modified soils of central Amazonia: a model for sustainable agriculture in the twenty-first century. *Philosophical Transactions of the Royal Society B: Biological Sciences* 362, Nr. 1478, 187-196.

Glaser, B., 2014. Soil biogeochemistry: from molecular to ecosystem level using terra preta and biochar as example. *In:* N. Benkeblia, ed. *Agroecology, Ecosystems, and Sustainability. Advances in Agroecology*. Boca Raton: CRC Press, 1-40.

Glaser, B. and Birk, J.J., 2012. State of the scientific knowledge on properties and genesis of Anthropogenic Dark Earths in Central Amazonia (terra preta de Índio). *Geochimica et Cosmochimica Acta* 82, 39-51.

Glaser, B. and Woods, W.I., 2004. *Amazonian dark earths – explorations in space and time*. Berlin, Heidelberg: Springer.

Glaser, B., Haumaier, L., Guggenberger, G., Zech, W., 2001. The "terra preta" phenomenon: a model for sustainable agriculture in the humid tropics. *Naturwissenschaften* 88, 37-41.

Gould, R.A., 1980. *Living Archaeology*. Cambridge: Cambridge University Press.

Grewe, K., 1986. Zur Wasserversorgung und Abwasserentsorgung in der Stadt um 1200. *In:* H. Steuer, ed. *Zur Lebensweise in der Stadt um 1200. Ergebnisse der Mittelalter-Archäologie. Bericht über ein Kolloquium in Köln vom 31. Januar – 2. Februar 1984*. Zeitschrift für Archäologie des Mittelalters: Beiheft 4. Köln: Rheinland-Verlag, 275-400.

Grimm, J. and Grimm, W., 1854. *Deutsches Wörterbuch. Erster Band A – Biermolke*. Leipzig: S. Hirzel.

Grimm, J. and Grimm, W., 1885. *Deutsches Wörterbuch. Sechster Band L. M.* Leipzig: S. Hirzel.

Hahn, H.P., 2005. Dinge des Alltags – Umgang und Bedeutungen. Eine ethnologische Perspektive. *In:* G.M. König, ed. *Alltagsdinge. Erkundungen der materiellen Kultur*. Studien und Materialien des Ludwig-Uhland-Instituts der Universität Tübingen 27. Tübingen: Tübinger Vereinigung für Volkskunde, 63-79.

Håkansson, T., 1997. Soil Micromorphology with Special Reference to 'Dark Earth'. *In:* U. Miller, H. Clarke, A.-M. Hansson, M. Johansson, B. Ambrosiani, T. Hackens, eds. *Environment and Vikings with special reference to Birka*. PACT 52 (Birka Studies 4). Rixensart: PACT Belgium, 151-154.

Hayden, B. and Cannon, A., 1983. Where the Garbage Goes: Refuse Disposal in the Maya Highlands. *Journal of Anthropological Archaeology* 2, 117-163.

Hodder, I., 1982. *The Present Past: An Introduction to Anthropology for Archaeologists*. London: B.T. Batsford.

Hodder, I., 1987. The Meaning of Discard: Ash and Domestic Space in Baringo. *In:* S. Kent, ed. *Method and Theory for Activity Area Research. An Ethnoarchaeological Approach*. New York: Columbia University Press, 424-448.

Höfler, E. and Illi, M., 1992. Versorgung und Entsorgung der mittelalterlichen Stadt. Versorgung und Entsorgung im Spiegel der Schriftquellen. *In:* Landesdenkmalamt Baden-Württemberg, ed. *Stadtluft, Hirsebrei und Bettelmönch – Die Stadt um 1300. Katalog zur Ausstellung in Zürich und Stuttgart 1992.* Stuttgart: Konrad Theiss Verlag, 351-364.

Höfler, M., 1888. *Volksmedizin und Aberglaube in Oberbayerns Gegenwart und Vergangenheit.* München: Otto Galler.

Hösel, G., 1987. *Unser Abfall aller Zeiten. Eine Kulturgeschichte der Städtereinigung.* München: Kommunalschriften-Verlag J. Jehle.

Humes, E., 2012. *Garbology: Our dirty love affair with trash.* New York: Penguin.

Karg, S., 2015. Überlegungen zur Kultur- und Anbaugeschichte des Leins. *In:* A. Rast-Eicher and A. Dietrich, eds. *Neolithische und bronzezeitliche Gewebe und Geflechte. Die Funde aus den Seeufersiedlungen im Kanton Zürich.* Monographien der Kantonsarchäologie Zürich 46. Zürich Egg: Baudirektion Kanton Zürich, 27-31.

Kaschuba, W., 1988. *„Deutsche Sauberkeit" - Zivilisierung der Körper und der Köpfe. Nachwort zu Georges Vigarello: Wasser und Seife, Puder und Parfüm. Geschichte der Körperhygiene seit dem Mittelalter.* Frankfurt: Campus-Verlag , 287-321.

Keller, R., 1998. *Müll – Die gesellschaftliche Konstruktion des Wertvollen. Die öffentliche Diskussion über Abfall in Deutschland und Frankreich.* Opladen, Wiesbaden: Westdeutscher Verlag.

Klinke, R. and Silbernagl, S., 1994, eds. *Lehrbuch der Physiologie.* Stuttgart, New York: Georg Thieme.

Kluge-Pinsker, A., 2003. Zum Stellenwert von Fäkalien, Schmutz und Müll im mittelalterlichen Alltag. *In:* S. Wolfram and M. Fansa, eds. *Müll – Facetten von der Steinzeit bis zum Gelben Sack. Begleitschrift zur Sonderausstellung vom 06. September bis 30. November 2003 in Oldenburg anschließend in Hanau.* Schriftenreihe des Landesmuseums für Natur und Mensch Oldenburg 27. Oldenburg: Isensee, 87-97.

Körlin, G. and Weisgerber, G., eds. 2006. *Stone Age – Mining Age.* Montanhistorische Zeitschrift: Der Anschnitt. Beiheft 19 (Veröffentlichungen aus dem Deutschen Bergbau-Museum Bochum 148). Bochum: Deutsches Bergbau-Museum Bochum.

Kosiba, S.B., Tykot, R.H., Carlsson, D., 2007. Stable isotopes as indicators of change in the food procurement and food preference of Viking Age and Early Christian populations on Gotland (Sweden). *Journal of Anthropological Archaeology* 26 (3), 394-411.

Kuchenbuch, L., 1988. Abfall. Eine Stichwortgeschichte. *In:* H.-G. Soeffner, ed. *Kultur und Alltag.* Soziale Welt, Sonderheft 6. Göttingen: Otto Schwartz & Co., 155-170.

Kuchenbuch, L., 1989. Abfall. Eine stichwortgeschichtliche Erkundung. *In:* J. Rüsen, J. Callies, M. Striegnitz, eds. *Mensch und Umwelt in der Geschichte.* Pfaffenweiler: Centaurus-Verlagsgesellschaft, 257-276.

Laporte, D., 1978. *Histoire de la merde.* Paris: Christian Bourgois.

Laporte, D., 1991. *Eine gelehrte Geschichte der Scheiße.* Frankfurt am Main: Frankfurter Verlagsanstalt.

Lehmann, J., Kern, D.C., Glaser, B., Woods, W.I., eds., 2003. *Amazonian Dark Earths: Origin, Properties, and Management.* Dordrecht: Springer Netherlands.

Leube, A., 2019. Garz und das Jahr 1928. Die Ausgrabungen auf dem „Schlossberg". *In:* Stadt Garz und Heimatverband Garz, eds. *700 Jahre Stadt Garz / Rügen. 1319 bis 2019.* Elmenhorst: Edition Pommern, 33-42.

Meier, T., 2008. Einige Bemerkungen zum Umweltverhalten der Menschen im Mittelalter. *In:* T. Knopf, ed. *Umweltverhalten in Geschichte und Gegenwart. Vergleichende Ansätze.* Tübingen: Attempo, 135-157.

Müller, U., 2018. Gerberei im späten Mittelalter. Überlegungen zur Anwendung der Theorien sozialer Praktiken für die Erforschung handwerklicher Tätigkeiten. *In:* M. Bentz and T. Helms, eds. *Craft production systems in a cross-cultural perspective.* Graduiertenkolleg 1878. Studien zur Wirtschaftsarchäologie 1. Bonn: Dr. Rudolf Habelt, 233-259.

Murray, P., 1980. Discard Location: The Ethnographic Data. *American Antiquity* 45 (3), 490-502.

Oexle, J., 1992. Versorgung und Entsorgung der mittelalterlichen Stadt. Versorgung und Entsorgung nach dem archäologischen Befund. *In:* Landesdenkmalamt Baden-Württemberg, ed. *Stadtluft, Hirsebrei und Bettelmönch – Die Stadt um 1300. Katalog zur Ausstellung in Zürich und Stuttgart 1992.* Stuttgart: Konrad Theiss Verlag, 364-374.

Rathje, W. and Murphy, C., 1992. *Rubbish! The Archaeology of Garbage.* New York: HarperCollins.

Rathje, W. and Murphy, C., 1994. *Müll. Eine archäologische Reise durch die Welt des Abfalls.* München: Goldmann.

Ruchhöft, F., 2019. Warum Garz nicht das berühmte „Karentia" ist. *In:* Stadt Garz and Heimatverband Garz, eds. *700 Jahre Stadt Garz / Rügen. 1319 bis 2019.* Elmenhorst: Edition Pommern, 43-46.

Scheub, U., Pieplow, H., Schmidt, H.-P., 2013. *Die schwarze Revolution aus dem Regenwald.* München: oekom.

Schiffer, M.B., 1987. *Formation processes of the archaeological record.* Albuquerque: University of New Mexico Press.

Schneeweiß, J., 2020. *Zwischen den Welten. Archäologie einer europäischen Grenzregion zwischen Sachsen, Slawen, Franken und Dänen.* Göttinger Schriften zur Vor- und Frühgeschichte 36. Kiel, Hamburg: Wachholtz.

Schoeninger, M.J., 2010. Diet reconstruction and ecology using isotope ratios. *In:* C.S. Larsen, ed. *A Companion to Biological Anthropology.* Chichester: Wiley, 445-464.

Schrader, M., 2006. *Plumpsklo, Abort, Stilles Örtchen.* Suderburg-Hösseringen: Edition Anderweit.

Schuchhardt, C., 1944. *Aus Leben und Arbeit.* Berlin: Walter de Gruyter.

Sommer, U., 1991. *Zur Entstehung archäologischer Fundvergesellschaftungen. Versuch einer archäologischen Taphonomie.* Universitätsforschungen zur Prähistorischen Archäologie 6 (Studien zur Siedlungsarchäologie I). Bonn: Dr. Rudolf Habelt, 53-193.

Sosna, D., Brunclíková, L., Galeta, P., 2019. Rescuing things: Food waste in the rural environment in the Czech Republic. *Journal of Cleaner Production* 214, 319-330.

Stöllner, T., 2003. Mining and Economy – A Discussion of Spatial Organisations and Structures of Early Raw Material Exploitation. *In:* T. Stöllner, G. Körlin, G. Steffens, J. Cierny, eds. *Man and Mining – Mensch und Bergbau. Studies in honour of Gerd Weisgerber on occasion of his 65th birthday.* Montanhistorische Zeitschrift: Der Anschnitt. Beiheft 16. (Veröffentlichungen aus dem Deutschen Bergbau-Museum Bochum 114). Bochum: Deutsches Bergbau-Museum Bochum, 415-446.

Sydow, J., ed., 1981. *Städtische Versorgung und Entsorgung im Wandel der Geschichte.* Stadt in der Geschichte 8. Sigmaringen: Jan Thorbecke.

Thompson, M., 1979. *Rubbish Theory. The creation and destruction of value.* Oxford: Oxford University Press.

Thompson, M., 1981. *Die Theorie des Abfalls. Über die Schaffung und Vernichtung von Werten.* Stuttgart: Klett-Cotta.

Thompson, M., 2003. *Mülltheorie. Über die Schaffung und Vernichtung von Werten.* Essen: Klartext.

Thüry, G.E., 2001. *Müll und Marmorsäulen. Siedlungshygiene in der römischen Antike.* Zaberns Bildbände zur Archäologie. Mainz: Philipp von Zabern.

Werner, F., 2011. *Dunkle Materie. Die Geschichte der Scheiße.* Zürich: Nagel & Kimche.

Wiedner, K., Schneeweiß, J., Dippold, M.A., Glaser, B., 2015. Anthropogenic Dark Earth in Northern Germany – The Nordic Analogue to terra preta de Índio in Amazonia. *Catena* 132, 114-125.

Windmüller, S., 2003. Abfallkultur. Volkskundliche Aspekte des modernen Mensch-Müll-Verhältnisses. *In:* S. Wolfram and M. Fansa, eds. *Müll – Facetten von der Steinzeit bis zum Gelben Sack. Begleitschrift zur Sonderausstellung vom 06. September bis 30. November 2003 in Oldenburg anschließend in Hanau.* Schriftenreihe des Landesmuseums für Natur und Mensch Oldenburg 27. Oldenburg: Isensee, 113-121.

Windmüller, S., 2004. *Die Kehrseite der Dinge. Müll, Abfall, Wegwerfen als kulturwissenschaftliches Problem.* Europäische Ethnologie 2. Münster, Hamburg, Berlin, London: LIT.

Wolfram, S. and Fansa, M., eds. 2003. *Müll – Facetten von der Steinzeit bis zum Gelben Sack. Begleitschrift zur Sonderausstellung vom 06. September bis 30. November 2003 in Oldenburg anschließend in Hanau.* Schriftenreihe des Landesmuseums für Natur und Mensch Oldenburg 27. Oldenburg: Isensee.

Woolgar, C.M., Serjeantson, D., Waldron, T., eds. 2006. *Food in Medieval England. Diet and Nutrition.* Oxford: Oxford University Press.

Yoder, C., 2010. Diet in medieval Denmark: a regional and temporal comparison. *Journal of Archaeological Science* 37 (9), 2224-2236.

Die Zeit, 2005. *Das Lexikon in 20 Bänden.* Bd. 01 A-Bar. Hamburg: Zeitverlag.

Zimring, C.A. and Rathje, W.L., eds. 2012. *Encyclopedia of Consumption and Waste: The Social Science of Garbage.* Los Angeles, London, New Delhi, Singapore, Washington, D.C.: SAGE Publications.

Ideology and identity in grammar: A diachronic-quantitative approach to language standardisation processes in Ancient Greek

Dariya Rafiyenko and Ilja A. Seržant

Abstract

This paper sets out to disentangle the natural developments leading away from encoding semantic relations by inflectional case towards encoding them by means of prepositions, on the one hand, and the impact of the Attistic language ideology on the development of prepositions on the other. Our aim is to describe the major standardisation trends in the grammar of prepositions in a corpus-based study.

While the Archaic, Classical and Hellenistic periods are characterised by the natural expansion of prepositional patterns across various semantic and syntactic domains, the language of Postclassical Greek is subject to different standardisation processes and ideological influences. Already by the Hellenistic period, we observe the tendency towards consolidation of variation in prepositional usage, being an effect of adopting some of the standards of Koiné. The Roman period, by contrast, again increases variation: Different authors and texts imitate the ideals of the Archaic and Classical periods to varying degrees (Atticism). Accordingly, we refer to the Roman period as a period of *creative standardisation*. The conventionalisation of a set of Attistic patterns takes place only from the Early to Late Byzantine periods. The Late Byzantine period attests more than twice as little variation than the Roman period. Finally, we argue that the expansion of prepositions is not only determined by language change and Atticism but that genres channel the ex-

Dariya Rafiyenko
Institute of Classical Philology and Comparative Studies
Byzantine and Modern Greek Philology
Leipzig University
Beethovenstrasse 15
04107 Leipzig, Germany
dariya.rafiyenko@uni-leipzig.de

Ilja A. Seržant
Institute of Slavic Studies
Kiel University
Leibnizstraße 10
24118 Kiel, Germany
serzant@slav.uni-kiel.de

pansion of prepositional patterns. Historians and early religious texts are the most progressive and less amenable for imitating earlier periods. By contrast, writers of poetry and orators are much more conservative, more resistant to language change and tend to imitate the earlier language layers more faithfully.

Introduction

Language standardisation is a historical and sociolinguistic process by which an over-regional variety emerges with a codified orthography, lexicon and grammar. Ideally, a standardised language shows no diachronic, diatopic or diastratic variation. However, an absolute standardisation can never be achieved (cf. Georgakopoulou 2009, xiii) and it is, therefore, more appropriate to speak of standardisation as an ideology, i.e., 'a set of abstract norms to which actual usage may conform to a greater or lesser extent' (Milroy and Milroy 1999), and thus as a continuum and not a categorical matter. The linguistic material adopted as the set of norms in the standardised variety is often selected consciously on the basis of some linguistic authority, such as the literary tradition and particular writers, in a process of constructing self-identity (see Peterson et al., this volume). One of the salient motivations behind this conscious selection is the wish to link oneself to the tradition and thereby to a particular social subgroup. Revalorisation of varieties that are associated with particular speakers may serve

> 'not just as symbols of group identity, but as emblems of political allegiance or of social, intellectual, or moral worth' (Woolard and Schieffelin 1994, 61, see also the references therein, in particular, on Greek see Strobel 2009, 95; Horrocks 2010, 100).

While research about constructing identity and linguistic ideology primarily focuses on phonetics and lexicon, grammar is less frequently discussed in this context. In this paper, our aim is to investigate the impact of the literary tradition on the grammar of Postclassical Greek, i.e., to explore grammatical Atticism (cf. Strobel 2009, 97). Our aim is to grasp the main statistical tendencies and to disentangle the effects of the expansion of ideological norms from the effects of grammar-driven language change in a bird's-eye perspective as well as to better understand the ways that the mechanisms of the ideological expansion intervene with a grammar-driven language change.

More specifically, we focus on one particular domain of grammar, namely, prepositions. The emergence and expansion of prepositions in Greek has been subject to extensive research (among others Luraghi 2003; Bortone 2010; Seržant and Rafiyenko in press). Ancient Greek underwent substantial changes in its grammar from marking semantic relationships primarily by means of case in its early stages to marking them primarily by prepositions in the Postclassical period. The reduction of the inflectional case system of Ancient Greek may already be observed in the earliest attested period of Mycenean Greek (Hettrich 1985; Hajnal 1995, 16ff). The general tendency to reinforce the old inflectional cases with prepositions already became strong since Homer (Morpurgo Davies 1983, 288; Bortone 2010, 155-156). This process led to the abandonment of the most part of the old case system of Ancient Greek in the course of time. Literary texts do not immediately mirror this change, and literary tradition considerably skews the picture – an aspect that we take under closer inspection below.

We investigate the impact of Atticism on the use of prepositions in a corpus-based study. Atticism refers to the ideological movement in language usage that arose by the end of the 1st century BC to revive lexical but also grammatical properties of the classical language. The motivation behind this movement was that the classical language came to be considered as the ideal variety as opposed to the administrative Koiné that was dissociated from any literary tradition (Schmid 1887-1897; Swain 1996; Schmitz 1997; Silk 2009; Strobel 2009). Originally, the conscious imitation of the classical language produced a new literary register noted as Learned Language, which combines ancient and sometimes artificial, hypercorrect patterns with those actually used in everyday life and adopted from Koiné (cf., i.a., Strobel 2009; Benedetti 2020; García Ramón 2020).

Greek has an exceptionally long documented history, like no other Indo-European language (Morpurgo Davies 1985, 75) with a large digital collection of texts for all periods (Thesaurus Linguae Graecae, http://stephanus.tlg.uci.edu/, henceforth TLG). This allows us to approach our research questions quantitatively by using a dataset created on the basis of a subcorpus of TLG (Rafiyenko and Seržant 2021). The reason for applying a usage-based approach is that the variation we observe is – as expected for any linguistic ideological norms – not graspable with categorical judgements but is rather probabilistic in nature. Moreover, the corpus-based method provides for falsifiable claims. Our study follows previous philological research on prepositions that crucially relied on corpus counts (cf. various statistical studies on prepositions in Xenophon, Isocrates, Thucydides, and some other Attic prose, e.g., Abel 1927, 215; Bortone 2010, 177-182; Koch 1889, 35; Lutz 1891, 6; Mommsen 1895, 6; Martínez Valladares 1973, 192; Sobolewskij 1890, 65; Westphal 1888, 2).

We proceed as follows: in the first section, we describe our subcorpus and the prepositions to be investigated here. In the next section, we discuss the evidence and the results. To do so, we first discuss the common trends for all prepositions at issue and then deal with particular prepositions. The final section presents our conclusions.

Our corpus

For our study, we selected 18 prepositions (Table 1).

We chose the older layer of prepositions, sometimes – traditionally – referred to as "proper prepositions" (cf. Smyth 1956, §1681-1698), while more recent prepositions, such as μεταξύ, μέχρι, ὁμοῦ, and ὄπισθεν (cf. Smyth 1956, § 1699-1702), have been left out. The former occur more frequently in the corpus than the latter ones. The only exception is ἀμφί, which is found less frequently and disappears from the colloquial language very early.

Our data stems from TLG (Thesaurus Linguae Graecae) with 104,526,008 words as of June 2017. Our subcorpus consists of ca. 34 million words (as of June 8, 2018). The selected prepositions occur 2,199,561 times in our subcorpus, as opposed to TLG, where they occur nearly three times as often. The overall relative frequency of the 18 selected prepositions accounts for 66.3 words per thousand in TLG and for 64.9 per thousand in our corpus. The entire dataset underlying this study is published in Rafiyenko and Seržant (2021).

Dictionary form	Absolute Frequency		Relative frequency	
	TLG*	Our corpus	TLG*	Our corpus
ἀμφί	8,873	3,456	0.08	0.10
ἀνά	16,600	4,100	0.16	0.12
ἀντί	79,545	18,201	0.76	0.54
ἀπό	372,201	95,391	3.56	2.82
διά	614,259	197,677	5.88	5.83
εἰς	765,179	242,155	7.32	7.15
ἐκ	565,350	180,566	5.41	5.33
ἐν	1,148,618	383,822	10.99	11.33
ἐπί	601,443	195,489	5.75	5.77
κατά	693,853	208,372	6.64	6.15
μετά	296,690	93,895	2.84	2.77
παρά	306,674	94,929	2.93	2.80
περί	399,581	129,811	3.82	3.83
πρό	68,632	21,378	0.66	0.63
πρός	609,650	208,368	5.83	6.15
σύν	56,718	15,379	0.54	0.45
ὑπέρ	95,356	35,854	0.91	1.06
ὑπό	230,820	69,852	2.21	2.06
Total	6,930,042	2,198,695	66.29	64.90

Table 1. The frequency of prepositions (the counts for TLG are given as of June 1, 2017); the relative frequencies are per 1000 words.

TLG has been lemmatised automatically and is, therefore, not always reliable in case of homonymy and/or homography. For this reason, we selected those prepositions that do not tend to have homographical forms with other words.[1]

The selection of authors – 70 in total (Table 2) – was motivated by the following criteria. First, the length of the texts should be reasonably long as to allow for statistically significant judgements. Secondly, we somewhat preferred authors with an affinity to the spoken register of the period rather than the authors of highly stylistically affected texts (consequently, we have predominantly chosen prose texts and less poetry). Thirdly, in order to balance biases arising from different text genres, we selected sets of authors for each period that are comparable thematically and genre-wise to the extent that the text attestation of Ancient

---

1   There are two exceptions. First, the prepositions *en* and *eis* are homonymous with the numeral εἷς, μία, ἕν. However, this homonymy (947 homonymic forms in total) is not significant given the overall number of occurrences of *en* (383,961) and *eis* (242,320) in our corpus. The error does not exceed 0.15%. The other homonymic pair is the apocopated allomorph ἀν'/ ἄν' of the preposition ἀνά (cf. Smyth 1956, §75D) that graphically coincides with the modal particle ἄν. The relative frequency of the allomorph as opposed to the total frequency of the preposition ἀνά in our subcorpus is also extremely low.

Greek allowed us to do so. Each author has been attributed to one of the seven idealised historical periods based on what is known about the author's life span:[2]

i.   Archaic period (8-6 century BC; *e.g.* Homer, Hesiod),

ii. Classical period (5-4 century BC; *e.g.* Plato, Thucydides),

iii. Hellenistic period (3-1 century BC; *e.g.* Diodorus, Nicolaus Damascenus),

iv. Roman period (AD 1-3 century; *e.g.* Plutarch, Arrianus),

v.   Early Byzantine period (AD 4-7 century; *e.g.* Johannes Malalas, Johannes Antiochenes),

vi. Middle Byzantine period (AD 8-11 century; *e.g.* Symeon Logothetes, Michael Psellus),

vii. Late Byzantine period (AD 12-15 century; *e.g.* Georgius Pachymeres, Gregorius Palamas).

Division into periods is based on the division into centuries as given in TLG. We selected the authors in such a way that we would have at least one author per century (while certain centuries have many more authors).[3]

Some of the authors do not entirely match the criteria mentioned above. For example, the selection of texts for the Archaic period is less faithful with regard to the above-mentioned second and third criteria. Moreover, Homer's texts are certainly not homogenous dialectally and, possibly, diachronically. The New Testament is also problematic with regard to its homogeneity. However, as both are important witnesses of their periods, it was important to include them.

Texts collected in our corpus belong to different literary genres. Based on the information provided by TLG, we attributed each of the 70 authors to one of the eight categories that roughly correspond to the commonly adopted genre designations (Table 3). Each author has been attributed one singe genre, which is a minor simplification.[4]

As we argue below, the genres may be grouped together into two larger clusters. The first cluster contains historiography, religious texts and the texts of the authors who wrote in different genres. It is the largest cluster of the two. The second cluster is considerably smaller and contains such genres as poetry, oratory, philosophy and some other genres.

---

2   We had to make some ad-hoc decisions in ambiguous cases, *e.g.*, when the lifetime of an author cannot be properly determined (*e.g.* Hesiodus or Heliodorus), when one text has been written over a span of more than one century (the Septuagint and the New Testament), or when authors cannot be unambiguously attributed to one of the periods because they lived in the transition between two periods (*e.g.* Menander or Flavius Josephus).

3   The word count per century ranges from 0.1 to 12.9 million words (AD 4) with an average of 1-2 million words per century.

4   Within the scope of this study, it was not possible to systematically test whether one and the same author considerably diverges in prepositional usage across different genres (for those authors who wrote in different genres). The preliminary evidence does not seem to speak in favour of such an assumption. Thus, we tested whether Xenophon has largely the same frequency of prepositions in his *Anabasis* vs. all his works. The frequencies do not significantly diverge from each other with 48/1000 vs. 50/1000, respectively.

TLG-number	Latin name (TLG)	Word count (TLG)	Relative frequency of 18 prepositions per thousand	Genre (corpus)	Dating		Our periodisation
					Century (TLG)	Century (corpus)	
0012	Homerus	199,251	49.86	EPIC	8 BC	8/7 BC	Archaic
0020	Hesiodus	26,626	45.18	EPIC	8/7 BC?	8/7 BC	Archaic
0085	Aeschylus	81,504	41.07	TRAG	6-5 BC	6 BC	Archaic
0003	Thucydides	150,196	71.82	HIST	5 BC	5 BC	Classical
0010	Isocrates	120,506	63.10	ORAT	5-4 BC	5 BC	Classical
0016	Herodotus	185,554	64.50	HIST	5 BC	5 BC	Classical
0014	Demosthenes	296,539	52.69	ORAT	4 BC	4 BC	Classical
0017	Isaeus	32,744	50.21	ORAT	5-4 BC	4 BC	Classical
0019	Aristophanes	116,951	36.65	COM	5-4 BC	4 BC	Classical
0026	Aeschines	48,845	61.73	ORAT	4 BC	4 BC	Classical
0032	Xenophon	315,469	50.36	HIST	5-4 BC	4 BC	Classical
0059	Plato	591,143	42.89	PHILOS	5-4 BC	4 BC	Classical
0086	Aristoteles et Corpus Aristotelicum	1,076,439	61.15	SCI	4 BC	4 BC	Classical
0540	Lysias	78,074	65.21	ORAT	5-4 BC	4 BC	Classical
0541	Menander	80,882	28.93	COM	4-3 BC	4 BC	Classical
0593	Gorgias	9,616	44.41	ORAT	5-4 BC	4 BC	Classical
0543	Polybius	316,866	90.89	HIST	3-2 BC	3 BC	Hellenistic
0552	Archimedes	109,980	84.15	SCI	3 BC	3 BC	Hellenistic
1264	Chrysippus	192,890	54.26	PHILOS	3 BC	3 BC	Hellenistic
0527	Septuaginta	623,781	82.51	REL	3 BC/ AD 3	2 BC	Hellenistic
0060	Diodorus	464,305	82.05	HIST	1 BC	1 BC	Hellenistic
0577	Nicolaus Damascenus	34,939	71.73	HIST	1 BC	1 BC	Hellenistic
0007	Plutarchus	1,036,815	58.42	VAR	AD 1-2	AD 1	Roman
0074	Arrianus	141,772	77.83	HIST	AD 1-2	AD 1	Roman
0526	Flavius Josephus	475,709	74.55	HIST	AD 1	AD 1	Roman
0612	Diochrysosto-mus	179,346	47.38	ORAT	AD 1-2	AD 1	Roman
0031	Novum Testamentum	137,938	75.37	REL	AD 1	AD 1	Roman

Table 2. Authors included in our corpus.

TLG-number	Latin name (TLG)	Word count (TLG)	Relative frequency of 18 prepositions per thousand	Genre (corpus)	Dating		
					Century (TLG)	Century (corpus)	Our periodisation
0062	Lucianus	281,064	51.92	VAR	AD 2	AD 2	Roman
0385	Cassius Dio	546,840	65.64	HIST	AD 2-3	AD 2	Roman
0551	Appian	226,924	78.22	HIST	AD 1-2	AD 2	Roman
0554	Chariton	34,966	47.10	NOV	AD 2?	AD 2	Roman
0561	Longus	19,858	45.37	NOV	AD 2?	AD 2	Roman
0638	Flavius Philostratus	180,200	58.12	ORAT	AD 2-3	AD 2	Roman
2042	Origenes	1,280,101	77.46	REL	AD 2-3	AD 2	Roman
0532	Achilles Tatius	41,869	53.52	NOV	AD 2	AD 2	Roman
0658	Heliodorus	76,434	56.90	NOV	AD 3?	AD 3	Roman
0641	Xenophon Ephesius	16,569	56.25	NOV	AD 2/3	AD 3	Roman
0722	Oribasius	503,549	68.35	SC	AD 4	AD 4	Early Byzantine
2017	Gregorius Nyssenus	788,739	76.09	REL	AD 4	AD 4	Early Byzantine
2018	Eusebius	1,233,487	75.24	REL	AD 4	AD 4	Early Byzantine
2035	Athanasius	734,398	69.27	REL	AD 4	AD 4	Early Byzantine
2040	Basilius Caesariensis	710,152	71.20	REL	AD 4	AD 4	Early Byzantine
2062	Joannes Chrysostomus	4,071,012	55.84	REL	AD 4-5	AD 4	Early Byzantine
2200	Libanius	763,855	51.39	ORAT	AD 4	AD 4	Early Byzantine
4089	Theodoretus	1,300,876	56.57	REL	AD 4-5	AD 4	Early Byzantine
4090	Cyrillus Alexandrinus	2,334,974	72.33	REL	AD 4-5	AD 4	Early Byzantine
4138	Ephraem Syrus	427,012	68.49	REL	AD 4	AD 4	Early Byzantine
2871	Joannes Malalas	102,553	76.40	HIST	AD 5-6	AD 5	Early Byzantine
4029	Procopius	292,548	68.31	HIST	AD 6	AD 6	Early Byzantine

Table 2. continued.

TLG-number	Latin name (TLG)	Word count (TLG)	Relative frequency of 18 prepositions per thousand	Genre (corpus)	Dating		
					Century (TLG)	Century (corpus)	Our periodisation
4394	Joannes Antiochenus	106,954	70.01	HIST	AD 7	AD 7	Early Byzantine
2934	Joannes Damascenus	690,220	63.29	REL	AD 7-8	AD 8	Middle Byzantine
3043	Georgius Monachus	352,928	70.89	HIST	AD 9	AD 9	Middle Byzantine
4040	Photius	1,113,380	62.18	VAR	AD 9	AD 9	Middle Byzantine
3070	Symeon Logothetes	132,538	76.17	HIST	AD 10	AD 10	Middle Byzantine
3115	Symeon Metaphrastes	38,451	56.38	HIST	AD 10	AD 10	Middle Byzantine
2702	Michael Psellus	910,320	57.90	VAR	AD 11	AD 11	Middle Byzantine
3135	Joannes Zonaras	378,901	63.86	HIST	AD 11-12	AD 11	Middle Byzantine
2703	Anna Comnena	145,850	67.34	HIST	AD 11-12	AD 11	Middle Byzantine
4083	Eustathius Thessalonicensis	1,950,642	67.58	VAR	AD 12	AD 12	Late Byzantine
3142	Georgius Pachymeres	653,046	66.84	VAR	AD 13-14	AD 13	Late Byzantine
3236	Nicephorus Callistus Xanthopulus	472,239	67.21	VAR	AD 13-14	AD 13	Late Byzantine
3254	Gregorius Palamas	694,387	67.75	REL	AD 13-14	AD 13	Late Byzantine
4145	Nicephorus Gregoras	575,593	54.88	VAR	AD 13-14	AD 13	Late Byzantine
3169	Joannes VI Cantacuzenus	498,759	67.66	VAR	AD 14	AD 14	Late Byzantine
3251	Philotheus Coccinus	448,689	61.28	REL	AD 14	AD 14	Late Byzantine
3195	Gennadius Scholarius	1,624,669	69.90	REL	AD 15	AD 15	Late Byzantine

Table 2. continued.

Genre (number of authors / word count)	List of authors
MAJOR CATEGORIES	
HIST (18 authors / 6.1 million words)	Herodotus (5 BC), Thucydides (5 BC), Xenophon (4 BC), Polybius (3 BC), Diocorus (1 BC), Nicolaus Damascenus (1 BC), Flavius Josephus (AD 1), Arrianus (AD 1), Appian (AD 2), Cassius Dio (AD 2), Joannes Malalas (AD 5), Procopius (AD 6), Joannes Antiochenus (AD 7), Georgius Monachus (AD 9), Symeon Logothetes (AD 10), Symeon Metaphrastes (AD 10), Joannes Zonaras (AD 11), Anna Comnena (AD 11)
REL (15 authors / 17.1 million words)	Septuaginta (2 BC), Novum Testamentum (AD 1), Origenes (AD 2), Gregorius Nyssenus (AD 4), Eusebius (AD 4), Athanasius (AD 4), Basilius Caesariensis (AD 4), Ephraem Syrus (AD 4), Joannes Chrysostomus (AD 4), Theodoretus (AD 4), Cyrillus Alexandrinus (AD 4), Joannes Damascenus (AD 8), Gregorius Palamas (AD 13), Philotheus Coccinus (AD 14), Gennadius Scholarius (AD 15)
VAR (9 authors / 7.5 million words)	Plutarchus (AD 1), Lucianus (AD 2), Michael Psellus (AD 11), Photius (AD 9), Eustathius Thessalonicensis (AD 12), Georgius Pachymeres (AD 13), Nicephorus Callistus Xanthopulus (AD 13), Nicephorus Gregoras (AD 13), Joannes VI Cantacuzenus (AD 14)
SMALLER CATEGORIES	
ORAT (9 authors / 1.7 million words)	Isocrates (5 BC), Aeschines (4 BC), Demosthenes (4 BC), Gorgias (4 BC), Isaeus (4 BC), Lysias (4 BC), Dio Chrysostomus (AD 1), Flavius Philostratus (AD 2), Libanius (AD 4)
SCI (3 authors / 1.7 million words)	Aristoteles et Corpus Aristotelicum (4 BC), Archimedes (3 BC), Oribasius (AD 4)
PHILOS (2 authors / 784 thousand words)	Plato (4 BC), Chrysippus (3 BC)
EPIC, TRAG, COM (5 authors / 505 thousand words)	Homerus (8/7 BC), Hesiodus (8/7 BC), Aeschylus (6 BC), Aristophanes (4 BC), Menander (4 BC)
NOV (5 authors / 190 thousand words)	Achilles Tatius (AD 2), Chariton (AD 2), Longus (AD 2), Xenophon Ephesius (AD 3), Heliodorus (AD 3)

Table 3. Genres covered by our subcorpus (based on the categorisation found in TLG). Lemma: COM: comedy, EPIC: epic poetry, HIST: historiography, NOV: Roman novel, ORAT: orator, PHILOS: philosopher, REL: religious texts, SCI: scientific texts, TRAG: tragedy, VAR: various texts.

Unveiling the hotspots of variation

The grammatical system of encoding semantic roles of participants in a sentence changes in the course of time in Ancient Greek (*i.a.* Delbruck 1893, 647-665; Kühner and Gerth 1898, 526; Smyth 1920; Schwyzer and Debrunner 1975 [1950], 419-436; Chantraine 1958; Dunkel 1979; Horrocks 1981; Vincent 1999; Luraghi 1996; 2003; Hewson and Bubenik 2006; Bortone 2010; Rafiyenko and Seržant 2020). Originally, in the Archaic and, to some extent, in the Classical period, many roles are primarily coded by inflectional case, while prepositions are used for rather specific, semantically more fine-grained distinctions (*e.g.* for spatial relations such as *inside, above, below, etc.*).

By contrast, in the later periods, the inflectional cases lose a number of their original domains in favour of prepositions that gradually take over increasingly more grammatical functions. For example, the recipient of the verb 'to give' is typically marked by the dative case in the Archaic and Classical periods. However, after the Hellenistic period, prepositions are frequently employed to signal the same role (such as *prós* 'to', *eis* 'to'). The gradual disappearance of the dative case from colloquial language is an important step here (cf. Humbert 1930; Blass and

18 prepositions by 7 periods. Median.

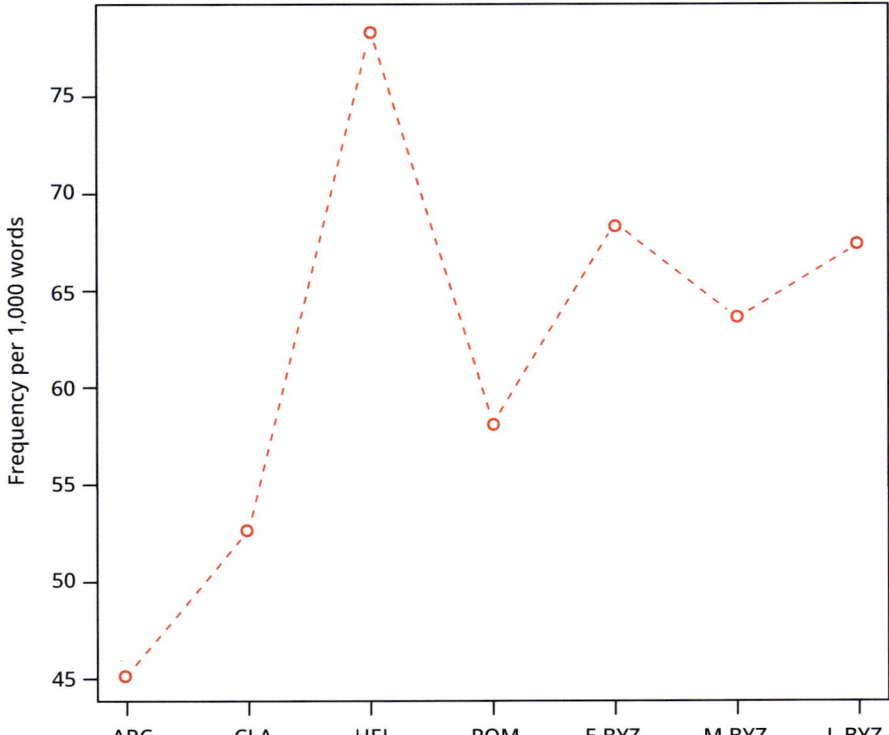

Figure 1. Median of the relative frequencies of each preposition by period (graph: the authors).

Debrunner 1979; Cooper and Georgala 2012; Seržant and Rafiyenko 2021), notwithstanding some increase during Roman times, the Byzantine period and in the New Testament, which is due to the impact of the conservative literary tradition (cf. Horrocks 1997, 49). Another example is the allative meaning 'towards' and the illative meaning 'into'. Both spatial relations could originally be expressed by the bare accusative case in Early Greek. However, already during the Archaic period, these relations tend to be marked periphrastically by the respective prepositions such as *prós* 'to' for the allative and *eis* 'in(to)' for the illative meaning. Yet another example is part-whole relations. These were originally expressed by the (partitive) genitive case, while, starting at the latest from the Hellenistic period on, the prepositions *apó* or *eks* 'from' are used for the same purpose (Nachmanson 1942). Many other examples can be added. As a consequence of these kinds of processes, the frequency of prepositions increases considerably across various periods.

In what follows, we estimate the frequency effects of these types of processes across the periods, authors, genres and for particular prepositions. Instead of looking at particular constructions and contexts, our goal here is to scrutinise frequency trends in a bird's-eye perspective and to draw some general conclusions about the impact of language ideology on the change that in itself is primarily grammar-driven. Methodologically, our approach is somewhat similar to some of the quantitative approaches in stylometry.

We first approach the diachronic variation via the overall relative frequency of prepositions (per 1000 words) across all periods. Figure 1 represents the median frequency of our prepositions per one thousand words:[5]

---

5   We choose the median frequency over the mean frequency because it better represents the variation in the data.

What we find is that there is considerable variation across the periods: the curve of expansion of prepositions is obviously not a simple function dependent on the time variable. Thus, the number of prepositions does not steadily increase across all periods as one might have expected: after the steep increase from the Archaic up until the Hellenistic period, there is a substantial breakdown in the Roman period. After this, the expansion of prepositions continues to rise again up into the Late Byzantine period.

This overall picture can be interpreted as follows. First, we observe a steep increase of the frequency of prepositions from the Archaic to the Hellenistic period. This increase in frequency mirrors the grammatical change by which semantic roles of event participants become increasingly marked by prepositions at the cost of the bare cases. This is a purely grammar-driven process of language change that many other Indo-European languages underwent in a similar way (*i.a.* Seržant and Rafiyenko 2021). Crucially and secondly, the breakdown during the Roman period represents a dramatic shift in preferences. Prepositions must have been abandoned from various contexts in which they had already become regular during the Hellenistic period. No doubt, this shift must be due to the rise of the Atticistic ideology, which is generally known to have had an enormous conservative effect on all domains of grammar and lexicon. In our case, it must have led to the abandonment of prepositions from some of their newly established contexts and to their retrograde replacement by case-inflected forms with the aim to imitate earlier, Classical usage. Finally, although it can be observed that the expansion of prepositions sets in after the Roman period again, this expansion is not so pervasive anymore and does not reach the frequency of the Hellenistic period. Given that the relative frequency found in the later Byzantine periods does not reach the peak of the Hellenistic period, it can likely be assumed that the Attistic influence remained in operation even after the Roman period (*i.e.* during the Early, Middle and Late Byzantine periods). This is certainly due to the Attistic ideology that is still alive in the later periods. However, it might also be an indication of the fact that at least some of the puristic norms introduced during the Roman period by a small, highly educated elite penetrated into the linguistic usage of some other social groups, thus gradually transgressing the conscious ideology and turning into the unconscious norm of some speakers (see Peterson *et al.*, this volume). We explore this conventionalisation of the consciously introduced patterns below.

Of course, the overall relative frequencies do not tell us anything about the particular changes of different prepositions and the constructions in which they occurred. Thus, it is certainly possible that particular constructions and prepositional meanings or even particular prepositions, under a closer inspection, might show trends that would deviate from the overall picture observed in figure 1. Since our goal is to capture the overall picture, our method is unavoidably too coarse-grained to capture these specific aspects. Having said this, in order to exclude the possibility that some of these specific factors would skew the overall frequency picture of its period, we rely on median – instead of mean – frequencies.

Now we turn to the breakdown of the Roman period. In order to better understand the specific processes responsible for the breakdown in the Roman period, we zoom in on particular authors. Figure 2 illustrates the relative frequency distributions of particular authors within their periods:

At first glance, we observe a lot of author-specific variation. The sparsest use of prepositions is found in Menander and Aristophanes (less than 40/1000), the highest number of prepositions in Polybius, Diodorus, Archimedes, and the Sep-

Table 4. The degree of dispersion between the authors for each of the periods.

Classical	Hellenistic	Roman	Early Byzantine	Middle Byzantine	Late Byzantine
42.89	36.62	41.88	33.0	19.78	15.01

tuagint, all belonging to the Hellenistic period (more than 80/1000). By contrast, Menander (4 BC) has the lowest number of prepositions (30/1000).

Apart from these two extremities, there are interesting tendencies in each period. Thus, the majority of the authors of the Classical period are evenly distributed in the range from ca. 29 to 72 prepositions per thousand words. This indicates that the grammaticality norms for prepositional usage in this period were rather fuzzy. It was acceptable that some authors used almost twice as many prepositions as others, while apparently still remaining within the norms of grammaticality.

Moreover, the periods are not alike with regard to the very degree of the attested variation, which is calculated as the dispersion between the maximum and the minimum frequency for each period (Table 4):[6]

While the later Middle and Late Byzantine periods are characterised by a considerable decrease in variation, the earlier Classical, Hellenistic, Roman and Early Byzantine periods attest a much higher degree of variation. The Classical period has the widest spectrum of frequencies. Side by side with the authors that use extremely few prepositions (e.g. Aristophanes, Menander, and Plato), there are authors that use a high number of prepositions (e.g. Thucydides, Lysias, and Herodotus). Notably, the authors of the Classical period do not form groups by less vs. more frequent prepositional usage, but are rather evenly distributed within a wide range. This means that a lot of variation was allowed in this period and we cannot speak about one single "grammar of prepositions" that would be common to all authors. Accordingly, we observe no standardisation processes here.

This situation changes in the Hellenistic period quite substantially. In this period, there is less dispersion among the authors, indicating a process of language unification. Most of the authors cluster around very high preposition frequencies (e.g. Polybius, Diodorus, Archimedes, the Septuagint, and some others). Crucially, while the Hellenistic period stands out among all periods by the highest median frequency of prepositions (median 82/1000, see Fig. 1), the degree of dispersion, conversely, decreases by more than 10% when compared to the Classical period. In other words, despite an enormous expansion of the use of prepositions during the Hellenistic period (from 53/1000 in the Classical to 82/1000 in the Hellenistic period, see Fig. 1), the grammar of prepositions undergoes a certain degree of unification in this domain. We assume that this effect is due to the emergence of the super-regional variety, Koiné, which had a strong consolidating effect for all registers and varieties of the period.

We now turn to the next, Roman period. One might expect that the same trend towards less variation and a more unified grammar would hold here as well. However, to the contrary, while the median number of prepositions drops abruptly to 58/1000 in the Roman period from 82/1000 in the Hellenistic period (Fig. 1), the degree of dispersion increases from 36.62 in the Hellenistic period to almost 42 (Table 4), reaching the degree of dispersion of the Classical period again. Thus,

Figure 2 (opposite page). The relative frequencies of 18 prepositions per author and period (per 1000 words). Genres are colour-coded: dark green for poetry, red for historical accounts, blue for religious texts, light green for oratory texts, and black for others (graph: the authors).

---

6   The degree of dispersion has been calculated as the difference between the maximum and the minimum relative frequency for each period. For example, the maximum frequency of prepositions is 71.82 per 1000 words in the Classical period, while the minimum is 28.93 per 1000 words. Hence, the dispersion among different authors in this period is 42.89 per 1000 words. Note that we excluded the Archaic period from consideration here because it artificially shows very little dispersion due to the very limited number of texts and authors.

18 prepositions in 70 authors

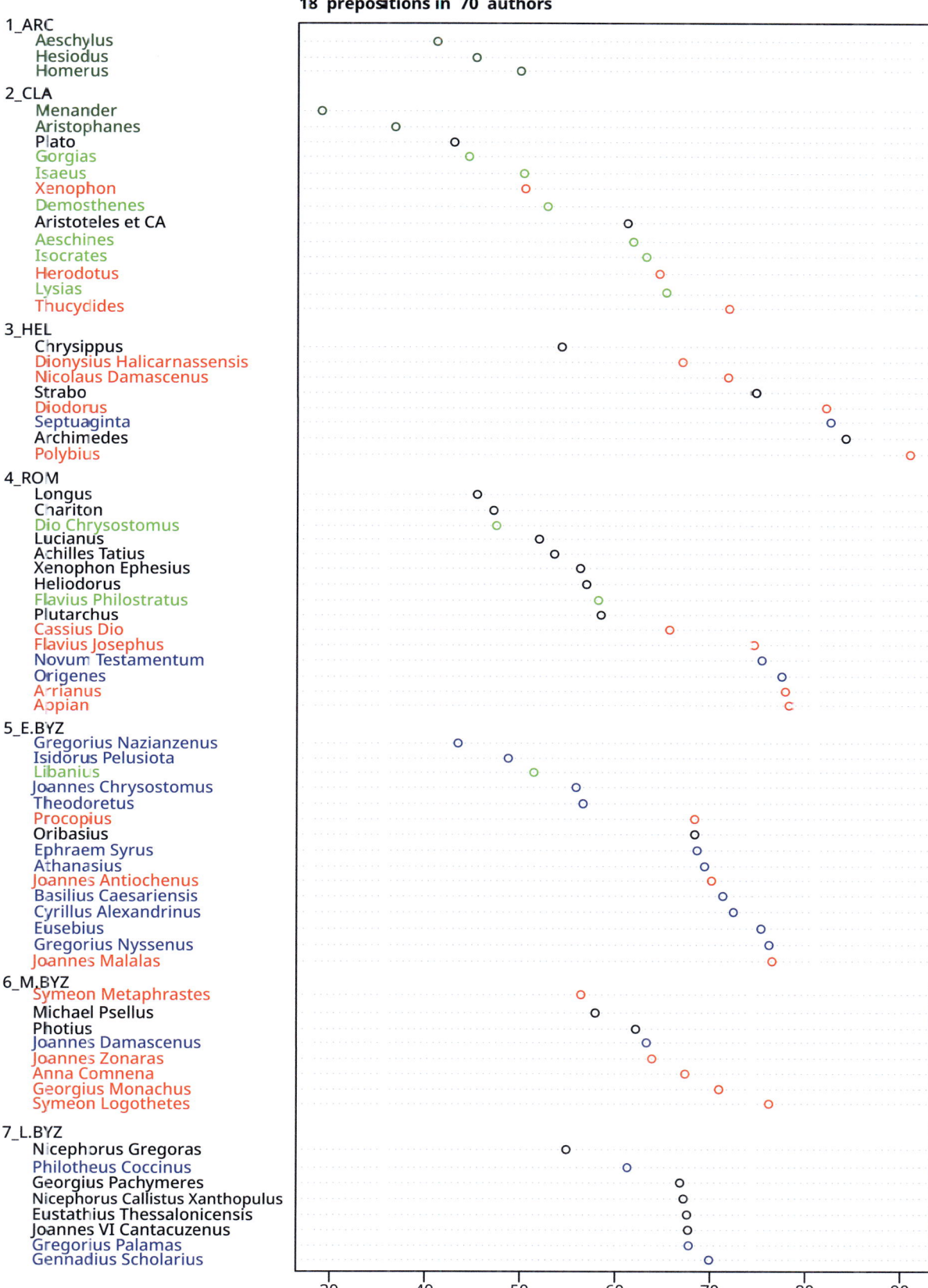

1_ARC
Aeschylus
Hesiodus
Homerus

2_CLA
Menander
Aristophanes
Plato
Gorgias
Isaeus
Xenophon
Demosthenes
Aristoteles et CA
Aeschines
Isocrates
Herodotus
Lysias
Thucydides

3_HEL
Chrysippus
Dionysius Halicarnassensis
Nicolaus Damascenus
Strabo
Diodorus
Septuaginta
Archimedes
Polybius

4_ROM
Longus
Chariton
Dio Chrysostomus
Lucianus
Achilles Tatius
Xenophon Ephesius
Heliodorus
Flavius Philostratus
Plutarchus
Cassius Dio
Flavius Josephus
Novum Testamentum
Origenes
Arrianus
Appian

5_E.BYZ
Gregorius Nazianzenus
Isidorus Pelusiota
Libanius
Joannes Chrysostomus
Theodoretus
Procopius
Oribasius
Ephraem Syrus
Athanasius
Joannes Antiochenus
Basilius Caesariensis
Cyrillus Alexandrinus
Eusebius
Gregorius Nyssenus
Joannes Malalas

6_M.BYZ
Symeon Metaphrastes
Michael Psellus
Photius
Joannes Damascenus
Joannes Zonaras
Anna Comnena
Georgius Monachus
Symeon Logothetes

7_L.BYZ
Nicephorus Gregoras
Philotheus Coccinus
Georgius Pachymeres
Nicephorus Callistus Xanthopulus
Eustathius Thessalonicensis
Joannes VI Cantacuzenus
Gregorius Palamas
Gennadius Scholarius

Instances per 1,000

30   40   50   60   70   80   90

it may appear that the Attistic ideology indeed succeeded in making the language of the Roman period very much similar to that of the Classical period.

Yet, the situation of the Roman period is systematically different from the Classical period. While the Classical period shows no clustering of authors into usage groups, the Roman period exhibits clear-cut groups. Two major groups of authors emerge here: (i) Appianus, Arrianus, Origenes, and the New Testament are consistent in using many prepositions (red and blue dots in Fig. 2), while (ii) Longus, Chariton, Dio Chrysostomus, Lucianus, and some others (black and green dots in Fig. 2) are conservative and employ far fewer prepositions. The first group is much closer to the colloquial language, while the second group is clearly heavily influenced by the Attistic ideology. Accordingly, we refer to the first group as *non-classicising* and to the second group as *classicising*. Notably, the median frequency in the texts of the non-classicising authors is still below the median frequency of the Hellenistic period. This suggests that even the non-classicising group has been influenced by the Attistic ideology as well, albeit to a smaller degree than the classicising group, of course.

We now summarise the evidence from the periods. The high degree of dispersion in the Classical period reveals the actual variation in the language that was undergoing the change from marking semantic roles by bare cases to marking them by prepositions. In other words, the high degree of dispersion in the Classical period is the effect of language change that, expectedly, only gradually affects different speaker layers. By contrast, in the Roman period, the actual diachronic change has been accomplished and the Attistic ideology is responsible for the variation. The high degree of dispersion in the Roman period is due to the selective effect of Atticism. While non-classicising authors and texts (*e.g.* the New Testament) do not depart much from the everyday, colloquial language that primarily relies on the use of prepositions, the classicising authors, by contrast, skew this picture by copying the classical, case-driven patterns and consciously avoiding prepositions. This divide yields the high degree of dispersion that we observe. The classicising authors are responsible for the strong decrease of the median preposition frequency in the Roman period (ca. 58/1000) compared to the Hellenistic period (ca. 82/1000) (Fig. 1). Crucially, the dispersion and variation in frequency is layered here very differently from the Hellenistic period.

Similarly, the distinction between the *classicising* vs. the *non-classicising* authors is observed in the Early Byzantine period as well. Unlike the Classical period, but similar to the Roman period, the Early Byzantine period attests a clear clustering of its authors into groups. Here, too, such authors as Gregorius Nazianzenus, Isidorus Pelusiota, and others group around low preposition frequencies, whereas Johannes Malalas, Gregorius Nyssenus, Eusebius, and others form a group by using many more prepositions.

Within the course of the Early, Middle, and Late Byzantine periods, the frequency of prepositions increases slightly above the level of the Roman period. One thus observes only very little infiltration from the colloquial register, which primarily relies on prepositions (as we know from entirely colloquial texts of the period such as papyri). The median frequency of prepositions remains largely on the same level up to the end of the Byzantine period (Fig. 1). This means that the literary language of these periods develops towards a conventionalised standard and becomes more robust against further influences from the colloquial language.

This is supported by another piece of evidence. The degree of dispersion among authors and texts drastically decreases through the Early, Middle, and Late Byzantine periods from 33 to 15 (Table 4). This means that these periods attest in-

Figure 3 (opposite page). The relative frequencies of 18 prepositions. Genres are color-coded: dark green for poetry, red for historical accounts, blue for religious texts, light green for oratory texts, and black for others (graph: the authors).

18 prepositions in 70 authors

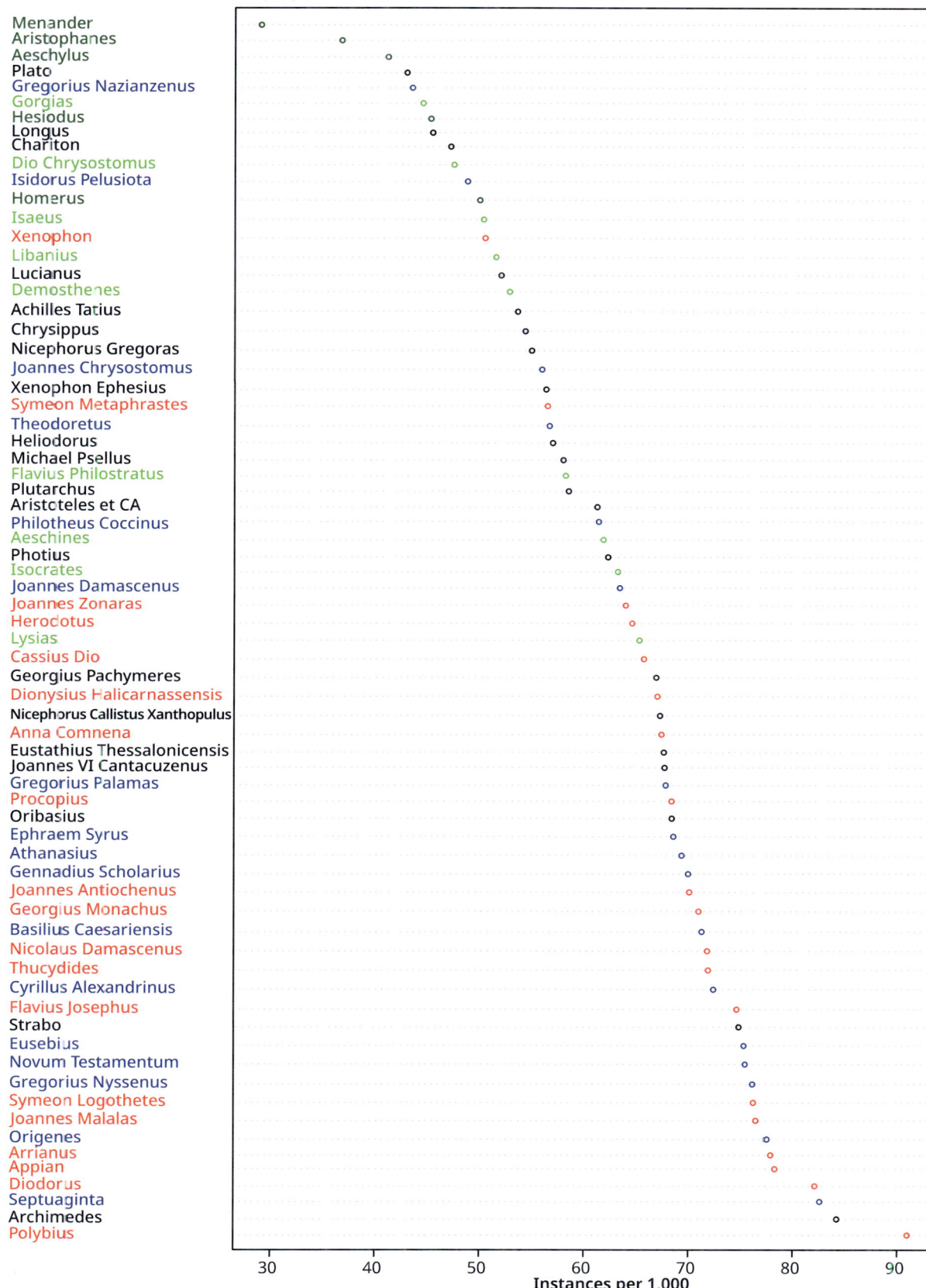

Instances per 1,000

creasingly less variation in prepositional usage despite the fact that the (median) preposition frequency slightly increases. In other words, despite the slight expansion of prepositions from the Early to the Late Byzantine period, we observe a consolidation of usage.

We take these facts as evidence for an ongoing process of standardisation in which the impact of Atticism observed so strongly since the Roman period plays an important role. The use of prepositional patterns stabilises. In effect, authors start exhibiting similar preposition frequencies and come much closer to each other in this respect than it was the case in any of the previous periods. Moreover, while the Roman period was a period of individual approaches to Atticism – something that might be referred to as *creative Atticism* – the Late Byzantine period is rather characterised by what we call *conventionalised Atticism*. Particular Atticistic patterns became the convention and thus the norm of usage by this period.

To conclude, we roughly observe two major periods in the development of prepositions in Ancient Greek. The first period embraces the time span from the Archaic to the Hellenistic period and is characterised by a rapid, grammar-driven expansion of prepositions due to language change. The second period consists of two layers of processes: the grammar-driven expansion continues its operation, but it is at the same time inhibited and re-constrained by multi-layered effects of the Attistic ideology. In effect, the time span from the Roman period to the Late Byzantine period shows only slow expansion but a lot of standardisation with a strong impact of the literary tradition.

The process of standardisation is a highly complicated process that deserves a much larger study than ours. However, our figures allow us to make one important claim about its pathways. We observe that text genres channel the standardisation of prepositional patterns. Figure 3 visualises the effect of the genre:

Thus, authors associated with poetry (dark green in Fig. 3) have much lower preposition frequencies than writers of any other genre. Poetry authors form a consistent group – including the tragedian Aeschylus as well as the comedians Aristophanes or Menander – in that they all score lowest when compared to other authors of the same two periods (the Archaic and Classical periods). Low prepositional usage in poetry has been explained by Herbert W. Smyth (1956, §1656) as an attempt to retain "the more primitive form of expression", although, based on our data, it is not quite clear what kind of primitive form was exactly to be retained by poetry. For example, Menander exhibits a preposition frequency lower than any other author in our corpus, and even lower than what we find in Homer or Hesiod. It is more likely that poetry is subject to linguistic norms that are in part motivated by the conservative – and, possibly, hypercorrect – usage imitating the early tragedians and epic writers. Our evidence supports the view that very early standardisation processes in one particular domain of the language already coined a super-regional variety, namely, the poetry language, which reaches as far back as the Early Classical period (cf. Silk 2009, 16-17).

By contrast, the orators of the Classical period are too heterogeneous and do not form a group (green dots, Fig. 1). Even though they seem to follow the general trend of the Classical period, exhibiting lower preposition frequency than the authors of the later periods, they, however, do not form a consistent group within the Classical period. Some of them tend to be more conservative (Demosthenes, Isaeus, and especially Gorgias), whereas others (Isocrates, Lysias, and Aeschines) align to historians of their time and show higher frequencies.

Historians (red) exhibit the highest frequency in the use of prepositions, followed immediately by religious texts (blue), and are consistently found at the top of their respective periods. For example, Thucydides employs many more prepositions than other authors of the Classical period; the same is true of Polybius in the Hellenistic period and Johannes Malalas in the Early Byzantine period (cf. Horrocks 2010, 100). This suggests that historians are the closest to the colloquial usage and the least amenable to Atticism across all periods.

Furthermore, there are consistent genre-based and chronologically contemporaneous groups of authors that have similar preposition frequencies. One such group that scores low in the use of prepositions is represented by the novelists of the Roman period: Heliodorus, Xenophon Ephesius, Achilles Tatius, Lucianus, Chariton, and Longus. Another such group consists of the Early Byzantine theologians Ephraem Syrus, Athanasius, Basilius Caesariensis, Cyrillus Alexandrinus, Eusebius, and Gregorius Nyssenus.

Finally, the genre of religious texts deserves some attention here. Our evidence suggests that this genre follows the usage of historians until the Early Byzantine period. Thus, the Septuagint is typical for the Hellenistic period by having the same preposition frequency as Diodorus and even a bit less than Polybius. What is more, the frequency of prepositions in the New Testament or in Origenes – one of the most influential figures in early Christian theology, apologetics, and asceticism – is almost equal to the frequencies in the texts of contemporaneous historians such as Appian, Arrian or Flavius Josephus. Similar to historians, the frequency of prepositions in the New Testament decreases as compared to the Septuagint despite the fact that the New Testament is a later text than the Septuagint. This again corresponds to the overall trend of the period: the Roman period generally attests fewer prepositions (Fig. 1).

It is only first in the Early Byzantine period that the authors of religious texts start to split into two groups. On the one hand, the classicising ones, *i.e.,* those that use significantly fewer prepositions than the average of the period (*e.g.* Gregorius Nazianzenus, Isidorus Pelusiota, Joannes Chrysostomus, and Theodoretus) and, on the other hand, the non-classicising, *i.e.,* those that use more prepositions (*e.g.* Gregorius Nyssenus, Eusebius, Cyrillus Alexandrinus, Basilius Casariensis, and others). We conclude that, originally, religious texts presented a homogeneous group which, however, was not necessarily a group of its own, independent from historians. First in the Early Byzantine period, we observe that aspirations towards classicising language sets off religious texts from historical texts.

Zooming in into the frequency levels of particular prepositions

In this section, we focus on the frequency behaviour of particular prepositions from our set in order to see how these were influenced by the Attistic ideology.

As is already known from the literature, the preposition *amphí* disappeared by the Hellenistic period (Fig. 4):

The fact that it reappears in the Roman period and is then used until the Late Byzantine period is certainly only due to the Attistic ideology. This is the only preposition whose frequency and usage is entirely due to the Attistic ideology.

With all other prepositions, only particular usage patterns have been subject to Atticism and, subsequently, the process of standardisation. Attistic influence

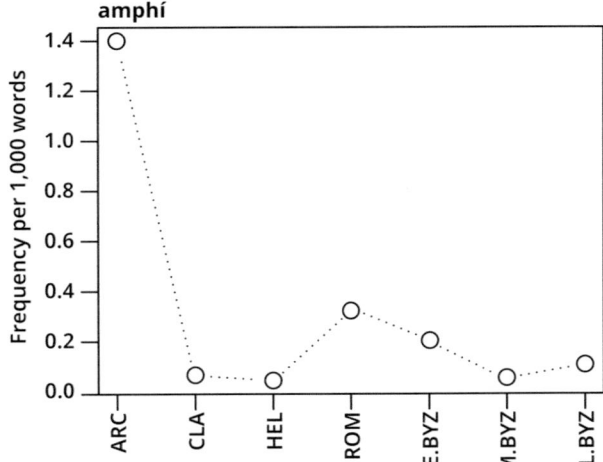

Figure 4. *amphí* 'around, about' (graph: the authors).

is visible in the trend reversal found in the Roman period as compared to the preceding Hellenistic period.

Consider the frequencies of the prepositions *antí* 'instead of', *pró* 'in front of' or *hypér* 'above, over' across the periods (Fig. 5). The usage frequency of these prepositions during the Hellenistic period decreases considerably (with a decrease of ca. 23-35% as compared to the Classical period). This indicates that particular usage patterns of these prepositions were no longer in use in the Hellenistic period. By contrast, the Roman period continues with the same frequency as the Classical period as if there had been no Hellenistic period in between:

From this, we tentatively conclude that some patterns were "borrowed" from the texts of the Classical period and became part of the learned-language grammar during the Roman period, despite the fact that they already disappeared during the Hellenistic period. As above, we observe that the usage adopted in the Roman period largely continued into the Byzantine periods (except for *hypér*) and thus becomes the standard in writing.

Conversely, the following prepositions increased considerably in frequency from the Classical into the Hellenistic period. In contrast, their frequency considerably diminished in the Roman period, thus almost returning to the frequencies of the Classical period. This means that a number of the Hellenistic usage patterns must have been considered inappropriate in the Atticistic ideology and became dispreferred during the Roman period (Fig. 6):

A similar picture is obtained for *katá* 'below, along'. Accordingly, we conclude that these prepositions or, more precisely, some of their usages were wiped out by the Attistic ideology and the subsequent process of standardisation.

So far, we have discussed prepositions that are characterised by a switch in their usage trend during the Roman period, either by considerably increasing their usage frequencies (*e.g. amphí*) or decreasing them (*e.g. apó* or *prós*). Interestingly, there are also prepositions that did not undergo any substantial change in their frequencies during the Roman period. For example, *pará* 'at' does not show any considerable changes in frequency (Table 5):

A similar picture is obtained for *epí* 'on' or *eis* 'in'. We may conclude from this that these prepositions, in contrast to the others, have not been subject to Atticism at all or just to a minor degree. Such a selective treatment of grammatical items of the same type is not atypical for the ideological impact.

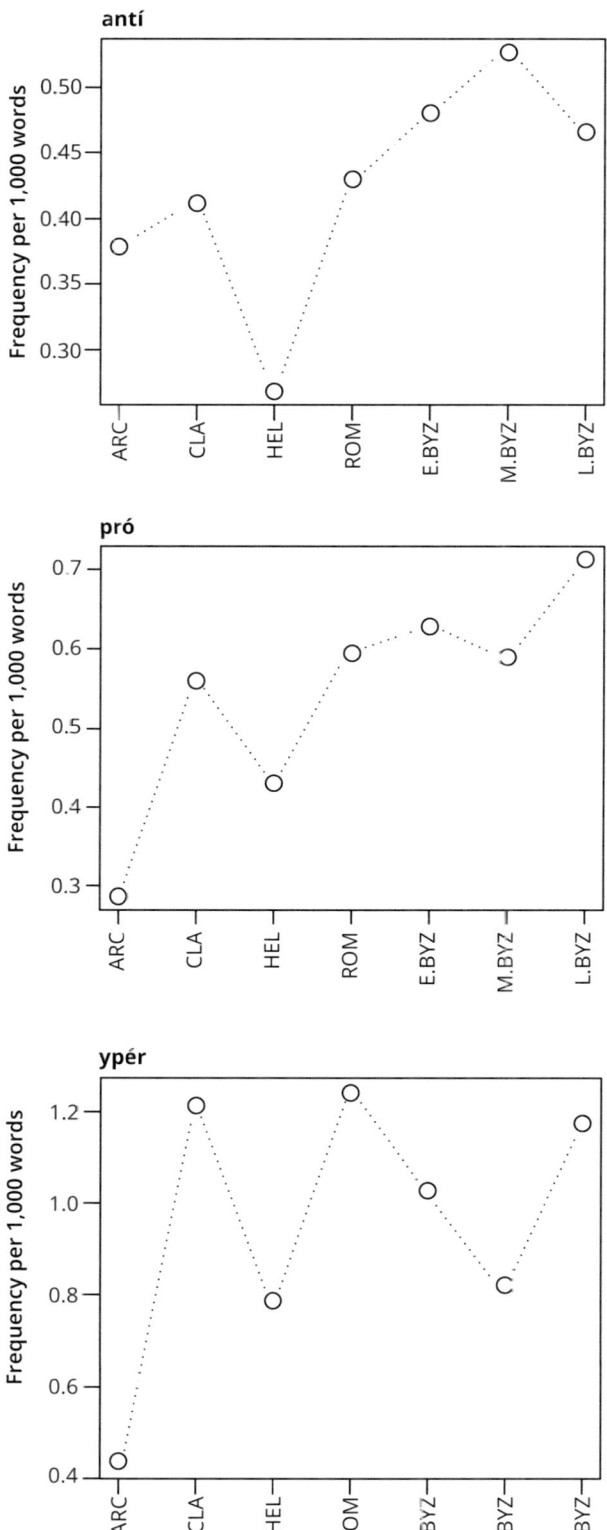

Figure 5. Relative frequency of *antí* 'instead of', *pró* 'in front of' or *hypér* 'above, over' (graph: the authors).

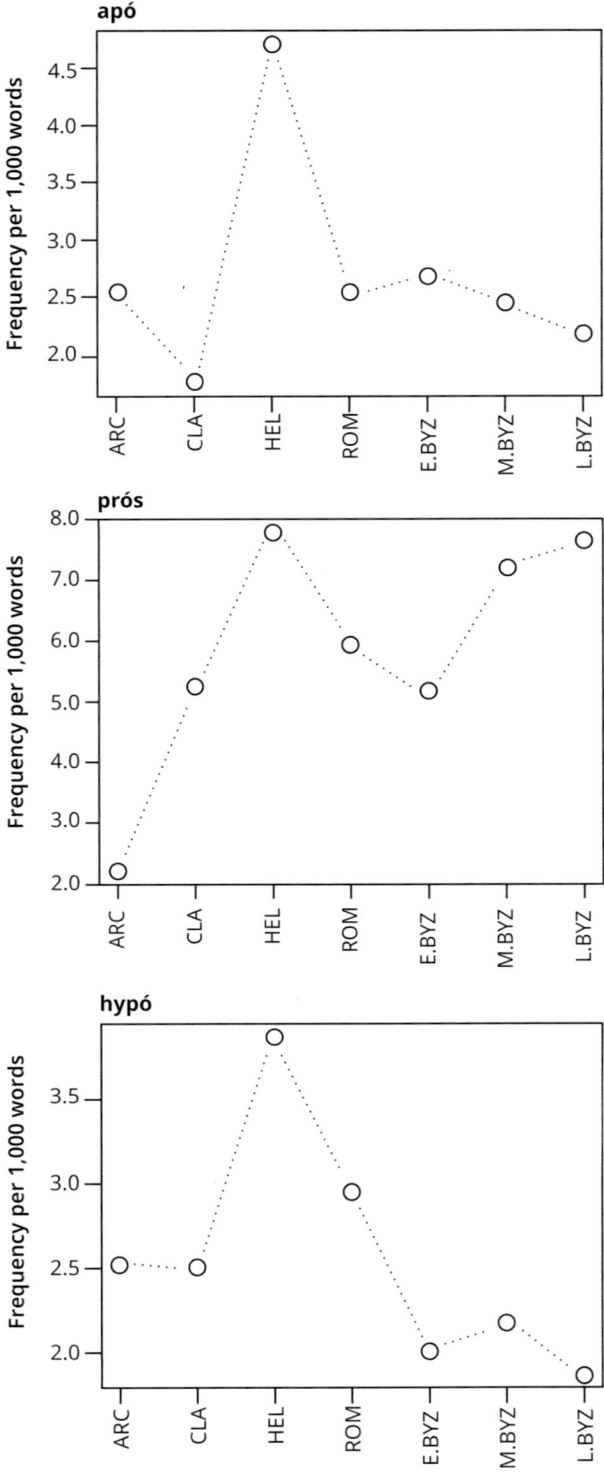

Figure 6. Relative frequency of *apó* 'from', *prós* 'to' and *hypó* 'under, from' (graph: the authors).

Classical	Hellenistic	Roman	Early Byzantine	Middle Byzantine	Late Byzantine
2.60	2.95	2.85	2.81	2.75	2.88

Table 5. The relative frequency of *pará* 'at' across the periods (per 1000 words).

Conclusions

Inspired by the quantitative approaches in stylometry, we assumed methodologically that despite different particular histories as well as semantic and constructional developments of particular prepositions, the overall median frequency of all 18 prepositions is a legitimate proxy for the major processes in the grammars of different periods, authors, and genres.

We have shown that the frequency of prepositions in Ancient Greek was not solely determined by language change, *i.e.*, by the grammar-driven development away from encoding semantic roles by inflectional case towards encoding them by means of prepositions. By contrast, we have argued that the ideological impact and standardisation processes heavily influenced the outcome. The Roman period is crucial in this regard (see Fig. 1). We observe that this period considerably skews the trends in the development of prepositions, which we take to be due to the Atticistic linguistic ideology.

More specifically, we distinguished two major developmental steps in the expansion of prepositions in Ancient Greek. First, the time span covering the Archaic, the Classical and the Hellenistic periods is characterised by the grammar-driven expansion of prepositional patterns across various domains. By the Hellenistic period, this process is very much advanced at the cost of the bare case. This is observed by the steady increase of the corpus frequency. Moreover, we found that the Hellenistic period is characterised by a lower degree of dispersion among its writers than the Classical period. It is during the Hellenistic period that Koiné emerged into the superregional variety, which, we assume, had a negative effect on the degree of variation in this period.

The second step, by contrast, is a development of a different sort. It starts during the Roman period as a creative ideologisation in favour of the "ideals" of the Archaic and Classical periods and leads to a great deal of variation among the writers of the Roman period. Eventually, particular Attistic patterns became conventionalised in the writings of the Byzantine periods – something that we see in the decrease of the dispersion factor. This development indicates that the norms had been developed and accepted over a wider social layer than the original one. Thus, the original trend towards the expansion of prepositional marking is reversed in the Roman period. There is a considerable decrease in the overall corpus frequency of prepositions as compared to the chronologically earlier Hellenistic period, which is then gradually fixed in the Byzantine periods only to a certain extent. More specifically, while some few prepositions that became rare or even extinct in the Hellenistic period are "restored" in the Roman period, most prepositions decreased their frequency in the Roman period when compared to the Hellenistic period and thereby acquired frequencies that were close to the original frequencies of the Classical period. This is because a number of prepositional usage patterns of the Hellenistic period were retrogradely abandoned and replaced by bare cases during the Roman period.

Moreover, we found that the frequencies are not solely determined by the grammar-driven language change or by the language ideology, but that genres channel the expansion of prepositional patterns. Thus, different genres considerably deviate from each other in the frequency of prepositions. Historians and early religious texts are the most progressive and less amenable to ideologising the earlier periods. By contrast, writers of poetry and orators are much more conservative, more resistant to language change, and tend to imitate the earlier language layers more faithfully.

Interestingly, we also found that the Attistic ideology was apparently not concerned with all prepositions because some of them do not show any considerable effect of the Roman period on their frequencies.

We approached the impact of the Atticistic ideology on the grammar of prepositions with a bird's-eye view without concentrating on particular patterns and occurrences. Our aim was to quantitatively evaluate the overall ideological impact on Postclassical writings and to uncover the major pathways here. The very sociolinguistic mechanisms of these pathways have been left out here for reasons of space, see, however, Alexandra Georgakopoulou and Michael Silk, eds., (2009) for a collection of the relevant studies, *i.a.*, Claudia Strobel (2009).

References

Abel, F.M., 1927. *Grammaire du grec biblique*. Paris: Gabalda.

Benedetti, M., 2020. The perfect paradigm in Theodosius' Κανόνες: diathetically indifferent and diathetically non-indifferent forms. *In*: D. Rafiyenko and I.A. Seržant, eds. *Contemporary Approaches to Postclassical Greek*. Trends in Linguistics series. Berlin, New York: De Gruyter, 205-220.

Blass, F. and Debrunner, A., 1979. *Grammatik des neu-testamentlichen Griechisch*. 15th ed. Göttingen: Vandenhoeck und Ruprecht.

Bortone, P., 2010. *Greek Adpositions. From Antiquity to the Present*. Oxford: Oxford University Press.

Chantraine, P., 1958. *Grammaire Homérique. Tome II: Syntaxe*. Collection de Philologie Classique, IV. Paris.

Cooper, A. and Georgala, E., 2012. Dative loss and its replacement in the history of Greek. *In*: A. van Kemenade and N. de Haas, eds. *Historical Linguistics 2009. Selected Papers from the 19th International Conference on Historical Linguistics*. Amsterdam: Benjamins, 277-292.

Delbruck, B., 1893. *Vergleichende Syntax der indogermanischen Sprachen*. Erster Theil. Strassburg: Karl J. Trubner.

Dunkel, G.E., 1979. Preverb repetition. *Münchener Studien zur Sprachwissenschaft*, 38, 41-82.

García Ramón, J.L., 2020. Grammatical und lexical structures on change in Postclassical Greek: local dialects and supradialectal tendencies. *In*: D. Rafiyenko and I.A. Seržant, eds. *Contemporary Approaches to Postclassical Greek*. Trends in Linguistics series. Berlin, New York: De Gruyter, 303-336.

Georgakopoulou, A., 2009. Introduction: Greek Language-Standardizing, Past, Present and Future. *In*: A. Georgakopoulou and M. Silk, eds. *Standard Languages and Language Standards: Greek, Past and Present*. Centre for Hellenic Studies, King's College London Publications 12. Surrey, Burlington: Ashgate.

Georgakopoulou, A. and Silk, M., eds., 2009. *Standard Languages and Language Standards: Greek, Past and Present*. Centre for Hellenic Studies, King's College London Publications 12. Surrey, Burlington: Ashgate.

Hajnal, I., 1995. *Studien zum mykenischen Kasussystem*. Berlin, New York: Walter de Gruyter.

Hettrich, H., 1985. Zum Kasussynkretismus im Mykenischen. *Münchener Studien zur Sprachwissenschaft*, 46, 1985, 111-122.

Hewson, J. and Bubenik, V., 2006. *From case to adposition – the development of configurational syntax in Indo-European languages*. Amsterdam, Philadelphia: John Benjamins.

Horrocks, G., 1981. *Space and Time in Homer. Prepositional and Adverbial Particles in the Greek Epic.* New York: Arno Press.

Horrocks, G., 1997. Homer's dialect. *In:* I. Morris and B. Powell, eds. *A new companion to Homer.* Leiden, New York, Köln: E.J. Brill, 193-217.

Horrocks, G., 2010. *Greek: A History of the Language and its Speakers.* 2nd ed. Oxford: Wiley-Blackwell.

Humbert, J., 1930. *La disparition du datif en grec (du Ier au Xe siècle).* Paris: Librairie ancienne Honoré Champion.

Koch, M., 1889. *Der Gebrauch der Präpositionen bei Isokrates. Erster Teil: Die einfälligen Präpositionen mit Einschluss der Präpositionsadverbia.* Berlin: R. Gaertners Verlagsbuchhandlung Hermann Heyfelder.

Kühner, R. and Gerth, B., 1898. *Ausführliche Grammatik der griechischen Sprache. Satzlehre. Zweiter Teil. Syntaxe.* Reprint 2015. Darmstadt: WBG.

Luraghi, S., 1996. *Studi su casi e preposizioni nel greco antico.* Milan: Franco Angeli.

Luraghi, S., 2003. *On the Meaning of Prepositions and Cases. The expression of semantic roles in Ancient Greek.* Amsterdam, Philadelphia: Benjamins.

Lutz, L., 1891. *Die casus-Adverbien bei den Attischen Rednern.* Würzburg: Bonitas-Bauer.

Martínez Valladares, M.A., 1973. Las preposiciones en Tucídides. *Revista Española de lingüística año* 3 (1), 185-94.

Milroy, J. and Milroy, L., 1999. *Authority in language. Investigating Standard English.* London: Routledge.

Mommsen, T., 1895. *Beiträge zu der Lehre von den griechischen Präpositionen.* Berlin: Weidmann.

Morpurgo Davies, A., 1983. Mycenaean and Greek prepositions: o-pi, e-pi etc. In: A. Heubeck and G. Neumann, eds. *Res Mycenaeae. Akten des VII. Int. Mykenologischen Colloquiums in Nürnberg vom 6.-10. April 1981.* Göttingen: Vandenhoeck & Ruprecht, 287-310.

Morpurgo Davies, A., 1985. Mycenaean and Greek language. In: A. Morpurgo Davies and Y. Duhoux, eds. *Linear B: a 1984 Survey.* Louvain-la-Neuve: Cabay, 75-125.

Nachmanson, E., 1942. *Partitives Subjekt im Griechischen.* Göteborg: Elanders boktr.

Rafiyenko, D. and Seržant, I.A., 2020. Postclassical Greek. An overview. *In:* D. Rafiyenko and I.A. Seržant, eds. *Contemporary Approaches to Postclassical Greek.* Trends in Linguistics series. Berlin, New York: De Gruyter, 1-18.

Rafiyenko, D. and Seržant, I.A., 2021. Dataset for the paper "Ideology and identity in grammar: A diachronic-quantitative approach to language standardisation processes in Ancient Greek" [Dataset]. Zenodo. Available at: http://doi.org/10.5281/zenodo.4974880.

Schmid, W., 1887-1897. *Der Atticismus in seinen Hauptvertretern von Dionysius von Halikarnass bis auf den zweiten Philostratus.* Fünf Bände, Stuttgart: Kohlhammer.

Schmitz, T., 1997. *Bildung und Macht. Zur sozialen und politischen Funktion der Zweiten Sophistik in der griechischen Welt der Kaiserzeit.* Munich: Beck.

Schwyzer, E. and Debrunner, A., 1975 [1950]. *Griechische Grammatik: auf der Grundlage von Karl Brugmanns griechischer Grammatik.* Teil 1. Band 2: *Syntax und syntaktische Stilistik, vervollständigt und herausgegeben von Albert Debrunner.* Vierte, unveränderte Auflage. München: Beck.

Seržant, I.A. and Rafiyenko, D., 2021. Diachronic evidence against the source-oriented explanation in typology. Evolution of Prepositional Phrases in Ancient Greek. *Language Dynamics and Change,* 11 (2), 167-210.

Sihler, A.L., 1995. *New comparative grammar of Greek and Latin.* New York, Oxford: Oxford University Press.

Silk, M., 2009. The Invention of Greek: Macedonians, Poets and Others. *In*: A. Georga-kopoulou and M. Silk, eds. *Standard Languages and Language Standards: Greek, Past and Present.* Centre for Hellenic Studies, King's College London Publications 12. Surrey, Burlington: Ashgate, 3-31.

Smyth, H.W., 1920. *A Greek Grammar for Colleges.* New York, Cincinnati, Chicago, Boston, Atlanta: American Book Company.

Smyth, H.W. 1956. *Greek Grammar.* Rev. by G.M. Messing. Cambridge: Harvard University Press.

Sobolewskij, S., 1890. *De Praepositionum Usu Aristophaneo.* Mosquae: Typ. Univ. Caesar.

Strobel, C., 2009. The Lexica of the Second Sophistic: Safeguarding Atticism. *In*: A. Georgakopoulou and M. Silk, eds. *Standard Languages and Language Standards: Greek, Past and Present.* Centre for Hellenic Studies, King's College London Publications 12. Surrey, Burlington: Ashgate, 93-108.

Swain, S., 1996. *Hellenism and empire : language, classicism, and power in the Greek world, AD 50-250.* Oxford: Clarendon Press.

Vincent, N., 1999. The evolution of c-structure: prepositions and PPs from Indo-European to Romance. *Linguistics*, 37 (6), 1111-1153.

Westphal, F., 1888. *Die Präpositionen bei Xenophon (im besonderen ana, pro, yper, amphi, anti, meta, syn).* Zwanzigstes Programm des städtischen Gymnasiums in Freienwalde zu Oder. Freienwalde zu Oder, 1-21.

Woolard, K.A. and Schieffelin, B.B., 1994. Language Ideology. *Annual Review of Anthropology,* 23, 55-82.